A Time
of Change

Books by Harrison E. Salisbury

A Time of Change: A Reporter's Tale of Our Time   1988

The Long March: The Untold Story   1985

China: 100 Years of Revolution   1983

A Journey for Our Times   1983

Without Fear or Favor—The New York Times   1980

The Unknown War   1978

Russia in Revolution 1900–1930   1978

Black Night, White Snow: Russia's Revolutions 1905–1917   1977

Travels Around America   1976

The Gates of Hell   1975

To Peking—and Beyond   1973

The Eloquence of Protest—Voices of the 70's *(Editor)*   1972

The Many Americas Shall Be One   1971

War Between Russia and China   1969

The 900 Days—The Siege of Leningrad   1969

The Soviet Union: The Fifty Years *(Editor)*   1967

Behind the Lines—Hanoi   1967

Orbit of China   1967

Russia   1965

The Northern Palmyra Affair   1962

A New Russia?   1962

Moscow Journal: The End of Stalin   1961

To Moscow—and Beyond   1960

The Shook-up Generation   1958

American in Russia   1955

Russia on the Way   1946

Harrison E. Salisbury

A Time of Change

A Reporter's Tale of Our Time

A Cornelia & Michael Bessie Book

PERENNIAL LIBRARY

Harper & Row, Publishers, New York
Cambridge, Philadelphia, San Francisco, Washington
London, Mexico City, São Paulo, Singapore, Sydney

A hardcover edition of this book was published in 1988 by Harper & Row, Publishers.

First PERENNIAL LIBRARY edition published 1989.

Library of Congress Cataloging-in-Publication Data
Salisbury, Harrison Evans, 1908–
   A time of change.

   "A Cornelia & Michael Bessie book."
   (Perennial Library.)
   Includes index.
   1. Salisbury, Harrison Evans, 1908–
2. Journalists—United States—Biography. I. Title.
PN4874.S266A3 1989   070'.92'4 [B]   87-45660
ISBN 0-06-091568-4 (pbk.)

89 90 91 92 93 FG   10 9 8 7 6 5 4 3 2 1

For Charlotte, my love, and comrade
on these pages

Contents

Acknowledgments

To mention all of those who have been of help in composing this book would be to repeat most of the index. Let me single out, then, some of the most notable: my colleagues and friends at *The New York Times*—Clifton Daniel, Peter Kihss, David Halberstam, Emanuel Freedman, Frank Adams, Turner Catledge, A.M. Rosenthal, James Reston, David Schneiderman, Charlotte Curtis, who read the manuscript chapter by chapter until her death in 1987, Iphigene Sulzberger and her husband, Arthur Hays Sulzberger, and Susan Dryfoos. There is no way that I can repay the assistance of my many Chinese friends who made the China chapters possible, but I will single out Yao Wei, Zhang Yuanyuan and Jeanette Sui for special mention. David C. Humphrey of the Lyndon Baines Johnson Library at Austin, Texas, was extraordinarily helpful. So was Susan Levin, who typed most of the manuscript, Ann Finlayson, who edited it, and of course, that remarkable man Simon Michael Bessie.

A Word of Explanation

I have spent most of my life on the front lines of reporting, and it has often been a stormy passage. I was thrown out of the University of Minnesota as editor of the college daily for my uppity campaigns against the administration. I nearly lost my first journeyman's job for my reports on the Great Depression in my hometown of Minneapolis. Stalin and Molotov threatened to expel me from Russia in World War II. Some editors of *The New York Times* wanted to fire me for my reports from Moscow; Moscow banned me from Russia for the same reports. Birmingham entered millions of dollars in libel suits because I warned that the city was going to blow up in race violence—which it did. Lyndon Johnson and the Pentagon exploded when I went behind the enemy lines to Hanoi during Vietnam.

So it has been, and that is the way it should be. If a reporter is not a "disturber of the peace," he should go into cost accounting. I said at the time of Hanoi that, if I was getting nothing but bouquets, I must be missing part of the story—the vital part.

My heroes in journalism have been muckrakers—past and present: William Howard Russell of the London *Times* who exposed the boobery of the general who ordered the Charge of the Light Brigade; George Jones, the editor of *The New York Times* who exposed the Tweed Ring; Upton Sinclair who published the scandal of Chicago's meat packers; Lincoln Steffens who wrote *The Shame of the Cities;* Ida Tarbell who documented the Standard Oil monopoly; and Paul Y. Anderson who uncovered Teapot Dome. I revere men like David Halberstam, Neil Sheehan, and Seymour Hersh, who reported the reality of Vietnam and, above all, I honor Homer Bigart who reported the wars of our time honestly, bluntly, no fifes-and-drums.

Not a popular lot.

I cherish John Reed and Edgar Snow and Herbert Matthews, who plunged into birthing Revolutions and brought out news not everyone wanted to read.

In these pages I write of reporting in this day, of complex and unpopular issues and men I have tried to understand and interpret. I would be shocked if every reader applauded my judgments.

This is the second personal volume that I have written. The first told of beginnings in Minnesota, of what I have come to call the Minnesota spirit, skeptical, contrarian, often out-of-step, hostile to the Bigs—Big Cities, Big Power, Big Money, Big Government. I told of reporting in World War II and of long, difficult years in Stalin's Russia and that of Nikita Khrushchev and Leonid Brezhnev. Here I describe the America to which I returned from Russia in the mid-fifties, of the New York I explored, of national issues—Washington, Eisenhower, Stevenson, the Kennedys, Lyndon Johnson, Richard Nixon, civil rights, Vietnam, the revolutionary ferment of the 1960s and 1970s, and finally China, the mecca of childhood aspirations, Mao Zedong Zhou Enlai, Deng Xiaoping. I offer some clues to the mysteries of *The New York Times* of which I have so long been a part—once in, never out.

If I conclude on a positive note, it is based not so much on specific evidence as on my faith in the continuity of our democracy and my optimistic nature. I agree with my "Uncle Hiram" of 150 years ago: We have come so far, it is reasonable to think we will go farther.

Above all I seek to spell out the virtue and total necessity for our society of reporting the unpopular event at the most—especially—at the most difficult touchy moment. It is easy to ride with the mob, but that path leads to Hitler and Stalin and the tosspot puffins we've so often put our money on. To me the First Amendment is our richest jewel.

Never has this principle been asserted with more plain honesty than by the late Murray Gurfein. In his opinion, upholding the right of *The New York Times* to publish the "classified" Pentagon Papers, Gurfein wrote:

> The security of the Nation is not at the ramparts alone. Security also lies in the value of our free institutions. A cantankerous press, an obstinate press, an ubiquitous press must be suffered by those in authority in order to preserve the even greater values of freedom of expression and the right of the public to know.

Thomas Jefferson did not say it better. I have carried this quotation in my wallet since the Saturday afternoon, June 19, 1971, when Gurfein read it from the bench of the U.S. District

Court in New York. It was his first opinion after being appointed by Richard Nixon. Gurfein had stayed up the night, writing it, and, he told me not long before he died, he was very nervous but totally sure he was saying the right, the *only,* thing. Hardly a week goes by that I do not read over Murray Gurfein's words again. They should, I think, be chiseled above the entrance of every newspaper in America.

1 | The Red-Eye

I snuggled down in the wide seat of the 707, my chin in my hand, flying through the night on the red-eye from San Francisco. It was after midnight, the early hours of Wednesday, January 11, 1967, and I was flying home from Hanoi after a fortnight behind the enemy lines in Vietnam. My mind, dulled by the monotone of the jets, roved aimlessly back to Hanoi and ahead to New York. I could have been killed in Hanoi as I crouched in a concrete manhole while the B-52s flew over. I could be destroyed in New York by the firestorm my dispatches had set off.

Nothing in thirty-five years as a reporter had prepared me for this complex and contradictory journey into the land of our enemies and back into the torment of my own country. Everything was exaggerated, everything was larger than life: my Christmas Eve dispatch about the bombing of Hanoi and the civilian casualties; the destruction of President Johnson's myth that we hit only targets of concrete and steel; the shock waves that had shaken America and the world; the geyser of rage that had spewed out of the White House and the Pentagon.

What lay ahead I could not guess, hunkered down in the upholstered womb of the 707. *The New York Times* had dispatched me on this strange and ominous mission. Now it was standing solid as its fortress on 43rd Street. Or was it? Clifton Daniel, managing editor and my friend from World War II in London, had directed me to get back as fast as I could—and duck the press. The bombardment of cables and messages which penetrated into Hanoi had told me that this was an occasion as unpredictable as a typhoon. The *Times* had battened down for rough seas. The future course of the war, the fate of the Johnson administration, even improbably the prestige of *The New York Times* and my career as a newspaper reporter might be at risk.

On my way back from Hanoi I had paused in Hong Kong to complete my final, summing-up dispatches and got a taste of what lay ahead. I had met three reporters, men I had known for years. They shocked me with the vehemence of their questions, their skepticism of my reports, their ugly doubts of my integrity.

1

To some, I discovered, I was Hanoi Harry, reporting for the *Ho Chi Minh Times*.

When I flew into San Francisco, I found that Wally Turner, the *Times* man, and Robin Kinkead, PR man for Pan-American, had everything in hand. They whisked me down the crew's staircase and into Wally's car before any passengers left the plane. In the catacombs of the airport I found Tom Wicker, the *Times* Washington correspondent. He was flying out to Saigon for the first time, and we had a long talk.

The situation was bad, even dangerous, Wicker said.

"Lyndon Johnson is so mad, he'll chew you up and spit you out before breakfast," Wicker said. "He'd like to send a B-52 over to Forty-Third street and show *The New York Times* what a real surgical bombing strike is like."

"That's right," Wally drawled. "You be careful. That man's like a copperhead on a hot rock."

Dangerous. They kept repeating that word. The Washington *Post* (and some other papers) had joined the clamor. "They are jealous of the *Times* and your beat," Wicker said, "but that doesn't make it any less serious." Editorials in the *Post*. Snide stories by my old colleague, Chal Roberts. Art Sylvester and I had jounced for hundreds of miles together in the buses covering Presidential campaigns. Now he was leading the attack for the Pentagon.

"You watch out," Tom Wicker said. "It's a lynching party, and Lyndon wants blood."

I didn't tell them that Lyndon was the man I had to see. I was bringing back from Hanoi information meant only for his big ears, information that could affect war or peace. Scotty Reston had already set up a secret date for me with Secretary of State Dean Rusk. But Lyndon was stonewalling. Scotty told me later that the President was so mad Press Secretary Bill Moyers didn't dare put the question of a meeting with me to him.

It looked as though LBJ wouldn't even be willing to find out that a window had opened up if he wanted to bring the war to an end. He wasn't going to let himself hear about it.

I had to agree that things were worse than I had imagined, and I had known they would be bad. We talked for a couple of hours in the infrastructure of the airport. Then Wicker left for his departure lounge, and Wally drove through a maze of baggage trains, fuel trucks, cargo hustlers to my 707.

"We're putting you on the food elevator," he said. "You'll go up with the hot lunches. You'll be on board before any of the passengers. There's a crowd of reporters at the gate, and they are mad as hell because you gave them the slip when you arrived."

The food handlers didn't blink an eye when I was lifted up. I entered the plane through the steward's galley and found my seat halfway back in the cabin, settled down, and began to read the San Francisco *Chronicle,* which had mastered the art of making up page 1 without a single item of news. For a few moments the *Chronicle* carried me away from the real world. Then the passengers began to board. The red-eye was almost empty that evening, and soon I could hear shouting. The reporters. They were demanding to be let aboard. "I know he's on the plane," I heard one angry voice. "His name's on the manifest, and there isn't any other plane to New York." The din rose. I scrunched down in my seat. I was not about to be discovered. The shouting hit a crescendo. As the plane was ready to leave, a young man with disheveled blond hair darted into the forward compartment looking about him wildly. "I know he's here," he cried. "He's got to be here." I slumped down in the seat so that my head was below the level of the seat ahead but an impulse rose in me. As a stewardess and a husky passenger agent shoved and pulled the young man from the plane I wanted to shout, "Here I am! What do you want to ask?" So many times I had stood in the footsteps of the young reporter, my passage barred by a burly police officer or a bumptious guard. I resisted the impulse. This was no ordinary reporters' combat. I was, I knew now, up against a raging bull, and I was the banderillero who had flicked the cruel arrows into LBJ's shoulder. I heard a deep roar as the engines ignited, and the plane began to move slowly over to the active runway, then down the pathway of red and green lights to the takeoff. I was very happy I had made it through San Francisco. In New York I would have to run the gauntlet. The San Francisco reporters would have telephoned their colleagues to catch me at JFK.

Not quite a month had passed since I had gotten the cryptic cablegram that had changed my life and, incredibly, for a small space of time, the world. The cable instructed me to go to Paris. A visa for Hanoi would be waiting for me.

I had dropped everything. Put the new investigation of Jack Kennedy's assassination on the shelf (where it gathers dust to this day). I had telephoned my son, Michael. I could not come to his New Year's Eve wedding. Charlotte would have to take over the wedding, and Charlotte would have to take over Christmas for my younger son, Stephan. There would be no Christmas for Charlotte and myself in this, our third year of marriage. I dropped everything, bought a ticket for Paris, and flew away, on to Hanoi and the turbulent events still in progress. I had been lifted into world orbit.

Over and over the events of Hanoi ran through my mind like the seamless loop of a newsreel. It hadn't been what I expected. So stubborn these people. So warm and human but so stubborn even as their backs were to the wall. Not from our bombing. Not even the lazy dogs, the most terrible of all, the lazy-dog bombs that spewed out 300 pups, each the size of a baseball, twisting and turning and suddenly blasting steel splinters into your liver or your throat. What hung over Hanoi now was a threat worse than any LBJ could devise—the threat that the flow of rice (and other supplies) from China would be cut off, cut with a Chinese sword. No rice meant starvation. Did LBJ know that? Of course not. Would he believe it? Probably not. If he did, would he negotiate? Or would he turn up the heat of bombing and let Vietnam starve and bleed to the end? Dare I tell LBJ? I rolled the dilemma over and over in my mind and felt the fear levels creep up. He might, I thought, destroy me rather than hear the words I was carrying to him. And how would I handle the reporters massed at the entrance gate at JFK. No chance of escaping them a second time. I was headed into an ambush, and I was more frightened than I had been 20 days ago when the plane touched down in Hanoi, not a light showing. Vietnam soldiers with bayonets on their rifles clattered into the plane and turned the beams of powerful electric torches in my eyes. I stumbled out blindly and wondered how long I had to live.

I suppose that I must have slept, for I suddenly felt the depressurization. My ears began to vibrate. We touched ground and taxied up the runway. The plane came to a halt. The lights flashed on. I picked up my old Remington portable, the one the UP gave me in 1942 before I went to London as a war correspondent (it was stolen property—I had never given it back) and walked out of the plane and into the waiting area. It was empty. Not a reporter in sight. No one except my Charlotte, straight as a young poplar, eyes gleaming, a quiet smile on her lips. We hugged, and there were tears in our eyes.

"Well," I said, "I'm home, darling."

"I missed you," she said.

"I missed you," I said.

"Particularly on Christmas," she said.

"Likewise."

We didn't say anything more. The luggage came up on the belt. I lifted my heavy bag, we struggled out to a cab and held each other all the way to our brownstone at 349 East 84th Street. I don't know whether we slept that night or not. I don't think we did. We went to bed. I didn't say anything for a long time. Neither did Charlotte. Then she began: "That Johnson. I could kill him with my own hands." Charlotte was as clear as crystal. Her opinions were cut with a diamond. No equivocations. "If I could get my hands on him . . ." Don't say it, I told her. Don't say anything. Nothing. A chill ran up my spine. I was thinking of Russia. Maybe the house was bugged. No way we would ever know. The words of Wally Turner and Tom Wicker echoed in my mind. It was dangerous. Charlotte went on. She wouldn't stop. I put a hand over her mouth. Don't, I whispered. Don't say a word. Don't you understand? They are going to destroy us if they can. Who knows what they can hear? Her eyes started from her head. I nodded solemnly and put my finger to my lips. Not a word. I was acting as I had learned to act in Russia. Just don't say anything that can be repeated. Be silent. Don't even whisper. I think now that I was hysterical. I'm sure Charlotte thought so. She looked at me with wild eyes. Who was this man she had married on that cool sunny April day in 1964? Less than three years and now this. What next? I could not tell her. It was dangerous. That was all I knew.

At ten o'clock in the morning I was striding through the lobby of *The New York Times* at 229 West 43rd Street. On the lobby wall was Mr. Ochs' favorite quotation: "Every day a fresh beginning; every morn a world made new." I wondered. I wondered. I had hardly entered the city room when Abe Rosenthal rushed up. I had known Abe since he was a pencil-thin youngster at the United Nations in Lake Success twenty years ago. He was a little chubby now, city editor of the *Times* and moving up fast.

He threw his arms around me. He was a very emotional man.

"What *have* you done, Harrison?" he cried. "What *have* you done?"

It was a good question. The answer was not easy. It led a long way back to the time when I came home to this city room to start a new career after six years in Russia, the last years of Stalin, Stalin's death, and the start of what came after.

What *had* I done and where would it lead? I had to see Clifton Daniel and begin to sort out the answers. And beyond that I would have to examine the bigger questions: What had propelled me into this dramatic role? Where had I come from and where was I going?

2 | Mr. Hagerty's Desk

It is easy to exaggerate. My first chapter seems too dramatic when I read it through. But I think this is a measure of the distance which now lies between the eighties and the violence of Vietnam, the passion, the blood anger, the frustration, the timbre of voices, the emotional storm that almost wrenched the American structure apart. Nothing so sundered the country since Fort Sumter. In January of 1967 neither I nor anyone I knew or trusted felt certain where it might end.

I had been watching the tensions build in the United States for a decade, amazed at the volatility, feeling I had no compass to point the direction we were taking. I thought myself superior to most in measuring what was happening, but perhaps I was mistaken. I felt I could see the world in broader perspective. I'd gone abroad as a correspondent in World War II, and then, after a short interlude in New York, I had spent nearly six years in Russia in a kind of no-man's-land of the Cold War. I knew at first hand the fear and terror of Stalin's last years. I never went to sleep in my gloomy chamber, Room 393 of the Hotel Metropol, without wondering whether I might awaken to find war's bony hand clutching the down comforter from my bed.

I had been distanced from American life in those years, but I thought this should give me objectivity and insight. Today I am not so certain of this. In Moscow I had felt only the distant echoes of Joseph McCarthy, the purge of the Old China Hands, the Alger Hiss case, the Rosenberg affair, the headlined paranoia of Senator Eastland.

By the time I got back to New York, the banality of the Eisenhower era had begun to cool the fevers. I was sent over to Princeton to cover Alger Hiss's first speech on being released from prison. The campus swarmed with police. Press excitement was high. I asked a young *Princetonian* editor about the mood of the students. He carefully elevated his legs in their gray flannel trousers and pebbled Cordovan Oxfords to the top of his desk, drew deeply (and languidly) on his Chesterfield, and gently expired a single word: "In–diff–er–ence." I thought it summed up an epoch.

If this was the America to which I returned in the mid-fifties what had landed me in Hanoi in late 1966? How did it come about that for a blinding moment I had become the focal point of the great agony of Vietnam? Certainly nothing like this had seemed to be in the cards when I returned to New York after the long stint in Moscow. I had come home to a big splash—my stories about the end of the Stalin era—a fourteen-part series billboarded all over town, a very big splash. But now I had to go to work. I had to get acquainted with *The New York Times* and with the United States. I did not—so I felt—know either my paper or my country.

A day or two after the November election in 1954 I left my cubbyhole at the Algonquin Hotel and headed west into Times Square, taking a little bow at the pie slab of Times Tower and the square Adolph S. Ochs had persuaded the city fathers to name for his newspaper.

I walked down 43rd Street to No. 229 where, since 1911, the *Times* had been published, a bit to the right of Manhattan's center if you are going down to Greenwich Village but a bit to the left if you are going uptown to Park Avenue. The geographic metaphor, I thought, suited the *Times* perfectly.

My errand that November day was to report to City Editor Frank Adams, a chubby, sensitive man with ruddy complexion, a fondness for two or sometimes three martinis for lunch, and a stubborn will to present the truth and nothing but the truth (although sometimes a long-winded truth) on the pages of *The New York Times.*

For six years I had been reporting for the *Times,* but I did not know Adams nor did he know me. I had never worked as a reporter in New York. I had been the *Times* man in Moscow, and now, so I thought, I had put Moscow behind me and was going to discover America. I had faced Stalin's Russia; I had covered World War II; I had survived Al Capone's Chicago and FDR's New Deal. But I felt a bit daunted by the fifteen-story citadel of the *Times* and the *Times* editors who, I imagined, could make Captain Bligh look like a pantywaist. I was about to celebrate my forty-sixth birthday. I was the father of two boys. I had been a newspaperman for twenty-five years, but my pulse was racing as the elevator door closed and a soft-spoken, fine-looking Negro (the word at the time) named Jesse Hughes pressed down his brass lever and rode me up to the third floor. Jesse Hughes was one of the many blacks Mr. Ochs had brought from his native Tennessee. All the *Times* elevator operators and porters had come from Tennessee, but there were no blacks in the city room, none on the advertising staff nor in the circulation department. The whiteness of the *Times* was glaring, but I did not notice it. This was the way things were. Nor did I note the scarcity of women. The *Times* employed two or three female reporters in the city room, but most women, except secretaries and clerks, worked in the ghetto of the "women's department" where they wrote about the New Look, recipes for pumpkin pie, how to bring up the children, and weddings on Long Island. These were the days before the *Times* became the Emily Post of nouveau chic, hiring platoons of women to write about Zabars, tofu, aerobics, and anorexia, spending hundreds of times what it cost Mr. Ochs to bring to the world the news of Albert Einstein's theory of relativity and Charles Lindbergh's flight to Paris.

There had been a moment in World War II when the city room was overrun with copy girls from Smith and Vassar, replacing young men who had gone into the Army. The influx was short-lived. It ended when, as Gay Talese swears, it was discovered that an enterprising supervisor had installed a complaisant copy girl in the Hotel Dixie (later the Carter) across the street and was offering her favors on a pay-as-you-come basis.

On this bright morning I passed into the city room freely—no receptionist, no guard rail, no buzzer, just walk right in. So, too, at the street level—no uniformed guards, no bulletproof glass, no plastic idents, no sign-ins, doors open twenty-four hours a day, 365 days a year, Christmas and New Years included.

The city room was essentially unchanged since it was built fifty years before—an industrial floor, air-conditioned but not soundproofed. No planters, no hutches, no cubicles, no static-free wall-to-wall nylon carpeting to protect the environment of the computers. No computers. No offices except for that of Managing Editor Turner Catledge tucked away along the 43rd Street side. No color-coded decor. The whole room, ceiling and walls, painted in flat off-white. Factory brown, heavy-duty linoleum covered the tongue-and-groove oak flooring, the linoleum strapped down with wide brass belts. Functional. A plain honest hall for plain honest work, no flash, every desk like every other desk, more proletarian than Lenin's Russia, as egalitarian as Mao's China. Later I would delight in exhibiting this room to visitors from Moscow accustomed to the conventional Soviet class differences—special offices on special floors for senior writers, secretaries hovering over important editors, uniformed soldiers with rifles at the entrance. At 229 West 43rd Street no offices, no secretaries, no research assistants, nothing classy, and on this November morning 200 empty desks and swivel chairs, row on row, awaiting the editors and writers to report for work, each tilt-top desk fitted with an identical standard Remington, each top inset with green Fabrikoid, a perfect surface for editing oatmeal copypaper.

For twenty years this room would lie at the heart of my work, whether I was on the Pacific rim with Dwight D. Eisenhower, whistlestopping in Ohio with Richard Nixon, wangling my way into Albania, jolting across the Gobi, dining in Peking with Zhou Enlai, or running for the air raid shelter in Hanoi. Always, I came back to the city room. Wherever I might be, I could close my eyes and watch my story progress from desk to desk. I could see the copy editor count out the letters of the headline, marking the copy (as they still did) with the magic initials BLR—"By-line Requested." The fiction, wearing ever thinner, persisted that signatures were awarded for merit. Some reporters worked for years without seeing their name in print.

The room into which I walked that day extended one block from 43rd Street to 44th and opened up before me a quarter block wide, an unbroken acre under a fifteen-foot ceiling studded with brass sprinkler nozzles and aluminum shadow-free lights. Columns two-feet square supported the lead-heavy composing room overhead, a floor of elderly craftsmen (average age almost seventy), operating a regiment of linotype machines, casting type, justifying the lines, setting the bright metal filigree into page forms on massive steel chases, wedging in the cuts, locking the pages for stereotyping, a chamber of Gutenberg magic as mysterious as the bazaar at Isfahan (and somehow resembling it). Later I would watch the glass-walled, air-purified, static-free computer housing creep into that space, inching forward, month-by-month, as graying typesetters averted their eyes, each advance scrubbing more names from the payroll until the echo of giants' ten pins no longer rumbled from the fourth floor.

* * *

Above the city desk I watched the electric display board carrying the numbers 1 to 60. As press time neared, the page numbers winked off faster and faster, and the steel chases carrying finished pages from makeup to stereotyping reverberated over our heads. The reporters looked up again and again to the display board. Blink—page 8 went blank. Blink—page 14 was gone. Finally, only pages 1, 2, and 7 (a "jump" or continuation page), still were lighted. Then BLINK—all three went blank together. The paper was closed. All pages complete. Where had my story landed? Was it Page 1? The building began to tremble. The decibel count rose. The presses in the subbasement were rolling. There came a roar like the distant waking of a lion and the faint breath of printer's ink misted up the elevator shafts. The first edition was running! In a moment the senior copy boy (a middle-aged man) burst into the room, slamming down ink-wet papers. Silence descended. Reporters and editors buried their heads in the pages—reporters looking for their stories, editors looking for errors.

Over the years every detail of the city room and the editing process engraved itself in my mind. When I returned to New York from whatever outlandish place the search for news had propelled me and walked into the city room, I felt, like a child playing hide-and-seek, that I had got home free. I had made it safely again. I was back in that place where every inch and every person was so familiar that I knew from a turn of a head or the pitch of a voice whether anything significant was happening.

When I got back from Birmingham, Alabama, in 1960 in the civil rights days and found a $3.5 million libel suit slapped against me, Turner Catledge beckoned me into his office and said: "You know this, of course, but I want to tell you the paper is standing behind you." When I came back from Hanoi, Clifton Daniel told me the same thing.

On that November day of 1954, the city room was empty. The *Times* was a morning paper, and in those days reporters and editors seldom came to work before noon or 1 P.M. For a moment I thought I had mistaken my appointment with Mr. Adams. Then I saw a cluster of men beside an aisle desk. Frank Adams stepped forward and carefully introduced them, one by one. First was James A. Hagerty. James A. Hagerty was seventy-seven years old. For thirty years he had been the *Times* chief political writer, a man of awe to politicians and reporters. Even Herbert Hoover called him "Mr. Hagerty."

In that era before computers, exit polls, TV projections, sophisticated polling techniques, James A. Hagerty was the king of elections. A rangy upstate New York man, born at Plattsburgh, tall, with high Lincolnesque cheekbones and craggy jaw, James A. Hagerty "called" the elections, usually hours and even days ahead of everyone else. Mr. Hagerty never revealed his secret, probably because it was essentially just being Mr. Hagerty, a man who devoted his whole intelligence and life to politics. Telephone calls to a few old pols, a check of a handful of townships which he knew were bellwethers, a careful look at the turnout figures, study of the AP returns, a firm grip on the shiny seat of his blue serge pants, and Mr. Hagerty could tell you how New York would go and then how the nation was going. James A. Hagerty could read Tammany better than Tammany could read Tammany. In a lifetime he missed only one: He picked Dewey over Truman in 1948.

If there was a man who reflected the philosophy Mr. Ochs incorporated into his *Times,* it was James A. Hagerty. He was a frugal man, he knew the value of a dime and of a word. He spent neither carelessly. He spoke graciously to me and shook my hand. I am not sure that he had ever heard my name. Moscow is a long way from Canajoharie.

Adams now introduced me to Russell Porter, a grave withdrawn man with a long, long face and brooding eyes (he was to die in a few years of a fall from his apartment window; everyone was at pains to point out that the window had a low sill). He offered me his hand silently. Porter was as legendary as James A. Hagerty. Porter was the *Times* reporter on touchy, controversial, libel-prone stories. Totally reliable. Never a mistake. He had covered splashy trials like the Hall-Mills murder case in the 1920s. Mr. Ochs's sedate "newspaper of record" carried pages of meticulous reports of dramatic murders. Mr. Ochs called this "sociology." Some of Porter's stories contained more wordage than the whole "Living" section of the *Times* in the 1980s. (The *Times* used smaller type in those days.) In the 1940s and 1950s Porter covered the big McCarthy cases, Alger Hiss, the Eastland investigation of Communists on the *Times.* He was a Catholic and very conservative.

Adams did not have to introduce me to Peter Kihss. I had known Peter from the early sessions of the United Nations. I was covering for UP, Peter for the *Herald-Tribune* and Abe Rosenthal for *The New York Times* (No. 2 to Tom Hamilton). I had unlimited admiration for Peter Kihss and great sympathy for Rosenthal, so full of ability and so possessed of ambition I sometimes thought he would burst. Now in 1954 he was on his way, absent from New York, having at long last escaped from United Nations servitude, beginning a brilliant career in India, Poland, and Japan.

There wasn't a reporter I knew who did not respect Peter Kihss and fear him in head-to-head competition. No one ever beat Kihss on a story. Peter was Greenwich Mean Time. We set our watches by him. Tall as James A. Hagerty, Peter was always stooped. His glasses must have been a quarter-inch thick, and he leaned forward to see better, his eyes bulging from their deep sockets. His lean cheeks, long nose, arching forehead gave his face a skeletal look. Peter was a gentle man, but when he thought he was being lied to, he pierced his subject with his laser eyes. Few could hold out against him. He never forgot a detail and could dig up original notes of ten years back to reinforce his memory. He had no equal in journalism. He was embarrassingly modest. He quit the *Herald-Tribune* to come to the *Times* because he did not think the *Tribune*'s editors were serious about the news. No one can count the times he walked off the *Times* on questions of principle (I am certain he was always right). To their credit the *Times* editors let the dust settle and then wooed him back.

I do not think that Leo Egan was any more interested in meeting me than James A. Hagerty. Egan was all politics. He had been groomed to succeed Hagerty. He was middle-aged and middle-sized. He possessed a sandy complexion, blue eyes, silver-rimmed glasses, and a serious face. He smoked a lot, and I was to become used to his hours on the telephone with the politicians. The ferocity with which he attacked his typewriter delighted me. He hitched up his trousers, glanced into space for inspiration, poised his hands high over the keyboard, then plunged his fingers at the keys like dive-bombers.

This was a distinguished company. I felt very much a new boy. As I stood there, I heard Frank explaining that Mr. Hagerty was retiring. He had come in this morning for a postmortem on the election of Averell Harriman as governor and to clean out his desk.

"It's all ready," Mr. Adams said. "From now on it's going to be your desk."

The little group turned to me with warm faces, murmuring congratulations. "Just fine," said James A. Hagerty, his long face blessing me with a smile.

I thanked Frank Adams and told Mr. Hagerty I would take good care of his desk. I tried hard not to show how pleased I was. The city staff had not been my idea of heaven. After Moscow, I thought I might get London or Paris or Rome or possibly Washington—the diplomatic beat or the White House. Mr. Hagerty's desk made all the difference. No one outside the *Times* would ever understand, but as long as I lived no higher honor could come my way. In 1986 I was elected to the American Academy of Arts and Letters and assigned chair No. 3 which had been *Edith Wharton's chair.* There was no way in which I could explain to my fifty distinguished colleagues why Mr. Hagerty's old oaken desk meant more to me.

A few days before he died in 1983 of heart disease, Peter Kihss sketched in his crabbed hand his recollection of the city room where we worked. It tallied precisely with mine. The city desk, four desks banked together, was the center. Toward 43rd Street lay the independent domains of the foreign and national editors. The territory north to 44th Street overlooking Shubert Alley was city territory. Here sat score upon score of reporters in unbroken phalanx, facing south, facing the city desk. Adams liked to keep twenty or twenty-five reporters in reserve at all times in case the *Titanic* sank again or the *Hindenburg* blew up. Beside the city desk were two contrary clots of desks, facing east. One was the rewrite bank headed by the remarkable Meyer Berger who, like Russell Porter, could easily fill two full pages or more with details from the courtroom. At the Al Capone trial in Chicago, I watched in wonder as he took the whole thing down in shorthand. I never knew another American reporter who could do this.

Beside the rewrite bank were two short rows. Here sat the top political reporters and a band Turner Catledge came to call his "fire brigade." These men could cover the sinking of the *Andrea*

Doria one day and fly to Vienna to handle the Hungarian revolt the next. To that company I came in November, 1954. A bit later, Homer Bigart, the greatest war correspondent of his (or any) day, left the *Herald-Tribune* and joined us.

After the introductions I sat down at my desk, pulled up the top, and tipped the standard Remington into place. I put in a sheet of copy paper and typed out: "Now is the time for all good men to come to the aid of their party."

The machine worked fine. It had a new well-inked cotton ribbon, the keys had been cleaned and oiled. I was ready for work.

I sat at my desk all day. Nothing happened. The pace of the city room quickened. Reporters sauntered in and began to telephone. Copyboys circulated. Editors consulted. Copyreaders sat down at their circular desks, meticulously arranging pastepots, scissors, black No. 1 wound-paper copy pencils in regimental rows, tidying up the neat blocks of copy paper, fitting on their green eyeshades, hitching up shirt-sleeves with elastics, laying a steel ruler beside the shears, getting ready for action. I didn't know a dozen faces in the big room. I had no notion of the skein of relationships that underlay this ordered chaos, the subtle distances and distancing, the silent competition of editor and editor, the interplay of reporter-and-reporter and reporter-and-editor, the twisted histories that were captured in human word banks, the unwritten protocol, the pecking orders, the arrangement of desks and chairs, the neat human corners and deliberately vague boundaries that constituted the living fabric of the city room, the prejudices, unspoken rules about "minimizing the Jewishness" of bylines, the neat balance of a Jewish editor, a Catholic editor, and a Protestant editor. To me all was grand and glorious.

I got bored with gazing. I put another sheet of paper in my Remington and batted out a letter to my son Michael, a cadet at the Howe Military School in Indiana. I finished the letter. Nothing happened. I read and reread the *Times*. I listened to the typewriters clicking. All day I sat. At 7 P.M. Mr. Adams suddenly appeared at my desk and said, "Good night, Mr. Salisbury."

I could not have been more startled. He passed quickly to other desks, stopping here and there, and I saw the reporters thank him, flip shut their desks and head for their lockers. So that was it. Good night meant the end of my first day in the city room on 43rd Street.

3 | Garbage: NYC

The foreign country which I began to explore from my new base of Mr. Hagerty's desk could not have been more distant from Hanoi. In those late days of 1954 I could hardly, I am afraid, have distinguished between Hanoi and Saigon. I was totally preoccupied by the environment of 43rd Street, New York City, and the U.S.A.

I had been fretting at Mr. Hagerty's desk for several days with nothing to do when on the afternoon of November 10, 1954, Mr. Adams called me over and handed me a buff-colored memo which read, in part:

> Some of our travellers returning from abroad this summer have commented that New York is the dirtiest city they have ever seen. This brings up again the problem of making a survey of how New York handles its street cleaning and garbage disposal.

"See what you can do with this," Mr. Adams said, swaying gently in his swivel chair. He had just come back from a martini-and-hamburger lunch at Gough's, across 43rd Street from the *Times,* a no-frills bar-and-grill patronized by *Times* printers, *Times* photographers, Mr. Adams and his assistant, Colonel Marshall Newton, and a few other sturdy souls.

"See what you can do with this." Words I was to hear many times from Frank Adams. "I don't believe in telling adult reporters what to do with a story," he said. "They know better than I how to handle it."

Mr. Adams was acting in the tradition of Mr. Ochs. His principle was to hire men in whom he could place his trust. He hired no other kind. If he trusted a man, he did not spend his days looking over his shoulder. He respected his men and rare indeed was the occasion when his trust was misplaced. There was no revolving door in Mr. Ochs's *Times.*

If you examine *The New York Times* index, you will find this entry: "GARBAGE: NYC. H. Salisbury, series, Dec. 6–8, 1954." These were the first stories I wrote for the *Times* after I got back from Moscow.

GARBAGE, NYC, as I discovered much later, was an assignment which originated with Iphigene Ochs Sulzberger, the extraordinary daughter of founder Adolph S. Ochs, wife of Arthur Hays Sulzberger, Mr. Ochs's successor as publisher, and mother of Arthur Ochs (Punch) Sulzberger, contemporary publisher of the *Times* and grandmother of Arthur O. Sulzberger (Young Arthur), publisher-presumptive, of the *Times*. From her father's death in 1935 Iphigene Sulzberger, under provisions of the Ochs Trust, became, in effect, owner of the *Times*. Fifty years later, she still was.

Until my return from Russia, I had never met this woman, whom I came to worship. She had been a Barnard student before World War I and fell under the spell of Woodrow Wilson and his New Freedom. She urged her father to bring the (then) young radical, Walter Lippmann, onto the paper and abandon the *Times*'s cast-iron conservatism. That didn't happen, but Iphigene Sulzberger held to her views. She backed Al Smith. Her father kept cool with Coolidge. She went for FDR. Her father stuck with Herbert Hoover and his high starched collars. She voted for Adlai Stevenson, her husband for Eisenhower. When her son Punch swung the paper to the right, she voted for Carter and Mondale. Richard Nixon was not for her and neither Ronald Reagan's treacly voice nor Hollywood profile melted her heart. By this time Iphigene Sulzberger was into her nineties. She was proud of her son's success in turning the *Times* into a money-making enterprise such as her father would have admired, but nervous about its conservative drift. Her favorite *Times* editorial director had been her cousin, John Oakes, foe of Westway, foe of tinhorn Central American dictators, champion of civil rights, painfully objective, agonizingly humorless. Mr. Integrity. Another favorite was Sydney Schanberg, fearless in Cambodia, fearless among New York's Condo Kings. She was less than happy when Punch (with an assist or two from Abe Rosenthal) eased out Schanberg, tired of his crusade against the real estate high (and low) rollers. But she did not break her self-imposed rule of noninterference. Once Iphigene told me why she had not liked her father's brilliant editor, Carr Van Anda. She felt Van Anda looked down on Adolph Ochs for his lack of formal education. True, she said, Van Anda was a genius, but he had not treated her father with respect. She did not consider Managing Editor Edwin L. (Jimmy) James in Van Anda's class. James was too much a patron of racetracks, bookies, and the Paris boulevards. Turner Catledge, nurtured in the same liberal Southern traditions as herself, she loved and felt comfortable with. But she thought he was not quite fair to the family in his memoirs. She was, I came to know, very fond of Clifton Daniel, Catledge's successor, another Southerner, from Zebulon, North Carolina. She and Clifton shared a birthday, September 19 (twenty years apart). She thought Clifton was very gallant and a fine dancer. Her longtime favorite on the paper was James (Scotty) Reston, the Washington bureau chief and columnist, adviser to her husband and herself (as well as to Presidents and Presidential hopefuls), a cozy, pipe-smoking power broker behind the scenes in Washington and in the bright cretonne rooms of the Sulzberger estate, Hillandale, in Stamford. She never felt at ease with the *Times* editor of the 1970s and 1980s, A. M. Rosenthal. His passion, his flamboyance, his emotionalism, and his neoconservatism were not to her taste. Brilliant, yes, she was willing to concede that, as she did for Van Anda. Rosenthal was her son's choice, and she would not interfere, but she did not think her father would have put the paper in hands so frenetic. It was not *Times* tradition for editors to be in the gossip columns, splashed over magazine covers, up-front personalities. There was too much froth and breathlessness. Not enough starch. When Ann Rosenthal, a true life *Abie's Irish Rose,* finally drew the line and shut the door against her husband, Iphigene in her firm but gentle way called Ann, not Abe, to say how sorry she was. Carol, Iphigene's daughter-in-law, sympathized with Abe.

When Iphigene spoke to Turner Catledge about the filthy New York streets (she brought this to his attention almost every year after debarking in New York at Pier 49 from the *France*), she knew he would never mention her name, nor did he. In fact, Catledge did not connect his own name with the assignment. He passed it through one of his assistants. That, Iphigene felt, was the way to run the *Times.* No shouting. No histrionics. No posing. No breast-beating. Hints. Indirection. A quiet word. That was the way Mr. Ochs had run the paper, and his daughter did not think Mr. Ochs's style could be improved.

So it is not surprising that it was a good many years before I learned that Iphigene's quick eye, sense of public concern, and deft hand lay behind my initial assignment in the *Times* city room.

The first thing I did with GARBAGE, NYC was run for the clips—the files of all that the *Times* had printed previously. The story, I quickly found, had been done only fifteen months previously by Peter Kihss who now sat beside me in the city room. Peter had done a massive job. But the streets were as dirty as ever.

If the thought flickered across my mind that it was a long, long haul from the Kremlin to Manhattan garbage, it vanished in the joy of getting out on a story.

I decided that if I was going to cover GARBAGE I would do it in style. No *Times* reporter had ever ridden a garbage truck. I would. I couldn't wait to climb aboard at 7:30 one morning and rumble uptown under the West Side Highway to the upper reaches of Columbus Avenue and the area west of Central Park. Today it is so gentrified, at least in part due to the ceaseless stories in the *Times* about brownstone restoration, upwardly mobile delis, food boutiques, and Yuppies, that I find it hard to recognize the route of my first garbage truck. We crunched into a no-man's-land of vacant lots and landscapes that reminded me of the Warsaw ghetto. Riding a garbage truck, I found, was a good deal like riding a Sherman tank— the same clatter, exhaust fumes, and ponderous pace. I kept thinking we might come under fire from Molotov cocktails hurled from gutted roofs.

I began to lose track of what country I was in. These were facades I had seen in London's blitzed East End, pulverized Kharkov, the blasted bunkers of the Wilhelmstrasse. But, looking to the distance, I saw the towers of New York's pleasure palaces, marching up Fifth and Park Avenues.

I did not understand what all this meant. But I knew it must be the flip side of that brave, bright America which I had held close to my heart like a personal icon during the long days I spent in the shadow of Stalin's terror.

My garbage crew was having a lark, dolled up in white coveralls for the benefit of *The New York Times.*

"It's a jungle up here," Joe Cappola said. "You could send

the whole department in, and they would never get it cleaned up."

I spent a morning with the crew. At noon I jumped down and thanked the team. They smiled and shrugged their shoulders.

We all knew they hadn't made a mark on the detritus of the world's richest city. As I watched Joe and Mike and Sam heave can after can into the jaws of our crunching machine I became aware of an awesome fact. Only America spewed out such waste, useless, valueless flotsam of our consumer society. Only in America did these mountains of cardboard, tin cans, old newspapers, packing materials totter higher and higher. And only lately.

When I was a boy, growing up in the decaying Oak Lake section of Minneapolis, I carefully stacked the newspapers and tied them with string. I flattened the cardboard and fiberboard and put it in another pile. Magazines went into a third.

In spring the junkman came through the alley, an immigrant Jew from the Pale of Settlement in Russia, from some gray village near Pinsk, with a broken-down wagon, a broken-down horse, a jangling bell hung below his seat, and his shrill cry: "Old papers. Old papers. Brass. Old iron. Rags."

He halted at the gate beside our back door, and I lugged out the debris of winter: bundles of newspapers, 20 cents a hundred pounds; bundles of magazines, 40 cents; bottles, 2 cents; brass; gunny sacks filled with old rags. There wasn't much that the junkman wouldn't buy. Everything had a value, and before I finished college, Sam the junkman was owner of a scrap iron yard, and his son was my classmate at the University of Minnesota.

Everything had a value. That was what had changed. Now nothing had a value. It all went into the maw of this quivering machine. I asked my companions: Isn't junk worth anything anymore? They laughed. Not much. Sure, during the war people saved paper and sold it.

"That's the trouble," Joe said. "You can't sell paper any more. And twenty-five percent of this waste is paper."

That was it. We were drowning in our abundance. In Moscow or France hardly anything on our load would have been discarded. Certainly not the old davenports, the bed frames, the cabinets, the bric-a-brac. Why, I thought, the sidewalks of New York could furnish your whole apartment in Moscow (I didn't know that New Yorkers did this very thing). Moscow, I thought, would pick these trash mountains clean. And so would any city of Asia or Africa or Latin America.

All of it would be carted away—except the garbage, the old food, the remnants of the TV dinners. But even this would be picked over. Orange peel—priceless in Russia where oranges came on the market once a year at $3 an orange (in those days). In Russia every orange peel was saved; preserved, candied, used to flavor vodka. Coffee grounds—my God! Coffee was black gold. Old bones would go into the soup pot. Along with potato peelings, soggy winter vegetables, frozen cabbage leaves.

A year or two later I took some Soviet newspapermen on a Circle Line cruise around the island of Manhattan. When they saw the graveyards of crushed, disposed-of automobiles, their eyes popped. They knew Americans threw away tin cans. But automobiles!

I thanked my guides to the world's most abundant and wasteful society. I didn't try to tell them that, when I was six years old and growing up in Minneapolis, one of my chores was to take the garbage, neatly wrapped in yesterday's Minneapolis *Journal,* and deposit it in the galvanized can just behind our back gate. Nor did I mention that, when my mother asked me what I wanted to do when I grew up, I replied: "I want to be a garbage man."

No one could have devised a better introduction for me to the technological America which had grown up in the years of my absence.

Not until I rode the garbage truck did I begin to perceive that New York might be moving to the edge of a fearsome division—a small class of the hyperwealthy and an expanding underclass. But, I admit, this view in 1954 was only a whisper of a premonition.

GARBAGE: NYC splashed over page 1 of the *Times* on December 6. It ran four to six columns a day for three days. Big picture layouts. Tables of statistics. Archaeological implications. (I got scholars to expatiate on how they had reconstructed the history of Athens and Rome from their middens.) What kind of a picture would be reconstructed of New York when its middens were excavated in the year 3000?

The story caused a lot of comment, a lot of mail, a lot of gossip inside the paper. Mr. Adams, I discovered, was bowled over.

He felt the series proved his proposition: Give a reporter his head. Leave him alone. He'll do a story you could not have dreamed of.

I was delighted. There was nothing better than reporting in America. I could walk down a street, poke my nose into anything, and write it up the way I thought it should be written up. No danger of a warning shot from some trigger-itchy sentry. No rows with censors. No communications snafus. No angry letters calling me a dirty red for writing under the Moscow dateline. No steel-teethed bureaucrats to lecture me on shaping up or facing expulsion. This was America. Nothing to hide. Nothing to fear. I could not wait for another assignment on the streets of New York.

4 | What Are Yonkers?

It would be a mistake to suggest that I found the America to which I returned after the years in Russia a foreign land. Quite the contrary. Like most of us who have spent a long time away from our native shores, particularly in a scene as alien as the Soviet Union, I came back to the U.S.A. with a passionate love for what I had left behind. I could now put a value on American freedoms, American life, American spirit, because I was matching it against a society where these virtues were lacking. In the U.S. I could breathe. In Russia my lungs almost burst. My Russian experience made me a patriot, even a corny patriot, and I plunged into the rediscovery of my country with the enthusiasm of a prisoner who has just burst the barbed wire of Gulag.

Not all my discoveries were confined to the United States. I had never read a line of Oswald Spengler until that most improbable man, Frank Adams, set me on my exploration of Megalopolis. Yes, I knew Spengler had written *The Decline of the West.* I knew he was, like Malthus, anathema to the didacts of the Marx-Engels-Lenin-Stalin Institute, a prophet of pessimism antithetical to their radiant Communist hymns, fueled by vodka and fear of Gulag.

It was Yonkers which turned me to Spengler. All I knew about Yonkers, when Adams set me loose on that leathery Dutch town on the Hudson just above the Bronx, was the old vaudeville chestnut: "What are yonkers?" I had to pull down the linen-backed wall map of metropolitan New York just beyond the city desk to discover how to get there.

It seems ridiculous that I found my way, rather unwillingly, to Spengler through Yonkers, New York, a decaying factory town of 165,000. Today I can see little of Spengler in my Yonkers stories. If there had been, they would have raised an even louder clatter than they did. I tried to take an upbeat view of Yonkers. There was light at the end of the tunnel. Somehow Yonkers would emerge shiny-eyed, embracing the soaring future of the twenty-first century, and I was not too timid to suggest that

Yonkers after fifty-five years of the twentieth was still mired in the nineteenth.

What had drawn Frank Adams' attention to Yonkers? A triple catastrophe. Yonkers' biggest enterprise, the Alexander Smith carpet works, a bulwark since the Civil War, the largest carpet factory in the world, had scuttled off to Greenville, Mississippi. Lower taxes, cheap labor. The Cross County Center, a spruce $50 million shopping center, was opening up, sending the venerable Yonkers merchants into shock. And the New York State Thruway was blasting six concrete lanes down Central Avenue, chopping the town into two quivering segments.

I took the "I'm all right, Jack" line on Yonkers. Sure, Alexander Smith had moved out, but Otis Elevator, No. 2 in town, was staying on. (It skedaddled a few years later.) Not to worry, the shopping mart would create new jobs. But I couldn't sweet-talk the Thruway. That was forever. It isolated the "old nesters" in their roosts along the Hudson. Newcomers beyond the Thruway, beyond "the Alps," a high rocky ledge, went their own way—high incomes, New York commuters, Scarsdale, Bronxville, Tuckahoe addresses—politically part of Yonkers but not many householders could have found their way to Getty Square and City Hall.

I dusted my sketch lightly with rouge and powder, but nothing could hide the death agony of one more geriatric American city, done in by new high tech, new life-styles, new cost factors, new ideas. In Russia Yonkers would have been good for another hundred years. In America Yonkers would never recover. Yonkers was as obsolete as tail fins soon would be. I didn't say that because I didn't understand it much better than the men and women who had worked four generations for the tight-fisted Scots from Glasgow, who set up their carpet shop ninety years ago and hauled in fellow Scots by the boatload, shipping them straight from Ellis Island to Yonkers to spare them the sinful temptations and higher wages of New York.

My articles drummed up a storm. I had walked the streets of Yonkers and tactfully (I thought) touched on some of the old sores—the cleavages between the steely Presbyterians and the growing Catholic population (Yonkers was now more than 60 percent Catholic); between the Irish and the Italians, the Poles and the Russians, the nesters and the carpetbaggers, the haunting echo of anti-Semitism. I took enough notes to write a Middle-town-on-the-Hudson. I sensed undercurrents of despair like those of the 1930s. Depression days. I couldn't quite put my finger on the causes, and that drove me to Spengler—probably by way of Lewis Mumford, whose *New Yorker* articles on American cities I had long admired.

I didn't understand how typical Yonkers was of parts of America touched by blight—the shoe towns of Massachusetts, the textile towns of New Hampshire, the hat towns like Danbury, Connecticut. I didn't realize that decay was creeping through the upper tier of New York State. Before anyone quite perceived it, the smug, prosperous cities of the Ohio Valley and the Great Lakes would begin to turn sere and yellow. Parking lots where no one parked. Buildings where no one worked, the gaunt visage of those red-brick piles along the Connecticut, the Penobscot, the Merrimack, and the Blackstone. The first lights missing from the thousand-paned windows, millstones beginning to green with moss, millraces overgrown in reeds.

I couldn't fathom all that. But I could hear the plaintive cry of people who did not understand, the anger of an old worker: "I've never filled out a form in my life!" He had worked at the carpet shop. His father worked at the carpet shop. His grandfather. His great grandfather from Dundee. A thousand case histories. People tried not to look as they passed along the fifty-six acres in the center of town where the closed carpet shop stood. There were grand plans for new enterprises. Some of them came to pass. They were thrifty and canny, these Scots and Swedes and Irish and Italians and Poles. The Yonkers bankers could not believe the figures. Deposits actually rose in the three years when 6,000 lost their jobs.

Bewildered, dazed, frustrated, frightened, quarrelsome. All or any of these adjectives described the people of Yonkers. I used few of them. I let them tell their stories on their own. Yonkers had long been divided—Rivertown, the "old nesters," and "Beyond the Alps," over the granite ledges where the dormitory families from New York lived, fashionable suburbs. Some of the New Yorkers, it was whispered—and more than whispered in Rivertown—were Jews. Not many people directly told me the Jews were to blame for Yonkers' trouble, but the question was there, not spoken, hanging in the air. Allusions. "Us" and "them." Old town was very Catholic. Parochial schools—St.

Paul's, St. John's, St. Eugene's, Christ the King, St. Peter's, Sacred Heart, St. Denis', St. Barnabas', on and on, twelve elementary, four high schools, nasty rows over the public schools, taxes, quality of education. Neighbors against neighbors.

And there was Sarah Lawrence. No girls' college in America more advanced, more progressive, more chic, more controversial. Sarah Lawrence—red, radical, revolutionary, God knows what they taught the girls about sex. The American Legion up in arms, spewing filth about Commies and concubines. (They used a four-letter word.) Harold Taylor, president of Sarah Lawrence at twenty-nine, still president at forty-one, cool as steel, soft-talking his way through the garbage. I met one of his aides, Ed Solomon, who steered me through the tangle. ("But don't use my name. It won't do either of us any good.") Sarah Lawrence was across the Alps, a Bronxville post office. Blue-collar Yonkers (they still wore blue collars in Yonkers) thought it was a den of sin. I didn't interview Harold Taylor. I can't imagine why not. There wasn't much about Yonkers he did not understand. Nor did I talk to one genuine red revolutionary who lived in Yonkers—Earl Browder, whom Moscow had kicked out as leader of the American Communist Party. He could have told me a thing or two. He had two sons in the Yonkers schools. They got along OK. Felix was an honor student. "We don't hold his father against him," an old nester told me with pride.

I think these men might have given me a little deeper insight into what was happening in Yonkers. When I turned to Spengler, I sensed there must be a connection between this tottering relic on the Hudson and those Manhattan wastelands I had traversed in my garbage truck. Spengler spoke of the shiftless . . . the meaningless life . . . repetition of rudely mechanical tasks . . . vulgar and brutal diversions . . . the desolation of the cities . . . the inevitable decline down the path of Alexandria and Rome . . . the descent into nihilism and decadence.

Well, Alexandria Yonkers was not. Nor could I accept Spengler's pessimism about the West. I had seen nihilism in Stalin's Siberia. The blank faces of the young factory workers blurred with vodka. The Spenglerian barrens of Novosibirsk and devastated Kharkov. There I could believe in the Decline of the West. But not in America. Not in my land enlightened by the vision of the city on a hill. Not America. Today, I confess, I am not always so confident.

* * *

Yonkers ran for four days in *The New York Times*. A good many thousand words. I was used to being called a red, a Communist, an agent of the Kremlin. But here was something else:

Listen, Hebe,

Ordinarily I would have no truck with a man who hides his racial and religious origin behind the synthesis of historic names. Your masquerade will fool no one. Your Uncle Arthur. Where did he get the Arthur? The 21st century will have a cure for all that.

The *Times* talks of a Protestant and Catholic problem in Yonkers. There is no such thing. There is a Jewish problem. You people have created it. You have drawn the sword.

There will be repercussions to your articles that won't be salutary to the *Times* or to the Sulzberger type of Jewry. That type can never replace the American Eagle and the Six Pointed Star.

Of course the letter was not signed. Nor was one attacking "creeping Sulzbergerism" and "Jew Republicanism." Another denounced my "veiled call for us Jews to take over Westchester county." And one said: "Leave us alone, Mr. Salisbury. There is no Statue of Liberty or even a road sign at the entrance to Yonkers reading 'Send us your poor, your uneducated, your downtrodden, your bums and goons.' You keep 'em. We don't want 'em."

I had grown up in a Jewish ghetto, a settlement of Russian Jewish emigrants, in my native Minneapolis. I had gone to Sumner School on Sixth Avenue North, one of two or three gentiles in my class. I was used to being a goy in a Jewish community and very comfortable there. I had never thought of the *Times* and the Sulzbergers as Jewish or non-Jewish. But now, I was a Sulzberger masquerading as a Salisbury. This was new.

There was a smell of something I had seen in Russia—the cartoons in *Krokodil,* the Moscow "humor" magazine in which Russian Jewish writers who wrote under pen names like Ivanov or Petrov were "exposed" as "faceless cosmopolitans" whose real names were Finkelstein and Ginsburg. They were pictured with long noses, baggy trousers, and clawlike hands. But here I was in America. The year was 1955. Had I stumbled on an incubator where the vomit of Hitler and Stalin was still kept warm? It gave me a start.

* * *

The dark stain did not long possess me. Soon Frank Adams
had me chasing the dazzle of Manhattan again, this time a golden
bubble, the story of those towers I had seen glittering in the distance from the turret of my garbage cruncher. He designated me
to write a piece on the midtown skyline, the new New York, the
glass houses shouldering up Park Avenue, destroying what
Spengler would have called the "barracks of the rich," the old
New York Central apartment houses, a parade of gleam and
light—the emerald jewel of Lever Brothers, Seagram's classic
sheath of bronze, the glass and aluminum palazzos of soap and
booze, following each other to midtown like timid elephants,
trunk-to-tail, trunk-to-tail (and long since following their tails
on to the golf-and-grass of Stamford and White Plains).

Today we have tired of glass boxes, but then they gave me
sheer joy. After my paean was published, John Phillips, a dream
of a writer long since lost to the *Times* by his biblical visions,
retyped my story and sent it to me from the Brooklyn shack
from which he covered the homeland of "Dem Bums."

(No more Brooklyn shacks, daily coverage of the boroughs
long abandoned.)

Phillips said I might think I was writing prose but it was "a
fair brand of poetry too." So he retyped my story as free verse:

> Twenty-five years from the golden twenties
> to nuclear fifties
> have sculptured more deeply
> The man-made cordillera
>   That is Manhattan . . .

> The cannonade
> of riveters guns
> Echoes over Park Avenue
>   And led by the titans of
>   Soap
>   And oil
>   And whiskey
> A new headquarters area for blue-chip corporations
> Arises . . .
> All glass and glitter.
>   Led by the goliaths of petroleum
>   And detergents

The parade to midtown
Grows bigger . . . and . . . bigger

But it has robbed New York
Of Murray Hill
(Which survives only as a telephone exchange),
Gone
Are the Vanderbilts
    And the double-deck busses
    From Fifth Avenue

Soon
The iron lace
Of the Third Avenue El
Will join that
Of the long macerated Sixth.

And, as if heeding my unspoken wish, Adams sent me to
board the last train of the Third Avenue El, a journey as sloppy
and sentimental as the handsome girl who brought out a pitcher
of martinis at the 59th Street station. When she could not slither
into the packed train, she and two companions poured out the
drinks and toasted the El as the whistle tooted, and the last train
pulled out.

As Long John Phillips wrote, all my story needed was music
by Gershwin.

Let Spengler molder in his grave, I thought. This is New
York. There had never been a story like it, and it was mine.

5 | A Midnight Walk in Red Hook

At a little before midnight I slid off my stool at a lunch counter on 9th Street, Red Hook, Brooklyn, pulled up the collar of my gray herringbone topcoat, pushed open the frost-glazed door, thrust my hands deep in my pockets and started toward the Smith-9th station of the Coney Island El.

Ninth was a street of slatternly brick houses with old wooden stoops sited close by the approaches to the Erie Basin, not yet abandoned on this bitter evening in February 1958, with wharves and warehouses beginning to rot from disuse, not even a bar to show a sign of life, no traffic, not a footfall, dark windows, no one in the street, shadows. The wind tugged at signs and shimmered the street lights. I felt the hair rise on the back of my neck. I thought of a night in wartime London, long after midnight, the sudden scream of sirens, the drone of German bombers, the crunch of bombs coming nearer, and no place to run.

I felt the brass taste of fear in my mouth. I walked down the center of the street, a tall hurrying figure, casting anxious looks at dark doorways and dim side streets, listening for the sound of a heel cleat on the pavement. No one walked the streets of Red Hook after ten o'clock. This was no-man's-land, terrain of the dockside gangs, the Mafia, and of the violent adolescent gangs which had made slum New York their killing ground.

I knew Red Hook, I thought, pretty well. I had spent a month on these streets, but I had never walked alone at this hour and would not now had I not lost track of time. Ahead lay the steep and endless steps to the wind-swept El platform, the highest in the city, high above the haunted hulks of abandoned factories. I climbed the long row of steps and stood alone an endless quarter hour until the train screeched in. I still faced the eighteen-minute ride to Times Square, waiting for a knife-armed mugger to stomp the empty cars. When I scrambled up out of the subway at 12:30 A.M., the temperature on the Bond Clothing sign flashed 21 degrees above zero. I was drenched with perspiration.

There came a time when I would relate Red Hook to Hanoi, but not this night. In 1958 Vietnam was still French Indochina

30

to me and a long, long way from Brooklyn. Only later did I come to see that a thin red line tied together the teenage fighters in New York streets and their peers in the Cochin jungles. In Red Hook it was called "heart;" in Hanoi it was called "revolutionary zeal."

Frank Adams had called me to his desk one afternoon in the first week of February 1958.

"I suppose you've been reading about this," he said, pointing to the ink-black double banner that filled the upper half of page 1 of the *Journal-American:*

TEEN GANGS SHOOT IT
OUT IN N.Y. STREETS

I had. The headlines had grown bigger and bigger since George Goldfarb, a conscience-ridden high school principal, had taken the elevator to the top of his six-story apartment building, walked out on the roof, carefully placed his furled silk umbrella on the parapet, set his silver-rimmed spectacles (he was myopic) beside it, and stepped into space. He died the moment his body hit the cement of the inner courtyard.

The spirit of this unassuming man had been broken before a special grand jury impaneled by Judge Samuel Leibowitz, a man not noted for public tact. Instead of reporting at 10 A.M. for another session of torment about the violence in his school, Goldfarb had taken his life. His act touched off a tempest. You could not pick up a newspaper or turn on TV without being drowned in angry rhetoric about terror in the schools and violence in the streets.

By now I had become part of Turner Catledge's "fire brigade." If a train plunged through an open drawbridge in Jersey, I rushed to Perth Amboy. If Hungary blew up, I dashed for Fort Dix to interview arriving refugees. I went to Washington to cover John Foster Dulles and crossed and recrossed the country with Adlai Stevenson in his second run against Eisenhower. I could never decide whether Stevenson would make a good President, but I grew to admire him as a human being. Adlai's first grandson was born Sunday before election. My eighty-year-old mother, a wild Stevensonian, handed me my silver baby spoon and said: "You give him this for the new baby. It will make him feel better if he loses." I waited in the Blackstone Hotel in Chicago on election night until the returns made Ike's victory certain, then brought out the present for Adlai's new grandson. "My mother said this would make you feel better," I said. Adlai swore that it did, but there were tears in his eyes.

Frank Adams pointed at the *Journal-American*'s headlines and said: "See if you can find out what's behind all this."

Those words sent me into Red Hook and a winter of prowling East Harlem, Bedford-Stuyvesant, the old East Side slums. Night after night I caught the Coney Island train at Times Square and rode to the plateau of Smith-9th, hurrying down the long wooden escalator into 9th Street and up toward Red Hook Houses, a huge city project a couple of blocks away. I pushed open the door of Schroeder's candy store, letting in a blast of cold air, and looked around.

The first time I saw Schroeder's it was 6:30 of a very chilly evening. Half a dozen youngsters stood outside the shabby store, silent, hands in pockets, cold, shoulders hunched, teetering back and forth, heel-to-toe, heel-to-toe, eyes darting over me, then peering into the distance, alert, quick to detect movement in the streets, quick as a patrol in a combat area—which in a sense they were. The street was their turf. Beyond lay the turf of the Chaplains. These were Cobras, a fighting gang. Their only stated purpose in life was to protect their demesne against enemies. Frontier guards. The Khyber Rifles of Red Hook.

I had come there, into their turf, to this outpost to get acquainted, to learn if I could what they were about and what it was that was raging in the streets of New York. That first night not one word was spoken between us, not by a Cobra, not by me. I had been brought there by a city youth worker—otherwise, I would have been "made" (identified) as a police detective, and the Cobras would have melted into the shadows before I reached the candy store. "Play it cool," the youth worker had said. "Don't say anything. Don't ask any questions. Let them come to you."

By the fourth evening the Cobras and I were "tight," we were friends, even allies in the medieval style of language and concept of these adolescent outlaws. I spent evening after evening with them. They poured out their life stories to me as I bought them coffee and burgers. The first thing I learned was that they were always hungry. As long as I had quarters and dollars for coffee and burgers, they would consume them. It was not unusual for a Cobra to wake up hungry and go to bed hungry, never having a bite to eat all day. One slug of Smokey Pete (cheap wine) on those empty stomachs, and they were higher than heroin.

Most evenings I got a ride home with a youth worker. Or a couple of Cobras would walk me back to within a block or so of the Smith-9th station, but not all the way; the approaches to the El were the turf of the Chaplains. Any Cobra found in the zone was a free-fire target. He might be killed, and the incident could trigger a gang war. Serious business. No Cobra would think of venturing into this enemy turf without his "piece," a Beretta pistol or a zip gun—a homemade weapon, the barrel fashioned from the stem of a car aerial and a trigger activated by heavy-duty elastic bands, firing a .22 cartridge or a steel pellet, inaccurate but deadly.

I spent a month on the shrouded streets of Red Hook. It was a foreign country—its own language, customs, government. Chico and Trigger (who commuted an hour each night to be with the Cobras) and Blood and Zorro and Monk and Dice and Smokey, the president of the Cobras. I never saw Red Hook by day. If I missed a night on the corner, my Cobras "sounded" me: "What's a' matter? Where ya' been, man? You lettin' us down? We thought we were tight, man." They meant it. In their narrow world the appearance of a reporter from Manhattan was like that of a man from Mars. They missed the hot coffee and burgers. Most of all they missed my ear. They could talk all night. I was the first person who ever listened. They told the stories of their lives. The old man they had mugged. The Chaplain they had knifed. They hadn't intended to kill him, but there was nothing to be sorry about. He would have done the same to them. The girls they had impregnated. They pricked their condoms with a pin "just to give Dee-Dee a little surprise." They told me their aspirations. First choice: to be a cop. Second: to be a big-time gangster. Each career put a gun in their hand. They had never heard of Mao or his aphorism: All Power Comes from the Barrel of a Gun. But they lived by it. In the evenings police squad cars cruised Red Hook, nosing slowly up and down the streets, halting at any group of youths, piling out, gun and billy in hand, smashing at the Cobras, the Chaplains, any adolescents in reach, demonstrating that power did, indeed, flow from the barrel of a gun or the walnut end of a nightstick.

I saw some of the places the Cobras called home. Up a project staircase (never use the elevators—they are latrines, nauseating with urine and feces) to the dirty flat of a stepmother prostitute. Blood slept on a sagging sofa in the daytime. The sofa was otherwise occupied at night. Zorro slept three in a bed with a brother and sister in the flat of a woman they called "auntie." Most of the Cobras preferred the street or an abandoned building. The gang was their life, their family, their security, their present, their past, and their future, if there was to be a future. Here they had love, comradeship, a cause, shared danger, shared hatred, everyone shook-up. None could make it in real life, but that made no difference. In the gang they were all for one and one for all. Heart was what mattered—bravery, or, more realistically, manic insanity, a willingness to steal a policeman's pistol from his holster and risk being shot if you failed.

I got to know Smokey and Blood almost as well as I knew my own sons. In those nights on the stools of the lunch counter, I became, in effect, a surrogate father but a father who had no influence on their conduct. Their lives were patterned deeply by the eroded skeleton of the society in which they existed, the fighting gang. And, as I found, the gang was not a slum product. Combat-prone bands of adolescents flourished in the suburbs, and I had seen them, I realized, in the Soviet Union, in the Moscow streets. The key to the emergence of these groups was the destruction of the family, and this destruction was as common in wealthy Winnetka or Scarsdale as it was in Red Hook. In the Soviet Union it was commonplace, and there, as in the American slums, the breeding grounds of the most violent, most homicidal adolescent conduct was the housing project. If anything, the Soviet gangs with their "Finnish" knives spilled more blood than did their American cousins.

What startled me most about the Cobras, the Chaplains, and the Bishops was the way in which they mimicked the adult world—not the world of today but that of Richard the Lionhearted, the world of chivalry. The Cobras lived by territorial warfare patterned precisely upon the feuds of the Scottish clans of Sir Walter Scott. They fought by archaic rules, set battles and the tilting of champions to determine questions of right or wrong. They spoke and dreamed images of a lost world of knights and ladies. The gang was a fiefdom ruled by a chief (they called him the president) with a chief of staff (the vice president), a war minister (the equivalent of Cap Weinberger) and an armorer (custodian and collector of weapons and ammunition). They possessed scouts and spies, double agents and slaves. They guarded the (public) honor of their ladies as if they belonged to the Round Table. They spent their days protecting their turf, on the alert for threats and insults. They boasted ambassadors and foreign ministers, who negotiated treaties with brother gangs. It was the fantasy of many police that some day the gangs might rise in a huge rumble against them. Of course, this was far beyond the organizing ability of these unstrung and shook-up young men. Had some Pied Piper come along, he might have led them off on a new Children's Crusade. I mentioned the Crusade, Pied Piper, the Knights of the Round Table to Chico and Trigger and Blood and Zorro. They had heard of none. Most had never been outside their own neighborhood. They could not read the street signs. The thought of being trapped on the subway tens of blocks from their turf terrified them. They called me the reporter from the *News*. They had never heard of the *Times*. They liked to look at the pictures in the *News;* they couldn't read the print.

In this time I avoided, for the most part, the social work apparatus. I spent my days on the streets, in the candy stores, in the projects, and later in some of the schools and settlement houses with youth workers and police.

When I went to the old East Side slums, I made a discovery. Social deterioration was not so bad there as in the housing projects. The projects compacted 10 and 12 stories of poverty, broken homes, relief families. No mix. The moment a family's income began to rise, out it went; only the lowest income people were permitted to occupy this housing. The project became a cesspool of the poorest, no leaders, no corner druggist to help girls when they missed a period or boys with their first clap, no candy store proprietors to look away when a starving kid snatched a Mars bar or to hit him on the head if he stole another.

No one to give a kid a quarter for delivering an order or sweeping out the store. No one to slip a quiet word to a mother that her daughter was hanging around.

Aleksandr Solzhenitsyn once wrote a story about the single upright woman in an old Russian village, the one with character and conscience, without whom no village or city or country could endure. That was all it took—one Puerto Rican mother in Forsyth Street, an old grocery man in Morningside, an Episcopal priest in Henry Street, that street which was a slum 150 years ago and was still a slum, only the ethnic character changing year by year from Irish to Jewish to Italian to Puerto Rican. It didn't take much to bring light to a dark street. The New Deal had thought the name of the game was slum clearance, new buildings, brick-and-plaster, get rid of the cockroaches, the leaky roofs, cracks in the walls, stinking drains, slumlords. But the new high-rise housing barracks had bred more ills than moldering railroad flats—every social, medical, economic problem known to man, and no one to lend a helping hand. The few social workers were gone by 4 P.M. That left the cops to beat up the kids every night.

But no one in the city seemed to notice this—not the bureaucrats busy building up or protecting their power bases, not the politicians (where were the votes?), not the uptown churches far far away from the mean streets. The only voices heard were those of a social worker here or there still clinging to the spirit of Jacob Riis and Lillian Wald and some youth street workers, brave and imaginative but powerless.

And the press? *The New York Times* published column after column of dreary reports from city and social agencies. Who plowed through the tedious words? The rest of the press and TV were in it for the headlines, the sensations, the knifings, the muggings, the beatings, the shootouts, sadism, vengeance, scapegoating those who could not understand the world into which they were born.

I did not have to walk the streets of Red Hook long to understand that society had no use for the Cobras and the other castoffs of an unequal, irresponsible system. Nor was there anything new about this. The bully boys of New York 100 years earlier, so tough the police would not even enter Hell's Kitchen, were the same shook-up remnant of humanity. So were the gangs of London in the eighteenth century, of Paris in the seventeenth century, and the riffraff that shouted, *"Bei Jidov"* as they beat the Jews in the streets of Moscow before 1905.

I thought of Lincoln Steffens and Upton Sinclair and Jacob Riis and Frank Norris and Ida Tarbell and Theodore Dreiser and the great exposés of American vice and corruption, *The Shame of the Cities,* the venal governments, the venal trusts, the conspiracy of Greed against which a generation of American muckrakers had struggled, exposé after exposé, the investigation of the Triangle Shirtwaist fire, the bloody strikes of Paterson, New Jersey, and Lawrence, Massachusetts—what had it all gained? I knew my articles would generate a response—probably a big response. But what would happen after the excitement died down? Would this change anything?

I come of the generation which thought that the New Deal was the answer. At long last we were turning our imagination and energy to resolving our social ills and cleaning out the dark, festering corners to try to bring the city on a hill to life on this earth.

What had it availed? Slums, slums, slums; the perversion of our dearest national treasure, our youth, went on and on. I could not believe that the creation of an equitable society lay beyond our grasp. I knew better than most that the answer was not in a new utopia. I had seen how man transformed a utopia into a caricature, a bizarre Orwellian nightmare. I had seen in Russia the tragic perversion of the idealistic dream of the young Russians of the nineteenth century, who gave their lives to cleanse the social evil from their land, idealism and bravery turned to the mockery of the Gulag. Who had created a just society in which human beings could attain their true potential and look ahead to a bright future? China? I did not know China at this point. Scandinavia? Only a Swede could make Sweden's way work. America? We had possessed the dream, we had prepared our foundations, but the gap between ideal and reality was growing. Benign attempts to cure one social ill sowed the seeds of another. The architects of the bright future could not—even with computers—predict what new disease might be born in the cure of the old.

Nearly thirty years after Red Hook, I spent a winter in Florence, and there on narrow, twisted, incredibly beautiful old streets I discovered the medieval ancestors of my shook-up Cobras. Here 500 years earlier under the banner of the Medici, the wars that raged at the foot of Smith-9th had been fought out—with, perhaps, more artistry, certainly against a tapestry of beauty, but fundamentally the same contests for turf, for demesne that animated the Bishops and the Chaplains. The boppers of 1958 would have felt entirely at home on the stones of Florence in 1458. There was no peril in Red Hook with which Lorenzo and his men would have been unfamiliar. I could, I thought, have written my story 100 or 200 or 300 years earlier. Only the names were new. And, I ventured, I could write it in the year 2100, and the same would be true.

Society, I began to perceive, is more durable than the transient schemes of men. Aggressive bands of drifting young men have been, I am sure, a social phenomenon since cave days. The cast-outs survive only as a group. Individually they have little or no judgment, few capabilities. Their virtue is "heart." That is, they put their lives at risk without thought. They have been thrown by society onto the ashheap of history, but they still possess a potential which can be put to use. They make remarkable soldiers. The wars of Europe have been fought by this young blood. Napoleon led young males into Russia. Hannibal led them over the Alps. With them Alexander conquered the known world. Hitler won Germany and threatened Europe with his *Jugend*. Mao Zedong led them on his Long March in China. They were called Little Red Devils. Some fought at Valley Forge and Manassas. They made up the last regiment that defended the Winter Palace in Petrograd against the Bolsheviks, and they fought their hearts out in Stalingrad. As Hitler was putting a bullet in his head, they were still manning machine guns outside the bunker.

They were the backbone, as I would later learn, of Hanoi's war against the U.S.A., wiry daredevils, often not more than twelve, thirteen, or fourteen, the fighting rats of the tunnel wars of Cu Chi.

But there was a difference between the Cobras, the Red Devils, and the tunnel rats. The Red Devils (and the youngsters of Valley Forge and Manassas) had a national cause and a national leader. True, these leaders might be young. True, some might call their causes dubious. But there was a structure, a philosophy, and charisma which the bopping gangs of Brooklyn and the Bronx could never match.

The Shook-ups of the New York streets (and of Chicago, Atlanta, Liverpool, and Moscow) led themselves. Their cause was survival. They had an innate instability. In the late 1950s most street gangs drank heavily, the leaders much less. Gangs began to fall apart if the leaders' judgments dissolved in alcohol. Drugs were just beginning to come in, but drug use was barred by most gangs for combat reasons. Stoned adolescents could not fight.

A year or two after my winter in Red Hook the elaborate, almost courtly structure of the street gangs began to fall apart, as more and more youngsters were caught up in narcotics, users and sellers. This was death to the gangs. No longer could discipline be maintained. By the midsixties the bopping gangs of New York were no more, gone, dissolved by heroin and cocaine. The network of street youth workers was dissolved as well. Only remnants of social work remained, the streets more and more resembling a terminal moraine of Western civilization.

My Red Hook Shook-ups had gone very quickly. Six months after that February of 1958, I could find only a handful. A couple had committed suicide. One had been killed (probably) by a Bishop. Others had vanished. Several were in prison. The casualty rate was as high as in the tunnels of Cu Chi.

But not all were gone. One Puerto Rican who came from a sturdy family (a strong mother, a working father) made it through City U. An enormously attractive black, out of Henry Street, survived. I had been present one evening when Father Myers struggled for the soul of Reno. The police had arrested his friend Chico, in retaliation for their appearance on a TV program. Reno had finished high school and hoped to go on to college. But anger over the police action brought Reno and his gang to the edge of explosion.

I listened for four hours as Father Myers, cool, calm, unblaming, reminded Reno again and again of his resolve to break from the streets, to go to college, to lead his friends out of the gangs. Then Reno, passionate, eloquent: "We did our best, and you did your best. But now there is trouble, and there is going to be more trouble. Nothing but trouble. You can't stop it. And that's the way it is."

In the end Father Myers won. Reno did not go back to the streets. Or perhaps he did but in another way. In 1971 at the height of Cambodian spring, I had a telephone call from Cornell. It was Reno. He had persisted. He had taken his degree at Cornell, and now he was an academic counselor working to maintain a cool, just as he had in the dark streets of St. Augustine's parish.

The Shook-up stories did have impact. For several days in Brooklyn and East Harlem, gang kids ran around with copies of the *Times* under their arms. They couldn't read them, for the most part, but they had friends pick them out. I had disguised the identity of gangs and their members, but they recognized themselves. They didn't like the picture. Some vowed to come to the *Times* and have it out with me in "a fair one." What made them especially angry was that I didn't give them credit for their bopping achievements. I waited for them to show up at 229 West 43rd Street, but they never did—that journey from Red Hook to Times Square was too much. I got a letter from "The Click of Lords and Debs" who claimed as turf "from 149th Street and Third and Willis Avenue to the Harlem river" in the Bronx. They were sore because I had not mentioned them. Another Bopper wrote:

> Mr. Salisbury:
> How Dare You? Saying Chaplins have heart when they are Punks and slobs. Especially the fort green chaplins and Marcy chaplins and all the chaplins. How could you say they have heart every time they fight us they run even though they got 5 to 1. If you got Nerve you print this letter.
> The People of Franklin and Myrtle avenue.
> Johnny Pegleg
> Little Oliver
> Jimmy Beans
> Eddy Feeth
> Jim Randy The Cool Cat.

I sent the notes to Arthur Sulzberger, saying I thought they would amuse him. "I'm afraid the word 'amuse' doesn't belong here," he replied. "I am rather saddened by the letters."

Robert Moses didn't like the series. He didn't like some of my remarks about big public projects (his specialty). His recommendation: more police on the streets and better athletic facilities. The promotion department of the *Times* shipped out 10,000 reprints of the series in ten days, a record. The Manhattan district attorney's office took 400. The *Times* even had a modest circulation gain in places like Harlem, Brooklyn, lower Manhattan, and the Bronx, but I warned Nat Goldstein, circulation director, that it wouldn't last. It didn't. Publisher Arthur Sulzberger and his wife, Iphigene, liked the series a lot. So did Managing Editor Turner Catledge and Clifton Daniel, who had returned because of ill health from Moscow, where he had succeeded me, and starting his internship for the managing editorship under the curious title of "Assistant to the Foreign Editor." Abe Rosenthal, tiring of India and agitating for a new post (he got Poland and a Pulitzer), wrote: "My God, man, this versatility is just stunning! What are you trying to do? Prove that there is still room on the paper for reporters? Up Salisbury!" My old friend Cy Sulzberger, nephew of the publisher, who had played a big role in getting me onto the *Times* in 1949, sent cheers from Paris. He particularly liked my material on delinquency in Russia. In Moscow they liked my material on delinquency in the U.S.A. Never before had they reprinted anything I had written. Now the magazine *New Times* republished several installments (but nothing about street gangs in Russia). A year later I ran into the editor and asked him if he was going to pay me. What currency would you like—Romanian? he asked. Then he took me to an Uzbek restaurant and served me a lunch of boiled sheep's eyes.

One letter came from Grover Hall, editor of the Montgomery, Alabama, *Advertiser.* He wanted a copy of my articles about "the New York student princes" and used it to berate New York for trying to tell Alabama how to handle the race problem when it had such terrible problems of its own. That was my first contact with Grover Hall. Two years later, when I went to Alabama, he wrote an editorial about *The New York Times:* "Lies, lies, lies."

By that time memory of the Shook-ups on New York's streets had almost faded away. Nothing had changed. But the problem of the South was coming up like thunder.

6 | Damn the Law

The time stamp on my registration card at the Tutwiler Hotel in Birmingham, Alabama, reads 9:53 A.M. April 6, 1960, a Wednesday. I had flown in from Baton Rouge, Louisiana, and a bellhop showed me to Room 1117. I had not yet unpacked my bag when the front desk called: Would I mind changing my room? There had been a mistake. I grumbled a bit, allowed myself to be moved to Room 1060, sat down at the telephone and went to work. It would be sixteen years before I understood why I was moved from Room 1117 to Room 1060.

I thought that by 1960 I had a pretty good grasp of what the United States was about. I had done a lot of political reporting and knew Adlai Stevenson and, improbably, Richard Nixon quite well. I had had a good look at my native Minnesota and the Middle West and been shocked by the abandonment of smaller farms and their consolidation into tracts of 300 to 360 acres and amazed at the corn/hog prosperity in Iowa where, as I reported, every farmer seemed to own a Cadillac—a finding which so enraged the Iowa farmers that they took a full page advertisement in the Des Moines Register-Tribune in protest. I had studied the deep social cleavages in the big cities and come to realise that the United States was not the paradise it had seemed to me during my long Moscow years. I had watched with concern the rise of violence in the South in the wake of *Brown* v. *the Board of Education* and the outburst of intolerance, still largely confined to the South.

But at least, I thought, we were making progress. I had been in Eastern Europe in 1957 at the time of Little Rock. Everywhere I went, I met denunciation of the United States for its "racist" policies.

Finally, in Bucharest, at a dinner given by Romanian journalists, I spoke out. Yes, there was racism, and there was violence. No American condoned that. But the reason must be understood. The violence was the product of our effort to change the oldest prejudices known to man, prejudices of color, creed, ethnicity, and religion. No nation was so diverse as we, and now we

42

were moving to make our principles of democracy, equality, and freedom more than words enscribed on a piece of parchment. Where else, I asked, had such a Herculean task been undertaken—to change attitudes thousands of years old, dating, perhaps, to the cave men? Certainly there was violence and bloodshed and certainly there would be more, and the task would take a very, very long time. Look around, I said; what is being done in your part of the world? Instead of criticizing Little Rock, I suggested, they should attack their own prejudices as we were attacking ours.

I spoke from my heart, and I think my words got through. I received a standing ovation, and in Bucharest, at least, I heard no more about American racism.

I had not been in the front ranks of *The New York Times* coverage of the South. As far as possible, Turner Catledge placed these stories in the hands of well-trained, courageous reporters of Southern birth, experience, and accent. Not until I returned to New York in late 1954 had I realized what a Southern tradition had been bequeathed to the *Times* by Mr. Ochs. He himself was born in Tennessee, founder of the Chattanooga *Times* (still owned by the family and published by his granddaughter, Ruth Holmberg). Iphigene Sulzberger made two or three trips a year to the city where she spent her earliest years (she was born in Cincinnati because Mr. Ochs didn't trust the Chattanooga doctors). Her Chattanooga-born grandsons, Stephen and Michael Golden, played an important role among the thirteen cousins into whose hands the *Times* ultimately would fall, and were deeply imbued (as were all the cousins) in the Ochs tradition and not too happy with the conservatism of Punch (although happy with his business success) and the ego-trip editorship of A. M. Rosenthal.

Of the paper's four editors in the half-century after 1930, three had been Southerners—Edwin L. James of Virginia, Turner Catledge of Philadelphia, Mississippi, and Clifton Daniel of Zebulon, North Carolina. Rosenthal, the fourth, was born in Canada and raised in New York City; as he said plaintively one night in the spring of 1986, "I think I'm the last Yankee who will edit the *Times.*" Not everyone would describe the Canadian-born New York-raised Abe as a Yankee.

Well, Alabama is a long way from my native Minnesota. And

I confess I never tried to conceal my Yankee background from Southerners. My grandfather and my great uncles fought for the Union in the Civil War, most of them in Wisconsin volunteer regiments. But my sentiments bore no resemblance to the caricature drawn by John Temple Graves, editorial columnist of the Birmingham *Herald-Post,* who in April 1960 described my Minnesota as "the most South-hating of the States."

I had been given a minor role in the remarkable survey of Southern sentiment conducted under Turner Catledge's direction in the aftermath of *Brown* v. *the Board of Education* in 1955. Catledge went down to his hometown of Philadelphia, Mississippi, and came back believing that things were working out, that the South would opt for peaceful transition, not violence. He sent a ten-man team into the South to test this assumption. The team was headed by that extraordinary ex-Marine officer (and son of a Marine officer) John Popham, whom Catledge a decade earlier had named *Times* roving correspondent in the South—the first and for many years the only correspondent of a major news organization covering the South. Both Catledge and Popham believed the day of Southern transition was inevitable. The *Times* would be prepared. Iphigene Sulzberger shared that belief and so did her husband, Arthur, who had personally in 1955 desegregated the obituary columns of the Chattanooga *Times.* No longer would black and white deaths be listed separately. The action cost the paper 8,000 in circulation, not regained for years.

The vision of the New South, free of race oppression and hatred, prospering industrially and economically, was an article of faith in the Sulzberger family as it was in the minds of Catledge and of other liberal Southern editors like Ralph McGill of the Atlanta *Constitution,* Harry Ashmore of the Little Rock *Gazette,* and Hodding Carter of the Greenville, Mississippi, *Delta Democrat.* With considerable hesitation I had come to embrace this view.

Popham had been traveling the South since 1946, 50,000 miles a year by road before the days of the Interstate system. There was hardly a cow patch or a shade tree mechanic below the Mason-Dixon line he did not know or a mayor or sheriff who did not know him, his Jim Dandy hat, and his extraordinary Tidewater Virginia accent, which his successor, Claude Sitton of Georgia, once compared to "dollops of sorghum syrup sprayed from a Gatling gun."

I performed only one function in the *Times* survey. I sat at Popham's elbow, as he struggled to synthesize the tens of thousands of words from the reporters, and helped him shape the mass into an overview, in which Popham proclaimed that the country was confronting a profound and inevitable social revolution with which, he believed, the Southern leadership was coming to terms. (But he offered a caveat: There could be vengeance in the deep South against moderate and liberal elements.) I agreed with that conclusion. In fact, I probably put some of those words into Popham's copy.

We all believed and hoped that we were correct. We were not. Years of pain and violence lay ahead.

Within a few months standpat segregationists were beginning to call the tune. Popham was always to blame President Eisenhower, his failure to give clear leadership. Ike left the field to hard-liners, Little Rock and all the rest followed, the cry of "The South Will Rise Again!" echoed over the land, and fiery crosses lit up lawns and hillsides.

As levels of violence rose, Catledge tried to keep *Times* coverage in the hands of reporters with Southern accents. It was much better to deploy Popham with his Tidewater tongue or Claude Sitton and his Georgia drawl than flat-toned Midwesterners like myself or hard-edged Balts like Peter Kihss, who faced down a mob at Tuscaloosa by challenging the whole Alabama student body to fight him, two at a time.

By the winter of 1960 there weren't enough Southern accents to go around. On February 1, 1960, at about three o'clock in the afternoon, four freshmen from the all-black Agricultural and Technical College in Greensboro, North Carolina, walked into Woolworth's, sat down at the counter, and asked for a cup of coffee. The waitress refused them. The students remained seated. Nothing like this had happened in history. Within a week young blacks were doing it throughout the South, walking quietly into drugstores and five-and-dimes, sitting down, politely ordering coffee, and sitting there when service was refused. Johnny Popham had never seen anything like it. Neither had Claude Sitton. Or the white power structure. The sit-ins leaped like crown fire in the forest, spreading headlines and consternation through the South. The young men were *so polite* and so persistent.

I was quickly preempted by the national desk, and a month

after Greensboro, on March 1, 1960, found myself in Nashville, Tennessee. No city in the South had developed race relations so sophisticated, smooth, and silky. Nashville had integrated its schools without a hitch. It was proud of a reputation as "the Athens of the South," a city of gracious, tree-lined streets, culture, taste, good manners, colleges (two of the best black colleges in the country), a city where voices were not raised. Its first sit-in came February 13 at the Woolworth, Kress, and McClellan lunch counters, polite young men from Fisk University.

I hurried straight from the airport to the center of town, where I found a crowd milling about a shopping complex—black students, curious passersby, police, and reporters. The lunch counter had been closed, the standard tactic with which proprietors met the sit-ins. A tall, thin, strongly built young man with notebook in hand introduced himself. He was David Halberstam, Harvard 1955. He had gone to Mississippi to learn the mechanics of reporting and now was working on the Nashville *Tennessean.* Within the year he would be off and running on *The New York Times,* first to the wars in the Congo and then to Vietnam with the best and the brightest. On this sunny, soft spring day Halberstam was tremendously excited by the sit-ins and eagerly began to tell me what was happening.

This was my first glimpse of the civil rights movement, which would plunge the country into an almost revolutionary state and take the life of Martin Luther King and all the others, black and white. On this balmy morning no one seemed to know how it had started (the young blacks thought it was their own personal idea). But someone that day, possibly David Halberstam, mentioned the name of Dr. Allen Knight Chalmers of Boston University's Divinity School. As time went on it became clear to me that his teachings about nonviolent resistance, patterned after Gandhi, lay near the heart of it all. Chalmers wrote me after Birmingham, saying, "You do a good job," and told me that Martin Luther King was his student. Then Chalmers was off to the Far East and I to West Virginia and the Kennedy-Humphrey primary, and we never did meet.

That morning I had only a taste of sit-ins, but I came back to Nashville a month later and confirmed my suspicion that, given the will, racial progress could be made. Nashville had been hit with the same blitz as other Southern cities, which had met it with bluster, bloat, billyclubs, and bullying. Nashville took it on the cool side. The universities and colleges helped. But most of all it was the city's tradition of civility. A professional man apologized: "I'm sorry for what brings you here." A woman wrote the Nashville *Banner:* "Nashville, the eyes of the country are upon you! Are you proud of what they are seeing? Until now I could look anyone anywhere straight in the eye and say, gladly, 'I'm from Nashville, Tennessee.' "

Imagination, I thought, that was the key—imagination and will. Elsewhere I would discover stereotypes and even stereotypes of stereotypes, spite words, "hollering nigger," the "bloody shirt," the clichés of a century of hate and conflict. I began to feel an echo of the days before and after Appomattox. I had grown up with the last of the *Uncle Tom's Cabin* tent shows, those nifty ones with two Uncle Toms and two Elizas. Uncle Tom was, I thought, a tired old joke. I had snickered when I found Uncle Tom presented at the Children's Theater in Moscow as a realistic slice of today's America, and now in the heat of the sit-in I found John Temple Graves proclaiming in the Birmingham *Herald-Post* that Harriet Beecher Stowe lived again in the prose of Harrison Salisbury.

I was out of the South for a few days, covering a blizzard that left Times Square looking like the North Pole. Then I went to Raleigh, North Carolina, again to a border region which prided itself on civility (these were the days before Jesse Helms) and where the moderation and intelligence of Chapel Hill and Frank Graham and the transplantation of the textile industry were laying the foundation of the New South. So Turner Catledge believed. So Iphigene Sulzberger believed. So, hesitantly, I believed.

In Raleigh for the first time I felt the cold whisper of terror—very faint but unmistakable. The story here was a court case which, it was thought, would go to the U.S. Supreme Court and establish the constitutionality of sit-ins. Jack Greenberg, the smart, aggressive counsel of the National Association for the Advancement of Colored People, was there to mastermind it.

When court adjourned after convicting two black students from Shaw University of trespass, Greenberg, myself and several blacks—decided to have dinner and talk things over. Where to eat? We could not go to the hotel or a white restaurant. That would have provoked an incident. What about a restaurant in the black area? This was not easy either. If a cruising police car spotted whites "segregating together"—in the classic phrase of the late Police Chief Theophilus Eugene (Bull) Connor of Birmingham—we would be arrested.

We went to a black restaurant anyway, carefully selecting a table hard to see from the street. It was an edgy meal. The proprietor was nervous. The blacks were nervous. I was nervous. No one wanted to cause a "mixing" incident and complicate the case of the right of two young black men to walk on the sidewalk of the Cameron Village shopping center. The sit-in movement was heading into uncharted legal waters, and lawyers like Jack Greenberg were improvising as they raced to keep up with it.

We hurried through our ham hocks, turnip greens, black-eyed peas, cornpone, and pumpkin pie and slipped away. I thought I now knew how the young *narodniki* felt in St. Petersburg in the dark days of the 1880s when Lenin's elder brother, Alexander, and his friends were conspiring against the Czar, expecting at any moment that the *shpiki,* the third section plainclothesmen, would pounce.

Next day I was on the road again, deeper into the South, each day the temper, the level of violence on the rise. I entered South Carolina, once the citadel of secession, now a satellite capital of segregation. Edges were more raw. The day before, 350 students at black South Carolina State College had been rounded up with high pressure, knock-down firehoses, arrested, and herded into the courtyard of the Orangeburg jail (the jail had only thirty-nine cells). I had left the New South but not completely. I had a long talk with Governor Ernest F. Hollings, handsome, young, hoping for a national career, trying to split the middle between the old nigger talk of Senator Cotton Ed Smith and the sleek New York idiom of the industrialists being lured by South Carolina's lazy tax laws and cheap labor.

We sat in his bright, airy statehouse office as he pondered his dilemma. Black students, he said, could violate any law they wanted so long as they sang hymns and carried Bibles. What about the police and their Bibles? Public order had to be maintained. He was trying for a balance, but my hunch was that the nightstick would prevail. Yet, in his pleasant office, in his troubled manner, little suggested that South Carolina was taking the first steps toward the terrible day in the Cambodian spring of

1970 when the guns would bark and twice black Orangeburg students would lie dying of bullets fired in the name of "law and order."

Three weeks later it was April 6, and I was checking into the Tutwiler Hotel, first to Room 1117 and then to Room 1060. I was, I confess, a bit leery about Birmingham, very much on guard. It was a rough town. No city had taken a rougher stand on integration. The commissioner of police, Bull Connor, an ex-radio announcer, ran a rough department. He swore segregation would prevail in his lifetime.

I had tried to argue myself out of coming to Birmingham. But there was no way I could not go in. Catledge had been impressed with my sociological reporting on Red Hook, Yonkers, and the City of the Future (reversing Lincoln Steffens, I had said of Los Angeles, "I have seen the Future—and it doesn't work"), and Catledge had liked my trial run in the South with the dispatches from Nashville, Raleigh, and Columbia, South Carolina.

So here I was, cut loose to pick some key Southern cities, analyze what was happening, and try to figure out what was likely to happen. I left New York with four possible cities on my list: Baton Rouge, Louisiana; Birmingham, Alabama; Memphis, Tennessee; and Marshall, Texas. I would make a final decision on the basis of developments. I had gone to Baton Rouge twenty-five years earlier to cover the Huey Long assassination. Now I wanted to see how it had changed and whether Huey's revolution had made a difference in race relations. (It hadn't.) Marshall, Texas, was on my list because race violence had erupted, Memphis was there because of Catledge. He had begun his metropolitan newspaper career there, coming up from Mississippi.

I could not persuade myself that Memphis was as significant as Birmingham. There had been only minor incidents in both cities, but everyone told me that Birmingham was Gibraltar, impregnable. It would take an earthquake to roll over Birmingham.

So I came to Birmingham. Claude Sitton told me that Bull Connor didn't like outside newsmen, better just turn up at his office. I didn't take that advice. I telephoned. He wasn't in. I said I would call back later.

Sitton had warned me to be careful in Birmingham, be careful when you are talking to people. That was in my mind as I began to make my calls, and I had another concern. The Alabama press was full of threats and denunciation of *The New York Times.* I had stopped over in Montgomery, the state capital, and found that officials were talking of a libel action because the *Times* had published a full-page advertisement, an appeal for funds for Martin Luther King. The ad was signed by forty or fifty notables, including Eleanor Roosevelt. It quoted from a *Times* editorial of March 19, 1960, on black demonstrations and called on Congress to "heed their rising voices."

Grover Hall, the vinegar-tongued editor of the Montgomery *Advertiser* (who had written me about the "New York student princes"), called the advertisement "Lies, lies, lies—and possibly willful ones." He demanded that the *Times* disassociate itself from the declaration. Alabama officials began to talk of sueing the *Times* for libel. To me this sounded plain nutty, but I took it as a serious reflection of the feverish temperature of the state, a clear warning to watch my step.

I was, I knew, moving across a field sown with hidden mines. The first person I met in Birmingham (twenty-five years later I still don't feel I should mention his name) warned me: "Birmingham is no place for irresponsible reporting."

"Be careful of what you say and whom you mention," he said. "Lives are at stake."

He did not tell me this over the telephone. I was (so I thought) on guard from the beginning about the telephone. I sensed, in the care with which people spoke, that they did not trust the telephone. It was a throwback to my days in Moscow, where I learned not to mention my name, not to mention the name of the person with whom I was talking. If we did not know each other well enough to recognize voices, we shouldn't be talking. I knew the dangers of careless contacts. In Moscow I never called a Russian from Room 393 in the Metropol Hotel. I always found a booth on the street. I thought of doing the same in Birmingham, then dismissed it. This was Birmingham. This was the United States. I would be careful, but I would not be paranoid.

I took a drive around Birmingham. I saw the brooding statue of Vulcan that looks down from atop Red Mountain—a symbol of the steel-and-coal industry that made Birmingham the Pittsburgh of the South. I lunched at The Club, where the bankers and businessmen, the "Big Mules" in their Brooks Brothers suits, talked over a martini or two and a king crab salad. I saw the $100,000 and $200,000 homes of Mountain Brook ablaze with shad, redbud, and the flowers of Birmingham's lush April. I passed through Honeysuckle Hills, the best black residential district (a federal housing project) and toured the one-block remnant of 18th Street, where the characters created by the writer, Octavus Roy Cohen—Florian Slappey and the "Sons and Daughters of I Will Arise"—used to entertain the nation in *The Saturday Evening Post* of my youth. I gazed on the gleaming white of the Birmingham jail of the legendary Judge Abernathy, who, it was said, used to hand a black defendant a pair of dice and invite him to roll the length of his stay in the jailhouse ("C'mon snake eyes!"), and the refrain of the old popular song reverberated in my mind as I looked on a Birmingham past that had almost vanished. (But three years later Martin Luther King was to write his "Letter from Birmingham Jail" as he sat there.) I saw the unpretentious headquarters of A. G. Gaston, the richest black in Birmingham, an authentic millionaire. It was sited only a stone's throw from the haunts of the fictional Florian Slappey. I drove through Bessemer, grim and sooty, and the great Tennessee Coal & Iron complex, still belching smoke and steam as if the future were forever.

I heard tales of Bull Connor (as he listed himself in the telephone book), and somehow I still couldn't raise him on the phone. I heard his celebrated aphorisms: "Damn the law—down here we make our own law." "White and Negro are not to segregate together." "Only legitimate holdups will be investigated" (in response to allegations that some Birmingham policemen had a hand in local robberies). Once he had been flushed out of a room at the Tutwiler, where he was spending the evening with an attractive young lady. Connor's conviction (and $25 fine) on a morals charge had been overturned by the Alabama Supreme Court, and he had squeaked out an electoral victory, the voters ignoring the finding of the Jefferson County grand jury that Connor was "a hard taskmaster, explosive and vindictive." Connor had publicly proclaimed to the blacks of Birmingham that "as long as you live and as long as Connor lives, there will be segregation in Birmingham and the South."

The more I saw and the more I heard, the more I knew that I was treading dark and bloody ground.

7 | Fear and Hatred

Full dark had fallen before my cab pulled up at a pleasant house in the Canabaw Heights section of Birmingham. The Reverend Robert Hughes's home was set back on a wide lawn beside a big field where a tall pine rose, stately and brooding. One night not long before, a cross had been set afire beside the gloomy tree. The next morning Bob's little girl went out to play. After a while she came in and told her father: "Daddy, we had a visitor last night. Jesus Christ was here."

"Why do you say that?" Bob asked.

"I found his cross on our lawn."

Bob, a slim, boyish man, swiftly answered my ring and admitted me, after peering to see if any car had followed me. He carefully closed the door and led me to his study, where a row of green filing cabinets ranged beside the wall. The shades were pulled and curtains drawn. I think Hughes had expected I would be driving myself rather than taking a cab from the Tutwiler.

Bob Hughes was a Methodist minister who had accepted the post of director of the Alabama Council on Human Relations, which dedicated itself to fighting the conditions which had caused one black to say that Birmingham had become "the Johannesburg of America." No one knew better than Hughes what was happening in and around Birmingham, the dangers, the tensions.

All that evening he talked in his soft, almost apologetic voice, telling me the Birmingham story: of the black mother and daughter who with their own bodies protected a teenage son from hooded men armed with iron pipes, clubs, and leather blackjacks into which razor blades had been set; of a middle-aged white man who flogged a black high school girl with a bullwhip in the open street when she had an argument with a white teenager; of a black working man who stood by as white men raped his wife ("I have to work here. I'm not filing any complaint"); of wiretapping; of letters he mailed that never arrived; of after-midnight telephone threats; of a young divinity student arrested because he visited a black friend; of murder; of the pusillanimity of some fellow clergy; of businessmen afraid to lift their voices for fear their stores would be ruined; of the Ku Klux Klan; of Bull Connor; of Bull's police; of the racist politicians, the intimidated power structure. No one was brave enough to speak out, the penalties were so extreme.

We talked until midnight. He drove me back to the hotel, swiftly scrutinizing the street and the neighborhood. He said he never knew what he might find outside his house.

That was the night I began to understand how different Birmingham was from my idealized image of an American city. The next morning I visited a rabbi, who led me carefully into his study, locking the door behind us. He had installed floodlights around the synagogue and hired a night watchman, after dynamite had been found in the parking lot. Bombings and threats had been reported at other synagogues. The same violence-prone individuals who beat up the blacks were perpetrating anti-Semitic attacks. I talked with the civil rights lawyer, Charles Morgan, on the telephone and listened to his Aesopian language, the veiled double-talk I had heard in Moscow from Soviet dissidents fearful of the KGB. (Morgan's support of civil rights defendants cost him his political career in Alabama.)

Back in Room 1060 at the Tutwiler I assembled my notes and began to write my story. Before I left Birmingham, I dictated most of it to New York—from the airport telephone.

My story began:

From Red Mountain where a cast-iron Vulcan looks down 500 feet to the sprawling city, Birmingham seems veiled in the poisonous fumes of distant battle. . . . More than a few citizens, both white and Negro, harbor growing fear that the hour will strike when the smoke of civil strife will mingle with that of the hearths and forges. . . .

The *Times* editors headlined my dispatch: "Fear and Hatred Grip Birmingham."

The story was published on page 1, April 12, 1960. Only one change was made.

Fairly high up I had written:

To one long accustomed to the sickening atmosphere of Moscow in the Stalin days the aura of the community which once prided itself as the "Magic City" of the South is only too familiar. To one who knew Hitler's storm trooper Germany it would seem even more familiar.

The national desk of the *Times* thought that was a bit strong and deleted it. I did not object. I too thought I was laying it on a bit thick.

All hell broke loose. The editor of the Birmingham *News,* E. L. Holland, chanced to be at Princeton for a conference on the New South. He read *The New York Times* and next day in an editorial column Holland wrote: "That headline in the *Times* says worlds: 'Fear and Hatred Grip Birmingham.' This is the big lie. Perhaps the biggest of all. Salisbury has done his damage. Moscow please copy." On the following day Birmingham read the story. Both papers reproduced it. The headline in the Birmingham *News* was "N.Y. Times Slanders Our City—Can This be Birmingham?"

Birmingham raged. My mail was filled with hate letters. The city demanded retraction. It asked Turner Catledge to send another reporter down to check up on my stories and expose their falsity. Turner Catledge turned them down. No retreat. He had confidence in his correspondent. He did publish a statement put together by William F. Engel, a Birmingham civic leader, and Clarence B. Hanson, Jr., publisher of the Birmingham *News.* But Birmingham didn't think much of the statement. Even Mr. Hanson's own paper denounced it. It didn't go far enough. "The city of Birmingham," said the *News,* "is a lovely city. It is a city in which fear does not abide." It called on citizens not to "demean [our] pride by resorting to the angry retort, the hot word, the blind retaliation."

The idyllic picture painted by the *News* was not shared by black citizens in Birmingham and a few others, but this did not deter the Birmingham city commissioners. Three weeks after my report was published, Bull Connor and the two other city commissioners filed a $1.5 million libel action against me and a $1.5 million suit against the *Times.* The three commissioners of Bessemer, Alabama, weighed in soon, each asking $500,000. That brought the total to $3 million for me, $3 million for the *Times.* Then a Birmingham city detective sued for another $150,000. The numbers added up. Governor John Patterson and the Montgomery city officials joined in a similar libel action against the *Times* for publication of the advertisement "Heed Their Rising Voices." They wanted another $3 million. That brought the total in Alabama to nearly $10 million and set the pattern for a new

Southern Strategy, designed to chill, control, and, if possible, suppress reportage of the civil rights movement. Before the Supreme Court brought this game to an end with the landmark *Sullivan* v. *The New York Times* decision, nearly $300 million in libel actions were outstanding against the media. Coverage had been chilled. I could not return to Alabama for four years. Few *New York Times* reporters went into the state, and news gathering was inhibited all over the South. In fact, to this day, despite the Supreme Court, a plague of libel suits has infested exercise of First Amendment rights, caused newspapers and electronic media millions in legal fees, and often dampened press enthusiasm for hard-hitting reporting.

I was quickly placed in double jeopardy. A grand jury was convened in Bessemer, Jefferson County, Birmingham's steel mill adjunct, and I was indicted on forty-two counts of criminal libel. I was subject to instant arrest if I set foot in Alabama. If I went to Birmingham to defend myself in Federal court on the civil libel, I would be clapped into jail in Bessemer in the criminal case for which I might be subjected to several hundred years of consecutive sentences. No one could remember anyone in modern times having been indicted in Alabama for criminal libel.

This was no joke. But it was trivial compared to what happened to the people with whom I talked in Birmingham. I thought I had taken precautions. I hadn't. Robert Hughes was served with a subpoena to appear before the Bessemer grand jury and bring all his records—that is, the names of everyone who gave money, everyone who contacted him for help, and all his sources of information. He refused and went to jail for thirty-six hours before Charles Morgan, the civil rights lawyer, got him out.

Morgan might have suffered the same fate, but I had not talked to him from the Tutwiler. The hotel records were subpoenaed. Everyone I called was brought before the grand jury, even Clark Stallworth, reporter for the *Post-Herald.* There was no way Clark could wiggle out. He had interviewed me ("Nikita Could be Elected Governor of Alabama, N.Y. Times Writer Says"). There it was under his byline with a photo of me reading the *Literaturnaya Gazeta,* which I had tucked into my briefcase to while away those long dull airline flights.

Stallworth's career was blunted for several years, "guilt by association." The North Alabama Council of the Methodist Church unfrocked Hughes, expelling him from the ministry, but gave him his reversed collar back on a promise to go to Africa as a missionary. He spent years in Southern Rhodesia. Two black clergymen with whom I spoke—Fred Shuttlesworth and J. Herbert Oliver—already were targets of Bull Connor. Shuttlesworth had been arrested more times than he could remember. He continued to be. Oliver once had been arrested and dragged off in his nightclothes. Now he was even more harassed. Ultimately he and his wife moved to Brooklyn and threw their energy into the northern slum of Bedford-Stuyvesant. (Shuttlesworth moved to Cincinnati.) Dr. Henry Stanford, president of Birmingham Southern College, was subjected to a vicious whispering campaign. His talk with me cost his college at least $1.5 million in promised contributions. Rabbi Grafman was called before the grand jury and browbeaten. One man whom I telephoned repeatedly (but never seemed to reach) was Bull Connor. He suffered no ill consequences. He was not called before the Bessemer grand jury.

To this day I cannot forgive myself for exposing honest, courageous citizens to the hazards of wrecked careers, physical danger, and changed lives. I simply was not as careful as I would have been in Moscow, but I did not believe—in fact, I still find it hard to believe—that Moscow conditions could prevail in a great modern city of my own country. This was naïveté. By 1960 I should have known better.

Times were tense in Birmingham. They were tense at 229 West 43rd Street as well. When the Birmingham and Montgomery cases arose, *Times* counsel, the venerable firm of Lord, Day and Lord whose partner Louis Loeb had handled *The New York Times* for many years, routinely contacted its correspondent firm in Birmingham, the best and most prestigious in Alabama. Sorry, the firm replied, they could not handle the *Times,* there was a conflict of interest. Loeb tried the No. 2 firm in Birmingham. Same answer. And so it went with the third. Lord, Day and Lord, got the message. No one in Alabama wanted any association with the *Times.* The *Times* was appalled. So was Lord, Day and Lord. "Nothing had ever arisen that was more worrisome," Loeb told me. "Nothing scared me more than this litigation." Finally, Lord, Day and Lord found a small litigating firm in Birmingham. As Cecil Roberts, a bright, taut-tongued Birmingham lady, put it, "They were the kind of lawyers who took black clients and got them life sentences instead of the death penalty." Beddow, Embry & Beddow, was indeed willing to take the *Times*. They were used to defending unpopular cases and doing it very well. A few years later Eric Embry, who handled my case, was elevated to the Alabama Supreme Court, a far more capable man, I am sure, than his colleagues in the blue ribbon firms.

I was not frightened by Birmingham. I had total confidence in the *Times* and its counsel. I had total confidence in my reporting. I knew I had the story right. I agreed totally with a man in Birmingham who told me privately: "Birmingham is going to blow—and I don't want to be around here when it does." I smiled to myself in January 1961 when David Lowe, working with Edward R. Murrow on a CBS documentary on Birmingham, told me he had found a grave defect in my Birmingham coverage: Conditions were much worse than I had reported.

Murrow said he had seen nothing to compare with it since Berlin under Adolf Hitler. People had been unwilling to meet publicly or talk over hotel telephones. Murrow met people at night, in shadowy park corners, obscure lunch counters. No one would come to the hotel. Nor did people want to meet in their own homes. Stocks of arms were being accumulated. Each side was now armed with machine guns. The working title for their CBS documentary was "The Johannesburg of America."

On Sunday, May 14, 1961, Birmingham did blow. The Monday morning headline in the Birmingham *News* proclaimed: "Mob Terror Hits City on Mother's Day." Thugs had attacked a group of Freedom Riders at the Birmingham bus station with fists and iron pipes and blackjacks. A giant of a man, reported the Birmingham *News,* beat whites and blacks against the cement floor, until his fists ran red with their blood. Connor's headquarters was two blocks away, but no policeman showed his face.

That Monday morning across the eight-columns of page 1, the Birmingham *News* asked:

Where were the police? The City of Birmingham is normally a peaceful orderly place in which people are safe.

Harrison Salisbury of *The New York Times* last year came to Birmingham and wrote two stories about us which said, in substance, that fear and hatred "stalked our streets." The Birmingham *News* and others promptly challenged this assertion. The *News* knows Birmingham people as others know them and they didn't fit that definition.

But yesterday, Sunday, May 14, was a day which ought to be burned into Birmingham's conscience.

Fear and hatred did stalk Birmingham's streets yesterday. . . .

The News asks when will the people demand that fear and hatred be driven from the streets of Birmingham.

Next morning I found on my desk in the big city room at 229 West 43rd Street a copy of the Birmingham *News* with its ugly black headlines. Attached to it was a memo:

> To Mr. Salisbury
> > Vindication!
> > > ECD   [Clifton Daniel]

Well, it was, and it wasn't. I had not written the Birmingham story in order to be vindicated. I had written it in hope that my words might change the course of events, that "fear and hatred" might be driven from the streets of Birmingham. I knew from private talks that my report did bring the city up short, that the reaction was not all bluster and bloat. There were people in Birmingham, including many who were angered by my reports, who felt them unfair, sensationalized, and biased, who now began to think more deeply about their city and what could be done. This did not cause a change in the tide of events—not immediately and not for a long time. The momentum was too great, the forces of intolerance too powerful.

My reports did not change Birmingham. Neither did the savage attack on the Freedom Riders nor the indignation of Birmingham over the event. More than headlines was needed, and, in fact, worse was yet to come—the terrible year of 1963, the year Martin Luther King was jailed in Birmingham and wrote from Birmingham jail of "the dark clouds of racial prejudice" and "the damp fog of misunderstanding." Two months later to the day, civil rights leader Medgar Evers was shot and killed outside his home in Jackson, Mississippi; five months and three days later, a bomb killed four black children at Sunday school services of the Sixteenth Street Baptist Church in Birmingham. On November 22, 1963, President John F. Kennedy was shot dead in

Dallas, and five years later Martin Luther King was to die, shot to death in Memphis, Tennessee.

It was still a long, long way home for Birmingham. Not until March of 1964 did the U.S. Supreme Court hand down its historic ruling in the Montgomery, Alabama, case of *Sullivan* v *The New York Times* (the case about the Martin Luther King advertisement).

This decision broadly affirmed the right of the press to criticize and report on activities and conduct of public officials. The principles of the Montgomery decision supported my right to report, as I had, on Birmingham. I came back to Birmingham for the first time in September of 1964, to appear in the U.S. District Court before Judge Grooms in the Birmingham libel case. Quickly the other plaintiffs were thrown out and only Bull Connor remained, a bulky man with an ovoid Roman head, incurably the politician, greeting my lawyers and myself as we came to court each morning with classic Southern affability, small talk about the weather, little jokes. For years now he had been teasing correspondents about what he would do when he took over *The New York Times.* Claude Sitton fell in with this hee-haw humor and asked Bull for a raise.

The trial lasted for a week. The *Times* lawyers and I stayed at the Tutwiler. I didn't bother to notice my room number. Nothing seemed to have changed in Birmingham. The lawyers had rooms on either side of me. We came to breakfast together, we walked over to court together, lunched together, dined together, and spent the evening in each others' company. A lot of togetherness.

The moment Judge Grooms announced the verdict [we lost], Louis Loeb and Tom Daly of Lord, Day and Lord and I jumped into a taxi and sped to the airport. After we boarded the plane, Loeb and Tom ordered drinks, settled back, and Louis wiped his brow with a handkerchief.

"You're perspiring, Louis," I said.

"You would, too, if you knew what has been happening," he said.

Federal court officers and the sheriff's office in Bessemer had made an agreement safeguarding me from arrest or interference during the trial. All seemed peaceful until three days into the trial. Then U.S. marshals received word that a posse of sheriff's deputies was on its way from Bessemer (just outside the Birmingham city limits) to arrest me and hustle me off to the Bessemer jail. Judge Grooms called a recess in court proceedings, directed the chief marshal to assemble his men, and repel the deputies by force if they attempted to storm the courthouse. He then got on the telephone and warned Bessemer that if their deputies appeared in his courthouse, his marshals would throw them into jail on charges of contempt of court. There was a little argument and hard breathing, but a few minutes later word came that the Bessemer posse had turned back.

From then on everyone was on the alert. The lawyers never let me out of their sight. Judge Grooms had put his marshals on twenty-four-hour alert to protect me if any new move was made to spirit me away from Birmingham.

Of none of this had I been aware. I had just thought that Loeb and Daly had been unusually solicitous.

"We didn't want to alarm you," they said. "We were afraid it might throw you off stride when you got on the stand."

A year later the U.S. Circuit Court of Appeals gave us a sweeping victory. Costs of $3,220.25 were awarded to the *Times* as well as vindication of my Birmingham reporting. I still cherish a photocopy of the check.

So, I thought, Birmingham had come to an end. It had begun, I hoped, the long, slow struggle of throwing off the evil past and trying to enter the New South which so many of us had envisaged. Of course the violence had not ended. It rose and fell all around the perimeter of Birmingham, it ebbed and flowed in Alabama and Mississippi. But, it seemed to me, the tide was beginning to turn because of the strong stand taken by the Kennedys and Lyndon Johnson. Bull Connor's image was waning. He suffered a stroke, got around for a while in a wheelchair as state utilities commissioner, and finally died.

Birmingham was no longer center stage. Neither was the South. Gradually the focus had shifted away from civil rights in the South to the North and to the whole country. It was Vietnam that rang the alarm bells now.

Long since I had forgotten that morning of April 6 when I checked into the Tutwiler Hotel and had been shifted from Room 1117 to Room 1060.

In 1977 the city of Birmingham decided to remodel a disused, decaying firehouse. The second floor of the building had been used as a dumping ground for old documents. Robert Corley, and J. R. Marvin of the Birmingham Public Library, were sent to see if any of the papers were worth saving. They climbed the dirty staircase and found the roof had leaked and papers in fiberboard containers were strewn in all directions. They pawed into the mess and discovered—fortuitously protected by the papers heaped above them—a treasure trove of civil rights history, seven years of secret archives of the Birmingham Police Department.

Here were tape recordings, transcriptions of listening devices, detailed reports by surveillance agents, taped telephone conversations, police records of surveillance of anyone thought connected with civil rights in Birmingham in the years 1957–63. Here was evidence of arrangements by the police for hotel and motel clerks to advise them if reporters or activists checked in, reports of undercover operatives who attended meetings of civil rights or black organizations. As a whole it constituted one of the most valuable and complete archives of the civil rights movement in the South.

Bull Connor had been dead several years by now. The era symbolized by his name was long since gone. Now he had inadvertently bequeathed to history a rare source of documentary materials. It was not complete. No record of my visit to Birmingham was uncovered. But the explanation for my shift in hotel rooms from 1117 to 1060 seemed clear. By mistake, I had been placed in a room without a bug. The desk clerk remedied that by shifting me to 1060.

Why weren't the tapes and surveillance notes on me found in the old fire station? We will never know, but I would guess that Bull kept them personally. Perhaps they were destroyed along with other caches of secret and sensitive information before he died.

This is not and cannot be a history of civil rights and Birmingham. Rather it is a chapter in the education of myself, in my never-ending struggle to understand my own country and our society so that I could better report and interpret it.

If you had asked me in 1960 or 1964 where to look for future progress of the races, for the elimination of the deepest abuses of humanity, I might have said Nashville or Charlotte, North Carolina, or even Greenville, Mississippi. Birmingham? Never! The imprint of Bull Connor was too deep. And I would have been wrong. It would have been reasoning with what passes for a logical, rational mind. But human beings do not move with computerized precision.

On the twenty-first anniversary of "Fear and Hatred" I was invited to return to Birmingham. Vulcan still brooded on Red Mountain but not much of my Birmingham was still there. Steeltown was dwindling. No longer was Birmingham raw and red neck. Now it was dominated by education and medicine, the greatest medical complex in the South in downtown Birmingham, 17,000 students. The old city, the wastes of cheap bars, vacant warehouses, the haunts of the Klan and the remnants of Florian Slappey's day—gone. Gone, of course, was Bull Connor, his name only a myth to a bright-eyed, black-and-white generation keyed to upward mobility, high-tech education, ignorant of the "dark clouds" and "damp fog" of which Martin Luther King wrote. Gone was the ancient Tutwiler, its giant brass cuspidors and seedy lobby. Gleaming glass-box skyscrapers caught the eye, and on the top floor of the biggest of these, the First National-Southern Natural Gas building, a luxurious auditorium had been turned over for a retrial of the case of Harrison E. Salisbury versus Birmingham.

It was hot, lush springtime, the temperature 89. Birmingham was a mass of azaleas, white and pink and lavender blossoms everywhere. The room was filled with button-down-collar young men and women, black and white, curious to hear the stories of a world they could hardly imagine. When films flashed on the screen showing Connor's attack dogs leaping at black crowds ("four flea-bitten old police dogs," as Arthur Hanes, once Birmingham's mayor, insisted on calling them), the young men and women, could not believe their eyes. *"That* happened in Birmingham?" a handsome black woman exclaimed. "Really? I can't believe it. Not here in *our* Birmingham."

I was glad that Arthur Hanes was there. His was the only authentic voice of the old Birmingham. I needed him to remind me that the Birmingham I had written about really existed.

On my flight back from Birmingham to New York I jotted down a few notes, just as I had when I flew back in 1960:

"My principal task was to convey to these young people the reality of what Birmingham had been. They simply do not know and cannot get it. This is the most striking measure of the distance Birmingham has traveled. And the young people, too."

Not that Birmingham was home and free. I heard talk of "survivalists" up in the red clay hills, training camps in racism and sadism. The Klan was not dead. Birmingham had a black mayor but (at that moment) no public transportation, previously used almost entirely by blacks.

No, I thought, Birmingham is not home free. But how many, many miles the city has traveled! Once again I was filled with hope for my country. Where else in the world could people come through such a caldron of hate and fear and emerge to this bright and sunny plateau?

8 | Death in the Family

I was never a Kennedy idolator. Idolatry is not my style. Among the Presidential possibilities of my day I placed Wendell Willkie and Adlai Stevenson ahead of any of those who actually held the office, with Alf Landon not far behind. I don't know whether they would have made good Presidents, but they had a human touch that was lacking in so many who won the White House.

I got to know Jack Kennedy in the Presidential campaign of 1960. I covered both Kennedy and Nixon in that year, and I was not wild about either. I often spoke of Kennedy as a "lace curtain Nixon," by which I meant I did not think there was much difference, if any, in their ideology. That was not true, but there was, I think, a nubbin of truth in my remark. Nixon was shabby in character but had a better grasp of the world. He had seen more of it and thought more. Kennedy had style; there were not many reporters he didn't charm, but he was lazy. I think that had he not been martyred, his Presidential rating would be much lower.

Most newsmen thought Kennedy loved them. That was not true. I have observed every President since Calvin Coolidge. None of them loved the press. FDR, Kennedy, and Reagan were the best at conning the reporters, Hoover and Carter the worst. One of Harry Truman's most amiable traits was his honest dislike of reporters. He put up with the marriage of his beloved Margaret to Clifton Daniel, but it was a bitter pill that Clifton was a newspaperman.

Jack Kennedy gave me a lift one evening from West Virginia, where he was campaigning against Hubert Humphrey. He was on his way to Washington. The plane was a puddle-jumper, and only the two of us were aboard. He spent the brief ride cursing "those sons-a-bitches," the newspapermen. He had a big envelope of clips which he pawed through and tossed away. Most of them seemed to be pieces about his father Joseph, and most of them, Jack felt, went out of their way to dig up the old Joe Kennedy scandals—his borderline bank manipulations, his speculative deals in Wall Street, the maneuvers that got him the Scotch whiskey franchises and the great Chicago Merchandise Mart (where in prohibition days, the building almost empty, a huge speakeasy with a 100-foot bar was the liveliest activity under its roof—I often ate my lunch there), and his role as a spokesman for America First and appeasement before FDR yanked him out of London as the U.S. ambassador. "Bastards," gritted Kennedy as he leafed through the reports. "Just a bunch of lies. They never tell the truth. Bunch of bastards." I didn't talk up the case for newspapering. It was his father, and he was a true member of the clan—the Kennedys against the world and, in this case, against the newsmen. But I had been given an insight into the true Kennedy feeling about the press. One thing was certain about the Kennedys. You were with them or against them. Totally. The press was on the other side.

I don't want to suggest that Nixon had any more love for the press. I think the feeling of the two men was mutual in this regard. But Kennedy could put on a bravado act, make a half dozen important Washington correspondents believe they were real friends (inside the clan). Nixon was a poor actor. His lies stuck out like cold sores. He was forever wrapping his anger at the press in a sleazy tangle of "I know what your problems are," or "Of course you have your job to do," "I don't mean to include you personally," and then out would come the hurt and anger. I guess you could say that, in his way, Nixon was the more honest man. Jack rarely let his distaste show in public.

I got to know Bobby Kennedy long before I met Jack. Bobby was assigned in 1956 to ride shotgun with Stevenson as "liaison" with the Kennedy politicians in big cities and particularly with the Catholics (often the same thing). Stevenson was vulnerable to the Catholic vote; he was a divorced man. Not infrequently Adlai coerced one of his sulky sons to campaign with him to show that he was a family man. Bobby was supposed to work the Catholic power brokers. Actually he did nothing of the kind. I never saw him lift a finger for Stevenson. The Kennedys did little to conceal their contempt for Stevenson. They thought he was a wimp and a loser. Bobby went along for the ride—to learn what not to do when his brother ran in 1960—and he didn't bother to conceal his feelings.

By 1956 the Kennedy machine was already in place, just waiting for Adlai's defeat to take off and start running for 1960.

(Within days of Adlai's defeat the Arthur Schlesinger, Jr.s and John Kenneth Galbraiths were jumping on the Kennedy wagon. I thought this was bad taste. They could have waited a few weeks.)

I remember one warm October evening in Ohio or Indiana, sitting on the railroad track with Bobby, one of those whistlestop tours that candidates used to inflict on themselves and their entourages. I had dictated my story to the *Times,* and Bobby and I sat talking, he plucking tough yellowing straws from the grass growing through the tracks and talking about the bumbles of the Stevenson campaign, Adlai's nit-picking at his speech text until he got up to speak, no rapport with the local machines (at least in part, Bobby's fault), the lousy advance work (poor crowds, lost luggage).

"We'll change all that," Bobby said, the elements of the 1960 campaign shaping up in his mind.

I didn't like Bobby. I resented his cynicism. I thought he and his brother should make a college try for Adlai. "What's the point?" Bobby said. "He hasn't got a prayer against Eisenhower." That was true, but I didn't like the arrogance. Nor did I like the arrogance of Bobby and his brother after President Kennedy named Bobby attorney-general.

I modified my opinion as I watched the brothers handle the confrontations in the South. They did not blink, and I gave them credit. Later, when JFK was killed in Dallas November 22, 1963, I watched Bobby mature in a way that I would not have thought possible. He shed the preppy touch-football image of Hyannis. We had a long talk on a ride up the Hudson River—a steamboat ride to spur the conservationist fight to save Storm King from the power people. I saw Bobby's eyes that day—the tragic shadows, the emotion as he spoke of Vietnam, his determination to bring an end to LBJ's escalation. The gung-ho days of his partnership with General Maxwell Taylor had gone. This was a man, not the Kennedy brat with whom I sat on the track on an October evening in 1956, chewing straw and spitting out the seeds. . . .

By the time Jack Kennedy was shot to death in Dallas at 12:30 P.M. of November 22, 1963, a lot had changed for me. Reluctantly I had bowed to Turner Catledge's insistence and taken on the post of national editor of *The New York Times*. (Catledge coined the title "Director of National Correspondence" so as not to hurt the feelings of Ray O'Neill, who held the title "National Editor.")

Catledge's proposal had reached me in Kabul, Afghanistan, where I was trying to persuade the authorities to let me go through the Khyber Pass. A small war was in progress. I never did get to the Khyber, going to Tashkent, Bokhara, and Mongolia instead. I had to accept Catledge's proposal—much as I preferred reporting. He had twice tried to make me an editor, and I knew I couldn't say no a third time. But I did get his pledge that once or twice a year I could abandon my desk and go off on a reporting trip. The promise was meticulously kept by Catledge and Punch Sulzberger, even after I set up the op-ed page and became an associate editor of the *Times*.

I had concluded before going to work for the *Times* in 1949 that the essence of journalism was reporting and writing. I wanted to find things out—particularly things which no one else had managed to dig out—and let people have the best possible evidence on which to make up their minds about policy. It was essentially a gloss on the old Scripps slogan: "Give Light and the People Will Find Their Way." I have never ceased to believe in it.

One day in November 1963 I was sitting at the long table in the third floor dining room of the Century Club, waiting for my lunch.

At that moment, just on one o'clock, the waiter having brought my purée mongole, Alfred De Liagre, the theatrical producer, elegant as always in English tweeds, rounded into the room, raised his voice over the cheerful hum of Century conversation, and said, a bit theatrically: "Gentlemen, I am sorry to interrupt, but the President has just been shot in the head . . . in Dallas." I dropped my napkin, leaped down the stairs, and ran the two and a half blocks west on 43rd Street to 229, up on the elevator, and to my national news desk just south of my old spot, the Hagerty desk which I had occupied for nine years. There I would remain almost continuously for the next several days.

I was used to violence in the South, violence in the country as a whole. It seemed to me that I had inhabited a violent world since I had come back from the deceptive quiet of the Moscow streets—violence in the slums of Brooklyn and Manhattan, a nationwide uprooting of populations, technological revolution in the farm belt, the bondage of the great cities in straitjackets of steel and concrete freeways, and now rising terror in the South.

Dallas . . . Kennedy . . . violence . . . it seemed an almost inevitable pattern, and my mind leaped instantly to the passion in Dallas that had raged since before Kennedy's election. Dallas had seemed like another country, ranting against *everything*. I knew of the threats and the hate ads that spewed out before the Kennedy visit. I had hardly gotten on the telephone to order staff to Dallas—everyone I could reach who could fly in by nightfall— than my mind spun with thoughts of a conspiracy by the radical right or even—I hardly dared formulate the thought—by some in the diehard LBJ camp who so hated the Kennedys. What it might be I did not know. But plots, conspiracy, coups raced through my head. From the vicious anti-Kennedy propaganda, there seemed to me but one short step to a conspiracy to assassinate the President.

The arrest of Oswald before the afternoon was over blew the gas out of my conspiracy balloon. In the supercharged Dallas atmosphere the raging Dallas billionaires might have created the atmosphere in which the Oswalds of the world were born and thrived. But that was another thing. I *knew* Oswald. I don't mean I knew this Oswald, but I had known other Oswalds in earlier years. I knew their fantasies, the paranoia, the tawdry sense of self-power. I had *met* Oswald in a dozen forms in the depression years. I had met him in the public library in Minneapolis, reading in the newspaper room (he never had money for newspapers), pouring over texts by Ignatius Donnelly or Henry George, the single taxer, furiously taking notes, digging his way through volumes of shabby theorists seeking the true villain of the age, the one who must be destroyed if his vision of a new day was to be fulfilled. I had talked with Oswald in 1932 in a ratty late-night bookstore on North Clark Street in Chicago, a gaunt young man with the deep-set eyes of a fanatic, holding a moldy volume in his hand and spouting about the conspiracy of the Morgans and the Jews against the gentiles; I had listened to him shout from a soapbox, a real soapbox, in Union Square, New York, in 1934, shouting: "Down with Capitalism!" He was some-

times old, sometimes young, always on the thin edge of survival,
eyes fixed on an image no one but he could see, mind dusty with
fragments of political theory, broken bits of philosophy.

Yes, I knew Oswald as soon as we got to his background, and
I gave my reporters assignments consistent with the Oswald
whom I knew, the universal Oswald. I told them to check the
public libraries in New Orleans near where he had lived, visit
secondhand bookstores, look at the squares where cranks hang
out and harangue, do the same in Dallas. He would be a bus person. Check the bus routes from New Orleans and Dallas and
Mexico.

The pattern paid off. He was precisely the Oswald I had met
in the bitter days of depression, his haunts the same, his confu-
sions the same—one moment stalking General Walker, the next
Nixon, the next Kennedy; pro-Cuba, anti-Cuba; pro-Soviet, anti-
Soviet. Could this confused Oswald be the man in a conspiracy?
Never—no matter how many shots had been fired from the
grassy knoll, no matter how many men were seen at the window
of the Texas Book Depository. Nor was his trail hard to follow.
It was broad, obvious, blazed wherever he went by his paranoid
inability to accomplish anything—except shoot the President of
the United States. When he took out a card in the branch library
near his Magazine Street flat in New Orleans, the first book he
checked out was a biography of Mao Zedong. Ten days later he
borrowed a Kennedy biography and another on the Huey Long
assassination. *Perfect.* Oswald could, of course, have been used—
as suspicion long suggested the Czar's *Okhrana* gave the drifter
Bogrov a chance to enter the Kiev opera house in 1911, knowing
he would assassinate Prime Minister Stolypin, or as Stalin's
OGPU let the young Nikolayev slip into Smolny and kill Leningrad's Party leader, Sergei Kirov. Certainly Oswald could have
been a cat's-paw, but I saw no trace of such a cunning trick.
Oswald hardly differed from the classic American assassin of
Presidents. After the assassination of Martin Luther King and
Robert Kennedy, President Johnson named a commission to in-
vestigate violence in the United States. The authors noted the
frequency with which the "lone killer" had struck at the White
House, Guiteau at McKinley, Czolgosz at Garfield, Zangara at
FDR, John Schrank at Theodore Roosevelt.

In an introduction to the LBJ report I wrote: "The notion

that violence and assassination is something new, something 'un-American,' a peculiar product of the present day, is demonstrably and remarkably mistaken. Violence has marked every step of the creation and building of American society. . . . Violence may not be 'as American as apple pie,' but it has been synonymous with the American experience from the earliest days."

That understanding has hardly been accepted by Americans. The notion that John F. Kennedy was killed by a single morbid drifter, his head stuffed with unbaked philosophy and tawdry phobias, is rejected everywhere. I think I understand this. On November 27, 1963, five days after Kennedy was killed, the first moment I had time and strength to put down what I felt, I wrote a memorandum to myself. I said that in the year 2000 the Kennedy assassination would still be a matter of debate, new theories being evolved how and why it happened. The lone, crazed killer would not then—or ever—be accepted. It offended nature. For the Sun King to be struck down by a vagrant with bulging eyes—no, the concept was repugnant to our very being. For a man so noble the cause of death must lie in high conspiracy, the most powerful courtiers, the great barons, the captains of the earth.

As a young reporter in Chicago, each year when the anniversary of Lincoln's death approached, I prepared for the annual ritual—the revelation of the "true story" of what had happened—an interview with a dying ancient in a log house in southern Illinois whose father had told him of the haunted, bearded, gaunt-cheeked man who had lived on into the 1880s, appearing suddenly in the village and living a life of solitude. "It was Lincoln," the dying man gasped. "My father knew him well." Or the legend of the grave, a hardy perennial. Lincoln's tomb had been secretly opened. *There was no body in it.* Or the tangled tale of conspiracy. It was not John Wilkes Booth—he was a fall guy for the man who engineered the plot, Lincoln's secretary of war, Stanton. There was always a new legend because with Lincoln too we could not accept the simple facts. They were not grand enough. They did not satisfy our sense of Homeric drama.

As I said in my memorandum to myself:

"I am sure that the echo of this killing will resound down the corridors of our history for years and years and years. It is so strange, so bizarre, so incredible, so susceptible to legend making. . . . It matches Lincoln's assassination."

I added: "We are running down every single item of Oswald's background that can be found. Strange story though it is, there is not one fact thus far which essentially changes the public story—or makes it any more understandable."

It was no surprise to me that the Warren Commission report did not halt the "revelations," the rumors, the legend making of the conspiracy theorists, now grown to a kind of carrion industry.

I did not think the Warren Commission had dug out any essential fact that the *Times* had not found in its intense coverage in the days and weeks after the assassination. The coverage had begun with classic reportage—Tom Wicker's on-the-scenes eyewitness. It could not be beat. Tom was the only *Times* man in Dallas that day. I made one contribution to Tom's beautiful story. At 5 P.M. I ordered him—no, *command* is the word—to halt reporting and start writing. No interruptions. Any new details we could put into the piece, if necessary, after it went into type about 8:30 P.M. that night. Just write every single thing you have seen and heard. Period. He did. No more magnificent piece of journalistic writing has been published in the *Times*. Through Tom's eye we lived through each minute of that fatal Friday, the terror, the pain, the horror, the mindless tragedy, elegant, blood-chilling prose.

To this day not one material fact has been added to *The New York Times* account of the assassination and the events that followed it. This record would be enhanced had it not been for Vietnam and my trip to Hanoi in December 1966.

Catledge and Daniel, now executive editor and managing editor respectively of the *Time,* decided to reinvestigate the whole affair because of the torrent of conspiracy yarns, challenges to the Warren Commission report and general hysteria about the assassination.

The decision was made in autumn 1966. Once again I was placed in charge of the Kennedy story. The veterans of 1963 were assembled, Peter Kihss, at their head. We listed every point that had been challenged by the conspiracy buffs and reinvestigated them. The work was nearing completion. Peter Kihss had roughed out the whole story by early December 1966. Then came the telegram telling me that a Hanoi visa awaited me in Paris.

"We'll just put it on the shelf until you get back from Viet-

nam," Clifton Daniel told me. By the time I returned from
Hanoi the furor about Kennedy had died down—it had had a
regular sequence of heights and depths. Daniel decided to let the
inquiry stay where it was until interest rose again. That moment
never seemed to return. The massive inquiry remains on the
shelf, unfinished, unpublished. I will say only one thing: nothing
in our new investigation undercut, contradicted, or undermined
in any fashion the basic conclusions of our original work or that
of the Warren Commission. The work is all there, solid as Gi-
bralter, and as I suggested in my memo of November 27, 1963,
there will still be questions raised, again and again, well after the
year 2000.

A footnote. I was filling in as national editor once again on
June 4, 1968. Robert F. Kennedy was speaking in Los Angeles,
and that night I stayed in the office until the Kennedy rally was
concluded and Bobby's speech finished. I then said good night,
slipped away, and took a taxi from 43rd Street to East 84th
Street. As I entered the house, the telephone was ringing: Bobby
had been shot. In ten minutes I was back in the office and stayed
the night.

It was worse than his brother's assassination. Bobby was so
young, so vigorous, he had come on so straight, he had grown up
so real, the act was so senseless, the repetition so banal, the plain
blunt facts of it no mystery, no chance for the mind to ponder
possibilities. Just the brutal act. The bullet. I sat at my desk,
talking with the reporters on the telephone, running through the
copy as it poured in, my mind numb, unbelieving, almost in
shock. A bit after 2 A.M. my phone rang. It was Jacqueline
Kennedy. I did not know her. She did not know whom she was
talking to. She just wanted some word. There was none to give.
Bobby was alive. But I knew he would not live very long. I could
not tell her that. She seemed on the edge of the world. I could not
imagine what she was passing through, her voice vague as a
child's, the image in my mind of her in the car in Dallas, dress
drenched with blood, her husband's shattered head in her lap.
Now this. About 3:30 A.M. she called again. There was nothing I
could do but talk, hoping perhaps my droning, flat, Midwestern
voice would somehow disconnect her from tragedy too deep for
any soul to endure. She hung up. I did not see her for years and,
of course, never spoke of the conversations, which probably ex-

isted for her in some plane where reality could not penetrate. After a while Bobby was dead, and there was nothing more to do at the office. I went home and told Charlotte and held her in my arms and cried. I had not cried for Jack, but I could not keep the tears back for Bobby. He was, I thought then and now, America's best and brightest future, and he was dead.

9 | Behind the Iron Curtain

I did not think, as I sat talking about Milovan Djilas with his wife, Stefica in their spartan apartment in central Belgrade, a Singer sewing machine in one corner, a rubber tree in another, that I was about to take my first step in a journey that would place me behind the American lines in Hanoi nine years later. I had gone to Yugoslavia in that pleasant summer of 1957 to fill in while Elie Abel, later to be dean of the Columbia Journalism School, went home on leave.

I spent my days poking about Yugoslavia, talking with Mrs. Djilas, her china-blue eyes sparkling like a child's, and with other Yugoslav intellectuals. That was the summer the name of Milovan Djilas was on all lips. *The New Class* had just been published in the United States, and Djilas was serving a three-year term in the Sremska Mitrovica prison (in the same cell he had spent 1933–36 as a revolutionary) because of his heretic conclusion that Marxism had given birth to a new class, an elite bourgeoisie comprising the ruling hierarchy of the Party.

Djilas' ideas had stirred a storm in Eastern Europe. "Milovan has talked enough politics in this flat to last a lifetime," his wife told me with a puckish smile. She was not worried about her husband—except for the cold. The prison at Sremska Mitrovica was not heated during the icy Serbian winter. This was the summer I met Vlado Dedijer, a craggy man with deep-set eyes, Tito's close companion and biographer, as controversial as Djilas. We talked to the early hours of morning, Vlado complaining that his head still ached from the bullet lodged there in a mountain firefight during World War II. He was still talking all night and complaining of the bullet thirty years later.

With a long lazy summer ahead, I decided to try my hand at penetrating the forbidden Balkan kingdoms of Communism that surrounded Yugoslavia. I don't know whose idea it was to send me to Eastern Europe—probably that of Emanuel Freedman, the solemn, long-faced foreign editor of the *Times.* He was a man as devoid of humor as the moon of water, a lovely honest man, astonished almost daily by his unpredictable correspondents and the impossibility of knowing what would happen next in the world. He was a most orderly man. Clifton Daniel once opened Freedman's closet and found twenty-two Savile Row suits hanging there, each on its own walnut hanger. Beneath each suit was the appropriate pair of good English oxfords.

Manny was a bit like city editor Frank Adams. He did not pretend to know what a correspondent might do with a story. He just put him into orbit and hoped for the best. So it was that I found myself poking about the Balkans. I loved Belgrade, strolling through the evening twilight in the Terazlie in the city's heart, where everyone, old or young, men or women, beautiful or ugly, sedate or flirtatious, joined in the *gulyan'e,* the promenade, not unlike that in the cities of Spain, up and down the street from which all traffic was barred.

I had been banned by Moscow since the 1954 publication of my exposé of Stalin's years, and it was a delicious experience to breathe the air of a Communist country which delighted in doing everything just the opposite of the Russian way.

Yugoslavia was surrounded by countries which had closed their doors against Americans. I decided to try the toughest one first—Albania. There hadn't been an American reporter in Albania since World War II, no U.S. relations since Mussolini invaded Albania in the 1930s. I sent wireless messages to the Albanian leaders, Enver Hoxha and President Mehmet Shehu, but I did not hold my breath for an answer. I traveled around Yugoslavia, got a big blister on my toe walking Belgrade's cobblestones, and, coming back from a trip, found to my astonishment that the Albanians were trying to reach me: I had a visa. I went around to the Albanian embassy. It looked like a fortress, heavy doors, steel shuttered windows. I had the feeling—maybe my imagination—that there were machine-gun nests in the recessed windows.

I rang the bell. A long wait. I rang again. Finally a small slot, something like a Russian *fortochka,* opened and a scowling face confronted me. I said: "Salisbury. American. Visa." No response. I said it three times, and the *fortochka* slammed shut. Long wait. I rang some more. The window opened again, the face peered at me. "Salisbury, American, visa." The door opened, and I was led into a central hall with a staircase to a second floor balcony fitted with four doors on each side and another at the rear. As I entered, eight doors opened, and eight small men, each dressed in a dark suit, emerged and exited through the door at the rear. The doors closed. Suddenly the rear door opened, and the eight men emerged. Each went into his office and closed the door. It was like a scene from a ballet by Meyerhold.

Finally a ninth little man emerged, motioned me to a chair, filled out a visa form on a piece of paper, sneering at U.S. passport restrictions. (My passport carried a prohibition against travel to Albania; when I got back to the U.S.A. the State Department lectured me for going to a forbidden country.) As I got up to leave, I heard a whispered sigh from the balcony. I did not turn back, but I imagined the eight little men tiptoeing out again through the doors to their eight little rooms.

I booked a ticket for Tirana. There were two planes a week, Wednesdays and Fridays. An Albanian plane in Tirana and a Yugoslav plane in Belgrade took off simultaneously and landed simultaneously. No trust.

I took off for Tirana on Wednesday, August 21, 1957, in a low mood. As I wrote in my journal: "Never have I started a journey in poorer heart, more despondent, less enthusiastic. I do not know what *chërt* (devil) it is that draws me into such crummy parts of the world. I am half-afraid of them. They upset and annoy me. My tolerance for police and bureaucracy grows less and less." (In November, 1985, as Charlotte and I flew out of Sheremetevo airport in Moscow, I said to her: "I just can't stand the police and the bureaucracy. This is my last trip to Russia." "That's what you said the last time," she told me with a grin. Six months later I was back in Russia.)

The first thing I saw as the plane set down in Tirana was three soldiers in dirty uniforms at the end of the runway, lolling in the grass with bayoneted rifles, watching the landing with shifty eyes.

Each night I spent in Albania I heard the chatter of machine guns in the mountains and an occasional mortar shell. For practical purposes Albania was more or less in a state of war with her neighbors, Yugoslavia and Greece. God knows what was going on in the hills. I began to understand the paranoia. My visit was the first and last by an American correspondent until the summer of 1986, when a Boston *Herald* man was allowed to attend a family wedding and write a few pieces.

Not only was Albania at war with her neighbors; she was, as I was assured by Petrit Aliu, the dark-haired, brown-eyed young man who served as my guide and interpreter, the No. 1 target of the CIA, which was trying to put King Zog back on the throne. I expressed astonishment that King Zog was still alive. The only interest Zog had ever stirred in the United States, I said, had been in the 1930s when it was reported in the tabloids that he smoked 300 cigarettes a day.

Petrit was infuriated. I had insulted him by not taking Albania's security threat seriously. He was certain the United States was devoting great time and resources to the Albanian question. (He probably had been told that I was a dangerous CIA agent.)

I retorted that most Americans didn't even know where Albania was. "The whole thing is ridiculous," I said. Actually, it was not ridiculous at all, as I came later to understand. Albania in 1948 had been the target of the first big CIA plot to overthrow a Communist government. We had been helped by the British, and it had been a disaster. Later the Russians tried the same thing. They bought up a clique of officers in Albania's gunboat-and-destroyer navy but failed as badly as the CIA. Hoxha and Shehu took the excuse to slaughter hundreds of fellow Albanians and broke connections with every country but Italy and Communist China. Beijing seemed far enough away not to be a threat. (But when Deng Xiaoping denounced Mao Zedong, Albania cut her ties with China as well.)

I met with Mehmet Shehu and tried to coax him into speaking English. He only essayed a few sentences (excellent American accent). I knew he had been educated in an American school in Tirana founded by the Junior Red Cross in 1921. When I got back to New York, I got ahold of *Laboremus,* the school magazine to which Shehu had been a frequent contributor in the early thirties.

Shehu, it turned out, had been a devout Sunday school pupil. In one long poem he concluded:

> It is not of our religion
> That God will ask:
> It is our behavior
> And how we did the task

He contributed an essay on "My Summer Vacation," work on the school farm, operating a tractor. He and his companions, he wrote, "Worked from sunrise to sunset with one hour out at midday. We ate with peasant farmers and slept on the straw, enjoying the beauty of moon and stars."

I would have given a good deal to have had Shehu's poetry and essays with me when I interviewed him in the presidential palace. For many years I sent him Christmas cards, I also sent cards to Petrit Aliu, my young Albanian translator. After four or five years Petrit Aliu's cards came back stamped: *"Destintaire inconnu,"* "inexistant." It took Shehu a bit longer to become "inexistant." He committed suicide, it was said, in 1984. Since then his name has vanished from the Albanian press.

Next stops: Bulgaria and Romania. Bulgaria had been famous for terror since the time of the Macedonians in the Ottoman Empire. I found it in 1957 a rather tedious market-gardening Communist country. Its principal export was attar of roses. I paid a visit to the Golden Sands, a new Bulgarian resort on the Black Sea, designed by Swiss architects. It would boast the first—and largest—gambling casino behind the Iron Curtain, enormously popular with tourists from bleak Ost-Europa. My only other memorable act was to hunt up a Bulgarian lady who had once worked for the *Times* and had been the girlfriend of an English writer in the long ago past. She was desperately poor, had suffered greatly for her connections with the West. I gave her some *Times* money and put her in touch with her old boyfriend.

Bulgaria had no diplomatic relations with the United States. Like Albania, it was theoretically barred to Americans. Romania had relations—but barely. In Bucharest I stayed at the venerable Athenee Palace hotel, still luxurious in a seedy Balkan way, and swam in Bucharest's great outdoor pool with its artificial waves. I went to Ploesti where so many American airmen had died in the longest (out-of-range of their bases) raid of World War II on the oilfields. As far as I could see, the U.S. deaths had caused only a few nicks in the vast oil refinery. I called on a muscular lady sculptor who was hewing a block of marble in her backyard studio with such ferocity I hardly dared enter. A year or so later she managed to get to Paris with the aid of a French admirer, there to continue her career with what success I do not know.

By this time I felt I had gotten to know the back waters of Communism, these little Communist kingdoms differing one from the other, but all shabby, all lackluster, all trading on misery not hope, distinguished by heavy-handed police and a heavy-labor proletariat. Was this what Lenin and his comrades had in mind when they carried out their coup in Petrograd on November 7, 1917?

As I noted in my journal:

"They believed that Europe and the whole western world stood on the brink of the apocalypse, which was to mark the end of man's subjugation by man. When the guns of the cruiser *Aurora* rattled the windows of the Winter Palace, the Communists believed they had fired a signal which would bring an echoing cannonade from Berlin, from Vienna, from Paris, from London and perhaps even from New York."

What had they gotten? Only poor, backward Russia until the Red Army in 1944 and 1945 marched into Bucharest and Budapest and Belgrade and Prague and the rest. The specter which Marx said "haunted Europe" now haunted the Communist world. Nowhere did I feel that haunting quality as in Budapest, still scarred and dazed from 1956, Americans not very popular, belief persisting that John Foster Dulles and Radio Free Europe had let the Revolution down by exhorting Hungarians to rise up, then offering no helping hand. Young people drank and loafed in the sidewalk cafés. In the Duna Hotel a cluster of prostitutes hovered around the bar: a teenage hippie, her sixteen-year-old brother shot down on a street corner by a plainclothesman; a tough blond with a broken nose and black lingerie; a stylish blond who never appeared before midafternoon; a fading blond, hated by the others for her *konkurentsia* (competition); a new-minted blond (she had been a redhead before the uprising). A Party man shrugged his shoulders: "Well, they have to take care of the foreign businessmen. It's their duty."

The American embassy in Budapest was a token presence. The only problem was looking after Cardinal Mindszenty, dour and ill-tempered in his forced refuge. I liked the tiny embassies in Bucharest and Budapest, a handful of eager young men and women devoted to reporting, no bulging presence of PX staff, housekeeping personnel, Agency operators, technical staff. I agreed with George Kennan, who once said that if ever he became Secretary of State, he would operate with a worldwide staff of 200 persons. No, he would not displace the pork-belly apparatus. He would let them go on exchanging useless reports amongst themselves while his elite conducted the business of the United States.

In Prague I feasted on *keks garazh,* a nine-layer chocolate cake, and attended services at the 400-year-old synagogue. I arrived in Warsaw at 6 P.M. October 5, 1957, to roaring shouts in the streets: *"Ges-ta-PO! Ges-ta-PO!"* The streets were lined with thousands of university students (and thousands who weren't university students). They chanted: "Ges-ta-PO!" to the thousands of police who confronted them. Sometimes they shouted: "MVD . . . MVD . . . MVD" (the initials of the internal security police).

Police rumbled through the Place of the Republic, a paved plaza big as Red Square, in olive-drab trucks, troop carriers, jeeps, command cars. The streets echoed with the blast of concussion bombs. I didn't know what was happening. But it seemed like a revolution. Tear gas grenades discharged clouds of mustard-scented mist.

It was, Sydney Gruson, the *Times* Warsaw correspondent, told me, a student manifestation, a protest against restrictions on the universities, the closing of the student paper, *Po Prostu.* But it was more than that. How much more remained to be seen. Sydney took me to the Journalists Club, jammed with people, and we sat at a table with his wife, Flora Lewis, and his assistant and friend, Tommy Atkins. It was pandemonium. People dashing in and out. The cannonade rising and falling. Rumors. Troops were firing over the heads of the students. Troops firing into the crowds. Masses of dead and wounded (not true), ashcans hurled from buildings on the police (true), barrages of bricks rattling off police helmets (true).

What was happening? The eve of a new Revolution? A dress rehearsal like that of 1905? People hurried up, whispered to Sydney and Flora, and ran out again. Twenty times Flora or Sydney left the table for quick consultations. Tommy Atkins came and went. His name was actually Seweryn Ben Izrael. He was a Polish Jew born in Łódź who got the name Tommy Atkins in the British army in England during World War II. He wore heavy horn-rimmed glasses. Years later he told me: "People thought I was a spy because I looked like a spy." He still looked like a spy after twenty years as a professor at Baruch College. We all looked like *The Third Man*—Sydney, blond, nordic, Irish as a shamrock, a Jew born in Dublin; Flora, auburn hair, sharp face, typecast ace reporter (which she was) and myself, long nose, trenchcoat, snap-brim hat, wandering in from the set of *The Front Page.*

My mind was awhirl. I didn't know what was going on. It might be just a student strike, but it felt like a revolution. In my journal I noted: "This rioting has a curious sense of unreality. What do the crowds want? Probably they themselves don't know." My nose prickled with the scent of tear gas, the streets littered with half-bricks, Gomulka, it was said, meeting continuously with his Politburo in secret session—about what? Within half an hour Sydney Gruson was cabling to New York the topic of Gomulka's discussions—an absolute cap on further talks with foreign correspondents, no more leaks, a crackdown on the press.

All evening I was asking questions. Atkins had few answers.

This was the Polish world Sydney and Flora had inhabited for eighteen months. I had arrived almost on the anniversary of the "Polish October" of 1956 when Khrushchev sent his tanks up to the gates of Warsaw. Gomulka, prison pallor still on his face, told him the Poles would fight if the tanks came further.

In those days Sydney Gruson had filed the most remarkable dispatches I have ever seen from the Communist world, documenting hour-by-hour, almost minute-by-minute, the inside story of the crisis: what Gomulka was doing; what the Polish military were doing; what they were telling the Russians; what the Russians were telling them. Sydney and Flora were Warsaw's lifeline to the West, the channel through which Gomulka could raise the alarm if Khrushchev and Marshal Zhukov tried to crush Poland as later they did Budapest. Khrushchev blinked, and the Gomulka experiment began. Now a year later Poland again stood at the brink—or did it? No one, not Sydney, not Flora, not Tommy Atkins, not anyone in that hubbub could say.

I spent a week in Warsaw, had an interview with Premier Cyrankiewicz, then I was on my way back to New York, my Balkan summer at an end.

Those months engrained deep in my consciousness the diversity of Communism. Albania was not Poland; Hungary was not Bulgaria; Poland was, had been, and always would be, Poland.

Today these ideas seem pedestrian (although, I confess, a concept which did not quickly penetrate the minds of the advisers of President Reagan—or perhaps, not the President's own mind). The notion so widely advanced, so powerfully argued by John Foster Dulles and other great simplifiers, Joseph McCarthy among them—that Communists all come in the same color: red— is not and never has been true. Nowhere have there been more violent quarrels, feuds, and disputes than among the Marxists, the didacts of the left. There were times when Vladimir Lenin did not seem to agree with any other individual in the world. That still goes for many theocratic Communists. Never after my Balkan summer would I make the error of thinking that there was one Communist world, whole and indivisible.

What nonsense we had taught ourselves. There was not a Communist country in Eastern Europe that would stay Communist if the Red Army pulled back its troops. As I wrote in 1957: "Instead of a policy, the United States sometimes seems to have imposed a quarantine over the whole area." The words echo hollowly today. Thirty years after the Polish October things haven't improved.

On Sunday, October 13, 1957, I went to the Warsaw airport and boarded an SAS plane for Copenhagen. With me was Sydney Gruson, his marvelous Irish color faded to a pasty white, as nervous a man as I have ever seen. Tommy Atkins, he told me, had been arrested. Sydney had excellent information. His turn, he had been told, would be next.

10 | "A Second-Rate Story in the Suburbs"

The chant of "Ges-ta-PO . . . Ges-ta-PO . . ." will, I think, echo in my brain for the rest of my life. In autumn 1957 I had not yet experienced the Japanese film *Rashomon,* the dramatization of the classic enigma of truth, the inescapable, ordained contradictions, life distorted to infinity in its own mirror. I knew in Warsaw as I walked through the October events that I was walking in a hall of facets, but I could not measure the angles of refraction, nor can I thirty years later be certain what was real and what was imagined.

It is this realization which has caused me to return to *Rashomon* again and again to study this metaphor of life and remind myself that there is no truth. There are many truths, some valid for one, some for another. *Things are not what they seem.* We suppose we learn this lesson in kindergarten the first time a magician projects a rabbit's ears on the wall with the shadow of his hands. But it is a lesson we must learn and relearn because always we keep searching for certainty, and certainty does not exist.

Was the Polish government about to collapse that October of 1957? Surely it does not seem so today. Yet on those evenings when the cries of "Ges-ta-PO!" reverberated outside the iron gates of Warsaw's university and echoed in the narrow alleys of the Old City it *could* have been true. Certainly as that troubled man, Gomulka, met hour after hour with his associates wondering if the security police could contain the rising violence, worrying whether troops would have to be summoned, worrying whether the uniformed forces would join the multitude as they had in Petrograd in 1917, worrying whether Khrushchev's tanks would rumble out of their camps and clank again down the autostrada toward Warsaw, worrying how many Poles would stand by the students and their suppressed paper, *Po Prostu,* and how many would stand with Gomulka and the "old Party"—yes, it is easy to see that when Gomulka stared past the Brussels lace curtains at the windows of the Central Committee, there was more than one Warsaw within his field of vision.

And this was true in the smoky dining room of the Journalists Club. To me it was a scene of excitement, tension, intrigue, but I could not read the code. Who were these people? Sydney Gruson and Flora Lewis I knew. Tommy Atkins I knew through them. But I did not know what was happening, nor as it turned out, did Sydney or Flora or Tommy. Neither they nor I could have imagined, sitting in the clutter of uneaten cucumber pickles, fragments of herring, plates that once contained eel in dill sauce, half-consumed bowls of borscht, cut-glass *ryumki* of Polish vodka, goblets of resin-heavy Polish wine, brandy spilled on the white tablecloth, ashtrays heaped in cigarette butts, that something was occurring that would affect all our lives, our fate, that one of us would go to prison, that two would hurriedly slink out of Warsaw, that the best correspondent in Poland would be driven from the country, and that Gruson's departure would open the way for another remarkable (but different) reporter, Abe Rosenthal, who in turn would be pushed out of Poland, like Gruson a victim of his own capability, caught in the delayed aftershock of the events that went forward on that October night.

Sydney and I sat side by side in the plane all the way from Warsaw to Copenhagen. I told him again and again that it could not be as bad as he thought; the Poles were not going to forget what Gruson had done for them in October 1956. Perhaps they would not pin a ribbon on his chest (as they should), but they would not arrest him; they would not demean him and themselves by such nonsense. Sydney was not convinced. His friends had told him that Atkins had been arrested for the specific purpose of preparing a case against Sydney: blackmarketing and—probably—espionage.

How could I convince Sydney his information was false? If there was anyone who knew Poland, it was Gruson. He and Flora had agreed: best for Sydney to slip out of the country with me. After all I was leaving directly from an interview with Prime Minister Cyrankiewicz. Certainly they would not arrest Sydney in my company. He always carried an exit visa in his passport—just in case. He would get out. Let the dust settle. If it seemed safe, he would come back. Otherwise, farewell Warsaw. We parted in Copenhagen. Sydney went on to London to wait things out, to quiet his nerves.

Gruson had done the best reporting of the decade from behind the Iron Curtain, but that did not win him a Pulitzer prize. Not because the Pulitzer judges did not understand he deserved it. He did not win because on the heels of Poland's October outburst came the Hungarian Revolution. The judges could not give the prize to Poland, because Hungary was a bigger show.

So the prize went to Russell Jones of United Press International who covered Budapest—a good, competent reporter who did a good, competent job. For years UPI had boycotted the Pulitzers on grounds (quite justified) that the judges were biased in favor of the Associated Press. This year (1956–57) UPI had ended its boycott. So, of course, for nonjournalistic reasons the judges honored Jones, not Gruson.

Next year the Pulitzer judges almost compounded the injustice to Gruson. For 1957 the *Times* submitted my Balkan dispatches, the scoops from Albania, Bulgaria, and all the rest. They also nominated Gruson again and several other foreign correspondents. The jury picked me as the winner. Fortunately there was reconsideration, and the award went to *The New York Times* for the overall excellence of its foreign reporting; the further slight to Gruson was averted.

Sydney spent ten days in London and then went back to an uneasy Warsaw. Tommy was in jail. Sometimes Gruson's Polish friends came to dinner, sometimes they did not. It was not the same, and it was not going to be the same. I knew Sydney was finished in Poland before I got back to New York, and I told that to Turner Catledge and Emanuel Freedman, the foreign editor.

"This unfortunate situation," I said in a memo, "arises directly out of Sydney's magnificant coverage and his unequaled contacts and knowledge of what is happening in Poland. I think it can be fairly said that for the last eighteen months no one in Poland, either in the Government, the diplomatic colony, or the press corps, has had as full a picture as Gruson."

But Gruson had become an embarrassment. There was no way the Polish government was going to permit Gruson's intimate and informed reporting to continue. The Poles would not arrest Sydney, but they would intimidate his sources and emasculate his reporting. A replacement, I told Catledge, was going to be needed.

Abe Rosenthal was in India while this was going on. He had been there for four years with Ann and his boys (Andy, the youngest, born in India in 1956). He and I were not really close, but we were part of the fraternity of foreign correspondents, the network; we wrote often, exchanged gossip, shared our aspirations, kept in touch. I loved Abe's India coverage and told him so. He liked my New York reportage—and my stories from behind the Iron Curtain—and told me so.

By the winter of 1958, Abe's discontent with India had boiled over. He was shopping for a new post. He had gutted India of its reportorial treasures as the British Raj had looted it of diamonds, gold, and rubies. No one since Kipling had mined the lands East of Suez as had Abe. By late March 1958, he was writing me that he was afraid he was getting a bit blasé about India and eager to "get another assignment to see new ports." In fact, he had just accepted—with many qualms—an offer by Freedman to succeed Gruson in Warsaw.

He made no secret that Warsaw was not his heart's desire and got into a testy argument with Freedman, complaining that he was not being considered a "senior correspondent," thus not eligible, for example, for Germany, to which Gruson was being transferred, or London, Abe's No. 1 choice. He accepted Warsaw, he said, because of its "story value," but added, "I won't pretend it fills all the hopes I had." To me he wrote of his qualms at following Sydney and what bothered him more, the constraints on covering news from Communist countries and the *smallness* of Poland. He had been roving a subcontinent and was used to the wide spaces (although, curiously, he did not, in his Indian tour, explore the romantic mountaintop kingdoms of Bhutan and Sikkim or muscle his way into troubled Assam—I've never understood why). India, he pointed out, took all day to fly across. Poland looked so small on the map. He hoped he could wander over Eastern Europe and maybe the Soviet Union too.

Years later he told me he had never wanted Poland, and once he told Dan Schorr he accepted the assignment with reluctance. He really didn't like Poland. "I didn't speak Polish," he remembered. "I was very disturbed. I could imagine them talking about me."

Poland for Rosenthal was a different Poland from what it had been for Gruson. Rosenthal spent two weeks in Warsaw meeting Gruson's friends and sources—Gruson generously turned them all over, although Abe never made much use of them. The Grusons gave Abe a big party, at which Sydney spoke with sentimentality of Poland and the Poles ("I like Poland and my Polish friends"). Rosenthal responded: "You aren't talking about Poland; you are talking about six Jewish revisionists." Gruson extolled the freedom of speech in Poland. "It's not freedom of speech," Abe snapped. "It's freedom of conversation. You can't get up on a platform and say what you think."

The difference in the Gruson and Rosenthal attitudes was spelled out in that initial encounter (Abe and Sydney had never met before). It deepened with time. Abe felt ill at ease in Poland. He had never been in a Communist country. He wrote me for a copy of my Iron Curtain series and for story ideas. He felt very much an outsider, although in his years at the United Nations, as Peter Kihss recalled, no one had had better sources at the Soviet Mission than Rosenthal.

In August Abe was still very, very tentative about Poland—even as he was writing what I regard as his finest story, a report of a visit to Auschwitz, which had moved him as few things in his life had moved him. How could he write of Auschwitz, he thought, everyone had done it years before. Tommy Atkins urged him to write. "How can I?" he said. "There's nothing to write. Just that awful silence." "Write that," Tommy urged. Finally Abe did, but he sent his story back by mail. "I can't have the office paying cable tolls on it," he said. "They would complain." He apologized to Manny Freedman in advance. "As I say," he told Freedman, "there is no news at Auschwitz, but never have I felt a stronger desire to write something."

Freedman, that conventional man, thought the piece was "a little offbeat for us," but gave it to Lester Markel who published it in the *Times Magazine* "back of the book."

Abe's attitude toward Poland didn't change. He would serve out his term, but he couldn't wait to leave. In November he got a $25 raise, bringing his pay to $275 a week. In December he asked Freedman for the Tokyo bureau as soon as it became open.

Abe couldn't get over the feeling of being hemmed in. He traveled to Prague, he visited Romania, he went to Yugoslavia. It didn't help much. He had to share the Balkans with two other *Times* men. He felt he was stumbling over their footsteps. In February 1959 he was writing me: "I don't feel a great deal of zest and scope in being part of a three-man team covering a second-rate story in the suburbs.

"There," he said, "I've said it. This is the kind of thing one usually tries to conceal from oneself. But once in a while it does good to get things off one's chest on somebody."

He had been in Poland for eight months, had written, he calculated, about 150 stories, six or seven magazine pieces and by the end of his tour would have done possibly 400 stories and a dozen or fifteen magazine articles. "I ask myself whether the story as it is now is worth it," he wrote. "I think that the Polish story as it is now is not juicy enough to occupy an active reporter. I feel very much in left field."

By this time Tommy Atkins was again in the hands of the Polish police. Looking back on it, the arrests of Tommy Atkins seem almost inevitable. The first time he was arrested he had been held five months and fourteen days—the maximum he could be held without formal charges—while they tried to squeeze some kind of case out against Gruson. When Tommy was arrested in December 1958, they tried to squeeze out a case against Rosenthal. Neither time did they succeed. Tommy wouldn't talk. He wasn't treated badly. These were not Lubyanka interrogators. They didn't torture him or deprive him of food. No beatings. One interrogator was very relaxed. "Well," he would say, "I've got to spend four hours with you—what shall we talk about?" They discussed literature and music and traded harmless items about each other's lives. Tommy's life resembled a yarn by John Le Carré. He'd been born in Lódź, son of a prominent Jew who became the leader of the ghetto under the Nazi occupation. The Jews acted with extreme correctness, believing this the key to survival. It wasn't. Tommy's father and all the Jews who had lived that long were slaughtered as the Red Army approached the city.

Tommy spent the war in England in the British Army. He came back to a void. No members of his family, no one he knew had survived. He had no friends left, no aim in life. He went to work for a Jewish underground organization smuggling Jews out of Eastern Europe into Palestine. He married a young woman with high Communist connections. No Party member himself, he began to move in her circles. He and his wife met Gomulka in the sanatorium where he was held before his arrest. After Gomulka was freed, Tommy met him again—now Tommy worked for the Communist Youth paper and with Sydney Gruson. There wasn't much Tommy didn't know about Poland and not many Polish figures he did not know first or second hand. He was sent to Moscow and then to China and Japan. When he came back in spring, 1957, he gave up the Youth paper, decided to emigrate to Israel but continued his association with Gruson (and later with Rosenthal). His request to emigrate got him nothing—except, perhaps, another page in his police dossier.

There was a difference in Tommy's two prison interrogations. The Gruson period centered on Gruson, bureau finances, currency dealings, people with whom Gruson met. The Rosenthal period covered these points (Atkins had made it his practice not to meet Rosenthal's friends or to have any knowledge of Rosenthal's transactions so he would have no information to transmit to any interrogator) as well.

But there were new twists. Tommy was questioned intensively about a murder case—the murder of the son of Boleslaw Piasecki, leader of a Polish Catholic group. Piasecki had been active in right-wing politics in Poland before World War II and in the right-wing Polish partisans. In postwar Communist Poland he headed Pax, a quasi-political organization, obviously cleared by the Soviets. His son was a student at Warsaw University. In March 1957 the son was lured into a car (by a trumped-up story of an accident to his father), kidnapped by two unknown men, shot, and his body dumped on the edge of town. This line of inquiry was soon dropped. At the time of the murder Tommy was in Japan.

The police also questioned Tommy about the Pavel Monat case. Monat was a Polish military attaché who had defected to the United States in the summer of 1959. This event happened while Tommy had already been in prison for seven months.

The effort to link Tommy with Monat had—although Tommy had no knowledge of this—considerable significance.

Poland seemed more drab, more dreary to Abe in the autumn of 1959. He lived in the house Gruson had rented for the *Times*. It was located on a dead-end street. Sometimes, Abe thought, his career was on a dead end. Poland, he remembered, was like a gray blanket. There was no joy or laughter. The second anniversary of the Polish October came and went. The days were very short at that time of year, lights turned on by two in the afternoon, dark clouds, cold, snow. Ann took Jon, the oldest boy, off to Vienna, he and she had to visit the dentist and she would do some

Christmas shopping. Christmas was the big Rosenthal holiday. In all their years abroad, Ann remembered, Abe never missed Christmas. Abe stayed behind with the younger boys. He had been writing stories about Poland's troubles. Gomulka's troubles. Things were not going well. The government had been nervous about Rosenthal's reporting for quite a while, had tried to get him to tone it down. There had been a row at the end of August when Vice President Nixon passed through Warsaw after visiting the Soviet Union. Gomulka got very angry, but the row was over a *Times* editorial, not a Rosenthal story.

Rosenthal had never met the lonely, tough-minded, individualistic, prison-hardened Gomulka. In fact, for whatever reason he never explained, he had not even asked to interview him (probably because he thought it would just produce Communist propaganda and Rosenthal's anti-Communism had been sharply honed by Poland).

Now in these darkest autumn days, Abe began to write about Gomulka and what was on Gomulka's mind, sensitive, revealing stories, etching an unforgettable portrait of the isolated leader, his insoluble problems, his growing touchiness, his outbursts at his associates (really his outburst agains the Polish fate).

They were remarkable vignettes, and no one who read them could fail to see Gomulka pacing his office, nervously smoking cigarette after cigarette, crushing hand to bony skull, suffused in frustration over problems for which there was no solution.

Whatever their source, and Abe has never spoken of that, the dispatches conveyed an extraordinary feeling (and that may well have been because Abe himself was feeling frustration similar to Gomulka's). Rosenthal pieces were too much for the Poles. Ann in Vienna got a telegram: "Come back to Warsaw at once." Abe had been expelled. Within a week—she with the two younger boys by train and Abe driving the family car with Jonathan— they were out to Vienna, first to an imperial suite at the Bristol ("a sitting room as large as a ballroom," Ann remembered) and then to a lovely house in the Vienna woods where the family made Christmas ornaments, Ann and Abe and Jon and Dan and Andy, because the ones from Warsaw hadn't yet arrived. Abe wrote some stories, including a scoop on the Monat case (probably from his friend Per Da Silva, the Warsaw CIA station chief who for security reasons was headquartered in Vienna), touching off a Polish campaign to link Abe with the defector and, in all probability, causing the interrogation of Tommy about Monat. The Poles, Abe reported, had given as the reason for his expulsion his too deep probing into high Polish politics. The Gomulka stories, of course.

Four months later Abe won the Pulitzer for his Warsaw coverage (the one I always thought really belonged to Gruson—although Abe had earned it fair and square). Out of his dead-end beat in "the suburbs," as he had called it, he was catapulted to fame. Henceforth he would be a "senior correspondent" and much, much more.

Tommy Atkins lingered in jail. He was told nothing of Rosenthal's expulsion. He stayed in prison until the spring of 1960 when Meyer Handler, the *Times* Vienna correspondent, negotiated his release and the reopening of the *Times* Warsaw Bureau. Tommy worked briefly for the *Times,* then for the U.S. embassy, finally escaping to Vienna in a packing case crammed in the back of a station wagon. And after many a dangerous and difficult adventure—to Israel, to Germany, to France—to the United States where after a valiant effort, supported by Gruson and Rosenthal, he finally got permission to stay, working his way by dint and determination to citizenship and a full academic professorship.

Not long ago Tommy told me about the fifth man at the table on the Warsaw night in October 1957, the propelling force of this particular Rashomon. The man had come and sat at our table for a long time. To me he was just a gray blur. I vaguely recalled someone sitting down with us. I could recall nothing of the conversation. Nor did Sydney remember him. But Tommy did, because he alone realized that something unusual was going on. I had been peppering Tommy with questions about what was happening. Tommy had answered some, ducked others. Many of my inquiries had sharp political edges, much sharper than I realized. Then this man, a Warsaw newspaperman with excellent connections, came up, introduced himself, and pulled a fifth chair up to the littered table. I asked more questions.

"And he answered them." Tommy recollected as we sat in a quiet Gramercy Park restaurant nearly thirty years later. "He answered all your questions. I knew something dangerous was going on. He should not have been so outspoken—his answers were remarkably complete and accurate. My jaw dropped. I did not know what he was up to."

What the Fifth Man was up to was very simple. He was acting as a stand-in for Tommy. When Tommy was arrested, he was accused of giving to me the answers the Fifth Man had offered. No denial by Tommy was accepted. They pretended that the Fifth Man was not there. No, they said, it was you, Seweryn Pomerancz (Tommy's name of record), who gave this dangerous foreign intelligence operative this intimate Party information.

The Fifth Man had come, done his job, left the table, and no trace of what he had said or even his presence remained in my mind.

11 | A Time of Change

I came back to New York with the feeling that it was time to give more shape to the random pattern of my life. I had become a kind of journalistic soldier of fortune, moved from Brooklyn to Budapest, from Garbage to Gomulka, by Frank Adams, Emanuel Freedman, and Turner Catledge. I loved living like the Three Musketeers, always plunging into a new adventure—but where did it lead?

I was a year shy of fifty. I had long been divorced. My two boys were growing up in the Midwest. I saw them occasionally, but I was leading a bachelor existence in New York (or wherever), still under the trauma of my failed marriage. Perhaps, I thought, I'm just not cut out for a permanent relationship, perhaps it demands more than I have the ability to give.

Now, at least, I must try to organize my professional life. I had gone to the *Times* because it *was* the *Times* and because I knew I wanted to be a correspondent and not an editor. I didn't want to make marks on papers or push them around. I belonged on the scene where I felt challenged, excited, at home. I loved to write, and I came back from Eastern Europe with a new sense of how important it was to see with my own eyes, hear with my own ears, touch with my own hands, before making a judgment.

But there was a problem. My speciality was the Soviet Union. I knew the territory (I thought) better than anyone in the business. I would match my judgment about Moscow against anyone's, in or out of government, American, European, or Asian. In fact I would match it against that of most Russians. But the Soviet bureaucracy would not let me set foot on Holy Russian soil. I had been banned since 1954. I felt like Antaeus, I had to touch the *chernozëm,* the black earth, regularly or I could not interpret Russia accurately. I did not believe (and I do not now) in the armchair "expert," the scholarly dilettante who examines dry bones of Marxist dialectic and proclaims eternal truths about the Politburo. To analyse you have to have a fresh eye, draw a little blood, and possess seat-of-the-pants luck.

Now, out of Warsaw, out of Budapest, out of Tirana, I began

to sketch for myself a broader horizon—the whole of the Communist world from the Elbe to the Bering Strait. If I could score a hat trick in Eastern Europe, why not in Asia, China, Mongolia, Korea, Indochina (just beginning to emerge from the distant thunder of Dien Bien Phu)? And somehow I would have to squirm between the barbed wire and get back inside Russia.

This, I thought, made sense. Side by side I would continue a healthy diet of grassroots America. You could not, I had become convinced, write from Kabul, Vientiane, Pyongyang, or Sofia with understanding unless you knew what was playing on Broadway and the price of wheat in North Dakota. If the cry "Yankee Go Home!" arose in Berlin, you had to know why they were chanting "Yankee Go Home!" in Tuscaloosa, Alabama.

It was—like it or not, and I did not pretend to like it very much—one world.

I had learned in this summer of 1957 that the Iron Curtain was leaky as a tin roof, that the Kremlin's sway ran just as far as the writ of the Red Army, no further, that the "Communist Gibraltar" was just a lot of grubby little dictatorships. More and more I began to wonder whether it was the reality of Communist power that frightened us or a nightmare conjured up by our overheated imagination.

I could not believe that this ramshackle structure would endure. One day it would topple down like Humpty Dumpty. I had invested five years waiting for Stalin's death and the extraordinary story that followed. If I took the whole Communist world as my oyster, I could be the man to report on the inevitable collapse of the century's colossus. That was worth a lifetime.

I don't want to give the impression that all of this, dovetailed neatly, tied down in logical propositions, filed away in tan folders in a green filing cabinet, was spelled out in my mind. I don't function that way. I am a disorderly, instinctive kind of person. But even I could see the parameters of this future and how I should position myself.

My Balkan summer had moved me into a new and different orbit. Henceforth the *Times* (and I, too) would begin to think of Salisbury as the man who could pick the lock and get behind the Iron Curtain and, who knows, perhaps the Bamboo Curtain and other curtains not quite so visible. As time went on, this would dominate my life.

* * *

I can't say that anything spectacular happened as a result of my musings, not for a time. Then Isaac Asimov gave my life a twist. Stephan, my eleven-year-old, spent Thanksgiving with me in 1958. My old friend of Moscow days, Tom Whitney, and I had bought a rundown farmhouse in Connecticut. The day after I had carved the turkey, I took Stephan for a ride through the autumnal countryside.

Stephan had fallen under the spell of Asimov, and he wanted to get a copy of the master's latest work. We were driving up Route 7 in the white TR-3, which I had proudly acquired a year earlier, hyperventilated in England's best tradition, a darling in the New England snowdrifts. When we got to Salisbury, Connecticut, I spotted Maurice Firuski's rare book shop, and we hopped out. A marvelous young woman, clear blue eyes, head and shoulders high, the walk of a rather mortal goddess (or at least that of a one-time Powers model) asked if she could help. It was Charlotte. We had not met for nearly four years, but her image was clear in my mind as the crisp November light. Stephan bought his book, and I knew that one way or another I had to see Charlotte again (if possible, again and again).

Charlotte was married, had several children (four as I found out), and, so far as I knew, was living a happy life. It was silly of me to think about her, but I did. Some months later I dropped by the shop again, and this time she invited me to tea in the cozy house where I had stayed the first time I came to Salisbury for a lecture in January 1955. We talked. I have no idea what we talked about, but I left with a feeling that we were going to meet again and that somehow, perhaps, it was not so hopeless a case as I had thought. Nor was it. Unknown to me Charlotte was in the process of moving out of her marriage. Before too long she and her son, Curtis, eight, would go off to Florence, to stay in Italy for some months, to live and work at Villa Mercede, an American girl's school. I hoped to get to Florence to see her but didn't. Visits to Moscow, Nikita Khrushchev, his trips to the U.S.A., interfered. Somehow this didn't make much difference. We were very cautious, both of us. We didn't want to make any mistake. And we didn't.

I feel shy about writing of happiness, unexpected, miraculous, but that is what the years have brought since that April day of our marriage in 1964. We have become a team, not only living together, sharing our six children, four of hers, two of mine, our great brood of grandchildren, our extended family, our almost Victorian kind of existence (except, of course, no "below stairs" staff), a life of intense intimacy and warmth such as neither of us could have dreamed. First we reclaimed an old Bohemian rooming house in Yorkville, of twenty-seven crib-sized rooms, restoring it to the splendor of 1880. After a decade we moved into a rambling house at the very corner of Connecticut, New York, and Massachusetts, under the shadow of the Berkshires, snowy, clean, and white in winter, shimmering green in summer. Charlotte's cool realism, her excruciating honesty ("I'm just a flat-footed Boston woman"), keeps me from flight into Cloud-Cuckoo-Land, and, I hope, my defiant optimism lightens the dark pessimism with which she faces the world, expecting the worst and preparing to meet it.

I cannot tell how many hundreds of thousands (maybe millions) of miles we have traveled together since 1964. We started out with a trip to Atlantic City, by bus, for the dreadful Democratic national convention at which LBJ humiliated Hubert Humphrey by dragging him like a slobbering hound around and around the convention hall before finally, with an offhand gesture, anointing him as No. 2 on the 1964 ticket, an omen of worse to come.

Again and again Charlotte and I traveled to distant corners of the earth, never for pleasure except that of each other's company, always on the trail of news and new barriers to surmount—Russia's farthest reaches, odd corners of Siberia (we love Siberia), the Gobi, the Himalayas, Mongolia (again and again, Mongolia), Sihanouk's doomed delicate Cambodia, Ne Win's eccentric Burma, Hope Cooke's Sikkim, Madame Gandhi's India, Korea, and, of course, China—first, all around its circumference during the mad days of the Cultural Revolution, then into China, dinners with Zhou Enlai, Soong Chingling, and Hu Yaobang, explorations of the Soviet frontiers, north and west, the stone trail from Lhasa in Tibet to Katmandu in Nepal and in 1984 the climactic retracing of the Long March, Mao's Red Army retreat of 1934-35, 7,400 miles into the most remote mountains and deserts. No better comrade than my Charlotte to be found in all the world.

Charlotte changed my life in an epoch in which change was the order of the day. The sixties would leave deep marks on

America. We had entered an age of unannounced revolution in political, economic, social, and personal relations—civil rights, race rebellion, women's rights, gay rights, Indian rights, student rebellion, an upheaval in morals and technology as had not been seen since the Industrial Revolution. It was a time of change everywhere and no less at the *Times,* an old order rapidly, painfully, erratically, and even hysterically giving place to new.

For me the changes within the *Times* began in 1962 with the cable from Turner Catledge that caught me in Kabul, asking me to take the job of national editor. I felt I couldn't turn him down, but first I went to Ulan Bator, the capital of Outer Mongolia, the farthest out capital in the world. It was winter—60 degree-below-zero winter. I stopped off at Irkutsk in eastern Siberia, cloaked in steam-frost from Lake Baikal, the world's largest body of fresh water, still unfrozen in the minus 60-degree frost. In a five-minute walk in icy sunshine, I froze my ears iron-white, worse than in a childhood of sledding in 30-degree-below Minnesota.

I put Mongolia ahead of the national desk, because I had found it to be a primary fault line in world politics. Here an earthquake could be detected quicker than anywhere. Two years earlier when I talked my way into Mongolia, I hadn't known what I would find except yaks, yurts, and yogurt. To my astonishment it had produced spectacular news. Mongolia, the distant, nomadic ward of Moscow, lacked modern skills, the heirs of Genghis Khan lived by horses and horsemanship. There were no better riders in the world, but they couldn't tell a hammer from a handsaw. Thousands of Chinese workers and Soviet soldiers were building roads, dams, bridges, factories, and housing for Mongolia.

Russia and China were staunch allies then, bound in eternal friendship and defense against the world, especially the U.S.A. But, as I discovered, they weren't speaking to one another. There was no friendship, no cooperation, just hostility. I went to the Mongolian national holiday, *Nadam,* and found the reception hall divided into two grim camps, Russians on one side, Chinese on the other. A beefy Russian general drank toasts to American-Soviet friendship, then put a pudgy arm around my shoulder and whispered confidentially; "Tell me, Mr. Salisbury, don't you feel more comfortable on *our* side of the room." Well, as a matter of fact, I did, because not one Chinese in Mongolia had been willing to say a word to me. They turned their backs and walked away on finding out I was an American. I was no more popular than the Russians.

This was not a charade out of Emily Post's *Etiquette*. These were symptoms of a profound split in Mr. Dulles' "monolithic" world of Communism, which he was sure had its headquarters in the Kremlin. I could hardly wait to file my dispatch. Of course, the State Department tagged me once again as a naif: "Everyone knows there can't be a real split." But my information was solid as the Pamirs. Angry polemics in 1960 made it all hang out, and Nikita Khrushchev underlined this by pulling 14,000 Soviet aid experts from China.

By the time I got back to Mongolia in 1961–62, the Chinese-Russian cross fire was hot and heavy. Still, there were those (and some exist even today in 1987) who slyly sidled up to me and asked whether I didn't *really* think it was all just "disinformation" to fool the trusting American people. I said, no, I don't think so.

No one had been there since my 1959 expedition, and I needed an update. Many young Mongols had sided with China then. I wondered if they still did and whether the Russians had made the Mongols send the Chinese workers home.

I did not meet the pro-Chinese Mongols of 1959. They had lost their jobs. Some had lost their lives. Moscow wasn't playing beanbag. Most of the Chinese work teams had gone home. I talked to Party Secretary Tsedenbal, a moon-faced man who looked a little like one of Chekhov's schoolteachers. I had first met him in Tirana, and I had seen him in 1959 in Ulan Bator when he talked earnestly about establishing U.S.-Mongol diplomatic relations. (Not until 1987 after more than twenty-five years were they established.) I would see him on all subsequent visits. Tsedenbal had been educated at Moscow University, was married to a Russian woman, spoke perfect Russian, and sometimes made speeches in Russian. No doubt where he stood—and yet . . . I hadn't met a Mongol who really didn't want a Greater Mongolia, dominated by neither Russia nor China. They had let the Russians in before 1911 to drive the Chinese out. Once the Russians got in (the Communists just picked up the Czarist Russian policy), the Mongols began to lean toward the Chinese. Mongols were split into three packages—Outer Mongolia under Russian influence; Inner Mongolia, part of China and rapidly filling with Chinese, and small Mongol enclaves in the Soviet Union called autonomous regions. The Mongols wanted to put the jig-saw together. There wasn't a chance either great power would cooperate. On my 1961–62 findings, I calculated it would be a long, long time before the Sino-Soviet alliance was revived—if ever. Naturally, the State Department did not agree.

When I got back to New York in the winter of 1962, I didn't know what I was walking into nor could anyone have forseen what lay ahead. The city room seemed as cozy and shabby as ever, cherubic Frank Adams still city editor, slipping off to a back corner at the end of day for a rubber or two of bridge, passing through the aisles in his patriarchical progress to give the reporters "Good night." Solemn, serious Manny Freedman presided over the foreign correspondents. Ted Bernstein, the iron-willed nervous boss of the bullpen, dictated the front page as imperiously as ever. Catledge with his Southern politician's soft-shoe, easy Mississippi accent pulled invisible wires from his cubbyhole office, and my old friend of London days, Clifton Dan-iel, training to succeed Catledge, seemed more busy, more active, more up-front than I recalled. Something suggested transition, and I took my appointment as national editor as the first move on a complicated chessboard that would lead Daniel to the top editor's chair.

I was right, but neither I nor anyone was ready for what was to come. Orvil Dryfoos, polite, patient, proper, was now pub-lisher, succeeding his ailing father-in-law. Dryfoos had brought in a "corporate management team" to run the paper. I hadn't seen much of "corporate managers," but they made me nervous. I thought they masked ignorance with self-assurance, multicol-ored flow charts, and slide presentations. Their bureaucratese ob-scured their lack of know-how. Not that the business manage-ment of Arthur Hays Sulzberger and his wife's cousin, General Adler, had been brilliant. Still they had kept the *Times* ahead of the competition (principally the *Herald-Tribune*) in the troubled New York field. Now the New York newspaper business was put to a terrible test—the "long strike," 114-days of idleness in 1962–63. I sat that out in the empty city room, as drear an epi-sode as I can remember, wondering who was going to pay the price. Everyone, as it turned out. The strike ravaged New York, only three papers survived in the end—the *Times,* the *News,* and the *Post.*

A few weeks after the strike, Dryfoos died of a heart attack. No successor waited in the wings. A couple of years before, in an advance obituary which I had prepared of Arthur Hays Sulzberger, I had noted how careful the *Times* was to train successors—Orvil Dryfoos to succeed Sulzberger, and Punch (Arthur Ochs Sulzberger, Dryfoos' brother-in-law) to succeed him—if necessary.

Catledge read the obit and called me in. "Who told you that?" he asked.

"No one," I said. "It's just obvious."

It had not been obvious to Turner. He thought I was on to something—which I wasn't. Catledge was the only one at 229 West 43rd Street who had paid any attention to Punch. He had been relegated to menial chores, no training for a major executive post. One day in 1957 or 1958 I came into the city room and found Punch with two men, unknown to me, standing by my desk, "Jim Hagerty's desk," looking out at the room. I liked Punch. I thought he had a hard row to hoe. He was pleasant and unassuming. We sometimes indulged in casual chatter. He often shared a drink with Catledge at day's end, and I sometimes joined the Catledge group.

"What are you up to?" I asked. Punch said they were going to replace the old oak desks and chairs with new formica-top steel furniture. I was appalled. I *loved* Mr. Hagerty's desk and all the desks. They were *perfect,* perfect for typing, for editing.

"I'm sorry about that," I said. "I've never had such a good desk."

Punch shrugged his shoulders in a what-can-I-do? gesture. "Saves a lot of time and labor for the cleaning ladies," he said. And probably because I looked forlorn, he crinkled his eyes and added, "Sorry." He was, too. And I was sorry for him. It just couldn't have been easy, the son of the publisher, in charge of housekeeping, painting, and cleaning at 229 West 43rd Street. Everyone liked Punch, everyone in his family, and almost everyone he met. But they didn't think he had much ability. The only one in the establishment who had a warm man-to-man relationship with him was Catledge. Both were divorced. They had evenings on their hands. I was divorced, too, and I had an affinity with Punch. Not that I thought he would make a great publisher. I was stunned when he was named, still with no preparatory training, to succeed Dryfoos, and yet some small voice told me none of us really knew this man, not Catledge, not his parents, not his sisters, and certainly not me. In a showdown, as time would tell, no matter how many bumbles Punch made, he came down with the right answer, the right man (often after firing two or three bad ones), the right policy after some wild goose chases. He had, I concluded, an instinct for decisions—if left to himself. But how many, many times those who thought they knew better politicked him into wrong choices which he ultimately had to correct.

In the beginning Punch had some very able men to help him. He relied enormously on Turner Catledge and, to a lesser extent, on James Reston, both outstanding, rivals for years but this had not limited their effectiveness. On the business side Punch had a far worse time. Not until he had worked through the whole legacy of the Dryfoos "management team" did he emerge with the solid, uncharismatic, pragmatic, and brilliant Walter Mattson, and the two piloted the *Times* to extraordinary heights of financial success, leaving in their wake an unbelievable train of systems men, corporate symposia, executive psychiatrists, consultants, and medicine men. These men taught Punch a lesson. He was seeking a magic button, a "way" to run the *Times,* a fail-safe system. It took a long time before this rather slight, dark, handsome, exquisitely soft-shoe man had to concede that there was no yellow brick road to the Emerald City.

I had been in place at the national desk about eighteen months when Abe Rosenthal came blazing back from Tokyo. I think "blazing" is a just word. He was like a Roman candle, shooting his sparks in every direction, no aim, no ear for the hubbub around him, as much a young man in a hurry as ever climbed up from the mean streets of the Bronx, from the rough poverty of an emigrant family out of Russia's Pale of Settlement, survivor of brutal illness, eyes like caramel candy (except when afire with anger), once so thin his schoolteacher said, "If you close one eye, you'll be a needle" (filled out now; later a tendency to pudginess).

I was delighted Abe was back. He was much more to my taste than the genial Frank Adams. My delight did not last. Somehow this was not the Abe I had known for twenty years. I had looked forward to working together, helping him to know New York again. No way. Abe was off and running on his own, suspicious of me and of almost all his colleagues. I had not been privy to the negotiations that brought Abe back. I did not know he had written Clifton from Tokyo, expressing great concern over rumors he said he had heard that "there is going to be trouble in the city room" (Clifton sharply rebuked Abe: "I think your conclusion is 100 percent wrong"). Years later Arthur Gelb told me how Abe persuaded him to become the other half of "Abe'n'Artie." "We can do anything. We'll create it all and do everything we want. We are going to make enemies."

They did. They did, indeed. They made enemies, they roughed up fine correspondents, they broke the spirit of bright young reporters, they drove talented men and women away until the third floor of 229 West 43rd Street reeked of envy, greed, jealousy, ambition, snideness, savagery, hypocrisy, and tawdriness. But they produced stories! Nothing stopped them. Not libel suits. Not complaints from the highest. They never quit. Sure, a lot of it was junk, including the famous thirty-nine witnesses who didn't stir to help a girl who was being murdered. But it was lively, readable, fresh, original, feisty, impudent, irresistible, and sometimes even important. The bottom line was that what Rosenthal-Gelb produced put the *Times* back in business. It wasn't the Ochs' *Times*. It wasn't Van Anda's *Times*. It wasn't Catledge's *Times* or Iphigene Sulzberger's. Sometimes it wasn't even the *Times*. Abe did not, although he was fond of saying it, "keep the paper straight," whatever on earth he meant by that. (No *Times* editor in history had ever felt it necessary to say anything like that.) In fact, Rosenthal's *Times* was often a good deal more like Pulitzer's *World* or Mr. Hearst's *Journal*. It rode hobby horses, to put it politely, and did not neglect private quirks. But, my, oh my, how it was read.

What I didn't know in the early sixties and found hard to believe in the late sixties was that the *Times* was on the line. It was softly settling closer and closer to the red ink. The New York newspaper field had been devastated, and inside the big old building on 43rd Street blood ran in the corridors. The question really seemed genuine: Could *The New York Times* survive? Or would it join the *World,* the *Herald,* the *Sun,* all those giants, that now were only ink-stained nostalgia?

I couldn't believe what my mind told me. But by the end of the 1960s, the *Times* was in terrible trouble. All the newspapers were in terrible trouble. And at the *Times* the tiller was in the hands of a young, untrained, untried publisher, and bulling his way to the top was the most hyperthyroid, emotional, brilliant, remarkable man who had ever headed the paper. Could the *Times* be saved? There were many in New York who thought not. By this time there were many in the *Times,* casualties of the infighting, who almost hoped the *Times* would go under and take the piratical new crew with it. I was not one of these.

12 | Nightmare in Sikkim

I awoke at 4 A.M. in a sweat, wide awake, feeling that the nightmare which had roused me was totally true, a premonition of events to come. I thought I knew its meaning precisely. The date was June 30, 1966, and the room in which I lay beside Charlotte, she peacefully sleeping, her breath smooth and regular, was the guest chamber of the palace in Gangtok, capital of the mountaintop kingdom of Sikkim in the Himalayas.

We had come there, Charlotte and I, as guests of King, or *Chogyal,* Thondup, and Queen, or *Gyalmo,* the former Hope Cooke, with whom Ellen, Charlotte's daughter, had gone to Sarah Lawrence. The bedroom was big and airy on the top floor of the modest Edwardian country house which served as the palace. On a staircase landing just outside was a massive white enamel urinal which flushed every five minutes, night and day—Old Faithful, Thondup called it when he came up, wrench in hand, to tighten a washer and slow down the burblings.

We were two months into a journey of 25,000 miles that was to take us around the rim of China. This had been Clifton Daniel's idea. No one had ever done it—and I don't suppose anyone has since. I had been trying unsuccessfully to get to Beijing. This expedition would give me a look at China through her neighbors' eyes. We would see the Forbidden Kingdom over the wall, and I would try my magic at getting into China and other sealed-off lands. Our passports were cleared for travel to Communist China, North Vietnam, and North Korea.

Now we had arrived at the high Himalayas, twenty miles as the falcon flies, from China (actually Tibet). For days the roads south to India had been closed by avalanches. This was the monsoon season, and I could hear the rain pelting on the tin roof as it had for a week. I had to get out. Somehow we had to get over those rock slides and out of Sikkim, down to India, and on our way. There wasn't a moment to lose. We had not received our visas for Russia. There had been delay after delay. I had applied in Washington. Nothing but smiles. No action. We left the U.S.A. without them. They will catch up with you, the pleasant

Russian in Washington said. We had been two months without word. We had to get out of the Himalayas. We had visas for Mongolia, but they were about to expire. They must be extended. And now this nightmare.

It was vivid as life. I had walked into the city room on 43rd Street, coming back from my orbit of China. The room was filled with people, typewriters hammering away, copyboys rushing back and forth. Not one person looked up. No one took notice of me. I glanced over the room. There was not a person in that indoor acre from 43rd Street to 44th Street whom I knew. No one looked up, and when they did they looked right through me.

I lay on my back, listening to the even murmur of Charlotte's breath, the patter of rain, the rhythmic gurgle of Old Faithful. I knew what the dream meant. There flashed into my mind a telephone call from Reston a couple of days before we left on the long flight to Hong Kong. We gossiped a bit, and then Scotty said, "What are you going to be doing when you come back?" Nothing new, I replied, back to my job. There was a pause. "Oh," he said. "I see. Well, I guess Abe is sitting in for you." "That's right", I said, "Clifton asked if he could sit at my desk and fill in while I'm nosing my way around China". Another microscopic pause, then Reston: "Well, good luck on the trip. See you when you come back."

I had not given Reston another thought. I was enchanted with the grand circuit, enchanted to be off in Asia with Charlotte, our first big trip, and I was sure that it would lead us into China—if not immediately, then before very long. And there just might be a chance for Hanoi. I had been working on China since 1949 and on Vietnam for nearly two years. As for North Korea, I would be entirely happy if I never went to Pyongyang.

It was not just these three closed kingdoms. There were others on the periphery of China—Cambodia, locked tight against Americans by Prince Sihanouk because he thought (correctly) that the CIA was plotting his downfall (he'd gotten a birthday package which blew up when servants opened it); Burma, the doors sealed by Ne Win to all foreigners, particularly Americans; and not many got to Sikkim and Mongolia.

It would be a grand coup, and I was glad to get away from New York. The atmosphere had changed. Too much pettiness. Sharp edges. Unaccountable happenings. Clifton Daniel had made me assistant managing editor when he became managing editor in 1964. "We'll do all kinds of things," he said. "Things no one will know about. We'll often be here working, late at night, working on secret stuff. It's going to be exciting." But he added an admonition: I would not be his successor. We were too much of an age (I was three years older than Clifton). When his term was up, the prize would go to a younger man. That suited me fine. I insisted that I continue to do two or three big reporting assignments a year. He gave his OK.

Later on, the inner power structure of The *Times* was radically altered. Catledge, supported by Daniel and Rosenthal, sought to grasp control of the quasi-independent Washington bureau headed by Reston. The maneuver failed in a dramatic sequence of events chronicled in detail by Gay Talese in *The Kingdom and the Power* and in my own *Without Fear or Favor.* Catledge, in effect, was kicked upstairs. Reston came to New York briefly as executive editor. Daniel fell into disfavor with Punch Sulzberger and Rosenthal, although a prime figure in the failed endeavor, won Sulzberger's favor. After a short interlude Reston gave up his New York post and returned to Washington to concentrate on his column. The field was thus cleared for Rosenthal to rise to the top as chief news executive of the *Times.*

In all these shennanigans I was only an observer, a very interested one but on the sidelines. I knew all the participants intimately; they were my friends and there was very little that went on that I did not learn, sooner or later. But I was not a player in the Big Casino.

What my dream in the palace bedchamber told me was the depth of my hidden fear of being dealt out in the fast-moving intrigue and the strength of my own emotions, which I had not understood until this moment. Now I saw clearly that I was at peril. Scotty, I thought, as I lay listening to the ceaseless tropical downpour, was right. Absolutely right. I was being shuffled off center stage in a most elegant manner, and Clifton had to know that this was going on. (Never under my most persistent questioning in later years would he admit what seemed so obvious to me. It hadn't been, he insisted, a maneuver to open up my spot for Abe.) But, of course, I thought, that was exactly what was going on. Rosenthal was sitting in my chair—not, thank God, Mr. Hagerty's chair. That was long since gone, and when I got back to New York, there might or might not be a chair for me.

I had to get out of Gangtok as fast as possible, avalanches or no avalanches. Let them get a helicopter. I had to hit the road. I had to complete my perimeter journey, and I had to make it ring bells. I had to make this trip the foundation for future successes. Otherwise, my dream was going to come true.

I looked at Charlotte, quiet beside me, and told myself there can be not one word of this to her. This was our first great expedition. We had been thrilled to be together, looking up at the stars, lying on our backs on the teakwood deck of the Toppings' junk in the Hong Kong waters, riding elephants like tourists at Angkor Wat, dissolving in the beauty of the royal Cambodian dancers against the stone frieze of their ancestors as the moon rose over the jungle ruins, watching the great peak of Kanchenjunga flash pink and gold in the 5 A.M. sun, sleeping in each other's arms high above the Pacific. But now I was on the line. We had to get out of Gangtok. The Mongolian visas were expiring. They could only be renewed in Moscow, and we had no Moscow visa. Catch-22.

We left Gangtok in fog and rain at 8 A.M., and by noon we had come back to Gangtok. The rain poured, the road was blocked by pyramids of boulders, all telegraph and telephone lines were cut, no one knew if planes were flying. Certainly nothing could get into Gangtok. There wasn't even a landing strip. The amiable, gin-drinking Chogyal, a kind of Himalayan Jack Kennedy, and Hope, the whispering Queen, looking like a girl out of a Sarah Lawrence fairy tale in her handsome *kuo* and carmine makeup, thought we should wait. Why hurry? Sometimes Gangtok was cut off for a week or more. My nightmare burned a hole in my mind. I was sorry. We *had* to get out. We had to. That evening a plan was made. We would take a very roundabout route. We would start at 4:30 A.M. If we were lucky, we might get through. Then in late evening the Indian Army general in charge of roads came in with a new plan. We would take the shorter road. There were blockages, but we would walk across them, and jeeps would pick us up on the other side. He seemed sure we could make our 1:30 P.M. plane to Calcutta.

It was murky when we started, our luggage with us in one jeep, an army colonel and two Indian soldiers in a jeep ahead. Rain came and went, fog seeped into the valleys and crept down to our ankles, water roared from the high mountains, and a tributary of the Brahmaputra leaped and surged beside the road. Gangs of soldiers worked to clear the debris. There was blockage after blockage.

We skirted rock falls, inching along the edge of 2,000-foot drops, shifting our weight toward the mountain side. Mile-by-mile we made progress, but my mind was filled with gloomy thoughts. Then we arrived at a mammoth slide. The whole mountain top had fallen in on the road where it skirted a cliff. Scores of workers, men, women and children, pawed at the mass with picks, shovels, and bare hands. We got out of our jeep, took shelter behind small trees, and they blasted away with dynamite charges, rock flying through the air like shrapnel. It would take days to clear the slide.

Our Indian officer conferred with the captain in charge, half a dozen skirted Sikkimese shouldered our luggage, and we were off over the treacherous rock like billy goats, the smell of cordite heavy in our nostrils, the officer in spotless uniform picking his way in the shattered stone, the fallen trees, the tumbled debris as though escorting us to the races. Miraculously, we got over, across the pile, still smoking from the dynamite blasts. How Charlotte managed I can't imagine. On the far side another jeep awaited, and we set off again, slithering down the mountains, halted time and again, waiting for smaller slides to be cleared and yawning holes to be filled.

Finally we were off the mountain and racing across flat country toward the airport. I relaxed. Then the motor sputtered, coughed, and died. Out of gas. Ten minutes to plane time. My heart sank. A Red Cross jeep came down the road, our escort flagged it, hopped in, and soon returned with a couple of gallons of gas. He poured it in, but the engine wouldn't start. Again and again he depressed the starter. Not a cough from the engine. Out we leaped. The luggage was transferred to the Red Cross jeep, and we hurried on. Plane time came and went. We were covered with mud, tearing down a flat dusty road at sixty miles an hour. God save us, I thought, if we hit a cow (sacred in India). We hit no cow, but we did slam to a halt a mile from the airport. The gate was down at a railroad grade crossing. No train in sight. No gatekeeper in sight. This was an old Pearl White serial. Our Colonel got out, serenely strolled across the tracks and disappeared. We stood in desolation. I had run out of encouraging things to say or think. We had lost another day and probably would spend the night in some hovel. Finally, our colonel came back, smiling. All was well. The plane hadn't arrived yet. Wouldn't get in for half-an-hour, maybe longer. Plenty of time to wash up and have a decent lunch before taking off for Calcutta. Miraculously, the gate went up, we chugged across the tracks (no train ever appeared), and all was well. We had a pleasant lunch and were on our way.

Back in Delhi that evening, July 2, I took myself in hand. I had been too gloomy. The dream didn't mean anything. It was just the product of my worry over the blocked roads, the monsoon, the long, complicated arrangements, the lack of Russian visas. Now we were in Delhi, there was time to spare, everything would work out. It didn't.

Tony Lukas, the *Times* correspondent, just beginning his spectacular writing career, greeted us. There was even a handful of mail. Letters from the children in New York. We devoured them. There was also a letter from Turner Catledge. I opened it warily. The last time I had received a message from Catledge while abroad had been in Kabul, proposing that I become national editor. I scanned the letter, and my heart sank. My dream had been on target. Scotty had been right. Turner was asking, just asking, mind you, whether I would be interested in giving up my news job and taking over the *Times*'s fledgling (and ailing) book publishing division. I had so many contacts in the publishing world. He thought I would be just the man for this.

So there it was. My premonition had been correct. What to do? The travel agent who was getting our visas for Moscow had not received them. What to do? I concealed my thoughts as best I could. I was in as tough a bind as I had ever been. Yes, I told myself, the publishing division might be fun and profitable—if that was what I wanted. But it was really just a Catledge gimmick to get me out of the city room and leave that chair and desk open. And, I told myself, if this trip flopped, if I could not get into Russia, if I could not get into Mongolia, if I had to cancel the sprawl of the vast frontiers of Russia and Mongolia with China, the most sensitive, hottest segment of all, the whole thing would fall to the ground. True it would have been a great travelogue. Sure, I had got into Cambodia. Sure I had made it into Laos. I had astonished everyone by breaking into Ne Win's Burma, thanks to an assist from Jim Linen, the *Time* executive, and a personal telephone call from New York to Ne Win. But

what did it add up to? Yes, Charlotte and I had been guests of
Himalayan royalty. We had had fun. An adventure. We had our
thrills and excitement, but when I got back to New York and
walked into the city room, no one would notice.

First things first. I spent the night tossing and turning. Fortunately, Charlotte was exhausted. I did not wake her. I made
my plan of action. I would cable Catledge and tell him I would
explore the publishing project the moment I got back. That
would put it on hold until I saw how the wind was blowing in
New York and whether my apprehensions were correct (I was
100 percent convinced they were). Abe was a young man in a
hurry. He had been expected to spend six months learning the
ropes of the city room. Frank Adams, his friend from United
Nations days, was delighted to have his protégé back. He looked
forward to working with Abe. But in three weeks Frank Adams
was gone, kicked up to the tenth floor to write editorials. Abe
couldn't stand having to sit beside the plodding Adams. Abe
knew what he wanted to do. He had recruited Arthur Gelb. He
had looked over the young reporters. He had picked those he
wanted to work with. Turner arranged for Frank Adams' immediate departure, hardly time for a farewell handshake. Adams
left the city room a bitter man. His consumption of midday martinis at Goughs went up.
    Next morning I checked with the Indian travel agent about
Moscow. The agent was very handsome, very suave, very certain
the visa would come through. No problem. I thought there was a
big problem and went to the Soviet embassy myself. The embassy
was equally benign. Not to worry. The visa would be ready. I was
not reassured. Not for a minute. Our Mongolian visas were valid
until July 7. It was already July 3. We had to get the Mongol
visas extended in Moscow. No way to do it in Delhi. I had dealt
with the Mongols and knew that even this small clerical detail
could not be solved instantly. My relations with Ulan Bator were
fine. But no one was more bureaucratic than the Mongols. We
had to have a couple of days in Moscow to attend to the Mongolian visas.
    That must have been the day I went to the Soviet embassy
again. The morning mail had brought a letter from Abe. He was
full of admiration for my Asian stories, particularly those from
Burma. He had known I would fall in love with India. (I

hadn't.) He put in a trifle or two of office gossip and added: "It's been fun for me, keeping your chair warm."

Everything will be fine, said the Russians that afternoon. If the visas don't come through, you can get them at the airport in Moscow. New regulations. They will issue the transit visas at the airport. A two or three-day stopover is automatic. I hoped that was true. My, how I hoped. But I only half-believed the men. Nothing so convenient had ever happened to me in Moscow. I believed the consul, because I had to believe him. The alternative was to abandon everything and go back to New York and the book business. The worst part was not to let Charlotte catch my worries. Charlotte is a great worrier. There were enough day-to-day worries on the trip without adding this kind of complication.

We took off from Delhi July 8. Our visas to Mongolia had expired the day before. We had no visas for Russia. It was as risky a gamble as I had ever taken. I did not know how it would work out. But I would *make* it work. I told Charlotte that, if worse came to worse, we would go to London and have a ball. I didn't tell her that the chances were 10 to 1 that we would go to London and not to Ulan Bator. I didn't tell her about the book business.

As she wrote in those days in her diary:

"I like to know where I am, what I am supposed to do, why and what is coming next. . . . We are always getting into cars, driving off to unknown places with people we can't communicate with, trusting everything to strangers and somehow or other it works out one way or another."

If she had only known.

It is a long, long haul from New Delhi to Moscow. We left in early morning and, even with the time difference, got into Moscow at midafternoon. Peter Grose, the *Times* correspondent, and Sara Shaikevich, my old secretary, met us. But there were no Soviet transit visas. We were confined to the transit lounge. It was Saturday afternoon. No way to contact the Mongol embassy. No explanation, no argument would change the minds of the airport officials. We had telephoned Foy Kohler, the American ambassador. Foy was an old, old friend. Couldn't someone telephone the Foreign Office? He laughed unpleasantly. "This is Russia, Salisbury, you know that as well as I do." Never have I been so frustrated. Charlotte was worn out—and we faced another twelve-hour flight to Ulan Bator. Nothing for it. At midevening we took off. What lay ahead I hated to think.

At the Irkutsk airport, we bumped into Bernie Reisman, just in from Ulan Bator where he had gone to do a documentary for ABC. He thought all his arrangements were OK. He had visas. Permits. Everything. The Mongols hadn't allowed him out of the airport and had shipped him back to Irkutsk. He had 16 mm cameras, not 35 as the documents provided.

Charlotte was exhausted. So was I. I assured her nothing like that would happen to us. No way. I had friends in Mongolia. (Privately I feared we would not be allowed out of the airport. We would be shipped back to Russia on the same plane. The Russians would not allow us out of the Irkutsk airport. Where they would ship us I had no idea.)

We flew down to Ulan Bator over the mountains and the flat steppes. It was a brief, even a pleasant flight. A nice woman in a blue Mongolian *del* served weak apple juice and Russian chocolates. We set down at the Ulan Bator airport in early afternoon. Everyone was pleasant. The Mongols got off the plane. Pleasant chattering Mongols met them. The Russians got off the plane. Pleasant Russians met them. Gradually people left the tiny airport, and we were alone. No one met us. No one paid any attention. We sat with our bags, and I wondered what to do. Finally a young Mongol, a student returning from Sofia, came to our rescue. He telephoned the tourist bureau and presently a polite tourist representative arrived, apologized, swept us up, passed us through customs, brought us into town, put us up in a big suite at the Ulan Bator Hotel on Suke Bator Square in the center of town. Our troubles were over. I could not believe it. The hotel manager waited on us. Everyone was solicitous. The load dropped from my shoulders. My God, I thought, we're in! Incredible! We had won the 10 to 1 bet. Either they haven't noticed the date on our visas or didn't care. We relaxed in exhaustion, slept twelve hours, awoke, had a good breakfast, bumped into Owen Lattimore, the old Sinologist and Mongologist, McCarthyite target and Russian target (his picture was still on the wall of the Mongolian Historical Museum, identified as a CIA agent, along with that of Roy Chapman Andrews), met the British and French ambassadors, both staying in the hotel. I lost so much tension I thought my knees would buckle.

* * *

Back at our room we found the hotel manager and an interpreter. The manager was very polite but firm. We had entered
Mongolia illegally. Our visas had expired. It was a most serious
crime. We would have to remain in the hotel until the proper
officials could be notified. Today was Sunday. No one was available. Tomorrow was the national holiday, *Nadam,* July 11. There
would be a three-day celebration. Whether anyone could be
located until after the holiday, he did not know. He was very
sorry. Very correct. Listened earnestly to my explanation. Rules
were rules. We had to stay inside.

Gloom settled down again, but somehow I thought there was a
glimmer of hope. I did not believe they would expel us. I consulted the British and French. They didn't think so either. We
relaxed a bit. We needed the rest. The next day, *Nadam,* Monday
July 11, it rained. It rained all day, a monsoon on this barren
desert land. We stood at our window. The great *Nadam* parade,
all of Mongolia, it seemed, passed before our eyes, wet, sodden,
banners drooping but singing in the rain. It was not an unpleasant front seat. Charlotte knitted. I tried to persuade myself that
we would overcome. We had gotten this far. We would not be
thrown out.

Next morning after a rather formal talk at the Foreign Office,
a vast apology by myself, all was forgiven. We got new visas.
Charlotte had a sinking spell. Never in her life (as she said) had
she been confined or restrained by any kind of government. The
moment passed. We went for a walk in the great square with
Lattimore. The rain was still pouring down. The Mongol national
games—horse racing, wrestling, archery—were postponed. The
rain came down and down and down.

The Tola River, normally as dry as the Los Angeles River,
runs through the heart of Ulan Bator. Now it surged over its
banks, several feet over its banks, factories flooded, apartment
houses collapsed, hundreds of people homeless, many drowned.
Army helicopters came to the rescue. Vast Suke Bator Square
was turned into a refugee encampment. The power station was
knocked out. No electricity. No telephones. No lights. No water.
The hotel kitchen out of service. The plumbing out of service.
Army generators tried to provide power. Army field kitchens set
up outside the hotel, which was filled with "distinguished
guests," delegations from Communist and Asian countries to the
Nadam festival. Lives had been lost, bridges swept away, high-

ways cut, the airport closed. Never had Mongolia experienced such floods. Thousands lost their homes. Suke Bator Square blossomed with yurts, soup kitchens, bedraggled people.

The flood disrupted the whole country. I filed a dispatch and got a good scoop. I didn't say what the foreign guests were telling me—that the Mongols were having such a good time at the big national day reception they paid no attention to reports of the rising Tola and danger to the city.

Travel was impossible, and after a week we took off for the Soviet Union, this time with proper visas (no problem at the Soviet embassy in Ulan Bator), flew to Irkutsk, went to Lake Baikal, took off for Khabarovsk but ended up in Vladivostok (strictly off limits to foreigners, especially Americans). A savage electrical storm prevented us from landing at Khabarovsk so we flew along the Sino-Soviet border, lightning flashing about us as I have never seen it, my nose to the window expecting at any moment to see Chinese antiaircraft batteries open up. They didn't, and we had several hours with the commandant of the Vladivostok airport, the colonel toasting us in glass after glass of vodka, *do adna,* bottoms up. We flew back to Khabarovsk, boarded the Trans-Siberian, down to the big port of Nakhodka, took a cheery Soviet steamer to Yokohama and on to Tokyo. We had completed the 25,000-mile itinerary just as I had planned, despite floods, avalanches, monsoons, Communist bureaucrats, nightmares—harvesting splendid stories, a splendid series, giving me a broader dimension of Communism and Asia, I felt, than anyone in the world yet had. I was not modest about this. It had been a perilous trip. A lot was at stake. But we had come through.

We arrived back in New York. No longer was I under the chilling spell of my Sikkim nightmare. I walked into the third floor of the *Times,* went to my desk (vacated by Abe), caught my breath, and went to work. I knew how I would handle the publishing assignment. The *Times* should get into the publishing field. I believed in that, but only in a first-class way. No half-measures. No fiddling around. The way to do it was to buy a good publishing firm, one compatible in character and objectives with the *Times,* one with good management in place. Nothing sick, broken down, or second-rate. Nothing cheap. The *Times* could take over the firm, give it *Times* backing, *Times* funding, let it grow and prosper. I knew exactly which company I wanted the *Times* to buy, and I knew the company wanted and needed the *Times*. A perfect fit. (My recommendation was for Harper & Row. I knew it well. Knew its executives and particularly Cass Canfield, its chief.) If Punch Sulzberger and Ivan Veit, the vice president in charge of the operation, liked my idea and were willing to go forward with it—fine. I would—for an appropriate (generous) sum—be glad to take it in hand for a fixed period, just long enough to be sure everything was going well. Then back to my own trade—reporting and writing.

I discussed the idea thoroughly with Cass Canfield. It appealed strongly to him. It came at a time when Harper & Row needed access to capital which we believed the *Times* could provide. Cass met with me and several *Times* executives very privately (I don't believe word ever got out about these talks). Cass was insistent that if Harper & Row were to be sold that it go to an institution compatible with its philosophy. He thought the *Times* was just right.

Unfortunately this was too big a deal for the *Times*. It was still in the process of becoming a public company. The purchase would involve a big exchange of stock as well as cash. Veit and Sulzberger were afraid to take such a big bite. They elected to buy a small company and "learn by doing." I don't know how much they really learned. In the end this and other publishing experiments cost the *Times* so many millions I don't dare put the figures down. Thankfully, I had no part in this; it was not my bag. Nor should it have been that of the *Times*.

There was something else on my mind, something more important. I hadn't got into China but now I thought that with the contacts I had made and the broader understanding I possessed of China, I had a good chance of breaking down the barriers. I hadn't gotten to Hanoi either. I might never make it, but I had reason to believe that I would. I had a secret promise that I would get to Vietnam before the year was out.

My Sikkim nightmare had not been all bad. Without it I might have given up in Delhi, taken the easy way out, booked passage for London, had a fine stay with Charlotte at the Savoy, shown her my favorite city, London, and my favorite country-side, England, and come home to empty out my desk and turn the keys over to Abe.

13 | The War Next Door

Vietnam . . . Vietnam . . . No one called it Nam in those days, and actually many people in Southeast Asia still thought of it as Indochina. But no longer in the United States. By now it was Vietnam to all of us, and more and more our lives, our thoughts, and increasingly our politics had begun to center on those two syllables, Viet Nam—the Land of the South as the Chinese call it.

Charlotte and I had not gotten to Hanoi on our Big Trip, but we had gotten close enough to hear and feel the war a few miles away. I had applied for visas in Phnom Penh, and soon, I was sure, I, at least, would be behind the enemy lines. I was not eager to take Charlotte with me, and the North Vietnamese were not eager for a woman visitor.

On one Cambodian evening we sat down to a banquet in the palace of the governor general of Svay Rieng, a pleasant man in his thirties with a round soft-featured face who reminded me of Prince Sihanouk. Svay Rieng was a provincial capital on Highway No. 10, a half a dozen miles from the Vietnam border.

All day we had been plunging in and out of the jungle along the Caiboc River in our Land Rovers, inspecting villages which had been bombed in what the U.S. Military called Operation Birmingham. I had seen my share of the dark and bloody ground of Birmingham, Alabama, but I could find no reference points to Bull Connor in the ruin of thatched-hut villages, leveled by stray (were they stray?) American bombs, the random rubble left by artillery shelling, burned-out vehicles, black and rusty, in talking to confused villagers who told us their confused stories, running with them for shelter (there wasn't any) at the sound of throbbing airplane motors, sighing with them in relief when the sound faded into the distance. We were not in Vietnam, but this was part of war Zone C, as it was called by Big Red One, the American division assigned to this location during Operation Birmingham.

This was no-man's-land where Viet Cong moved in stealth and Americans moved after them, the border being the meandering Caiboc River, twenty yards wide at one place, thirty at another, lush with water hyacinths, a faint brown streak from the air. The jungle was identical and unbroken on either side, and there was hardly a sign as to whether you were on Cambodian soil or Vietnamese soil: heavy, heavy vegetation, the thatch of the villages blending into the jungle, trails losing themselves in the forest, bunkers and trenches here and there (whether for Cambodian defense or Vietcong offense, who could say?). People with weapons kept appearing and disappearing, all looking the same, small and bronze, tattered cotton shirts and trousers, no way a careful American commander could know whether they were neutral or hostile. This was the war that had come to preoccupy America, this was its uncertain face, and this was what I was determined to examine from the inside. What *were* we doing? Did anyone know?

That day we had twelve hours of rugged travel, in and out of our vehicles, over what was said to be a trail along the border. Not until midevening did we return to Svay Rieng to see the palace, a fairyland of lanterns, red and green and blue, swaying from the mango trees. Within the palace, ceiling fans slowly stirred the turgid air, moving the fat flies from room to room. We had drinks from frosty glasses, a quick shower, and then seated ourselves at a mahogany table strewn with ivory camellias, and exotic lilies, the perfume heavy in our nostrils, the table laid with fine silver, cut glass, and Limoges, the wine from France, of course, waiters in white jackets, the governor general's lady, svelte, under thirty (Charlotte swore), pregnant with her tenth child, chic in black silk *sampot,* white embroidered blouse, and fine rubies, everyone cool, sophisticated, speaking French.

As we dined, I heard a distant rumble. Sometimes the table trembled, and the crystal lightly tinkled against the silver. Bombs were falling just down Highway No. 10 on the other side of the line. Oh, yes, our host said. It starts almost every evening about this time, about ten o'clock. It's been going on for a year or so. Sometimes, he said, I'm afraid the bombs may fall on us. It was a fear I heard many times in Cambodia, a fear that the war would spread across the vague frontiers into Sihanouk's peaceable kingdom.

Cambodia was still, as Sihanouk proclaimed, "an island of tranquillity" in the sea of war. One day we visited the State Museum in Phnom Penh. A Cambodian girl, gentle and young, led us through the antiquities, stopping now and then to caress the polished figures, passing her slender hands over their curves, so subtle, so sensuous. The image of that young woman is as clear in my mind today as it was in the time of Pol Pot when I closed my eyes and saw Pot's teenagers, no older than my Red Hook Cobras, glance at those lovely Cambodian hands without a callus, put a bullet through her head, and straggle on as the blood spread over the palace tiles.

All around China we had skirted the edges of war: warnings in Hong Kong that China would intervene; warnings in Bangkok that Thailand would change sides and go with China if we pulled out; warnings in Russia that the United States was out of control; warnings in Mongolia that China had gone out of control; warnings in Tokyo that nuclear war was too close for words.

It was against these warnings that I had come back to New York with a private guarantee, one which I shared only with Clifton Daniel. In Phnom Penh I had put my case to the North Vietnamese. I had prepared my way with care. I had tried to win the backing of every person who might have influence in Hanoi. There were quite a few. Early one morning I was sitting in the big city room of the *Times* when a slight young man in chinos, a tan open-collar sports shirt, and dirty white sneakers wandered in, looking for Scotty Reston. Scotty wasn't there, and I had a talk with him. He was Tom Hayden, the SDS leader, his publicity-prone career and Jane Fonda distantly ahead of him, just back from Hanoi. We talked for a time, and when I was launching my campaign to get into Vietnam, I enlisted his help. I did the same with Staughton Lynd, son of the *Middletown* Lynds, sociologist and visitor to Hanoi. I talked to David Dellinger, and I wrote to Wilfred Burchett, the Australian journalist deeply engaged in long-running, long-range combat with his Australian critics. In 1961 I had lunched with Burchett in Moscow and knew more than most about his relations with Communist movements—the Russians, the Chinese, the Koreans, and especially the Vietnamese. Burchett, I found, was already trying to assist my *Times* colleague Seymour Topping (whose father-in-law, the Canadian diplomat Chester Ronning, was in close touch with Hanoi) to get into Vietnam. But Burchett agreed to help me, too.

I had, of course, bombarded Ho Chi Minh and Premier Pham

Van Dong with cables and letters. I had sought the help of James Cameron, an English correspondent who had been in Hanoi about a year before. I had solicited several French correspondents, diplomats, and even two or three Soviet colleagues in Moscow.

As the years have passed, it has become clear to me that, if there was any single voice which spoke for me in tones which penetrated the minds and hearts of the Vietnamese, it was that of Anne Morrison.

Not many today may remember the name of Norman Morrison, an American Quaker who gave his life for peace. This was the period when yellow-robed Buddhist monks immolated themselves in the public squares of Saigon, sitting cross-legged on the pavement, calmly drenching their bodies with gasoline, touching a match and burning to death, passive and immobile as the flames leaped up.

Morrison, as devout in his belief in peace as a man could be, seated himself cross-legged outside the Pentagon one day, poured gasoline over himself and lighted a match in the manner of the Buddhist martyrs.

No American of that time was so venerated in Hanoi. Norman Morrison, as I found when I arrived in Hanoi, was regarded as a saint, an object of almost holy worship. I did not know Morrison nor did I know his widow. But John Corry, a warm and sympathetic *Times* reporter (his later emergence as waspish electronics scourge then unthinkable), knew Anne Morrison. Through Corry's good graces, she wrote a letter supporting my hopes for reporting from Vietnam. She vouched for me.

"As a Quaker pacifist," Anne Morrison wrote, "it is my belief that truth itself contains power to evoke change." She expressed her trust that *The New York Times* would bring my stories "unedited to the American people." Anne's words, I am certain, won my entry into Hanoi.

In Phnom Penh the Vietnamese had received me with politeness and even warmth. They could give me no immediate answer, but they felt my chances were good; perhaps I could come up to Hanoi almost immediately, within a few days. They would communicate with the Foreign Ministry and let me know. Charlotte and I spent ten days traveling about Cambodia but finally were told that we could not go to Hanoi then—a more favorable occasion would have to be awaited.

I now began to experience what might be called the Rashomon of the Vietnam war. Nothing in the news as published gave me a clue why this was not a "favorable" opportunity to come to the Vietnamese capital. Only later did I learn what was secretly going on. Chester Ronning, the Canadian, had just brought to Hanoi new American proposals for a halt in U.S. bombing in return for a halt in North Vietnamese operations in the south. As I waited in Cambodia, this proposal came to nothing amid bitter rhetoric, and on June 27 and 29 American bombers went into action, bombing Haiphong and the Hanoi area for the first time. Thus it was that Hanoi conveyed to me word that a more appropriate occasion for a visit would have to be found later on. As I would learn, this was not the first time nor would it be the last when peace missions touched off new bombings, new escalations by LBJ. It became almost a fixed pattern.

As for my visit Hanoi passed down the message: "It will occur before the end of the year."

I was too experienced to take those words at face value. I might or might not get into Hanoi in the next few months. It would depend on events over which I had no control and probably no knowledge and the decisions would be made by men whom I did not know and who did not know me. I was disappointed. I wanted to go when the iron was hot. Now it would cool down, and the moment would vanish.

Back in New York I did not neglect Vietnam. I resumed my rain of letters and telegrams. I hunted up more persons who might be helpful. The promise of a trip before New Year's was in my pocket but I was not going to let anyone in Hanoi forget it. I said nothing to my associates at the *Times* (except for Daniel). I am superstitious, and I do not believe in arousing exaggerated expectations. Time enough for others to know when and if a telegram came through. While waiting on Hanoi, I plunged into a study of book publishing by the *Times.* It took me two months to put together the Harper & Row proposal and have it turned down flat by Punch Sulzberger. I am sure he thought I was too grabby in wanting to run so important an enterprise without "business" expertise. But I took no backward look at the turndown. I was a reporter. I didn't want to be a publisher, and I had some splashy stories underway. I was heading up a team of a dozen *Times* correspondents who—if Moscow permitted—would go to Russia and size up the Bolshevik regime after fifty years. And I was heading a small group which was taking a new look at the Kennedy assassination, the Warren Commission report, and the cloud of "conspiracy" chatter that was spewing into the public media.

But most of all in that autumn of 1966 I was quietly pursuing Hanoi. This was the autumn when Vietnam began to overwhelm America, when it began to dominate television in the evening, to fill front pages and bring people to the streets and campuses to turmoil. Vietnam was hot, and it was getting hotter as Mr. Johnson and his generals sought to pour on the pressure and bring a fateful war to a victorious conclusion.

To me Hanoi had become a sphinx. Not one sign, not one message, not one hint. Nothing. I wrote my letters and sent my cables. I read the news reports, day by day, in the *Times*. I kept my ears peeled for gossip. I took to reading the *National Guardian,* which printed the reports from Wilfred Burchett. I thought there might be some clue in what he was writing, sometimes from Phnom Penh, sometimes from Hanoi, sometimes from unknown points in Vietcong territory. I subscribed to *Le Monde*. I read England's *Guardian* and the *Times* of London. I don't think I was any the wiser.

I was as ignorant as almost all Americans as to what was happening in Vietnam. I picked up through the grapevine word of Chester Ronning's failed mission to Hanoi in June 1966, but I had never heard of earlier efforts by the Canadian Blair Seaborn in 1965. The words "Mayflower," "XYZ," "Rangoon," "Marigold," "Sunflower"—the whole series of flower-coded negotiating endeavors—were meaningless to my ears (as to almost all Americans). I would have been amazed to learn that at that moment a complicated but futile sequence was being played out in Rangoon under the sponsorship of U.N. Secretary-General U Thant.

And certainly I did not know of the mirror-image dealings called Marigold, a complex bit of hugger-mugger, the full outlines of which are not entirely known even today. This had many players—American, Polish, Russian, Italian, French (probably), and, of course, Vietnamese. In some ways it seemed to insiders to be the most serious of all the secret peace initiatives. (So many were now under way, LBJ named Averell Harriman to coordinate them.) But in the end Marigold was shot down, a sunburst of recriminations coming to a head in early December 1966. I knew nothing about this during those long, puzzling autumn days. Nor do I know whether or how it may have affected my trip to Hanoi. But I have finally concluded that all missions to Hanoi, journalistic, diplomatic, or otherwise, in some mysterious and unseen manner were linked, if not in the minds of Ho Chi Minh and Pham Van Dong, then in the minds of LBJ and his diplomats, generals, and bureaucrats.

So far as the war was concerned, the combat, the commitment of American troops, the concentration of American warships and naval aircraft, the steady increase in participation of our great B-52 bombers went on with routine ferocity. No one—least of all myself, as the dreary 1966 autumn ran down from November into December—could see any sign that the cluster of men around Lyndon Johnson had doubts about what they were doing, any suspicion that all was not going well: that, indeed, there was no light at the end of the tunnel, that the daily body counts, the plastic statistics of the Five O'Clock Follies at Pentagon East in Saigon did not tell the story of a strong, unified leadership carefully quantifying the precise levels of napalm, high explosive, and artillery which in Lyndon's immortal words, would "make 'em holler uncle" and "bring home the coonskin." All was well in this most technological of wars. So it seemed.

One of the war's architects was Robert S. McNamara. For more than six months, unknown to the public, he had harbored deep doubts about the war and the prospect that it could be won. McNamara's views were as secret from me as from the country— and indeed from McNamara's closest aides—but the brightest of the brightest, the whiz among the "whiz kids" who brought Henry Ford's Motor Company back from disaster after World War II, the man John F. Kennedy picked to usher the American military establishment into the new technological age, had turned against the war.

Who can say precisely what is a turning point in so vital and so vast a case? Robert McNamara could not pinpoint that moment in talking to me in 1985. But he did remember, as did his closest aide, General Robert F. Pursley, his rising concern over ever vaster and noneffective employment of air power. Specifically Pursley remembered a time in the summer of 1966—July 4, to be precise. That day McNamara, with a broken foot hobbled into his office, holiday or no holiday. Pursley was there too, in a state of shock at the sudden death of his mother. That was the day McNamara asked Pursley to determine what intelligence lay behind the June 27 and 29 U.S. bombings of Haiphong and the Hanoi environs. Pursley asked Defense Intelligence. They had none. McNamara went to Richard Helms, head of CIA, and asked for CIA intelligence on the problem. This was, as later would be seen, McNamara's first positive act, which would lead to his order for the compilation of the Pentagon Papers (exploring the reasons for the Vietnam war; its conduct and its failures—to instruct future generations how to avoid the pitfalls of the present), to his open break with LBJ; it was the first crack within Johnson's iron framework, which ultimately led LBJ to his bombing halt of March 1968 and withdrawal from the 1968 Presidential race.

McNamara's action of July 4, 1966, was in response to the very American bombing that marked the breakdown of the Chester Ronning mission in June 1966, the bombing that blocked Charlotte and me from going on to North Vietnam from Phnom Penh. It triggered the reaction that turned Robert McNamara from a hawk to a dove.

For eighteen years I would not know this curious intersection in the lives of McNamara and my own. Not until we talked in 1985, trying to fit together the known and the unknown, the war as it seemed and the war as it existed below that mirrored surface, the war which I and millions of other Americans thought we were fighting, and the war as it came to be seen by those who were directing it.

This was the first of the separating images which, as time went on, showed me that in war, as in the simplest things in life, truth is multifaceted, a crystal that refracts light in many forms and many shapes, the quicksilver of the mind.

For all my talk and all my thought, I did not understand this in November and December of 1966. I still—against all probability—believed that the truth could somehow be quantified. Somehow as a reporter I could venture out into the field, even into the acrid jungles of Vietnam, torn by high explosive, roots fed by the blood of many men and women, many wars in a long and complex history, and bring back the truth; I would go into the country of Rashomon and tell my people what was its color and its nature. I was, I know now, very naive but so were the American people and, when you come to think of it, the human race.

* * *

I did not then know—nor would I for many, many years, not until I began to retrieve my FBI files under the Freedom of Information Act—that I had acquired a small tail.

General Ne Win and his wife, Katie, were coming to the United States and LBJ had invited them to dinner in late August. The White House decided to invite Charlotte and myself to the State dinner, probably because we had spent time with Ne Win and Katie in Rangoon. First there must be a security check. Mrs. Mildred Stegall, LBJ's liaison for security matters, sent our names over to J. Edgar Hoover. J. Edgar promptly replied to Marvin Watson, LBJ's special assistant. I don't know what his reply was—two thirds of it was blacked out in the copy I received—but we were not invited.

A small cloud in the sky, invisible to us, but soon there would be more, and they would not be so small.

14 | A Walk Down Pho Nguyen Thiep Street

We sat at one of those big round tables with the heavy black leather chairs to the rear of the Oak Room at the Plaza, Clifton Daniel and his wife, Margaret Truman, Charlotte and myself. It was Sunday night before Christmas, December 19, 1966, and the room was very crowded. Everyone from Jersey and the Island had come to New York that weekend to walk down Fifth Avenue, ogle the glitter in the Saks windows, watch the skaters at Rockefeller Plaza, and throw dollar bills into the iron pots of the Volunteers of America to the electronic sound of "It Came upon a Midnight Clear."

We talked about everything but what was on our minds—my departure on Monday for Hanoi. Clifton talked of the duchesses he'd known in London, and Margaret complained of Washington. She hadn't liked it in White House days, and she liked it less now. Charlotte and I hardly spoke. Too much on our minds.

I was going off into enemy territory, shooting territory, behind the Vietnam lines. I had worked my heart out to get permission, but the reality didn't seem so dashing. Yes, it would be the scoop of my life and a great feather in the cap of Clifton as managing editor of the *Times*. Yes, as Charlotte and I tried to convince each other, it might bring peace a step or two closer, but it was dangerous. It was not an expedition to be undertaken lightly. And I was leaving great burdens on Charlotte's shoulders—my son Michael was getting married on New Year's Eve, and we (that is, in my absence, Charlotte) were putting on the wedding. My younger son, Stephan, at Columbia, was going through a midschool crisis. Whether he would still be enrolled by the time I got back, I could not guess. I was miserable and full of guilt.

These thoughts were swirling around in my mind when I heard Clifton say: "You know, we don't go in at the *Times* for much in the way of promotion. But I think this trip to Hanoi is something special. When you actually get to Phnom Penh and board that plane for Hanoi, send me a cable. I think it would be worthwhile to raise a little fuss about this—we could run some spots on WQXR [the *Times*-owned fine music station] and maybe even put a few ads in the paper.

"It isn't every day that we get a man into Hanoi," he went on. "I think we could brag a bit."

I thought that was a fine idea. Time and again, it seemed to me, the *Times* had pulled off great scoops, and no one quite understood this because the *Times* played them sotto voce.

Clifton and I could not have been more naïve. If there was ever a story that needed no advertisement it was Hanoi. When it broke on Christmas morning, December 25, 1966, it broke on every front page of every newspaper around the world. It led the Vatican *L'Osservatore Romano,* it led BBC, it led every TV and radio newscast.

I got to Paris in the gray chill morning of Tuesday the twentieth. I spent the day shoving through the traffic between the Vietnamese and Cambodian embassies for my visas. That evening I dined with Henry Tanner and Dick Mooney of the *Times'* Paris bureau in Les Halles at the Pharamond. No one knew what I was doing in Paris. No one knew where I was going. Only six people on the *Times* knew, no one outside the paper. But of course all the Paris bureau had guessed. We drank mysterious toasts to "the success of your mission," then I caught a few hours sleep at my favorite Paris hotel, the Louvois on the Rue Richelieu (alas, no longer extant). Early in the morning, making my way through serpentines of school children at Orly, viewing the crèches (some looked like Picasso, some like medieval Florence). I boarded the plane for Phnom Penh. Not many passengers that morning.

It was Thursday noon before we touched down in tropical 100-degree Phnom Penh. Little Christmas spirit but the same mildewed Graham Greene atmosphere at the Hotel Le Royale as when Charlotte and I stayed there in June.

I had crossed beyond the threshold of my imagination. In the long flight across the Atlantic, in sleepless hours in the Louvois waiting for dawn, in the endless progress from Paris to Tirana, to Cairo, to Karachi, and finally Phnom Penh I had amused myself making up stories about the impeccably blond French stewardesses, the band of Albanian clowns and tenors flying out to Shanghai, the seedy Frenchman who slunk off the plane at Cairo and disappeared through immigration before I had a clear view of his dark skin and jet moustache; the too obvious English diplomat, six feet eight inches, who reminded me of Sir Hughe Montgomery Knatchbull-Hugessen, the World War II ambassador to Turkey who was so thoroughly flummoxed by his valet, Cicero, an agent of German intelligence.

Now relaxing over a Coca Cola on the terrace of Le Royale, watching a luminous young Thai goddess slowly kicking herself in a back stroke from one end of the pool to another, I was descended upon by the real spies and agents, men and women, who flourished in Phnom Penh.

If airtight security about my mission to Hanoi had been observed in New York, if my colleagues in Paris had nothing but intelligent guesses to go on, if no one in Washington had yet caught on (I had had my passport cleared for Vietnam months previously), there was absolutely no mystery in Phnom Penh as to who I was and what I was doing.

I don't know how many persons came up, shook my hand, and congratulated me. They knew I was leaving on the International Control Commission plane the next day, Friday the twenty-third, for Hanoi. The ICC plane was one of the great phenomena of the Vietnam war. From start to finish it provided service between Saigon and Hanoi with stops at Phnom Penh and Vientiane. It was neutral. The commission had been set up under the protocols of the 1954 Geneva Convention. Originally it possessed two silvery four-engined Constellations and four Bell helicopters. One Constellation had been shot down a few months previously and the helicopters were grounded for lack of pilots.

The single Constellation lumbered along. It made three round-trips Saigon–Hanoi-Saigon each fortnight. The Control Commission was run by India, Poland, and Canada. It carried a passenger from Phnom Penh to Hanoi for $235 and, except for a dilatory service from China via Canton and Nanning, it was the only way to get to Hanoi. There had been an Air Cambodge service when Charlotte and I visited Phnom Penh in June, but Prince Sihanouk suspended it after American fighters warned it off Hanoi during a bombing raid.

Le Royale was full of pleasant Poles, jolly Canadians, and mysterious individuals of unknown nationality. They all seemed to know more about me than I did myself. And they all connected my presence with a letter our United Nations representative, Arthur Goldberg, had sent to U Thant, supporting his peace efforts.

I didn't know such a letter had been sent. None of them paid heed to my protests of ignorance. They winked and looked at me slyly. Naturally I would deny it. But those simple denials just confirmed their suspicions. I was, in their minds, an unofficial messenger from LBJ to Ho Chi Minh. Not a doubt of it, and they wished me well.

I was, I confess, embarrassed. We had gone out of our way to make certain that the administration would not be compromised by my presence in Hanoi. I had spoken to no one in the State Department or the White House. Even Scotty Reston had not breathed a word to Dean Rusk or Walt Rostow. In no way would I be acting in Hanoi as a spokesman, unofficial or otherwise, for Washington.

Try to make the Poles or the Canadians or the Indians or the French believe that. I finally laughed and shrugged my shoulders. What else was there to do? I could think of nothing more unlikely and more irritating to LBJ than to find me in the role of his official emissary. I had never met LBJ beyond a formal handshake. He had put on a great campaign in his first days in office to win over the *Times,* telephone calls to the publisher, Punch Sulzberger, to Turner Catledge, two or three a day to Reston, so many phone calls that the *Times* people were embarrassed. Then, LBJ, realizing that he was getting nowhere, cut off the calls and entered the name of the *Times* and its editors in his ever-expanding black book.

That night I lay on the great brass bed of my room at the Royale and wondered what might lie ahead. In this decaying yet pleasant French colonial city, I had the impression that for all my research, my contacts, the expertise I thought I had acquired, I was, in a sense, a naïf. I seemed to have wandered into a chamber of mirrors in which little was what it seemed. There was *our* war in Vietnam, the one which, officially, we were fighting, the war reported every day in the *Times;* there was another war in Vietnam which, somewhere below the level of information and communiqués, seemed to be going on; there was the war the Vietnamese believed they were fighting; there were the versions which the Europeans perceived—East Europeans, West Europeans, and French—especially the French.

And then there were the Chinese. In the U.S.A. I heard nothing about the Chinese. Oh, yes, occasionally in Washington someone would warn that "if we go up to the north, if we invade North Vietnam, if we begin to bomb along the Chinese frontier, Peking will come in.

But in Phnom Penh that was not the China on the lips of the Poles and the French and the Cambodians. Sihanouk had designated China as Cambodia's best friend. But the question troubling these cynical, weary men, in their sweat-stained linen suits, their woven Panama hats, was a different one. What, after all, is happening in China and how will it affect Vietnam? Their question related to the turbulence which had boiled up in China just a year ago and, as of this date (late December 1966), showed every sign of escalating and escalating again. Where was it headed? Every one in Phnom Penh knew, as few in Washington yet recognized, that China was out of control, that China had halted Soviet shipments to Vietnam and threatened to do it again, that China had halted its own shipments to Vietnam and threatened to do it again, that China was implacably hostile to *any* contact or diplomatic initiatives to halt the U.S.-Vietnam hostilities.

"Wait till you get to Hanoi," one of the Poles told me, eyes sparkling (a good Pole, he loved diplomatic intrigue). "Wait till you get there. It has taken a lot of guts for Hanoi to invite you. I am sure the Chinese have told them to send you packing." (Frankly this thought had never entered my head.)

China, I quickly understood, was the hottest story in Hanoi. Not the China Washington had conjured up from Korean experience—not a China which was getting ready to send 1 million men into Vietnam if we got too close to the passes.

Not at all. This was the China which sat in judgment over Hanoi and Ho Chi Minh, the China which sat in judgment over Nikita Khrushchev and Leonid Brezhnev in Moscow, the China which had decreed that Khrushchev had abandoned Marxism and embarked on a capitalist program, the China which was tearing itself apart in the Cultural Revolution, the China which was denouncing its leaders Liu Shaoqi and Deng Xiaoping as "capitalist roaders," the China that was convulsed by a chaotic Marxism which viewed any hint of negotiations between Hanoi and Washington as treason.

This was not a China which I knew or understood. Nor was I alone. The Great Proletarian Cultural Revolution had started in Shanghai in November 1965. It had ripped China end to end. Not even in Communist Vietnam so close to China and so intimately

associated with China was it really understood. So I came to believe.

I did not understand it but still distant from Hanoi's boundaries, I was wondering if this might not be the most important
development which I might uncover.

I had hardly slept for forty-eight hours but even in the com-
fort of Le Royale I was fitful as a cat. I pulled out of my briefcase a copy of *Le Monde* which I had picked up in Paris. My eyes
bulged. Here was a dispatch from *Le Monde*'s special correspondent, Jacques DeCornoy, just back from Hanoi, an excellent dispatch. He told of the damage inflicted on areas near Hanoi by
American bombing: a textile center named Nam Dinh, south of
Hanoi, which had been badly damaged; a railroad town nearby
called Phuly had been destroyed—he had followed the railroad
south from Hanoi, had seen segments ripped up by American
bombs. Within a few hours they were back in operation. He had
a lot of good detail. I hoped he had not taken the edge off what I
would report.

The ICC plane was late the next day, Friday, December 23.
As I waited, a Canadian sergeant talked of incidents in which
ICC planes had been involved. The danger of attack was so great
that they did not fly into Hanoi until darkness had fallen. We
took off a bit after noon and got to Vientiane about 2:30, to wait
until dusk so that, we hoped, we would not be shot down. The
Poles invited everyone to their embassy for cold drinks or good
French coffee and pastry. More talk of China. More talk of the
danger of being shot down. Everyone, it was said, in Laos and
Vietnam carried a gun and shot at anything they saw in the sky.

I thought of giving U.S. Ambassador Bill Sullivan a ring. I
had had a long talk with him when I was in Vientiane the previ-
ous June, but I didn't like to call him from the Polish embassy.
By the time I got back to the airport, the Air America pilots
were beginning to pull in from the day's run—whatever it had
been. In those days there was no nonsense about Air America. It
was a CIA "proprietary." The planes were coming in, and a long
row of Mercedes had pulled up to meet the pilots and take them
home to their wives or their mistresses, to their sleek white villas,
and the moment to call Bill was lost. Well, I thought, he'll find
out soon enough that I've passed this way.

He did, indeed. There was, as I discovered years later

through FOIA documents, a convenient arrangement whereby Bill was advised (presumably by a clerk in Laotian passport control) of any one passing through Vientiane on the ICC plane. At 6:36 A.M. the morning of Saturday December 24, Bill dispatched a cable to Washington reporting I had transited Vientiane, apparently en route to Hanoi. The cable was received in Washington (because of the time differential) at 1:18 A.M. December 24 and sent on to the White House and the U.S. Information Agency.

This was Saturday, the eve of Christmas. LBJ had abandoned the Capital for his Texas ranch. There were only duty staffs at the Executive Mansion and the State Department. On no other day of the year was Washington more closed down. There is no evidence that the Sullivan telegram was relayed beyond receiving clerks, no indication that anyone picked up a telephone. The President slept soundly at his ranch and headed happily into his traditional round of Christmas festivities. In Washington the operational agencies closed at noon on Saturday (and they had hardly turned a wheel since noon on Friday).

All was quiet on the Potomac. By the time the Sullivan cable was tossed into "in" baskets on the bleary Monday morning after Christmas, I had been roaming North Vietnam for three days, having checked in at the fine old colonial hotel, the Metropole (now called the Thong Nhat [Reunification]) at midevening Friday night, December 23.

When I flew into London in early February 1943, the first walk I took was down Fleet Street to St. Paul's and to the city to see the bomb damage. When I went to Russia in 1944, the first thing I observed was the obliteration of Stalingrad—by bombs and artillery shells. When I went to Leningrad, I walked down Nevsky Prospekt to see the bomb damage (much damage but not very visible). Not much bomb damage in Moscow, but the rest of Russia was carpeted with rubble, every city—Kiev, Kharkov, Minsk, Sevastopol. When I got to Warsaw, I walked down the first morning to see what bombs had done to the ghetto. When I got to Berlin, I walked in the bomb-shattered Wilhelmstrasse and looked at the ruins. Bombs, I sometimes think, are as familiar to me as apple pie.

My first walk in Hanoi was down Pho Nguyen Thiep Street— to see the bomb damage. It wasn't much by my World War II standards. A few houses, a handful of people killed, I was told, at Nos. 44, 46, 48, and 50. Very unimpressive. All in all thirteen houses knocked down, thirty-nine families made homeless, five killed, eleven injured. It wouldn't have made a communiqué in Leningrad or Warsaw, nor in London during the Blitz.

Those cities had been bombed by the Nazi Luftwaffe in World War II. This was Hanoi, 1966, and the people had been killed and the houses destroyed, so the Vietnamese said, at about 3 P.M. on December 13 by American bombers.

I had been living, it seemed to me, for twenty years in a world in which somewhere bombs were dropping. From a military standpoint, the incident on Pho Nguyen Thiep street was not worth recording. Except . . . except that these were, so it was said, *American* bombs—*American* bombs falling in an area which our Defense Department said we had not bombed (for a while the Pentagon spokesman insisted it must have been the North Vietnamese who hit themselves with a misfiring SAM antiaircraft missile); moreover, as President Johnson had insisted time and time and again, our bombing was so accurate that all we hit was steel and concrete.

I did not believe the houses on Pho Nguyen Thiep street had self-destructed; I did not believe they had been knocked down by a North Vietnamese SAM; I did not believe that we were so accurate we hit only steel and concrete. I was, I am afraid, too old a hand on bombing. I had been very close to the U.S. Eighth Air Force during World War II. I knew the commanding generals, and I knew their public claims for the Norden bombsight. Hitting a target, they swore, was "like shooting fish in a rain barrel." But I knew, too, that pilots sometimes hit the wrong city, occasionally even the wrong country. I sympathized. It was not an easy business to fly deep into enemy territory through clouds of shrapnel, hundreds of guns firing to bring you down. It took courage, determination, great skill, and luck—lots of luck. But I never knew a pilot who seriously pretended he could bomb targets in or near a city or populated area without hitting nonmilitary targets and killing civilians.

It was not possible. I don't know whether LBJ understood this or not. He may well have convinced himself that U.S. bombs hit only steel and concrete and North Vietnamese in full uniform. He was capable of such an extension of belief. I was not. I saw nothing to surprise me on Pho Nguyen Thiep Street. Nor on any of the other streets in Hanoi, nor in the bomb-leveled villages and towns I saw in North Vietnam. Bombing is bombing, and war is war. It is not a neat or pleasant business, and there is no way that adjectives and patriotic words can paint it pretty. There is nothing heroic about a corpse that has lain a few days in the sun, no matter what uniform tries to contain it.

I wrote about the incident on Pho Nguyen Thiep street in my first dispatch to the *Times,* which was printed in the paper of Christmas day. I didn't put any spin on it. I wrote a Christmas story, the great crowds at the Cathedral of St. Joseph, the strings of Christmas lights—blue and yellow and green and red— the masses of flowers and the little Vietnamese flags with their golden stars on a field of red. I wrote about the young Hanoi wives sitting sidesaddle on the bicycles their husbands pedaled, bringing them back from countryside evacuation for the holiday. I wrote of the mood of the city, which seemed to me to be sturdy and purposeful, of the concrete manhole air raid shelters that lined the streets, of the broad French boulevards of Hanoi and the Christmas parties in the Metropole Hotel. Only after nine descriptive paragraphs about Hanoi, a city at war, did I present a vignette of Pho Nguyen Thiep street and a quiet view of other bomb damage which I inspected—a freight yard, a small and shabby truck park, and some damage to the Chinese embassy, the Romanian embassy, and a few other embassies in the diplomatic quarter. (A Canadian had picked up a hot fragment which came through his window and sent it back to his friends in Saigon with a note: "Look here, chaps, this is going a bit far.")

It didn't add up to much by military standards, by the air war standards with which I and my fellow correspondents had measured the bombardments of the last two decades. It was thin gruel. The ugly truth is that war is thin gruel. It is repetitious. Again and again the same thing—death and destruction. Only the geography changes, the terrible process of man's self-degradation which Ernie Pyle once put into three words. Sitting on the edge of a bed, a mosquito-netting enfolding a colleague who was suffering from dysentery in the Aletti hotel in Algiers, Pyle, just back from America and facing another combat tour, said he could hardly bear it, could hardly bear going back to the GIs. I just can't take it any more, he said, I can't take them. I can't take war. I can't listen to them. Every other word is fuck or shit.

The other day one of them said, over and over: "Fuck my shit. Fuck my shit." That's the bottom. The end.

So here I was on Pho Nguyen Thiep street. It could have been Threadneedle Street, London. Or Unter den Linden in Berlin or Admiralty Square in Leningrad. After Ernie Pyle, what was there to say? I wrote my dispatch, went through agonies of bureaucratic negotiation to get it transmitted to Paris for relay to New York, got a photo I had taken on Pho Nguyen Thiep street developed and printed and wirephotoed to AP for transmission to *The New York Times.* (By an unpleasant mistake AP distributed it as a Vietnamese propaganda photo; it took several days to clear up the error.)

When my chores were done, I went to a party being given by the Vietnamese for the small band of foreigners who found themselves on Christmas eve in the Metropole Hotel.

I have in my file a description of that party written by a German Communist correspondent whose name and visage have long since vanished from memory. He writes of "a mysterious man in his midfifties, a mixture of English lord and German schoolmaster; posture very erect, carefully trimmed gray-blond mustache, serious and cool, inquiring eyes behind rimless glasses."

In the gathering, he notes, are a Hungarian writer named Molnar, a Cuban poet, Felix Rodriguez, an Italian Communist correspondent, Trumbadori, the Australian Wilfred Burchett, and some Vietnamese officials. The German is atingle at finding himself in this room with "the man of the management of one of the largest American newspapers." What, he asks himself, can I be thinking when one of the Vietnamese blurts out an attack on the "American pirates who bring death and destruction to our country." He watches in fascination as I listen "calm, serious, without moving a muscle." What are my thoughts? How will I react? The Vietnamese finishes. There is a moment of suspense, then I rise, the German recalls, and utter a single sentence: "I'd like to drink to true friendship between the Vietnamese and American people."

A Communist sympathizer in the ranks of *The New York Times?* the German asks. No, "only a journalist who was influenced by what he had seen."

Well, perhaps the German didn't get it all right. I don't think he could have understood Ernie Pyle's words; I don't think he could have understood how nauseated I was to witness again this banal newsreel which history had played over and over in my lifetime now being put into reruns by men who did not understand the meaning of its banality or did not care.

It was late that night before I went to sleep. I could not get Ernie Pyle's words out of my mind. I still can't.

15 | Noël

At 4:30 of Christmas morning, December 25, 1966, I came down to the lobby of the Metropole Hotel and looked around for the guide who was to escort me on a trip south to a city called Nam Dinh.

I was not in a Christmas mood. This was the hour when I had awakened as a child at 107 Royalston Avenue in Minneapolis, slipped out of bed in my cold room, and stolen a peek at the tree in the parlor. The smell of those spruce needles was still in my nostrils.

On this morning there was no one in the Metropole's tile-floored lobby. A little earlier four American peace ladies had left for I didn't know where, and now I sat alone staring at a green Chinese urn in which a tropical pine had been planted and decorated with twists of red and white cellophane, probably stripped off cigarette packs. The only light came from a milky neon tube that flickered on and off around the ceiling.

It was a low. I never find Christmas easy, and I was missing Charlotte and the boys and the whole of our big family. And I could not get yesterday out of my mind. Not the little girl with the broken arm whose mother had been killed when her house was hit by a bomb. Nor the slightly older girl whose body was covered with black, green, and purple bruises from, it was said, the impact of ball bearings from one of our lazy-dog bombs. Not even the young woman whose eyes were glazed and whose mind was hazy, survivor of a family of five, the others, including her baby, having been killed by a direct hit. No, it was not the living horrors, painful as they were. It was the Revolutionary Museum where I spent an hour being shown the artifacts of the wars which, it seemed, had constituted the tapestry of Vietnamese history for hundreds of years—wars with the Thais, the Cambodians, and the Chinese. The French and we were tacked onto the saga as a tailpiece.

The weapons which the Vietnamese had devised over the centuries were ingenious and deadly. They killed slowly, cruelly with much pain, and they were so simple that any child could make them, sitting in the dust beside a thatched hut. A woman could construct an arsenal, hardly moving from the pot where the family's rice was cooking—long needlelike thorns tipped with poison and set upright in a wooden board to be concealed in a depression in the trail. The thorns penetrated the tough soles of barefoot Chinese or the leather boots of GIs, inflicting festering, crippling, often fatal wounds. There were invisible garrotes of silk or fiber, to be dangled from the limbs of trees to break the neck or sever the windpipe of a careless passerby on the trail. There were arrowheads, fashioned of fire-hardened wood, copper (going back to 310 B.C.), and flint, with sawtooth edges which ripped the flesh and muscles when the victim tried to pull them out (American Indians used the same technique), and elongated wire bird cages, decked with fishhooks—a leg plunging into this trap was hacked into morsels of meat when the victim sought to struggle free. Simple, deadly, dreadful. No electronics, no high tech, no military-industrial complex, no bottom line, no commissions. The Viets could not construct a lazy dog or a bullpup missile, but the thorns and nooses and cages were effective killers—at a cost-efficiency ratio McNamara would have admired.

I could not get these weapons out of my mind as I sat alone in the hotel lobby on this chilly morning. I had learned a lot about Vietnam in an hour's visit to the Revolutionary Museum. Why hadn't I known before of the hundreds of years of war between the Chinese and the Viets—wars always won (according to the museum) by Vietnam. But I saw from the map that the Viets had once occupied the Canton area—now they were hundreds of miles to the south.

I wondered what William Westmoreland knew of this history and McNamara and Rusk. I didn't have to ask myself about Lyndon Johnson. The only history he knew was the history of Texas. Perhaps he knew the history of Texas too well.

In 1969 James C. Thomson, Jr., one of LBJ's young China experts, chaired a seminar at the Council on Foreign Relations on how Vietnam decisions were made. The participants were a dozen bright junior aides to the top players of Kennedy-Johnson. Not one could recollect a time when such questions were brought into the decision-making process. The facts about Vietnam did not come up. Why? I asked, in astonishment. They looked at me with that condescension which the young display for an older person who really isn't with it. Why? Well, it wasn't considered necessary, they said. The U.S. possessed such overwhelming military power there was no need to take local peculiarities into account. The power could be applied in any manner the United States desired in order to achieve its goals. Whatever capabilities Vietnam might possess, whether Vietnam was a warrior nation (as it was), whether it had historically displayed iron resistance to an enemy (as Vietnam had for hundreds of years) did not signify. That history had *always* pitted Vietnam against a superior opponent made no difference. All of these factors could be answered by American firepower (95 percent air power). French experience in Vietnam? Forget it. The French were never consulted, never considered. They were losers. Why talk to them after Dien Bien Phu? What was there for Americans to learn? Nothing but sour grapes.

I wondered whether it would have made a difference had the McNamaras, the Johnsons, the Rusks, the Westmorelands, and the Rostows visited the Revolutionary Museum in Hanoi—would the lessons have penetrated their cast-iron convictions? I doubt it. American power threw such a shadow over the consciousness of these men, they believed they could impose the American will anywhere, anytime, anyway. It was supreme. To doubt it was to doubt God. Or their own existence.

It was still dark when we started down Route National No. 1, straight south for a destination that was as murky in my mind as the weather. All I knew was that Nam Dinh lay sixty miles to the southeast of Hanoi, eighteen miles inland from the Gulf of Tonkin, and southwest of Haiphong. It was, I was told, the third largest city in the North, a textile town with a population of perhaps 93,000, much bombed.

I knew that the Vietnamese were early risers, and it seemed to me that traffic had been continuous, day and night, since I had arrived. Now I found the highway jammed, Christmas day or no Christmas day—food, arms, ammunition, all kinds of mysterious cargo secured under olive-drab tarpaulins and festooned with leafy branches as camouflage, an endless stream of sturdy Soviet-made two and a half ton trucks. As the day wore on, I saw wagons, horse-drawn carts, man-drawn carts, woman-drawn carts, donkey-drawn carts, and bicycles—my God, there were bicycles! Fitted with balancing poles and struts, they could carry equal loads of 300 pounds or more on either side. And, of course, men and women with great burdens on their backs.

As the sky lightened, I perceived that we were passing through a panorama of war—houses and buildings blasted and burned, craters along the road, endless destruction, the everyday visage of the twentieth century. Our jeep joined the slow procession of vehicles.

We passed through a half dozen bombed-out villages. A railroad paralleled the highway (which ultimately arrives in Saigon) for long distances. It had been heavily bombed but not very accurately. The same was true of the highway. "In the general vicinity" seemed to be good enough for the military. Little woodburning locomotives chugged along, hauling toy trains. They didn't add much to the huge tonnage on the move.

The day was dark and drizzling and stayed that way as we drew into Nam Dinh, a factory town—plain, no fuss, no fancy, no furbelows, a duplicate of a hundred industrial towns in northern France, no architectural flourishes, plain brick factories, plain brick flats, plain brick dormatories. Beside the factories lay the embankment and dikes holding back the River Dao, perhaps ten feet above the town's street level. The Dao was no more impressive than the town. It was used for small shipping and transhipping, boat-to-truck, truck-to-boat.

The mayor of Nam Dinh was a woman, a petite dynamic lady named Tran Tri Doan. She had worked in the textile factories, a good-sized cotton textile mill and a small silk mill. There was also, she said, a rice mill but no military objectives. She was very firm about that, rejecting the thesis later advanced by the Pentagon that Nam Dinh was full of targets—petroleum storage facilities, the railroad, transshipment depots, and, of course, antiaircraft sites.

Hesitating a bit, I finally asked her age. She snapped, "Forty." I would have guessed closer to twenty-five.

Madame Tran impressed me. She knew her town. She was a font of statistics—population, production, housing, industry, schools, hospitals, kindergartens, births, and deaths. She had everything about Nam Dinh at her fingertips, and she was ready with her figures on U.S. bombing: dates and numbers of raids, damage and casualties. We walked through the town, visiting half a dozen areas. Each looked much like the other. As I jotted in my notebook: "We walked through the desert atmosphere of Nam Dinh." Most attacks on the town, the mayor said, had been made by aircraft of the Seventh Fleet, which lay offshore in the nearby Gulf. She reeled off designations of U. S. planes and military ordinance like an operations chief. The aircraft and their armaments, I quickly discovered, represented a new generation to me, but the destruction looked like Coventry or Rotterdam. No change.

I could believe that the obliteration of Nam Dinh had not been the intention of the Americans (although it would have been hard to convince the mayor of that), but, like it or not, Nam Dinh had been destroyed.

Later on there was to be a great deal of argument about Nam Dinh, and our air people stressed that we had to destroy the antiaircraft weapons which had been sited in built-up areas. If they had been put out in the open, people would not have been killed. I thought there was a circularity about this argument, a little like asking which comes first, the chicken or the egg. You are being attacked. To defend yourself you bring in ack-ack guns. Then the attacker comes back twice as hard, because, he says, he has to destroy the antiaircraft batteries. In this argument I found a faint echo later on of the rueful remark of the American lieutenant who said, in remorse, "In order to save the town we had to destroy it."

While I was standing outside Nam Dinh's city hall talking with the mayor, an air alert sounded. We went down into the bunker, and she continued her talk. She said it was the third alert of the day and that there had been one on Christmas Eve. I heard no ack-ack nor did I catch sight of a plane. Probably, I deduced, the alarm had been touched off by one of our reconnaissance drones, not a real plane.

I saw few people in Nam Dinh. The mayor said most of them had been evacuated as well as a good deal of the industry. Part of the textile mill had been moved. The rest was a shambles. Madame Tran insisted it was still in production, but I saw little sign of that. The silk mill was a skeleton but the rice mill was working, if slowly. That was it in Nam Dinh so far as I could see.

Late on Christmas afternoon, I got back to Hanoi and wrote up Nam Dinh, my second big story from Vietnam. I told about the mayor and the bomb damage in her city and reported the figures she had given me—fifty-one raids up to Friday before

Christmas, none of which, she thought, had been reported in the West. She put the casualty toll at eighty-nine killed and 405 wounded, a small figure considering the number of raids and the devastation I had seen. I wrote of walking through the streets and of my conversation in the bunker with Mayor Tran. My presence in the city and my observation of the damage was, I thought, clear to the reader. I didn't underline this, however. The *Times* had a long-standing rule that the reporter was to keep himself out of the story. "We don't want to read about the adventures of the reporter," Turner Catledge had said many times. "Just report the news."

Sometimes, of course, as in the case of Hanoi, the news and the reporter's experiences were intertwined.

After I had done up Nam Dinh, I put a fresh sheet of paper in my typewriter and wrote a letter to Charlotte, a little formal because I knew many eyes would be reading it. I told her how strange Christmas had been and how I had spent the day "looking at our American handiwork" which struck me as "about as senseless an outrage as you could imagine." That was how I felt about Nam Dinh on Christmas night, 1966, and that is how I feel about it today, twenty years later. More so, perhaps, now that I understand so much better what Nam Dinh was all about.

No dispatch from Hanoi appeared in the *Times* on Monday December 26; probably the Nam Dinh story was delayed by the holiday. Then on Tuesday, December 27, there was a double header on page 1—Nam Dinh and a parallel dispatch about our bombing on Route National No. 1. Both conveyed a negative impression of the results of our air offensive—civilian damage in Nam Dinh and failure of bombing to halt movement of supplies down the highway and railroad. I suggested that the basic flaw in the bombing seemed to be "failure to take into account the nature of the country and the people to which it is being applied." Had we been bombing the Pennsylvania Railroad and the major New York–Washington, D.C., highway, it would have been different. That would have caused enormous disruption and the "military consequences in wartime would be grave."

This was a judgmental conclusion, and it probably went a bit beyond the customary *Times* dispatch. But it was a correct judgment and an assessment which, although vigorously challenged by Air Force men, was held, as I would find out much later, by far more informed observers than myself. It was a very important finding in terms of how we were conducting the war and the results we were achieving. It was the kind of observation which an alert administration should have found priceless.

Each evening when I got back to the Metropole Hotel, having toured the country and carried out my interviews, I pulled out my little Sony shortwave and tried to get an idea of what was going on in the world. From Christmas day onward, I heard plenty about Hanoi, about my reports, about worldwide reaction but not very much from Washington. I attributed that to the Christmas lull.

On Wednesday morning I got a cable from Clifton Daniel, a low-key message cautioning me to be careful to give a source for any "controversial" casualty figures and avoid expressions which "readers might consider editorial" since the *Times* had frequently been accused of shaping news coverage to fit its editorial policies. "Stuff looks good," Clifton added.

The next day, Thursday, December 29, I received a message citing Washington denials of a couple of points in my Nam Dinh dispatch—my reports of bombed dikes and Mayor Tran's claim that Nam Dinh was a favorite Seventh Fleet target. There was also a word of praise for my "outstanding reporting." Next day, Arthur Hays Sulzberger, the publisher who had hired me for the *Times* (now retired), cabled that he had read all my Hanoi material and wanted to congratulate me. "I am sure they are having a profound effect," he added. "You are a lucky guy."

Lucky guy or not, my shorthand reading of this (coupled with some barbs I had picked up on the shortwave) was that critics were circling the wagon train; the *Times* was standing by me, but please be *very careful.* My reading, I soon found, was 100 percent accurate. I (and, to an extraordinary extent, the *Times*) was about to be subjected to a test by fire.

There was no way in which a *New York Times* correspondent could go to Hanoi in the midst of the controversial war without raising a storm. That was obvious to Daniel and me before I left New York, although, as I have suggested, we didn't understand how much turmoil my trip would generate.

We were naïve in that, as I have said, but there were special circumstances which contributed to the firestorm, some of them accidental, some deeply concealed secrets which only a few in government knew.

It was, for instance, an accident that I arrived in Hanoi in the backwash of the U.S. bombings of December. As I discovered once I got to Hanoi, the Vietnamese Foreign Office had been trying to reach me for several weeks.

A Foreign Office man told me over lunch, "We are delighted that you have come. We had thought you had lost interest in Vietnam."

"Whatever gave you that idea?" I asked.

"Well," he said, "we cabled you, and you did not reply."

I was shocked. I had replied instantly to the first cable I received, which was on December 15. Now it turned out that that wasn't the first telegram. The first had been sent in late November, but it had been dispatched to the business office of the international edition of the *Times,* then published in Paris. No trace of that message was ever found. Presumably a clerk, accustomed to handling advertisements and subscriptions, could make nothing of it and tossed it away. (This curious bit of information acquired momentary importance when, later on, some Washington officials contended that Hanoi had invited me in specifically to view the damage done in Hanoi by the U.S. raids of December and make propaganda.) In fact, the decision to let me come had been made well before the raids, and at a time, in fact, when there was good reason to believe that when I arrived, Hanoi and the U.S.A. would be sitting down in Warsaw for direct talks on ending the war. The coincidence of the bombing and my arrival in Hanoi and my reports on its results was bound to cause a dustup.

Another factor: When my stories began to come back from Hanoi, no one was minding the store in Washington. LBJ was on his ranch in Texas. He had had a row with his press secretary and protégé, Bill Moyers, over the war and other things. Moyers had not yet left the White House premises but was packing up, and his successor, George Christian, had become White House spokesman. Christian was an old hand with LBJ and the press, but foreign policy was not his strong point. Within ten days, largely as a result of George's ineptness in responding to my Hanoi reports, LBJ was consulting Walt Rostow about getting Christian expert support (so I discovered via the FOIA process).

By coincidence, the Pentagon was in a similar situation. McNamara was in Europe for a NATO conference and his press chief, Arthur Sylvester, was with him. Sylvester, like Moyers, had resigned and was preparing to turn his duties over to his able deputy, Phil Goulding. Neither the White House nor the Pentagon press shops were in shape to handle a major crisis.

I did not know Goulding, but Sylvester was an old, old friend. We had sat side by side on the press bus for hundreds of miles in the Stevenson and Nixon Presidential campaigns, he for the Newark *News,* I for *The New York Times,* usually occupying the first right-hand seat in the bus, for quick takeoffs to the side of the candidate and elbow room in which to unlimber our portables and write the story as we bowled along. Sylvester was a blue-eyed, red-cheeked middle-aged man, an old pro. We didn't stumble over each other's feet, and we didn't speak to each other when we were writing. Sylvester had a flair for arrogance, but we got on well. He had taken the Pentagon job, I believe, because the Newark *News* was getting shaky, and he didn't want to go down with the ship.

I don't think Art was a particularly good Pentagon press secretary. He made a speech in Chicago proclaiming the right of the government to lie to the press (and the people) in times of national emergency. I think he meant the danger of nuclear war, but his quotation inevitably lost its qualifications and was usually quoted as "the right of the government to lie." This hardly helped his credibility or that of the Johnson administration in the heat of Vietnam.

This disarray produced a hesitant, defensive, apologetic initial response quite atypical of LBJ. This was followed by massive overkill, feeding the fires of controversy as the administration tried to repair its self-inflicted damage. This was bound to make a difficult situation worse. I could sense from what I heard on BBC and VOA that LBJ was seething. I couldn't tell about McNamara. He was never mentioned. When I asked him about it nineteen years after the event, he could not remember my dispatches with clarity and expressed genuine amazement that anyone could have seriously questioned what seemed to him perfectly obvious.

McNamara's latter-day reaction was hardly that of the Pentagon at the time. Phil Goulding, some five years after the event in a book which he called *Play It in Low Key,* described my Hanoi trip as "a national disaster," a credibility disaster for the government, "the biggest public affairs mistake" of the Kennedy-Johnson period. He believed my Hanoi reports had undermined public trust in government declarations of policy on Vietnam and led to distrust of government in general.

"Additional lack of trust in the word of the Government was the dominant part of that reaction," Goulding concluded, but another part was deep disenchantment with the war itself. "The impact of the Salisbury stories was to present the United States Government before the world as a liar and deceiver. That in my view was tragic."

Goulding took upon himself much of the blame for this "disaster." He had known or feared that LBJ's policy of contending that the U.S. hit only military targets, "steel and concrete," was bound to backfire; he knew that we hit a lot besides steel and concrete, that you could not bomb without killing civilians and destroying nonmilitary targets. This should have been said and said repeatedly so that the public would understand the reality of war. The mistake, he felt, was one of public relations—to permit the people to believe that this war was different, that we did not burn down peasant huts and city flats. Some might properly have blamed LBJ for wanting to have it both ways—to wage war and pretend that war was pretty. Goulding did not take this easy out. He was the Pentagon's public relations specialist. It was up to him to persuade LBJ to adopt a public relations policy which would not blow up in his face. Whether it was morally wrong for the government to lie, Phil Goulding did not say. He looked at the question from the narrow perspective of nuts and bolts. What to do after the horse has been stolen from the barn? What to do? Goulding was pragmatic. He would fight fire with fire. If Salisbury's dispatches had undermined LBJ's credibility, he would undermine Salisbury's. Tit for tat. The option of saying yes, we were wrong, yes, we lied, yes, we misled the public never occurred to him. Nor did it occur to Lyndon Baines Johnson. The fact that it did occur to Robert McNamara was carefully concealed for many years. That part of the story appears only on these pages.

16 | The First Casualty

When I went to Hanoi, I was not a cub reporter. I was fifty-eight years old. I had had my lumps. I knew something about controversy. I had been involved in it since college days when I was thrown out of the University of Minnesota, because as a student editor, I challenged the power structure, the president and the board of regents. I had nearly lost my job with the United Press because of a piece on how the 1930s depression was affecting Minneapolis. The Minneapolis *Journal* took the position that the depression was somewhere else.

When I went to Moscow for United Press in 1944, I was almost thrown out by Stalin in my first weeks—because I didn't present a proper apology for a story our London bureau filed about Stalin and his generals. When I went back to Moscow for *The New York Times,* my life turned into a gauntlet of tomahawk wielders in the U.S.A., who said I was a Bolshevik (the Russians, of course, took the position that I was an American spy). And then there was Birmingham.

No, I should have been hardened to the row over Hanoi. But I wasn't. I knew that Senator Hiram Johnson of California had said during the World War I debate: "The first casualty when war comes is truth." And I knew that Winston Churchill, reversing the metaphor, had declared that in war "truth must be protected by a bodyguard of lies."

I knew that Hitler had succeeded by the Big Lie and that Lao-tzu, the famous Chinese philosopher of war, had preached that deception was the cornerstone of military success. I was well aware that disinformation was not invented by the CIA.

I had seen the lie used so often by governments and politicians I should have felt no sense of shock when it was turned against me during the Hanoi episode. Still I confess that Washington's performance amazed me and still does, although not so much now that I understand better what I walked in on.

Phil Goulding has given a vivid picture of the Pentagon's panic as it hunted for a way to discredit my Hanoi dispatches.

He deployed twenty or thirty experts, who went over my materials word-by-word and line-by-line, looking for something—anything—that could be used against me. It was, Goulding admits, hard going. His men checked out my reports on the Hanoi bombings. Not much ammunition there. They checked Nam Dinh— same thing. My dispatch on the paltry results of bombing Route National No. 1? Peashooter stuff.

Finally they hit pay dirt. Not in my reports but with a document which had been sent back in November 1966 by the U.S. military attaché in Moscow. It was a Hanoi propaganda release headed: "Report of U.S. War Crimes Against Nam Dinh City." Someone noticed that the figures in the pamphlet were identical with those I got from Mayor Tran Tri Doan. Eureka! Reporters were hastily called in, including, I am sorry to say, two men from the Washington *Post* whom I knew and respected. They were handed copies of the pamphlet. Here it is, they were told, here is where Salisbury got it all, a Commie propaganda sheet. The figures in his story and the pamphlet are identical. He's not a reporter, he's just a conduit for red propaganda the way he was in Moscow. (It was many years before my FOIA inquiries turned up the fact that White House press advisers were pushing this line and that the FBI had started a vacuum cleaner operation to see what dirt it could find on me.)

The gambit worked. Within twenty-four hours the Washington *Post,* the Washington *Star,* and some other papers were saying that Salisbury's stories were Communist propaganda. Clifton Daniel mildly commented, What kind of figures would Salisbury find in Hanoi but Communist figures? Never mind. The Pentagon had hit a live nerve, the old McCarthyite one. To this day in some dark corners, the legend persists that I never went to Nam Dinh, I never saw the bombing, I never collected information on my own—just copied it out of the old Moscow leaflet.

Soon Art Sylvester was making speeches about Harrison Appallsbury of *The New Hanoi Times.* And *The New Yorker* responded with a cartoon of an Army mess sergeant shouting to his cook: "It's direct from the Pentagon—scratch Salisbury steak until further notice."

Of course, none of this got the Pentagon off the spot, but it did not play badly in Peoria, and it gave supporters of the war something to shout about. It turned some eyes away from the sorry images I presented, even though no one could read my stories and be in doubt that I was there on the spot. I had not larded my paragraphs with attributions—"Tran Tri Doan said," "a North Vietnamese official said," the tag we learn in journalism kindergarten. Some critics called this "careless journalism." Others called it "treason." Tempers, it must be remembered, were pretty hair-trigger in those times.

For sixteen years the matter rested, forgotten by everyone but a few Vietnam controversialists and myself. There it would still rest had it not been for the vigilance of Charles Mohr of *The New York Times,* an old Vietnam hand. Pouring through thousands of pages of CIA documents declassified for use in the libel action brought by General Westmoreland against CBS, Mohr found a CIA report on Nam Dinh, a special study made coincident with (possibly triggered by) my trip to Hanoi. The study was finally completed on May 23, 1967. It was classified Top Secret and "No foreign dissemination." Had it not been for the CBS-Westmoreland case, it would still be gathering dust in the CIA files.

I could hardly believe my eyes when I read this document. Not only did it support my observations but the CIA's principal evidence was "Report on the U.S. War Crimes in Nam Dinh City," the very one the Pentagon had labeled "Commie propaganda." In the words of the CIA, Nam Dinh had been picked for their study because the statistics in the pamphlet, the casualty figures, the civilian damage, the air strikes "seem to be accurate when measured against detailed studies made on the basis of poststrike photography." "Casualties claimed by the North Vietnamese were also consistent with independent casualty estimates made by this agency, using Nam Dinh as a pilot study."

I had, in a word, been dead on target with Nam Dinh. And, as the agency made clear, the Nam Dinh situation had been known before I went there. The Pentagon declarations about the "accuracy" of its bombing of Nam Dinh, its claim that it was nothing more than "propaganda" that civilians had been killed, the astonishment of naval pilots that their bombs could have missed "military targets," the reconnaissance photos which the Pentagon showed to me in New York after my return to demonstrate that Nam Dinh could not have been bombed as I reported—the whole package put together to undercut my reports was eyewash. And some in the government (but not necessarily Goulding) knew it was from the start.

No wonder McNamara was amazed when I reminded him that there had been an attack on my credibility. These CIA reports were the very ones he had ordered up July 4, 1966, when he began to feel uncomfortable with the assessments by his own National Defense Intelligence Agency and their use to support "the Rostow line" for more and more bombing.

The CIA had used Nam Dinh as a pilot study, factoring in the aerial photos made by our pilots and our drones, the Hanoi "Report on War Crimes," and information from a Polish member of the International Control Commission. All fitted together, all mortised with my conclusions.

Among the CIA findings was a calculation as of January 1967 that our bombings in the North in 1965–66 caused 36,000 casualties of which 29,000 were civilians. Later the CIA refined this to total 31,300 civilians and 16,900 military in 1965–66 and the first quarter of 1967.

The CIA seemed to be reporting a different war from that of Goulding and the Pentagon. Goulding claimed, "We had taken the greatest possible precautions to avoid civilian casualties . . . never before in wartime had pilots operated under such tight bombing restrictions." The fact was we were killing twice as many civilians as soldiers.

"We did not then," he insisted, "and when I left the government still did not have a reasonable reading on the accuracy of the North Vietnam figures [on civilian casualties]. But one could certainly assume that the enemy was not understating his casualties in a propaganda sheet [the Nam Dinh war crimes pamphlet]."

Did the Pentagon have access to the CIA report? In the hall of mirrors which the U.S. Government had become, it is possible that Goulding knew no more of the CIA's study than I did. But he had access to the reconnaissance photography which the CIA used and which confirmed my reports.

The CIA had a totally different approach to Nam Dinh from that of the Pentagon. It said the textile plant had been "unintentionally" bombed in a U.S. air strike in July 1965 and that its operations had been dispersed to sites fifty to 100 miles away.

The CIA found that, in general, the "success of the U.S. bombing program was limited." Bombing had had no decisive effect on the North Vietnamese economy. It had not influenced the regime's attitude toward the war nor propelled it toward the bargaining table. "In fact, Vietnamese operations were now exceeding the results they had achieved before the Rolling Thunder [the U.S. bombing] program." And, said the CIA, the "outlook for success in meeting current U.S. bombing program objectives is not bright.

"The twenty-seven months of U.S. bombing of North Vietnam have had remarkably little effect on Hanoi's overall strategy . . . or on its confident view of long-term Communist prospects and on its political tactics regarding negotiation."

Indeed, said the agency (in terms very similar to mine), the bombing had not shaken the Vietnam conviction that "they will withstand the bombing and outlast the United States and South Vietnam. Nor has it caused them to waver in their belief that this test of will and endurance will be determined primarily by the course of the conflict on the ground in the South not by the air war in the North."

The CIA concluded that

· The air strikes had had no effect on Hanoi's ability and intention of maintaining "at least a rough military stalemate" in the South.

· There was no evidence that the bombing had impaired the morale of the Hanoi regime or the population.

· Despite the bombing Hanoi had improved its supply position because of an increase in deliveries by Russia and China and better organization.

· Strikes on oil storage tanks had not bothered Hanoi significantly; they simply received their oil and petrol in metal barrels, which they strewed along the roads and in the fields where U.S. planes couldn't find them.

When I read the calm, cool, calculated CIA analysis and matched it against my field reports, the match was about 95 percent. I didn't give Hanoi so much credit for building up its battle capacity under the rain of U.S. bombs as did the CIA.

The secret U.S. assessment of the war fitted mine like a glove fits a hand. But it bore little relationship to the fandango staged by Arthur Sylvester and Phil Goulding.

What was going on here?

Behind the scenes, as I now know, hidden from me, hidden from the American public, hidden from Congress, hidden from almost everyone in the Pentagon, the State Department, and the White House, a huge gap had opened up over the Vietnam war.

As I pieced it together years later from the revelations of the Pentagon Papers and documents from the State Department and White House, released under the Freedom of Information Act, two violently opposed views had emerged.

On October 14, 1966 (as the Pentagon Papers would reveal), McNamara had submitted a secret memorandum to LBJ etched in dark pessimism. Things were going badly in the South. The "pacification" program was running backward. Rolling Thunder bombing had neither significantly affected the infiltration of North Viet units to the South nor cracked the morale of Hanoi. "The enemy almost completely controls the night." McNamara proposed a bombing standstill and consideration of a total halt on bombing the North. Instead, he suggested bombing the neck of Vietnam on the chance that this would interdict supply and troop movements. Then, he said, we must give some credibility to our peace moves. In plain words he wanted to end the war.

McNamara no longer believed in the air war; he no longer believed Hanoi could be bombed to the peace table.

The Joint Chiefs exploded. They opposed every point made by McNamara. They wanted more troops, more bombing, more everything. Total victory.

A month later, November 17, almost on the eve of my departure for Hanoi, McNamara returned to the fray. He sent LBJ a memo that challenged the kill ratio the Army was reporting, suggesting the figures were vastly overstated, that four out of every five Vietnamese soldiers whom the Army said it was killing were not soldiers but noncombatants—porters, laborers, bystanders, and the like.

He argued that "I believe our bombing is yielding very small marginal returns, not worth the cost in pilot lives and aircraft." He estimated that the program was costing $250 million a month, and he saw no evidence that it was really hampering North Vietnam and the Viet Cong. McNamara, always quick with figures, estimated the total economic and military damage inflicted by bombing on North Vietnam to that point in the war at $233 million, considerably less than the cost to the U.S. *per month*.

McNamara did not convince Mr. Johnson. Walt Rostow and Robert Komer, the President's aides, opposed McNamara. So, of course, did the Joint Chiefs. LBJ did not cut back. Instead he increased the massive B-52 sorties from sixty to 800 a month as of February 1967.

It was into this stormy atmosphere that I charged with my Hanoi dispatches, laying them down, I'm afraid, with the deceptively easy roll of the lazy-dog bomb, so harmless in appearance, like a great basketball, then suddenly erupting into a hundred exploding baseballs, each packed with steel barbs and ball bearings, plastering the landscape in a crazy quilt of death.

No wonder Goulding and the Pentagon went into shock. Chance had timed the Salisbury missive for maximum impact.

But not I nor anyone outside the charmed circle had any notion that our high leaders and their generals were locked in so epic a conflict, one which would determine whether the Vietnam war would be pressed forward full throttle or be gentled down to give diplomacy a chance.

To this day McNamara's actual role, as an opponent of air war and escalation and as a supporter of negotiated peace, has not been accurately evaluated because of classification of key documents. David Halberstam in *The Best and The Brightest* correctly faulted McNamara for his role in the buildup and support of the Vietnam war but, writing before the publication of The Pentagon Papers and without access to the FOIA documents that I obtained, he missed the early start and strength of McNamara's turn against the war. McNamara's role is a subject well worth a close study in itself.

As I sat in my cold bedroom at the Metropole Hotel in Hanoi (I had left my trench coat on the ICC plane, and it kept shuttling back and forth between Saigon and Hanoi), nothing would have been less believable to me than the scenario I have finally managed to put together. Not a hint of a crack in the imposing facade of the U.S. establishment was visible. I knew that my reports had stung LBJ, but I saw no sign that, as the Pentagon Papers were to reveal, they had generated "an explosive debate about the bombing."

I did not know nor did the country that on November 17, 1966, Robert McNamara had told LBJ: "The increased [bomb] damage to targets is not producing noticeable results. No serious shortage of POL [petroleum products] in North Vietnam is evident, and stocks on hand with recent imports have been adequate to sustain necessary operations.

"No serious transport problem in the movement of supplies to or within North Vietnam is evident; most transportation routes appear to be open, and there has recently been a major logistical buildup in the area of the DMZ.

"The raids have disrupted the civil populace and caused isolated food shortages but have not significantly weakened popular morale. . . .

"The increasing amounts of physical damage sustained by the North Vietnamese are in large measure compensated in aid received from other Communist countries."

Nothing in my reports equaled in blunt skepticism McNamara's quiet words about the failure of the air war and the military stalemate on the ground. But McNamara's words were secret. They were rebutted by the Joint Chiefs and argued down by men like Walt Rostow and Dean Rusk. My words were public. The Pentagon did its best, but it simply could not destroy the inherent credibility and consistency of my reports. They fit together. A detail might be wrong, an emphasis distorted, but they far understated the administration's own secret, chilling, negative assessment. For all the rhetoric which the Pentagon unleashed, it was not possible for Mr. Johnson's propaganda to damage the impact of my stories.

LBJ was far too astute a politician not to understand that he was deeply vulnerable on the question of bombing, especially on the civilian casualties. Hardly had the President returned from Texas, than he launched an effort to shore up his position.

But he had a continuing problem with McNamara. McNamara was deeply upset (as the FOIA information reveals) over the bombing issue.

Alone among the men around LBJ, McNamara wanted the public to know the truth about U.S. bombing. He proposed that the administration make public the information which it already possessed (the fact that two years of bombing had caused 36,000 Vietnamese casualties of which about 29,000 were civilians).

McNamara wanted the whole record on U.S. bombing—results, costs, casualties—the works—made public, together with reconnaissance photographs which would disclose that most of the civilian damage was done in proximity to military targets. He submitted a draft of his proposed statement.

This wasn't palatable to LBJ. It was anathema to Rostow and to Komer, strong backers of bombing.

Rostow with the support of Clark Clifford shot down another McNamara proposal, that the President set up an ad hoc committee or group of "wise men" to examine the effects of the bombing and evaluate the whole U.S. bombing policy.

Clifford, as quoted by Rostow, said this would make LBJ look weak and uncertain. Clifford could see no political gain from the idea. Rostow convinced the President that if any bombing data was made public "no matter how the thing is packaged, *The New York Times* would tend to play it for the high figure." As for photographs "The *Times* would use it for its own purposes." Also, he was very much afraid the photographs would "show a lot of misses."

If for some unlikely reason LBJ decided to make casualty figures public, Rostow pointed out that two thirds of the civilians killed and wounded were, as he put it, "males engaged in war-related activity."

Rostow had a point about "a lot of misses." State Department cables sent to guide embassies in handling bombing inquiries conceded that there had been a great many misses.

A secret, no-foreign-dissemination report by Thomas L. Hughes, State Department's intelligence chief, to Secretary Dean Rusk December 30, 1966, reported that in the December 13 attack on the Yen Vien railroad yards in Hanoi, reconnaissance photos showed only three craters within the freight yards and forty outside the target area. In the December 14 raid American planes had jettisoned twenty-three 750-pound bombs when MIG fighters appeared. Hughes said that it "seems quite possible" that these bombs caused damage to the houses at the end of Doumier Bridge—that is, the houses which I had found destroyed on Pho Nguyen Thiep street, the ones which the Pentagon claimed had been destroyed by Hanoi's own SAM missiles.

The Hughes report that I obtained through FOIA was never published. It was not contained in the Pentagon Papers. It never saw the light of day. There *were* two wars: the one which the White House, the State Department, the Pentagon, carried on in public, and the second, quite different, conducted in secrecy and deceit.

At the end of World War II, the United States commissioned its famous Strategic Bombing Survey to evaluate the effect of American bombing on the war and the collapse of Germany. It pulled no punches. It demonstrated that until the last Germany managed to maintain its war effort, actually increasing production of key war materials, carrying on its remarkable transportation network, despite the rain of U.S. (and RAF) bombings, the firestorms which destroyed Dresden, Hamburg, and much of Berlin. The report was a landmark in military intelligence. It was designed to enable future generations to evaluate air power in the harsh light of reality and not in the capricious glow of publicity and propaganda.

McNamara left a similar testament to the American people in the Pentagon Papers, which he intended to guide us in future military-foreign policy, revealing our successes and our errors, giving us a realistic appraisal of what went wrong and what went right in Vietnam, the actual results of air power, the failures of our diplomacy, our errors of omission and commission.

It is all there—well, not quite all, as this account drawing on documents from the State Department and White House (not included in the Pentagon Papers) discloses.

I have conducted this examination of what was going on inside the administration—what was really known as contrasted with what was given to the public, the discrepancy between what the highest echelons of the Pentagon and White House knew and what they said publicly—using my newspaperman's observations on the scene in Vietnam as a kind of baseline to mark the deviations between public and private, between official and nonofficial reporting.

The contrast between my reports of bombing in Hanoi, Nam Dinh, and elsewhere in North Vietnam and the public declarations of the Pentagon and the White House is great. When the lid is lifted upon what was really known, what was really going on in the war, the discrepancy vanishes—or almost so. My reports were more optimistic about the American cause than were the private evaluation of our intelligence agencies and of McNamara, who was, as a civilian, President Johnson's deputy for the conduct of the war. I do not have access to the intimate realities as seen by the Joint Chiefs. We know their public positions in support of war and ever more war. But if their personal diaries should be made public—indeed, if they kept personal diaries—I should be surprised if their evaluations of Vietnam differed so much from those of Robert McNamara—no matter how they opposed him in public.

17 | Lies

I cherish in my archive two thin blue-paper notes, each bearing the seal of Her Britannic Majesty's government (one embossed, the other not), sent me by John Colvin, the British consul-general during my time in Hanoi.

The first invited me to lunch on New Year's Day, 1967. He was having the French delegate-general, François de Quirielle, and his wife, some Hungarians, and the Soviet military attaché. Or, if I preferred, we could lunch by ourselves another time. In the second note, dated January 5, 1967, he wrote in his spidery hand that I had left behind my wallet and a book after my visit. He knew they were mine because they bore my name, and I had enclosed my card. Would I please telephone and collect them that very day?

Colvin, a former naval officer and son of an admiral, was a thin, nervous man, a bachelor, dressed in a black turtleneck sweater, his hair—as I jotted in deliberately teensy illegible writing (so it could not be read if I lost it) in the memo pad which never left my pocket—"like Stef's." Stephan was my Columbia University son, who in the fashion of the day wore his hair rather longer than I thought attractive. "One just can't dress in Hanoi," Colvin explained.

There were few diplomats in the Vietnamese capital and fewer whom Colvin cared for. His bêtes noires were the Indians, and he did not fancy the French, warning me against them and particularly Madame Quirielle, whom he seemed to suspect of anti-American pro-Viet sentiments. (She had said that when the American B-52s were overhead, she longed for a gun to shoot at them.) Colvin looked harassed. His assistant was on leave, and Colvin was alone with a Vietnamese servant who spoke no English and whose French was such that, when Colvin asked him to bring a drink, he promptly lighted a fire.

My dispatches had provoked a blizzard of cables from London, and Colvin was working eighteen hours a day at deciphering and enciphering. Before I left Hanoi, as he told me, he had re-

157

ceived sixteen cables (to January 6) and dispatched twenty-six, many of them lengthy.

Things got more hectic after I met Premier Pham Van Dong, the day after New Year's, for four and a half hours. I had deliberately prolonged my talk, hoping that Ho Chi Minh would drop in. The Premier received me in the Presidential Palace across a broad green from the cottage where Ho lived. Sometimes Ho would walk across the lawn with his wispy beard and floppy inner-tube sandals, slip through the French windows, and join the conversation. But not the day I met Pham Van Dong.

The key point of my talk with Pham was cut out of my dispatch by the Foreign Office. "We have cut very little," the Foreign Office man said, "but unfortunately we have had to cut out the most important thing."

There was another cut, a question of taste, made by Pham himself. I had argued that the United States had been more forthcoming than Hanoi about negotiations. Pham interrupted me, apologizing, to say that he knew more about the negotiations than I did (which was certainly true).

"Each time," Pham said, "the Americans want to escalate, it is always accompanied by a peace move—from the Baltimore speech [in which LBJ spoke conciliatory words] *to the present.* * Of course, I understand this better than you because there are many things I can't tell you."

He added: "I am sorry to say this, but your President Johnson is a liar." He immediately apologized and asked that I not repeat this remark. Nor have I until this moment.

"The most important thing" which Hanoi cut from my dispatch was the first 200 words, in which I reported Pham Van Dong's declaration that, if the U.S. halted bombing and troop escalation, Vietnam would reciprocate. Of course, he did not use the word "reciprocate" but he repeated, under my questioning, four times that "we will know what to do" and that if the United States displayed "generosity," Vietnam would do the same.

"We will know what to do," "We will know what to do." It doesn't sound like a headline. It sounds innocuous. He was saying something, but he was saying nothing. If the Chinese, for example, asked a question, he could shrug his shoulders. He had deniability. But in order that I might not miss the importance of

---

*My italics. Pham was referring here to the December bombing, which ended Marigold (of which, of course, I had not heard).

his remarks, he had his Foreign Office man kill the passage and tell me that this was the "most important thing" in the interview.

Pham made another vital point. He said—very obliquely but perfectly clearly—that Hanoi was ready at any time without preconditions to meet privately, secretly (and preferably in Paris) with the United States—not peace talks but discussions which could lead to peace talks.

If this sounds arcane, it is because it is the language of diplomacy, the skill of letting your opponent know your position without being frozen into it. It is utterly divorced from polemics, propaganda, and public politics. It is the language which men like Talleyrand, Metternich, Henry Kissinger, and, yes, even Dean Rusk and Walt Rostow understand if they want to understand it. Why did Hanoi take the phrase out of my dispatch? To send a signal to LBJ and no one else. Especially not the Chinese.

I had met Colvin first a few hours before my interview with Pham Van Dong on January 2. Colvin was most hospitable, offering me his help in any way, including the use of his communications (a secure cipher). I thanked him but didn't think this was tactful. I was behind enemy lines and had to watch my step. I didn't want to arouse suspicion that I was sending back secret intelligence to the United States through British facilities.

When I got Colvin's note about the wallet and the book, I realized, of course, that he must want to see me urgently. Dutifully I made my way across Hanoi, through the streets, feeling as conspicuous as a clown at a funeral. It was a twenty-minute walk, and by the time I got to the consulate I was sure every eye in Hanoi had spotted me. I pushed through the gate and walked up to the door. It was locked, and no one responded to my knock. Looking around I found a small side door and tried that. No result. It was then that I noticed the blinds were drawn on all the windows as if there had been a death in the family. Nervous as I was, I felt certain Hanoi had concluded I must be a spy, and now the British establishment seemed to be locked and deserted. Nothing for it. I continued to root around and finally discovered a back door leading to the kitchen. I pushed my way in and shouted: "Anybody home?" There was a pause, then an angular figure in black turtleneck, long hair bobbing, scrambled out from under a Dutch half-door and greeted me. It was Colvin.

He invited me into his code room, serials strewn over every table and chair. His eyes had a desperate look. "I can't leave this place," he said. "I'm all alone." He couldn't leave the room with the codes scattered about. He couldn't leave the consulate. He couldn't leave Hanoi.

"I'm going out of my mind with all this," he exclaimed. He told me Rusk was urgently trying to contact me. Wanted me to use his (Colvin's) facilities to give him a fill-in on what Pham Van Dong had said. I was taken aback. I didn't think much of communicating third or fourth hand. I told that to Colvin and said he could tell Rusk I would be at his disposal as soon as I got to the U.S.A., probably by January 11. I promised I'd keep mum on the delicate matters which had been discussed with me. With that I left Colvin to his codes.

I never saw him again, but a few years ago I was startled to read an excerpt from his memoirs saying that my reports from Hanoi had been "drawn chiefly from North Vietnamese false-hoods." He reproved me for having "cloddishly" written him on my return to New York. I must plead guilty. I did write him a chatty bread-and-butter note, thanking him for his courtesies and asking him if there had been any further fallout from my visit. He did not reply.

Scotty Reston made an appointment for me to meet secretly with Rusk, January 13, 1967. He tried to set up one with the President but had no luck. Bill Moyers said, "I can't even put it to him." At first I thought this might reflect LBJ's hostility to Bill, but I was wrong.* Two weeks after I returned, Harry Ashmore, one-time editor of the Little Rock *Gazette,* and Bill Baggs, editor of the Miami *Daily News,* got back from Vietnam. They had arrived there in the same ICC plane that took me out. They had seen much the same bomb damage as I had, and they'd had the talk with Ho Chi Minh that I had hoped to have.

Ashmore and Baggs were on good terms with LBJ but the White House didn't want to see them either.

They went to Washington and had a talk with Senator J. William Fulbright, chairman of the Senate Foreign Relations Committee, no hero in the President's book. Fulbright, appalled

*For four weeks before Moyers left the White House, LBJ would not speak to him. LBJ was telling his intimates: "I made Bill Moyers. Why, Bill Moyers wasn't nuthin' before I made him."

to hear that the President wasn't meeting them, dropped in at the White House the next morning and urged Johnson to talk to Ashmore and Baggs. "They're both good Democrats, Mr. President, they have some important things to tell you," Fulbright said.

"Ah, gee, Bill," said Lyndon in his coziest good ol' boy tones, "you know I'd like to, but I just can't see everyone who comes back from Hanoi."

My talk with Dean Rusk didn't track very well. We were out of sync. He wanted to argue Vietnam with me: Would Hanoi admit they had troops in the south? Would they agree to stop helping the VC if we stopped bombing; would they do this; would they do that. I wasn't there to argue with Dean. I was there to fill him in on important information, information he felt was important when I was in Hanoi, but in which, as far as I could see, he had no interest now. Fortunately, Assistant Secretary of State Bill Bundy took good notes, asked sharp questions, and understood what I was talking about.

Rusk brought in Robert McCloskey, a PR representative, so that a news release could be given out about our talk. He seemed to think I was going to write a story or that Scotty would. I told him (with some firmness) that I was there only to report what I had seen and heard; this was for my government's benefit. With reluctance he sent McCloskey away. I don't know what was going on in Dean's mind. We'd never really been on the same wavelength, not since we first met at Lake Success at the United Nations in 1947. Dean had just joined the U.S. mission, and I was heading the United Press coverage. At the end of one day, we were leaning against the railing outside the UP office, and I asked him about U.S. policy on Israel. He looked me straight in the eye and denied what we both knew was true. We were old hands in the game. We each knew that we couldn't always be frank, but there were ways that diplomats and reporters talked to each other. Dean broke the rules, and I never forgot it.*

When I started the Op-Ed page in the *Times* in 1970, Vietnam was still a hot ticket. Dean was down in Georgia by then, on the law faculty. I called and asked him to do a piece for us—one

---

*Robert Manning, then of UP, wrote the exclusive story of which we spoke to Rusk. The conversation stuck in Manning's mind when, years later, he was asked to join the State Department. Rusk's first question was: "Would you be willing to lie for your country?" Manning replied that you didn't have to lie; you could always make your case honestly.

which would criticize *The New York Times* editorial policy. Dean got so angry he almost hung up. He said he would never appear on the page across from John Oakes' editorial page. The *Times,* he said, had almost brought on World War III by its opposition to the Vietnam War. But, Dean, I said, the Op-Ed page is specifically for you—so you can tell everyone what's wrong with the *Times.* "Never," he snapped. Well, I don't take never as never. I called him some weeks later. Same thing, only more angry. But never isn't never. A couple of years later, when I was conducting a PBS TV program called *Behind the Lines,* I went down to Georgia and had a wonderful talk with Dean and put it on the air. He had mellowed out. Maybe I had too. I asked him what had been in his mind when we met after my trip to Hanoi. He remembered my trip to Hanoi, but not our private talk. "I talked to so many people. . . ." he said vaguely.

My secret talk with Dean Rusk left a bad taste in my mouth. I had a sense of being used—and used badly—a sense which would have been even sharper had I then had access to some of the secret file. Why had Rusk been so anxious at first to find out the nature of my talks with Pham Van Dong? And so indifferent when we met? Why was he continuing to lay down propaganda against my reports from Hanoi?

It would be years before I discovered what was going on in the White House, the State Department, and the British Foreign Office during my time in Hanoi. Not until I finally managed to lay hands on a badly reproduced copy of the "diplomatic volumes" of the Pentagon Papers, the ones which Daniel Ellsberg did not release to *The New York Times,* did I begin to get some clues. The volumes came to light in Federal court hearings during the aborted prosecution of Ellsberg in the Pentagon Papers case.*

But these clues only became understandable when in 1986 and 1987 I obtained under the Freedom of Information Act a series of Walt Rostow memos to LBJ, which filled in most of the gaps.

Under cover of the propaganda blitz against me, LBJ, Rusk, and Rostow did, in fact, take my Hanoi reports with utmost seriousness.

*The documents subsequently were published by the University of Texas Press, edited by George C. Herring, under the title *The Secret Diplomacy of the Vietnam War.*

Unbeknownst to me, John Colvin had fired off an urgent cable to the Foreign Office in which he reported the gist of my impressions, as I gave them to him on January 2, before my meeting with Pham Van Dong. I had told Colvin that the Vietnamese—despite my repeated denials—were treating me as an unofficial emissary of Washington. I said I had the impression from my talks at the ministerial level that, if we halted the bombing and troop increases, Hanoi would make some military concession and would be prepared to negotiate. Colvin reported (accurately) my belief that Hanoi was eager to negotiate secretly but did not know how this could be arranged.

Colvin's report was passed on to the British Minister in Washington, Michael Stewart, who gave it to Bill Bundy that same day.

Bundy took it immediately to Walt Rostow, who sent it to LBJ with a memo timed 7:10 P.M. January 3. From what I know of LBJ's habits, he read it that evening, probably before dinner.

Rostow accompanied the report with a remarkable memorandum. Part of it is still blacked out by the "sanitizing" process but deletions do not obscure Rostow's recommendation:

> I have come to believe it conceivable, if not probable, that they [Hanoi] are trying to get out of the war but don't know how.
>
> By "don't know how" I mean they cannot openly negotiate with us. They must have a deal which saves them minimum face with the NLF [Viet Cong] and the Chinese to announce before negotiations are acknowledged. They lose their bargaining leverage if they are known to be negotiating, because the NLF might bug out.
>
> If this is so, the message we should send back is this, and no more. Your message to Salisbury has been delivered. You will be hearing from us soon.
>
> We should then send a direct message [several words blanked out here—probably "via U.S. embassy, Moscow"] in a sealed envelope. It should be a direct communication, unopened, without intermediaries, between the U.S. Government and Hanoi.

There was a suppressed excitement about Rostow's memo to LBJ. Clearly he thought he was on to something very important. He appended a six-page memo—which he had prepared several days earlier, so he said—which he called "Direct Contact with Hanoi—a Scenario."

Rostow insisted that he did not give his proposal "very high odds [but]—I think it is worth a try."

LBJ's response is not available. Probably they discussed it verbally. Next day British Foreign Secretary George Brown weighed in, pointing out that my report coincided closely with the package which Brown had put to Moscow (with Rusk's approval) in November. "This being so," said Brown, "we must take it very seriously." He offered British secure communications out of Hanoi for "clandestine discussions" either before or after I left Hanoi.

On the evening of January 4, unquestionably after consultations among Rusk, Rostow, and LBJ, the secretary handed over to Stewart in Washington a long message for Brown to transmit to Colvin. Colvin was to advise me that Rusk had received Colvin's report on my conversations (prior to the Pham Van Dong interview) and would appreciate a full report on any and all talks bearing on negotiations via Colvin's secure channel. Rusk asked Colvin to warn me of the danger of publicly discussing Hanoi's views, because of fear the Chinese might learn of them. Rusk wanted me to assure Hanoi that all such conversations were on a "clandestine basis."

If, said Rusk, senior members of the Hanoi government suggested direct clandestine talks with the U.S., "Salisbury is authorized by us to tell the North Vietnamese that he can convey this to us through the British secure channel." I was to advise Hanoi that "we place the highest priority on finding a mutually agreeable, completely secure arrangement for exchanging communications with them."

This message was received by John Colvin (because of the time differential) early January 5 and was the cause of his hugger-mugger note to me about book-and-wallet.

After our code-room talk, Colvin reported to Rusk that I would give the gist of my talk with Pham Van Dong only to him personally, that I did not care to use the British cipher, that I would talk of clandestine discussions only with Rusk, and I would not include this subject in my articles. Colvin reported that I thought that, if there was any receptivity in Washington, there were grounds for further exploration, but the results of my talks should not be exaggerated. Colvin told Rusk that I hoped to be in Washington by January 11.

Colvin advised the State Department he had not been able to pass on to me Rusk's proposal that I act as his private envoy in telling the North Vietnamese to communicate through me on the question of setting up private talks.

I am certain that this was not deliberate on Colvin's part. I think he just had not been able to decode the whole of the lengthy cable before we met. In any event I did not get this message.

I would have been extremely uncomfortable in the role of a go-between, although I confess the notion of "Harrison Appallsbury" being recruited for delicate, secret diplomatic duty on behalf of Dean Rusk and Lyndon Baines Johnson did have its charm.

I suspect that Colvin was both relieved and upset by my refusal to avail myself of his facilities. It denied him a chance to play middleman in what might have been an extraordinary chapter in the Vietnam story. But in the real world there was no way in which he could have handled extended cipher traffic among myself, Rusk, and the North Vietnamese.

After receiving my reply, Rusk sent a circular telegram to embassies along my likely routes back to the United States, asking them to offer me the use of their transmission facilities and caution me about divulging anything about North Vietnamese confidences until I could report to him and let the Department evaluate their significance.

He sent a quick message to Moscow and asked the embassy to deliver a private letter to the North Vietnamese for Hanoi, saying that the United States placed "the highest priority" on finding a mutually agreeable totally secure site for exchanging communications on the possible peaceful settlement of the Vietnam war. We were ready to meet the North Vietnamese at any place where both countries had embassies or any other place that was suggested.

I met with Rusk and Bundy at 5 P.M. on the afternoon of Friday January 13, two days behind the schedule I had permitted Colvin to send to Washington from Hanoi. We talked until 6:30 P.M. An essentially accurate report of our talk was on LBJ's desk after lunch on Saturday, January 14. It was signed by

Rusk but undoubtedly drafted by Bundy. Rostow forwarded it
to the President with this memo:

> Once again it confirms:
> —The possibility—if not the probability—that they are look-
> ing for a way out.
> Secret talks with us without an intermediary is the proper
> route.*

Whether Rostow was right or wrong about his recommendation we will never know. The path was not followed in a serious
way despite Rostow's excitement, Rusk's cooperation, and some
surface interest by LBJ at the start. What I learned once I had
patched together this secret history was that at the moment when
publicly Rusk and Rostow were denouncing my reports as "mood
music" and anti-American propaganda, in reality they were
using the information to try to fashion an approach toward negotiating, but, I'm afraid, this effort to find common ground with
Hanoi was scuppered by LBJ just as were all the others.

On one topic I had gone cautiously with Rusk—China. Nothing had so impressed (and frightened) me as Hanoi's almost total
dependence upon China. China controlled the bulk of supplies
that Hanoi must have to continue the war. China was the source
of the rice and foodstuffs that Vietnam could no longer produce
herself. She would starve without China. China was the source of
Hanoi's small arms, rifles, machine guns, grenades, mortars, ammunition. China was the source of railroad supplies, rolling
stock, rails, locomotives, and, I was told, maintenance crews.

This kept Hanoi in the war. And more. The preponderance of
Soviet and East European supplies came via China and the Chinese railroads—planes, artillery, SAM antiaircraft missiles,
radar, heavy machinery, petroleum products, and trucks. True,
the Soviets had shifted some shipments to ocean routes and Haiphong, but more and more this was being bombed by the U.S.

China, in the grip of the Cultural Revolution (and recognized
in Hanoi as a wild and dangerous phenomenon), had interrupted
her own shipments on occasion and also—more and more frequently—Soviet and East European shipments. Some had even

---

*In a telephone conversation with Bundy January 16, I reiterated what I had
told him and Rusk on the thirteenth: "Direct talks are best—no intermediary."

been returned to the Soviet Union. She had refused Moscow permission to open a trans-China air supply route to Hanoi via Xinjiang.

The Chinese were insisting that the Vietnamese adopt the most leftist policies of world guerrilla warfare, the theories of Lin Biao. China ardently opposed any diplomacy by Vietnam to end the war, any talks with the U.S., any negotiations: "Let it go on for 100 years. Capitalism is doomed." China warned Hanoi that if she opened talks with the U.S., she would risk a cutoff of Chinese and other aid which China transmitted.

Beijing was holding a pistol to Hanoi's back. It was, I was told by East European diplomats, a day-to-day gamble as to when China would pull the trigger. Only the adroitness of Ho Chi Minh and Pham Van Dong kept supplies coming.

I knew that the Chinese blackmail was real and dangerous. I was certain that if the Chinese discovered that Hanoi was seeking peace with the U.S., they would exercise their veto. I was sure Hanoi even then would not give up the war. She would retreat to the hills and jungles where Ho Chi Minh had fought so many years. It would be guerrilla war without end.

I had seen the silent split between China and the other Communists every day in Hanoi. The Chinese held themselves aloof from me. They held themselves aloof from everyone. They did not attend receptions or press conferences. They traveled in a group, six Chinese in a military command car. They spoke to no one. Moscow had printed news of my Vietnam reports. Not a word in Beijing. I thought of going back to New York via Europe. The Russians promptly offered a transit visa. The Chinese did not.

I spoke to Rusk about China. But I took it easy. I was afraid that if he and LBJ knew the peril China presented to Hanoi, they would stonewall Vietnam, throwing Hanoi, like it or not, into the arms of Beijing.

I received over 300 letters about my Hanoi coverage, three to one favorable. The *Times* received 1000 more in about the same ratio of pro and con. Normally there is a high preponderance of negative mail. Those who have a complaint are quicker to write than those who have a compliment.

When the Pulitzer Committee met in April 1967, the jury

picked my Hanoi stories for the award in international reporting. This decision was overturned by a 6–5 vote of the judges (in
which Turner Catledge, the *Times* representative did not participate). One judge, Ralph Pulitzer, Jr., raised the question in the
board of trustees of Columbia the next day. The trustees voted 6
to 5 to support the verdict of the judges. Arthur (Punch) Sulzberger of the *Times,* a trustee, did not participate in the vote.

I was asked to comment. I said that I held the judgment of
my colleagues at the *Times* above that of anyone else, and I had
won that.

Brooks Atkinson wrote to say the Pulitzers "are awarded by
timid men indifferently informed about what they are doing." I
think Brooks was wrong. The judges knew what they were doing.
They were voting their support of LBJ and the Vietnam war.

On the plane flying out of Hanoi I jotted down a few impressions. I felt, I said, a certain nostalgia about leaving. "It brings
an end to a period in which I have had a special sense of history,
of actually moving and influencing events. The only other time I
have had this sense was at the time of Stalin's death in 1953. I
think the sense has more basis now."

What to make of the Vietnamese? I asked myself.

"They have heart," as Smokey [one of the Shook-ups in Red
Hook] would say. Great heart. They fight with nothing. They
have spunk and the devil, and they will go down to defeat rather
than budge if you try to shove them.

"They are suffering. No doubt but they can take a lot of that.
Can we negotiate? Yes, but only with care and prudence. I don't
know if we possess that. . . ."

I exaggerated the effect of my dispatches. They played a role,
but a small one, in bringing the country to a more realistic view
of the war. It would be a long time before the war would end.

I was wrong about many things. A Vietnamese official told me
the war would ruin the United States as it had France—exhaust-
ing gold reserves, setting off inflation, dividing the people, poi-
soning politics. I laughed. He didn't understand. We were so big,
so rich. We could fight Vietnam and still have LBJ's Great Society.

I was wrong in the beginning to believe—and the belief was
strengthened by the Pentagon Papers publication, the CIA exposés, the strong antiwar movement, Watergate and Nixon's res-

ignation—that a new force had emerged in American life, a combination of investigative reporting and populist action which could turn the country around.

Twenty years after Hanoi I am not so sure. The words of the country's great investigative reporter, Sy Hersh, who exposed My Lai, haunt me. No one has done more to uncover the lies of war and peace, to bring reality to the public, to shoulder the responsibilities which the First Amendment to the Constitution places on the press, to live the journalistic creed of Adolph S. Ochs, founder of the modern *New York Times,* to "give the news without fear or favor."

Could, Hersh was asked at a Vietnam symposium in 1984, it happen again? Could we be led down the fateful path to disaster despite what had seemed to some, including me, the new courage and frankness of the press?

Yes, said Hersh. It could happen again and probably would. How? The government would lie, just as it had so often. It would just lie.

I'm afraid that the poet, Robert Bly, my fellow Minnesotan, got it right when he wrote:

The Chief Executive Enters, the Press Conference begins: The President lies . . . the ministers lie, the professors lie, the television lies, the priests lie . . . the attorney general lies. . . .

18 | "A Mean Man"

The fears I whispered to Charlotte the night I came back from Hanoi, that somehow LBJ would destroy us in the lava of his anger, quickly died away. I did not know that J. Edgar Hoover would poke around in wastebaskets for months, trying to find some tattered trail against me. I still have only a fuzzy idea of what the FBI was up to, but there is one telltale clue—their reports went to Marvin Watson, LBJ's confidential White House aide.

I did not know that, within a month of my return from Vietnam, LBJ had orchestrated another massive escalation of the war. What I did sense quickly in the winter of 1967, as I fanned out around the country, making talks, appearing on TV, and testifying before the Senate Foreign Relations Committee, was that people were in a state of tension. It was not just the war. The civil rights struggle had come north. Students had moved into political action, the streets were alive. Charlotte and our friends were joining the big demonstrations in New York and Washington. American flag decals blazed on over-the-road trucks, iron-on flag patches appeared on the tight-ass jeans of the young. On Saturdays people drove with headlights on to support the war. They spat at neighbors standing in town squares with lighted candles in peace vigils.

I had seen nothing like the anger, not even in depression days. Then the unemployed stood silently, patiently, cowlike until they were run down by the "Cossacks," the blue-coated, pot-hatted police with their nightsticks. Not until FDR and the CIO did workers storm the steel and auto works in the face of Thompson submachine guns.

What I saw now was different—broader, deeper, divisive, people against people, young against old, and middle class—very middle class—against blue collar.

I saw no sign of any move to lower the temperature. I had one alarming talk after another. I remember one with Bobby Kennedy. In May he told me that LBJ's decision in February 1967 to escalate the war was backed by a consensus—the Joint

Chiefs, Rusk, Rostow, and the President, everyone but McNamara. Rostow, said Bobby, had concluded that "the war is over but Hanoi does not realize it." Within six weeks U.S. victory would be at hand. LBJ, Rusk, and Rostow had concluded that it was true, Hanoi sincerely wanted peace. Ipso facto, Hanoi must be on the ropes. So—hit 'em now and hit 'em hard. This word (largely confirmed by FOIA and the secret Pentagon volumes) fed my terrible fear that my report of Pham Van Dong's desire for peace had reinforced LBJ's belief that a few more hard knocks would propel Hanoi out of the war. Instead of furthering peace and sanity, I had added fuel to war and madness.

What would LBJ do now? That question, Bobby said, was being argued. The alternatives: a "small invasion" of the North, probably carried out by amphibian forces just above the DMZ (LBJ was being told that China would not get excited). Or an invasion of Laos, the occupation of Cambodia, more and heavier bombing. Every target in North Vietnam except Hai phong and Hanoi had already been obliterated; there was nothing left to bomb.

McNamara (in the words of Bobby and Arthur Schlesinger) was opposed to these proposals. He wanted negotiations and his $3 billion electronic barrier to halt Hanoi from sending men and supplies south. McNamara told Schlesinger he favored negotiations in deepest secrecy. He was staying on only because, if he quit, Texas Governor John Connally would take over the Pentagon, and God only knew what would happen then.

My friend of the Stevenson campaign, Clayton Fritchey, had known Lyndon for years. "He is a mean man," Fritchey said, pursing his lips. "Mean all the way through and vindictive. He will never give up on Vietnam until he has punished them and made them submit to him."

I talked with Eliot Janeway, the political-financial analyst and longtime LBJ intimate, and his friend, Senator Vance Hartke of Indiana. They agreed that, when Lyndon set himself a goal, he never wavered.

"When he is down, he is most dangerous," Janeway said. They thought LBJ might be headed for a nuclear confrontation with Moscow. "It is the only way he can outdo Jack Kennedy."

* * *

By the winter of 1968 the situation at the *Times* was rapidly changing. Abe Rosenthal was moving upward, acting as deputy to Clifton Daniel, in charge when Daniel wasn't on hand, and Scotty Reston was about to embark on his brief, frustrating term as executive editor. The *Times* was an uneasy island in an uneasy America. This was the winter of Tet, the devastating blow by Vietnam, which cost tens of thousands of Viet lives and took thousands of American lives, the blow which the U.S. military insisted (and still insists) was a great American victory but which, in reality, ended the American effort to impose its will on Hanoi.

It was a turning point.

On April Fool's Day, 1968, several foreigners, including Jacques DeCornoy of *Le Monde,* the French photographer Roger Pic, the Australian Wilfred Burchett, and one or two Japanese journalists, plus the writer Mary McCarthy and Professor Franz Schurmann of California, were gathered in Burchett's big room at the Metropole Hotel in Hanoi, drinking a morning coffee and listening to President Johnson speak from Washington. It was 9 A.M. Hanoi time (9 P.M. in Washington).

Vietnamese kept bursting into the room, asking what the President was saying, and the foreigners translated as best they could. Mr. Johnson talked in his flat Texas accent, employing the slightly overblown language favored by his speech writers. He gave a brief review of the war, spoke of our determination to go the last mile, our efforts to make peace. He announced a bombing halt—a pause, really—to permit negotiations, an opportunity, if the enemy wished, to bring the war to an end.

At this point the foreigners turned off the radio, feeling they had heard Mr. Johnson's main points. Someone broke out a bottle of Bulgarian slivovitz and, as Mary McCarthy recalled, "We danced around and embraced each other; we did feel it was a victory."

Coming downstairs, they ran into a Vietnamese interpreter who had also listened to the broadcast. He told them of the President's announcement that he would not run for reelection. "We all laughed," Mary McCarthy remembered, "saying to each other 'isn't that typical of Vietnamese fantasizing'?" It took some time to adjust their minds. They knew LBJ was in trouble. They knew Bobby Kennedy had entered the race, but none really believed LBJ could be denied the nomination.

In a moment the situation had been transformed. Some still thought (as did I) that it was an LBJ trick. Others were not so sure. Harry S. Ashmore and William J. Baggs, the American newsmen back in Hanoi for a second time, were certain it was for real. They urged their view strongly on the Vietnamese.

The Vietnamese Politburo met for two days. Finally they too were convinced by LBJ's decision to yield the Presidency. They cabled their acceptance of his offer.

I watched this with amazement. I had not expected Hanoi to accept the offer, withdrawal or no withdrawal by LBJ. I had anticipated a totally different scenario: Hanoi would reject LBJ's proposal. LBJ and his aides would rally the country around him. If Hanoi would not negotiate even with LBJ's promise to retire, then what alternative did we have? Bomb them back to the caves! LBJ, I thought, would turn American opinion around. I could hear the rhetoric echoing in my ears—the call for victory, an end to peaceniks and mollycoddles, an annihilating bombing (like the Nixon-Kissinger Christmas bombing of Hanoi in 1972), a strike into the North, who knows what? And a ground wave sweep of Johnson sentiment across the country. The decal truckmen, the hyperpatriots, the eagle hawks would *demand* that Lyndon give his all for his country and run for another turn.

Fantasy, perhaps, but the idea lurked in my mind and grew stronger with the events-to-come in Chicago. I still think I was at least half-right.

LBJ's declaration did not restore harmony to the United States. With spring American campuses rose in turmoil. Everywhere I went—and I traveled the country end to end—there was violence. I did not have to leave New York for that. There was Columbia University.

At the end of April the Columbia students had occupied five campus buildings in protest against university plans for a new gymnasium. Of course that wasn't what it was about. It was a manifestation of the spirit of 1968. They were demonstrating against the war, against LBJ, against the military, against the chauvinism of American society, against the system. It was spring. They were rebels.

On the night of April 29, 1968, Abe Rosenthal was attending the opening of the musical *Hair*. He returned to the *Times* to find that Police Commissioner Howard Leary had tipped his good friend, Nat Goldstein, the *Times* circulation manager, that he was going to bust the Columbia sit-in at 1 A.M. Nat tried to get Leary to move up the bust to eleven o'clock so the *Times* could make the story in its second edition. Leary wouldn't budge. He didn't want to bust Columbia until next door Harlem had gone to sleep.

Abe dashed to 116th Street and spent the night at Columbia. He was powerfully moved—the debris, the violence, the obscenities of the students (every other word, as he recalled, was "motherfucker.") He stood in the shambles of President Grayson Kirk's office, and Abe's heart froze at the leather-bound volumes strewn on the floor, spines ripped and pages defiled. I think that did it. Like myself he loved books, had spent his teenage quarters in the secondhand bookstores of Fourth Avenue. Like me he cherished his Heritage Press edition of the classics. Later he told me it was the "anger and authoritarianism" of the students that upset him. I think it was the broken books. He was outraged when Arthur Cox's report on Columbia dismissed the damage to Kirk's office as "trivial." He wrote Cox insisting it had been at least $5,000 worth.

There was something else. He had, he told me, heard that he had been picked by the radical underground as a "target." This was startling news. I pressed him very hard as to who told him that. At first he said he couldn't remember but finally suggested it was an old friend, Arnold Beichman, who was doing graduate work at Columbia that year. But Beichman told me that Abe had got it backward. Beichman didn't think Abe was a target; he didn't think Mark Rudd and the Columbia students had any targets—the whole thing was spur-of-the-moment.

Abe was brimming with passion in early morning when he got a call from Clifton Daniel. Clifton's father had died, and Clifton had to leave immediately for Zebulon, North Carolina. He put Abe in charge of the paper. "I urge you in the strongest possible terms," Daniel recalled telling Abe, "not to write and not to print that story." Daniel then telephoned me, told me about Abe and Columbia, and said: "I don't want him doing it. See what you can do."

I couldn't do much. Abe wrote his story and brought it to

me to read "because I am out of practice." I read it. It was a torrent of emotion. He told of seeing Kirk standing in his office at 4:30 A.M., passing a hand over his face as he viewed the destruction: "My God, how could human beings do a thing like this!" (When I asked Kirk later, he had no recollection of this melodrama or of seeing Abe at Columbia.)

I gently tried to persuade Abe to reconsider the story—at least to tone down the Kirk scene. Abe said he would think it over, but he printed it just as he wrote it. Posters went up at Columbia: "Kirk and Rosenthal must go." Punch Sulzberger was picketed in his Fifth Avenue apartment, and Abe acquired a reputation as a rightist (he was later to dub himself a "bleeding heart conservative") and an antagonist to the young, a reputation which never left him.

Daniel and Sulzberger were not amused.

I wrote Daniel an apology: "I am sorry that I was unable to mitigate or stop this from happening. I think it was very bad conduct. The story was so emotional (the natural by-product of an emotional man staying up all night in an emotional atmosphere) that it was bound to cause all kinds of consequences."

On Wednesday, May 1, Charlotte and I had a big party at our 84th Street house. The place was jammed, people overflowing from one floor to another. Stephan was a senior at Columbia, in the thick of the sit-in, a friend of Mark Rudd and many other radicals. He and his girlfriend, Gretchen, arrived wearing their black "revolutionary" leather jackets, Stef with a Lenin cap, Gretchen with her auburn hair dramatically billowing down to her waist. They had been busted in the Columbia raid and had just gotten out of jail. People crowded around in excitement. What had it been like? What next? I thought of those February days in Petrograd, 1917, the last parties in the great flats off the Nevsky. Abe Rosenthal was downstairs in the kitchen talking with every young person at the party. He and Stef exchanged a few words. Not very cozy.

A very old friend came to New York from Moscow. He knew the United States well and liked it very much. He had a long talk with Stef.

"Never have I been so impressed," this man said, "with you people and your spirit, with the vitality of you young people, with the courage of Americans in struggling with the most difficult questions of the day. What other society would be so bold?"

Europeans, he said, had so long thought of Americans as crude, unsophisticated, materialistic. And now Americans were examining "the central philosophical issues of mankind."

"It is remarkable," he went on. "I am proud of you. You have a great country. Truly great. But be careful. Do not destroy it. I say that as a Russian. We Russians know the price to be paid for destruction. I do not want to see that happen in America."

As time went on, I would come to see this episode as a metaphor of the 1960s and of *The New York Times* in that heated period, and I would wonder how Adolph Ochs would have handled such emotionalism.

Ever since I arrived at the Union Station from Minneapolis on a frozen January 13, 1931, I have thought of Chicago as *my* city—the city of Sandburg and Frank Norris, of Upton Sinclair's *Jungle,* of Dreiser's *Maggie,* of Hinky Dink Kenna and Alderman John (The Bathhouse) Coughlin, of Al Capone and Cicero, of Ben Hecht and Charlie MacArthur and *The Front Page,* of Yellow Kid Weil and James Whitcomb Riley, the city of hyperbole, of the Big Wind, of Big Speculators, Big Crime, Big Politics, of Big Bill Thompson who ran for mayor on the promise "I'll punch King George in the snoot," of Mayor Anton Cermak and of a failed gangland plot to assassinate him on the City Hall steps (to which, I am amazed to say, I was privy, sort of).

Nothing that happens in Chicago really surprises me. But the 1968 Democratic National Convention was an exception. I expected trouble. I expected violence. I expected the nomination of Lyndon Baines Johnson. I was right about trouble and violence. I was wrong—but perhaps not that wrong—about Lyndon.

On the night of August 28, 1968, a Wednesday, I was sitting at my command post in the press section of the convention hall at the Chicago Stockyards. I *knew* there would be violence. It had been building up.

Robert Kennedy had been assassinated in June in Los Angeles. Martin Luther King had been killed in Memphis in May. The country was going up in smoke. One afternoon I was running to board an airplane in Newark when I heard a young woman ask the man she was with: "What's all that smoke?" He (and I) looked back. "Oh," he said, "it's just Newark burning

down. Let's hurry." From the takeoff I could see Newark's black
ghetto burning in the rage of King's murder.

That was my America in the summer of 1968. No way that
Chicago, Hog Butcher Chicago, Daley's Chicago, wouldn't ex-
plode.

I had arrived on the watch for a Draft Johnson movement. I
hadn't believed LBJ was sincere in his March 31 speech. I knew
there had been confusion and surprise in the White House and
State Department when Hanoi said yes to Johnson's limited
bombing halt. They had rejected this kind of thing before. I was
sure LBJ expected—was counting on—another turndown. So for
a month there had been sparring. Washington didn't want that
yes. Hanoi proposed a meeting in Phnom Penh. Washington suggested New Delhi, Rangoon, Tokyo. Hanoi responded with Warsaw. The State Department agreed, but the White House flared
up because Tass reported it before the White House spoke. I
thought the whole thing was going up the spout but at last both
sides agreed on Paris. No meeting was held until July, and now
it was late August and still there was deadlock.

Mayor Daley didn't seem to take LBJ's "withdrawal" any
more seriously than I did. Daley had backed Robert Kennedy
until Robert was killed, then switched to LBJ. He prepared a
monster birthday party for Lyndon at Soldier Field. It sounded
like a campaign kickoff to me. By this time the White House was
leaking to every visitor nasty stories about Humphrey. He was a
loser. "He cries too much." There was no doubt what the White
House was up to. I was not amazed when on an inspection of the
Chicago Amphitheater, I stumbled into a storeroom where LBJ
placards, banners, and posters were stacked to the ceiling. Everything was set for the convention to rise and sweep LBJ into the
nomination.

But nothing in Chicago went according to plan. The antiwar
forces—David Dellinger, Tom Hayden, and the Yippies led by
Abbie Hoffman—had mustered their supporters by the thousand.
Daley mobilized his forces—8,000 police, 5,000 Illinois guardsmen (some 5,000 U.S. regulars were alerted and held in reserve).
The convention hall looked like Hitler's last bunker, barbed wire
coils everywhere, barricades, checkpoints outside and inside the
hall. American politics had never seen such security.

Confrontation quickly became the order of the day. The decibel count went up and up. The higher it rose, the faster prospects

for a Johnson coup de theatre faded. The Secret Service would not guarantee his safety. He was confined to his Texas ranch, on the telephone to Daley, but the Blue Helmets washed LBJ out with their street brawls. Daley had to cancel the Soldier Field birthday party. Those tons of LBJ banners never left the stadium bins.

Charlotte had come to the convention with me. We both had misgivings. We were staying at a quiet hotel on the near North Side, just a block from the half-basement flat where I had lived in the Capone era. In those days my big story had been gang killings. Dion O'Banion had been gunned down a stone's throw away in the flower shop across from the cathedral on North State Street. The St. Valentine's Day massacre took place in a not distant garage. At night I had been awakened by bombings—the gang was organizing "protection" of the dry-cleaning shops. But the throb and surge of street violence as it built up in Chicago in August 1968 was something else. It crept closer and closer to our quiet sanctuary. I began to worry about Charlotte, her physical safety, the emotional impact of the brutality all around. On Tuesday she went to a movie and walked back to the hotel through streets filled with police and troops, and called me. She had decided to get back to New York. I sighed in relief. "There is no one there to respond to the cries of the discontented people," Charlotte wrote in her diary on the plane going home.

Behind cordons of police and barbed wire the convention hall was an island of quiet. Not so the central convention hotel, the Conrad Hilton, which spanned a long block on Michigan Avenue. The police beat and hounded young people from Lincoln Park down to Grant Park opposite the Hilton.

Tony Lukas, just back from the Congo wars, was handling the street story. He knew the protesters, the gentle pacifists, the wild radicals, the eccentric Yippies. He knew them all.

On Tuesday evening Wallace Turner, the best of the *Times*'s investigative reporters, was walking back to his hotel. He spotted three or four squad cars blocking a street. In a courtyard he saw a huddle of police and heard a patrolman say: "Sergeant, can I have me a hippie to beat the shit out of?"

The next evening it started.

Tom Wicker was standing at the big window of the *Times* news room on the twenty-first story of the Conrad Hilton, looking down on Michigan Avenue, when he saw the police charge past the National Guardsmen into Grant Park. Several hundred youngsters sat there singing: "God Bless America." The Daley men burst among them, beating, kicking, and dragging them by the feet to paddy wagons. "These are our children!" Wicker exclaimed. Next day he wrote a column headed: "These were our children, and the police were beating them." His colleague Ned Kenworthy rushed for the elevator, down to the street, two blocks up Michigan and over into the park. "Get out! Get out!" he shouted to the young people. "The police are coming. You're doing no good to your cause." (They were mostly Gene McCarthy supporters.)

Times reporter John Kifner was with the young people marching down Michigan. He watched the police charge, clubs and blackjacks swinging. He watched them drive young and old back against the Hilton and through the plate-glass window, shards splintering, police tumbling into the dark, air-conditioned, panel-lined bar, beating and slugging everyone in their path.

Kifner raced to a telephone. He got Charlotte Curtis on the line. She was filling in for Sylvan Fox, a deskman who had suffered a heart attack and been sent to the hospital by ambulance. Charlotte Curtis listened a moment to Kif and then handed the telephone to Lukas. "You better take this yourself."

At the stockyards I was going crazy. A *Times* photographer had been beaten and dragged off—no one knew where—by the police. I was on the phone to the hospital, to the police, to Lukas' post at Tribune Tower, to our main news room in the Hilton and, most of all, to New York, trying to convey to the editors that the story had shifted away from the convention hall, where the slow nominating process was underway, onto the Chicago streets. It wasn't politics this night; it was a riot. The editors found it hard to grasp.

Kifner was trying to get Lukas to understand. "I've just witnessed something unbelievable," Kifner told him. "The police have charged on a lot of innocent people and driven them through the glass window in the Hilton cocktail lounge, following them in and are beating them."

"Come on, John," said Tony. "Don't get carried away. Don't give me that stuff. I don't believe it."

"I saw it with my own eyes," Kifner insisted.

"You saw them inside, beating people up?"

"I did."

So Lukas wrote it. He knew Kifner was an experienced reporter. If Kifner saw it, it happened.

Kenworthy was writing what he saw, too, the young people singing, police charges, bystanders' reactions, 1,500 or 2,000 words. But trouble arose in New York. I got on the phone again and again, telling the responsible editors, Abe Rosenthal and night editor Ted Bernstein, that Chicago had gone into orbit. They didn't believe me. They thought the reporters had gone out of control. I told the editors to look at TV. The TV cameras were beginning to focus on the streets. Finally most of Lukas' story was published, but only a couple of paragraphs of Kenworthy. "We don't want to influence the convention balloting" was the excuse.

I knew it was hard for anyone to get the feel of Chicago that night, anyone who did not smell the teargas and vomit in the Hilton halls, who did not hear the crack of walnut sticks on skulls, who did not see the blood-stained carpets, who did not witness the police frog-walking people out of the hotel and into patrol wagons, flailing unfortunate youngsters, male or female, who appeared on the scene; you had to see the face of Mayor Daley, sitting in the front row of the Convention, mouthing "you son of a bitch" as Senator Abraham Ribicoff of Connecticut tried to remonstrate from the podium against the hatred loosed on Chicago that night by Daley and his men.

The gap between hot reality in Chicago and the cool of the air-conditioned offices in New York was wide as an ocean. A news analysis that Lukas wrote of the "blundering" of Daley and the "brutality of his blue-helmeted police" said Daley and his police had turned certain defeat for the young radicals into a startling victory. This language was too blunt for New York. "Blundering" became "miscalculation" and "Brutality" became "overreaction".

Nowhere in the *Times* the next morning was the true tragedy of Chicago delineated, the hideous blow to American democracy inflicted by Daley's truculence and the abandon of the young; the tawdry tainting of the nomination so grudgingly released by LBJ to hapless Hubert Horatio Humphrey. Nor did we catch the melodrama of LBJ's last hurrah, setting the stage for the triumph of Richard Nixon. I left Chicago convinced that LBJ was a "mean man." And I felt that I and my *New York Times* had fallen far short of our capability to present to the country a sharp-edge, unshadowed picture of Chicago.

On a spring day in 1983 I found myself in Austin, Texas. I visited the grand citadel that is the LBJ Library at the campus of the University of Texas, full of purring computers, white limestone vistas, corridors of power, dazzling splashes of boxcar glass, file upon file of LBJ papers (many security-classified into the next century), soft-spoken, efficient staff, memorabilia of LBJ's achievements—LBJ's dream of greatness set eternally in steel and concrete, microfiche, and computer software. I saw the LBJ ranch, neater than a pin, a middle-class heaven of split-level rooms with appropriate historic and not-so-historic rocking chairs and brass replicas, a long neat porch, and a grand cookout pit.

LBJ left nothing to chance. He signed off on his image of himself, an imperial image, before he died.

I got into the car and drove southwest across the landscape of plains without end, the air fragrant with the scent of a waving sea of Texas bluebonnets, spikey purplish bluebonnets, here and there fields of yellow and orange-red Indian paint and along the shoulders of the concrete highway the bountiful wildflowers sown by orders of Ladybird, whose signature on earth is "Highway Beautification."

Southwest I went to San Marcos, now a university, once LBJ's barren teachers' college, all classes given in Old Main, still standing. Old Main and a boardinghouse in the "German" style (palpably Victorian, bay windows, gingerbread, a stained glass staircase window, crotchety nooks, and enormous dining room) are the remnants of LBJ's day. I could see LBJ and the skinny Texas kids gulping down their food in the dining room—finished in five minutes, not a bean left in the pot, still hungry, gurgling thin, thin coffee from white crockery mugs, then off and away, to hit some books, evening jobs, a walk in the wallows with an arm around a skinny girl. Here, LBJ legend says, the future President ate and slept. But like all LBJ legends it is only half-fact. Most of the time he wasn't there. Where he slept, who got him his meals—well, no one now remembers or wants to remember, whether giggly girls or generous older ladies.

LBJ wasn't proud of Southwest Texas State University. It wasn't grand enough for a President's legacy. There is only one room dedicated to LBJ, mostly blown-up photographs from the White House, publicity spares. Not even a copy of the school paper, which he edited. Nothing in the paper but football, the contemporary editor, a feisty girl tells me. She looked it up. He was something, she says, a faraway look in her eyes. Once a young soldier pointed out his (LBJ's) helicopter in a row of pads. "Son," said LBJ, "they's *all* mine."

San Marcos wanted the LBJ Library. Fat chance. But LBJ haunts San Marcos. When he came back to Texas, Chicago behind him, the war behind him, Richard Nixon in the White House, Lyndon came back to San Marcos. He came back to teach the same skinny West Texas kids he had been himself. Once a week he came, gaunt, a little ill-at-ease, hunkering his long, disjointed frame over a schoolmaster's lectern, talking to them as if he was talking to his own image in a human mirror, talking, talking, talking until his words ran out of the big West Texas ears. There wasn't time enough to tell them everything. But he tried.

A week before the heart attack, someone snapped a shot of Ladybird and Lyndon, there at San Marcos. They look very happy. Lyndon had let his hair grow like that of those kids Daley's police beat down in Chicago. It grew in long sideburns and bushed out at the back of his head over his scrawny neck and the collar of his shirt. It is a picture that burns your eyes. A little hard to make out the long hair now—Ladybird hated it and had it retouched before the picture went up on the wall—but beneath the gray protoplasm of the brushwork you can see Lyndon's hair, as long and fuzzy as that of the kids who ended his last dream of glory.

I stared at the picture a long time. Then I went out and drove west toward the rise of land that erupts just west of San Marcos, the Hill Country where the Johnsons settled in the last century and where Lyndon grew up and lived before he came to San Marcos to learn how to be a schoolteacher, that strange plateau that rises on a line drawn by a ruler, up from the plain with its bluebonnets, waterless and windy, covered with scrub oak, twisted and gnarled, cactus, desert plants, gray-green, lifeless, too dry for the plow, too gray for cattle, the shimmering plateau where Lyndon Baines Johnson was born, the sun-blazed country where the lean boy's ambition was fed, the spirit which took this bag-of-bones youngster from threadbare farm to fame and fortune (a lot of fortune safeguarded and nourished by Ladybird), from zero altitude to the heights and which bred in him the envy, greed, drive, cunning, meanness, and ultimate humanity which turned his life into a comet.

I stared out at the endless hills, the endless gray, the glare of the sun, and then got back in the car. I felt better about Lyndon Johnson now. I knew where he came from, and looking at that sad and solemn picture of long-haired Lyndon and Ladybird, I thought I knew now where he finally went.

19 | An Inscrutable Mark

The first talk I had with Richard Milhous Nixon was on the cutting floor of the Degtyarsk copper mine in the Urals, 800 feet below the surface of the earth. The date was July 30, 1959, a hot day. The temperature on the surface was a humid 80 degrees; at the cutting face we were damp and chilly in our miners' clothes. I had watched Mr. Nixon take off his dark-blue summer-worsted business suit, his white Ban-Lon shirt and his black oxfords and don two-piece cotton longies with drawstrings at the ankles, heavy wool shirt, wool miner's breeches, knee-length rubber boots, mustard-colored jacket and miner's helmet with lamp and neckcloth. I was dressed the same. So were the thirty or forty officials, Secret Service, and Soviet security men.

We plunged down in the elevator cage to the 800-foot level and sloshed a half-mile to the face. "This may be the shortest way to California," Nixon said gloomily. It didn't sound like a joke.

At the pit face two miners shut off their screaming air drills and asked Nixon questions about nuclear arms. They had been put up to it, but the Vice President didn't mind. He cheered up, had a good chat, and started briskly on the long walk back.

"These men are fine fellows," he exclaimed. He meant it. "Boy, I'm telling you this is hard work. These miners earn their pay." He went on in a thoughtful tone (I was the pool reporter for the mine trip.) He had met Nikita Khrushchev in Moscow a few days earlier. Khrushchev had been a miner in the Donbas. He had grown up working in British and French-owned mines, had been treated badly, with twelve-hour workdays. That had an effect on a man's character, Nixon said. It made him tough and determined—but not necessarily a Communist. A man had to be tough to survive, and you must keep this in mind when you were dealing with someone like Khrushchev. We got into the electric lift and were whizzed back up. Nixon blinked in the sunlight, glanced about, and said: "We look like men from Mars." Then he headed for the changing room.

I had never seen Nixon before I met him in Moscow in July

1959. I had been abroad during his trademark moments—the Checkers speech, the Alger Hiss affair, Helen Gahagan Douglas. I didn't expect to like Nixon, but he was not the banal red-baiter I had expected.

It would be seven years before I understood what lay behind Nixon's ruminations about Khrushchev's toughness and hard work as a miner. The morning after he got to Moscow, Nixon went to the Kremlin for a courtesy call on Khrushchev. Two or three other reporters and I waited outside on the marble stoop of the Great Kremlin Palace for nearly an hour before he emerged. If I had known him, perhaps I could have guessed from his clenched lips, dark and stormy face, that something unusual (and newsworthy) had happened.

It was December 1966 before I heard the story. No Russian in 1959 was prepared to think anything good of Nixon, and Khrushchev was not an exception. He opened up by telling Nixon that he knew all about him—he was the enemy of the Soviet Union, the enemy of Communism, the white knight of Capitalism.

Nixon conceded that he didn't like Communism but as for Capitalism, well, he had grown up a poor boy, working in a small orchard, doing all the chores. Khrushchev snorted. He, Khrushchev, had grown up the poorest of the poor. He had walked barefoot. He had had no shoes. He had shoveled shit to earn a few kopeks. Nixon shot back that he'd been poor and barefoot, too—and had shoveled shit.

What kind of shit? Khrushchev demanded. Horseshit, Nixon said. That's nothing Khrushchev replied. He had shoveled cow shit—loose, runny, stinking cow dung. It got between your toes. I too shoveled cow shit, Nixon said tightly.

Well, Khrushchev grumbled, maybe Nixon had shoveled cow shit once or twice, but he, Khrushchev, had shoveled human shit. That was the worst. Nixon couldn't top that. He came out of the Kremlin in an angry trance. If this was the way Khrushchev started, how would he finish the visit?

That afternoon Nixon escorted Khrushchev through the opening of the first American exhibition in Moscow and engaged him in the famous Kitchen Debate. Later this was portrayed as an angry, chest-thumping confrontation. Actually it was a remarkably able presentation by each man of his viewpoint. I was probably the only American reporter who heard it all. I spoke and understood Russian (so I got everything Khrushchev said), and Bill Safire, who was the PR man for the kitchen display, lifted a velvet rope so I could slip into the kitchen and sit on the floor at the feet of the great men while they argued their cases for Capitalism and Communism.

I was surprised at how well Nixon handled himself and more surprised years later to hear that he went home with American Ambassador Llewelyn Thompson, whose guest he was at Spaso House, and got sloshed because he thought he had been a bust. Actually, he almost beat John F. Kennedy in 1960 with the face-to-face picture showing him punching a forefinger in Khrushchev's face to drive home a point. It became the icon of the Nixon age.

Soon I got to know Nixon quite well. Political figures have always fascinated me. No one is compelled to lead his life so publicly. Who else but Nixon would get down to his skivvies with a bunch of reporters hanging around, taking in every detail? Or like Lyndon Johnson waving his visitors into the bathroom with him as he squatted on the john? Or, like Huey Long, carrying on an interview as he toweled his rosy pot belly, stepping out of a shower? There's not much the observant reporter doesn't note about the pol he is covering. We are such magpies, our eyes darting to the frayed collar, the missing button, the hole in the shoe, a guilty look, flushes of anger, Freudian slips. If you cover a Presidential candidate day and night, you know him as an English valet knew his master, maybe better. You know his turn of speech, his inflections.

By a perverse fortune I came to know Nixon as I knew no other President, not all at once, but bit by bit and year by year, out of office, in office, the glory, the disgrace. On this Russian trip I gave him high marks. Khrushchev was not a patsy, and Nixon held his own, toe to toe. Nixon was a hit with the Russians. I came to think, as time went by, that Khrushchev could have been a successful politician in Iowa (after his visit there). Nixon could have won plenty of votes in Russia (if they had free elections). He is so nice, he is so handsome, he is so young, he is so American, he has such a marvelous smile. Nixon didn't get these raves in the U.S.A., but I heard all these remarks in the crowds that turned out for him from Moscow to Sverdlovsk. Those crowds bothered Khrushchev's cronies, especially the police. They sent goons out to heckle Nixon with unpleasant questions. At first Nixon was embarrassed, but he quickly sensed that the people were with him. They tried to shush the interrogators. "Why are you so rude?" "Shut up, he is our guest." "Give him a chance." So Nixon began to respond: "I'm glad you asked that question." And was off to the races. The police pulled the goons off after a couple of days. Nixon was scoring all the points.

When I traveled with Nixon on his 1960 campaign, I found he was a lot better in Russia than in the U.S.A. At home the crowds tensed him up. I watched him ball his fists, set his jaw, and hurl himself stiff-legged to the barriers at the airports and begin shaking hands. He was wound up like a watch spring, steeling himself for the ordeal. No ease. But in Russia he was self-confident, cool, enjoying himself and his audience.

Very curious. But there were a lot of curious things about Nixon. As time went by, I became convinced that he was the most interesting President of my time—puzzling, enigmatic, conflictive. I could spend a lifetime and not understand him.

In the spring of 1960, I bumped into a man at a dinner party, a Wall Street man, who told me that he had served with Nixon in New Caledonia in the South Pacific, where, as I knew, Nixon was attached to a naval supply base. "Nick ran a twenty-four hour poker game there," the man said. He was the only one I ever met who called Nixon "Nick." Nixon, he said, was a hell of a good poker player, but made his money running the all-night game, taking a cut out of every pot. A very smart fellow, the Wall Streeter said.

"Say," he said, suddenly, "is Nick still seeing that shrink of his in New York?" I hadn't a clue. Had never heard of a shrink. Much later, after Nixon entered the White House, I learned that for many years he had been seeing Dr. Arnold A. Hutsnecker, an internist by specialty but a doctor who numbered a good many high-tension men among his patients, men who possessed emotional and psychological problems.

At the moment of our talks, said the Wall Street man, "Nick has gone into his shell," and people were trying to get him out of it. Nixon, I gathered, had severe ups and downs, and it was not easy to pull him up when he fell into depression.

During his fall campaign against Kennedy, Nixon suddenly left the trail, came into New York, holed up in the Waldorf, and we didn't see him for a week. Perhaps, I thought, he had "gone into his shell."

I learned a great deal about Nixon when I found myself in 1983 holding the Richard M. Nixon chair at his alma mater, Whittier College, a small Quaker institution landlocked in East Los Angeles—an island of the 1900s where Nixon got his degree, where he met Pat, his wife, and where he began to display those traits which were to mark his adult career. Whittier doesn't change much—the same buildings, the same stores, the same sun-baked bungalows under the palms, survivors who knew Nixon in his campus years. There were still cousins and aunts around, and I talked with them. Some remembered and cherished the poor Quaker Nixon boy, with a determined mother, a ne'er-do-well father, and a brother who died of TB, money scarce as hen's teeth. Nixon worked hard. He was ambitious, and his mother was ambitious for him. He didn't like his father, probably he hated him. He adored his mother (he broke into tears when he mentioned her in his farewell speech to the White House staff as he left to go back to San Clemente).

Whittier had a small collection of Nixon memorabilia, which had been shipped out when the Nixons left the White House. It was kept in a locked room on the fourth floor of the library. You had to have permission and be admitted with a special key to see it. I saw it. Not much there—leftover gifts made to the Nixons by Arab sheikhs and African presidents. Hard to see why it had been sent. Not so hard to understand why it was locked up. Not everyone in Whittier was proud of Nixon, and the administration thought it better not to have the things on public display.

It seemed to me then (and now) that Whittier was the place for the Nixon Library (just as I thought Johnson's should be at San Marcos). Whittier had a real place in Nixon's life, both the college and the town. He had lived there and started his law practice there. It was small and reflected the aura of his early years, so poor, so ambitious, so envious of those more fortunate. On the campaign trail, I heard him tell, over and over, the story of his brother who had died of TB. His brother had always wanted a pony and died with his wish unfulfilled. Some richer kids were lucky. They had ponies. It was clear he was thinking of Jack Kennedy. It was also clear that Richard Nixon had coveted a pony and still felt cheated. I could understand the pony bit. I don't know how many contests I entered as a kid, hoping to win a pony. I never did.

I tried to persuade Whittier (and Nixon) that his library should go there. I found reluctance on both sides. To put a Presidential library in the tiny college would change it beyond recognition, and Nixon, a bit like Johnson, didn't think Whittier was grand enough. Yes, there was a good place for the library up on the hill—but what about parking? And could the money be raised for Whittier? Nixon seemed to doubt it. He mentioned the University of Southern California and Stanford. Both wanted it. I was sure he favored a bigger institution or his own site, his own place (San Clemente). I argued that Whittier had emotional and personal associations, a setting that would allow the visitor to understand what Nixon was about and where he came from. That didn't move him, and later I wondered whether the real objection to Whittier was that it told too much about Nixon, just as, perhaps, San Marcos told too much about Johnson.

Nixon had forgotten that FDR's library was at Hyde Park— a perfect place, he said. Where was Jack Kennedy's? Ah, Boston, well, that was right for Jack. I believe he still didn't think he could match the Kennedys, just as I believe he had felt he couldn't beat Jack in 1960. I remember talking with him after the first debates. He told how they had roiled his being, both before and after, so disturbing. "Of course, it's not that way for Jack," he said. A moment later he caught the implication of what he had said and lamely tried to cover it. He couldn't. Jack had put the whammy on him, and I think that made the difference in their close election, in which a switch of 20,000 or 30,000 votes would have changed the outcome.

Years later, I asked John Ehrlichman what could have put Nixon onto the path that led to the Plumbers, the Ellsberg affair, Gemstone, the Watergate break-in, the whole escalating mess.

"It was the Kennedy fixation," John said. "He never got over Jack and Bobby, and he was sure Teddy would do him in in 1972." There was something about Nixon and the Kennedys. Not rational.

Not rational. That, I came to understand, was the key. This was not unusual in politicians of intensity. Lyndon Johnson had displayed similar traits. There is a strain of paranoia in most ambitious men, and no one is more ambitious than a Presidential candidate. Lyndon possessed it, even Carter. (Reagan seems to be an exception, so possibly was Truman.)

I saw nothing of Nixon in his White House years. The line was drawn very strictly against press, old or new. I did, however, make the acquaintence of a man who knew him well and had observed him with insight since the Checkers days or even before. There was, he felt, something unusual about Nixon, a Dr. Jekyll and Mr. Hyde quality. On personal terms he often was very warm, very sensitive, very thoughtful. People who worked for him liked him. He had a good mind, and he knew the world better than any President since FDR. He had an instinct for politics and what would appeal to the country. That was the good Nixon.

But there was a bad Nixon, almost like the Herblock cartoons in *The Washington Post.* Nixon once told me he kept the paper out of the house so his girls wouldn't see Herblock. This was the Nixon who turned on reporters on the morning of his defeat for the California governorship and shouted: "You won't have Nixon to kick around any more." This was the Nixon of the dark Watergate stories, the man of obscenities that demeaned himself and his office, of the trip to the Capitol before dawn with his valet, Manuel, asking him to address the empty chamber and commenting, "I don't think that got over very well," the Nixon who pulled Kissinger to his knees in the Lincoln study of the White House to pray with him, who roved the White House at 3 A.M., talking to the portraits on the walls, and, quite possibly, the Nixon of the murderous Cambodian "incursion" and the Christmas bombing of Hanoi. Nixon's old associate suggested to me that Cambodia and the Christmas bombing might have been triggered by a compulsive need to prove his manhood.

But the President was also a man of privacy, a very private man, not at all like a Johnson or a Roosevelt who lived "by pressing the flesh" of supporters, men who like Antaeus lost their strength when cut off from their roots. Nor was Nixon like Kennedy or Nelson Rockefeller or Warren G. Harding or so many political men, possessed of a sex drive that propelled them from one bed to another. Nixon was not like that at all. He abhorred the arm-around-the-shoulder gesture (when he did it for campaign pictures he looked stiff as cardboard). He was no good at a Latino abrazo or the garlicky kiss of a French politician. Pictures of Dick and Pat in hugs or kisses are rare.

I came to share my friend's conviction that the Nixon mood

swings were rooted in childhood adoration of his mother and rejection of his father. He spurred himself to achievement to meet his mother's goals. He underlined his father's failures with his successes. But his methods! He liked to tell how hard he worked to help his mother make ends meet. But he never spoke of running away with a carnival to Prescott, Arizona, to be a barker at the Slippery Gulch Rodeo for a wheel of chance—*gambling*. Nor did he talk of his poker games in the South Pacific. *Gambling.* Nor of the tricks and trades and deals of politics. *Lying.* He rose in the world of politics. But he rose by methods that violated the morals of the hard-rock Quaker faith of his mother. She was not a pacifist Quaker, nor was her son. These were "fighting Quakes," transplanted from Indiana to Southern California about the turn of the century. But—and this was the point— these were very moral Quakers. They did not *gamble*. They did not *lie*. They did not *cheat*. They did not *drink*. They did not *swear*. They were honorable men and women in a world of sin.

From the day I met Nixon (and long before) he was a man laden with guilt. When I heard the good Quakers of Whittier talk about his mother, I understood a lot about him. There was hardly one of his mother's principles which he had not violated time and again. Did he tell his mother how he was earning a dollar an hour at the Slippery Gulch Rodeo? Did he tell her about the twenty-four hour poker game? Did he tell her of the cheats by which he won and held political office? Had there ever been so hopeless a conflict? Was it a wonder that he blurted out in Watergate days: "I'm not a crook!" But, of course, he was arguing with the shadow of his mother, an argument he could never win. No wonder he roved the corridors of the White House after midnight, seeking the support of the glossily varnished, dark-painted Presidents on the walls. No wonder he kept his tapes. The quick answer had been that he hoped to make a lot of bucks with tax write-offs when he turned the tapes over to the Nixon Library. I think the answer was very complex. In some twisted way he thought of them as his ultimate justification. If only his mother could listen, she would understand.

Oh, I suppose that sounds like windy sentimentalism, but it is not all sentiment, and I think it explains, in part, at least, the inexplicable—how so shrewd, intelligent, crafty a man could so entrap himself, make it certain that he would be punished, spin a web with devilish care, as only he could have done, a web beyond the capability of Ehrlichman and Haldeman, John Mitchell, and his adoringly faithful Rose Wood. Only Nixon could contrive it—the ultimate revenge of Mr. Hyde on Dr. Jekyll, or perhaps the other way around.

Late in 1974 after Nixon had retired to San Clemente, after the furor of Watergate had begun to die away, Nixon fell ill, desperately ill, close to death. His old friend believed Nixon wanted to die. The mood shift had occurred. Now he was "in the shell" of despondency. He understood what he had wrought; he saw no way out, nothing for which to live; guilt filled his veins like poison; he had betrayed the mother whom he idolized; he had failed her worse than his father. It was a tragedy from the Greeks.

But unlike Aeschylus, the Nixon tragedy did not end on a neat emotionally fulfilling note. Nixon did not die. Gradually, nourished by the faith of his wife and his daughters, he fought his way back. It was not easy. His loyal friends in Southern California, and their number included Ronald Reagan then governor, did their best to help. They had him to dinner. They invited him out of his den of despond. They tried to lessen his dependence on alcohol (a problem before, during, and after Watergate).

It took time. But it worked. Once again the Nixons pulled up stakes. They came east to New York. Bought a town house on 65th Street, back to back with Arthur Schlesinger, Jr., on 64th. Bought an estate at Saddle River, New Jersey. I began to see him after a ten-year break. Our last talk had been on an airplane flying from Indianapolis to Cleveland, September 13, 1968. The campaign against Hubert Humphrey was at cruising altitude, Nixon's election was certain.

It was an easy, reflective, relaxed Nixon who invited me up front to chat about foreign policy. He wanted to share his thoughts on Russia and China and match his views against mine. Prague had just happened—the Soviet tanks bringing to an end the brief Czech "spring." He was sorry about Czechoslovakia. He had hoped to get to Moscow before the campaign—if he had gone in August maybe this wouldn't have occurred. Anyway, Prague or no Prague, we had to negotiate. No question about that in his mind, but there must be consistency and better State

Department planning. It should be done at State, not the White House, and Defense had to be in on it.

When he took office (he had no doubt that he would, nor did I), the first task was to end the war in Vietnam. Otherwise it would paralyze him on foreign and domestic policy. It would become "Nixon's war" as Mel Laird, Nixon's defense secretary-designate, told me in January 1969. The war had to be ended, or it would hang over everything else and damage the whole Nixon program.

The Middle East was *the* danger spot—much worse than Vietnam—the only place where surrogates might drag the U.S. and U.S.S.R. into war against their will.

To negotiate with the Russians, we had to have all the strength we could muster. First, he would go to Europe and get De Gaulle, England, and Germany back on line. LBJ had neglected them. The alliance was a shambles. Next China. He knew exactly how dangerous the Russo-Chinese situation was. He would move on China as soon as possible. He would make the China opening as soon as he had taken care of a few other things—like Vietnam.

Nixon followed that plan—except for Vietnam. Why did it take him five years to sign a peace with Hanoi? I don't know. There is no clue in Nixon's memoirs or those of Kissinger. None in the studies I have seen.

When Nixon told me of his program, he had never laid eyes on Kissinger. That would not come until after the November election when John Mitchell, responding to a suggestion by Nelson Rockefeller (for whom Kissinger was a consultant), met Henry and introduced him to Nixon. The foreign policy was Nixon's, not Kissinger's as so many came to believe.

Did Henry persuade Nixon to go slow on Vietnam, urge delaying tactics, which ultimately strung out to 1973, the Cambodia incursion, and the Christmas bombing? I do not know, and I have not been able to find out. I do know that Kissinger in October–November 1972 negotiated in Paris a good settlement with Hanoi—indeed, the identical, almost word-for-word, settlement we agreed to in the winter of 1973. That autumn Ehrlichman and Haldeman were trying to destroy Kissinger, end his White House influence. They torpedoed the Vietnam settlement and opened the tragic path to the Christmas bombing. But who delayed the process in 1969, 1970, 1971, and 1972? Was it Kissinger or did Nixon for reasons not known (the Dr. Jekyll and Mr. Hyde effect?) scuttle his sensible intentions outlined on the plane September 13, 1968? When all Nixon's tapes are at long last placed in the public domain, we may find the answer—but somehow I doubt it will ever all be spelled out.

In the talks which I began with Nixon a decade after his airplane tour de horizon of 1968, the President exhibited the same perceptive, knowledgeable understanding which had characterized his early talks. Over the years he had written repeatedly on world affairs. He had continued to travel to critical areas, especially China, and to meet with important leaders.

He was—and would be always—properly proud of the opening to China and détente with Russia. While often cloaking his statements in vulgar language (profanity in private), he displayed a keen sense of world power. He wrote a book called *Real War* and matched it with one called *Real Peace,* admitting for possibly the first time that "it's the Quaker in me—but that's not a bad thing."

He was campaigning almost self-consciously for the role of American elder statesman. He wanted Watergate off his neck. His greatest disappointment was inflicted by Ronald Reagan and his men, who made plain they did not want or need his advice. He was compelled to stand by while the White House worked to dismantle the system of Great Power balance Nixon had, with Kissinger's help, even in the worst Watergate days, put into place.

The real irony came when Reagan, entrapped in the Iran-Contra scam, telephoned Nixon for advice. Reagan had succeeded in making Watergate look like a teenage prank.

China—that was Nixon's pride. When he spoke of China, I could not drive from my mind the memory of the Joe McCarthyite lynchings, which destroyed the lives and careers of our extraordinary corps of Old China Hands and of Nixon's role in it.

Now Nixon and Kissinger called on the survivors for aid. They sought out Edgar Snow, who had written *Red Star over China.* The wheel took a full turn but, alas, Ed Snow was to die of cancer in Switzerland on the eve of Nixon's takeoff for his meeting with Mao Zedong and Zhou Enlai.

There was irony, indeed. But, out of it all came what Nixon

properly considered the great monument to his Presidency—a new era in U.S.-China relations.

In 1984 I dined with Hu Yaobang, then general secretary of China's Communist Party, in his residence in the Zhongnanhai compound of the Forbidden City. We talked of Nixon. Hu was an admirer, thought him the best of our post-World War II Presidents. Hu and Nixon corresponded regularly, and Nixon sent Hu his books as they appeared. Hu had them translated, read them, wrote Nixon his comments. It was an extraordinary circumstance—Hu Yaobang, heading the world's largest Communist Party, a regular correspondent of Richard Nixon, the staunchest foe of Communism in the United States.

But, to me, it did not seem strange. It seemed natural. Nixon knew what he was talking about in China. Years before I had chided the late Premier Zhou Enlai a bit about China's relationship with Nixon. Not all Americans, I told him, were fond of Mr. Nixon. Zhou reproved me. "I don't care what he has done in the United States domestically," said Zhou. "We value him. He has been right about China."

And so he had. But still the questions trailed across my mind, not least now that Hu Yaobang, Nixon's Chinese correspondent, was no longer general secretary but had, like Nixon, been retired from his office before his term. Did the two men still write back and forth between New York and Beijing? I wondered. I wondered, too, what each man really thought of the other and of the world on which each has left a somewhat inscrutable mark.

20 | "The Meanest Queen"

When at long last in 1972 I arrived in China, Premier Zhou Enlai offered me an apology. "I'm sorry that we could not receive you earlier," he said, "but you are known as such a leading anti-Soviet champion, we were afraid it might upset our relations with Moscow."

I thanked him, but I knew that this was persiflage from a very sophisticated diplomat, the most skilled of our time, so thought Henry Kissinger. I agreed.

There was a nub of truth in what Zhou Enlai said, but he had no way of knowing that by my own reckoning I was more than forty years behind in getting to China. The delays (until the last years) had all been on my side, not the Chinese.

Two months after Black Friday in October, 1929, having no notion of what lay ahead, I wrote a Christmas letter to my Aunt Sue in New York, December 20, 1929, in which I informed her that, when I graduated from Minnesota in June, "I'm pretty much sold on the idea of getting a China or Japan job." Whatever happened, I added, "I won't be sticking around in Minneapolis."

I had China on my mind and had had since childhood. As a seven- or eight-year-old, hand in my mother's, I walked up Royalston Avenue, the Victorian street on which we lived, around past the livery stable with its smell of horses, over the small railroad bridge beside the red-brick firehouse my grandfather had built, and turned into Western Avenue at the Home Trade Shoe Store (I still have the well-oiled English hiking boots my father bought me there as a high school graduation gift), and up Western to the Chinaman's shop. I was a little afraid of the shop, but I was afraid to say I was afraid. It was a hole in the wall, the window filled with curious objects, jute-covered boxes, marked with bold black-painted Chinese characters, reddish fruits I had never seen before (litchi nuts), tin canisters splashed with labels in red and green (tea), festoons of garlic and long black strands which I believed were dried rat tails, tied end to end.

The store exuded scents that overwhelmed my adenoidal nostrils—tea, sandalwood, incense, spices. To the rear under a dangling naked bulb sat three Chinese, old, wrinkled, yellow, eyes narrow, heavy-lidded, on small stools around a low teakwood table playing fan-tan. They smoked long pipes. Opium, I was sure. Skeins of noodles draped from the beams. There were stacks of blue porcelain bowls, huge Sinbad jars, and bundles of chopsticks.

A bell tinkled faintly when we entered, and a man put down his cards and shuffled up behind the counter, his slippers going slap, slap, slap. I can still hear the shuffle of slippers on the scuffed floor. He came up opposite my mother, a flowery hat on her head, hands in white kid gloves, carrying a small petit-point purse.

For my childhood years the Chinaman's shop *was* China, a place of mystery, romance, excitement—exotic, a world which drew me like a magnet, so different from plain flat Minnesota. I had to see it.

At the Chinaman's shop mother bought candied ginger (too hot for my small tongue—my father loved it), candied kumquats in small blue-green earthenware pots tied with rattan, shredded coconut, bleached almonds, crystalized lilac and violet blossoms (only pinches, they were so expensive). Mother loved the dainty sugared blossoms. I could not wait for the next visit to the shop, but when I entered, timorous as a foal, I could hardly keep from running back into the sunshine.

There was another bit of China in the attic of 107 Royalston in my father's curio case—a bamboo opium pipe with silver mouthpiece, a pair of tiny red-and-green embroidered shoes (for a long time I thought they were the shoes of a Chinese lady whose feet had been bound), and a small cabinet of ebony and mother-of-pearl with tiny drawers and secret compartments. For years I hoped I might find a pigeon-blood ruby or a rare pearl in a hidden compartment, but I never did. This was the China of my youth, and my imagination grazed over it endlessly, so endlessly that when I entered the writing seminar at the university, my first sketch was about the Chinaman and his shop.

A man called Jefferson Jones on the old *Minneapolis Journal,* where I began to work as a cub reporter in 1927, steered my China dream into more practical channels. He had traveled in the Orient and was a good friend of J. V. Fleisher, publisher of the

Japan Advertiser of Tokyo. In the 1920s and early 1930s there were English language papers scattered up and down the Pacific rim, one or more in every city—Tientsin, Peking, Shanghai, Canton, Hankow, Swatow, Hong Kong, Kobe, Tokyo. Each year Fleisher, a graduate of the University of Missouri, came back to the United States to pick out a Missouri journalism graduate for his paper and to come to Minnesota for a checkup at the Mayo Clinic and a visit with his friend, Jeff Jones.

Jones promised that, when Fleisher made his trip in the spring of 1930, he would try to get him to pick me for Tokyo. I was in seventh heaven. My best friend, Gordon Roth, had just come back from the China coast. He had ridden the rods to Seattle, worked his passage to China on a freighter, jumped ship, spent half a year in Shanghai, and returned to the girl whom he had secretly married before leaving. Very romantic. I was ready to follow him to the far Pacific (I had no secret bride to return to).

It didn't work out. In 1930, probably because of the depression, Fleisher didn't come back. I had been tossed out of school for being an uppity student editor and was hard at work as a full-time reporter for United Press. Jobs were too precious to abandon for a gamble on the China coast. I told myself not to worry. I'd get to China with UP. The United Press was run by an elegant man called Karl Bickel, the first I ever knew who wore spats (pearl-gray), fawn-colored pigskin gloves, and a homburg. He carried a malacca stick, and there were twenties and fifties in his alligator wallet. I don't believe I had ever seen a fifty-dollar bill before.

Bickel was much at home in countries like Russia and China. He knew Karl Radek and possibly Bukharin in Moscow and Chiang Kai-shek, Madame Chiang, T. V. Soong, the editor J. B. Powell, and the warlord Chang Tso-lin in China. I told Bickel I wanted to go to the Far East, and he promised I would get there. As a starter he sent me to Banff, Alberta, in the summer of 1933 to cover a meeting of the Institute of Pacific Relations. There I met Hu Shih, China's leading poet, the first to write in the vernacular, a supporter of Dr. Sun Yat-sen and later Chiang's ambassador to Washington, and Henry Luce, a very young Henry Luce, with his young first wife (not yet married to Clare Booth), their toddling son (today he is Henry Luce II and middle-aged), and Henry Luce's father, the China missionary. I had long talks with the elder Luce. He knew everything about China, I thought. Hu Shih gave me a slim thin-paper, blue-covered collection of poems. It is still on my shelf. Later Senator Joe McCarthy was to attack the institute as a nest of Communists, but in those days it was all establishment. Newton D. Baker, Woodrow Wilson's secretary of war and general counsel of Scripps-Howard, which owned UP, was elected its president at Banff. Hu Shih and Henry Luce fired my imagination. But Bickel didn't get me to China. In a few months UP had sent me to Washington, and World War II took me to London, North Africa, the Middle East, and Moscow. I was as far away from China as I had been in Minneapolis.

China was my destination, but I seemed to have taken a very slow boat. Finally, Earl Johnson, UP news chief, decided to dispatch me from Moscow to Chongqing. Even that didn't work. As I waited in Calcutta to fly the Hump to China, Johnson ordered me back to New York to become UP's foreign editor.

In Moscow I had met Edgar Snow, author of *Red Star over China,* and we became good friends. I had read *Red Star,* and it had given shape to my ambition to go to China, of which I knew very little. I had taken the only course at Minnesota which touched on China (no language instruction in those days)—Far Eastern Diplomacy. It dealt with John Hay, the Open Door Policy, Commodore Perry, and Japan, not with contemporary China. I knew nothing of the Chinese Communist movement until I read Snow. There I heard for the first time of Mao Zedong, Zhou Enlai, Zhu De; there I heard for the first time of the Long March of China's Red Army, an event that would make a mark on my distant future.

Ed and I and Archibald Clark Kerr, the British ambassador who had come to Moscow from Chongqing, talked a lot. They believed Chongqing a more exciting place than Moscow. I accepted their opinion.

One hot July afternoon in 1944 I returned to Moscow from a long trip to Siberia and Central Asia and found the British correspondent, Alec Werth, giving a party for two new arrivals, Ella Winter, the English widow of Lincoln Steffens (she had married him very late in his life and very early in hers) and Anna Louise Strong.

I had heard of Anna Louise for years, a formidable figure, well over six feet tall, sturdily built, strong shoulders, great bosom, tower of gray hair piled up and up, piercing blue eyes, and a gruff voice that carried long distances in the open and resonated within walls. She talked like a drillmaster and possessed many of the human traits I most disliked. She was opinionated, domineering, a nonstop talker, had only the faintest interest in what others said, scorned inferiors (she placed most of the world in that category), dogmatic, what I called a "shouting Marxist" (she knew nothing of Marxist theory), anti-American, pro-Soviet, pro-Chinese, hostile to "capitalist journalists" like myself.

For some perverse reason I liked her instantly. Perhaps she reminded me of an equally statuesque woman, Dr. Anna Von Helmholtz Phelan, who conducted my writing seminar at Minnesota. They were of a size. In each I detected behind an awesome exterior a vulnerable little girl. Anna Louise was a very big little girl, who lived her life in a world of titans. Her total naïveté came close to destroying her and, I fear, many friends and associates, including her old, close, and loyal friend, Mikhail Borodin.

On that hot July day in Werth's big room, I had no premonition of what might lie ahead for Anna Louise and her friend Borodin. My romantic image of them and many others whom I would come to know—or know about—was drawn from the pages of Vincent Sheean's *Personal History,* which I had gulped down (like tens of thousands of Americans) when it appeared in 1935. There I read of the failed 1927 Chinese Revolution, there I read of Anna Louise and Borodin, the Russian agent sent by Moscow to superintend the Chinese Revolution; of Soong Ching-ling, widow of Sun Yat-sen; her beautiful sister, Soong Mei-ling, wife of Chiang Kai-shek; of Eugene Chen, the Trinidad-born English barrister who became Dr. Sun's foreign minister although he spoke not a word of Chinese; of Eugene Chen's sons, Percy and Jack; and, of course, of Rayna Prohme, with whom Sheean fell hopelessly in love; and of her husband, Bill, later to die in some mysterious underground revolutionary way in Manila. As I read Sheean's star-crossed pages, I ached with emotion. If only I had been in Shanghai in 1927! I did not meet "Jimmy" Sheean, as he was called, until the last dog-eared days of his life—the romance replaced by gin, sad relic of an era, his revolutionary friends long dead, their revolutions dim in memory, and he, the Beau

Geste of his time, having to be introduced and identified to young
people for whom the name of Rayna Prohme meant less than that
of some faded Hollywood star.

I met Borodin in Moscow, tall (so he seemed to me; the police
blotter gave his height as 5 feet 8 inches), gaunt, silent, sad eyes
that seemed to look past me to some distant horizon which only
he could see. I did not know on the evening when we met, during
an interlude at the Supreme Soviet meeting in the Kremlin in
January 1944, that Borodin's favorite phrase in China had been
"we must take the long view" (especially when all was going
wrong—Chiang Kai-shek turning on the Communists, the Shanghai slaughter, all the other horrors).

I can see him now with these deep-set, hawkish eyes, grim,
nothing genial, nothing warm about him, no small talk, no desire
to be sociable with an ignorant young American correspondent
whose only contribution to the conversation was hero worship.
He was then editor of the Moscow *News,* a clerk's job, and had a
post with the Sovinformburo, a wartime propaganda agency.
Even then he was a survivor, a man who had narrowly edged
past danger after danger but would not, quite possibly because
of the naïveté and loud tongue of Anna Louise, make it past the
next.

I never saw Borodin again. When I returned to Moscow in
1949, he was gone. I had heard on shipboard, en route to my new
post as *New York Times* correspondent, of the arrest, February 7,
1949, of Anna Louise by the KGB in Moscow as an agent of the
CIA. I said to myself: My God! If Anna Louise is being arrested
as an American spy, there isn't much chance for me! When I
arrived in Moscow, I found that Borodin and the entire staff of
the *Moscow News* had also been arrested.

Borodin was not as fortunate as Anna Louise. Not long after
Stalin's death, March 5, 1953, Ralph Parker, correspondent of
the *London Daily Worker,* whispered to me in a shadowy corridor
of the Metropol: "Don't you think Mikhail Borodin deserves an
obituary in *The New York Times?*"

"Of course," said I. I filed a brief dispatch, and to my surprise, the censors passed it. A bit later on a Siberian trip, I saw
the wooden stockade and watchtowers, the barbed wire and the
tommy gunners guarding the prison camp in Yakutsk where, it
was said, Borodin died, May 29, 1951.

There were rumors that the Chinese intervened when Borodin was arrested in February 1949, and that this had saved his life (for a time). I am not certain this is true. The Chinese, as I came to know, did not—or at least Mao and his supporters did not— have a high opinion of Borodin. They blamed his tactics for the failure of the 1927 revolution. But here, I think, they were being too casuistic, because Borodin was, in fact, the agent of Stalin to the revolution. Lenin had agreed to send someone to help Dr. Sun Yat-sen, but Lenin was incapacitated before he could do so. Stalin was the man who picked and sent Borodin to China.

It was Stalin's strategy and Stalin's tactics that Borodin carried out. It was true, as Mao and the others declared, that these tactics led to failure. (Borodin at Stalin's insistence supported Chiang Kai-shek long after Chiang had turned on the Communists.) And it was this which led directly to the debacle at Shanghai, the murderous assault of Chiang and his gangster allies on the Communists and workers, the split in the Nationalist movement, the ultimate collapse of the left wing-Communist government at Hankow, and the emergence of Chiang Kai-shek as heir to Dr. Sun Yat-sen's revolution. Stalin's motive for this suicidal (for the Chinese Communists) strategy? To avoid letting his rival Trotsky expose him as a rotten revolutionary, who had backed the wrong horse (Chiang Kai-shek) in China.

Naturally, I knew nothing of this when I met Borodin and none of it when I met Anna Louise. The Chinese Revolution, like all revolutions, is a puzzle box, and not even the participants necessarily know at all times what is true and what is not true.

When I arrived in Moscow in the winter of 1949 and began cautiously nosing around for information about Anna Louise, I did not realize that my curiosity would forge a link with this revolutionary Juno which would play a role in my long-standing ambition to get to China. Nor that, as I learned more and more of her dramatic and contradictory career, this would open for me long vistas into the world of revolutions, that of Russia and more particularly that of China.

The arrest of Anna Louise was too fresh in people's minds and the atmosphere of Moscow too tense for anyone to discuss freely what had happened.

I had assumed that Anna Louise felt at home in Moscow. She had lived there for a long, long time, had been in and out of

Russia for three decades, she had a Russian husband (I didn't know he had died in World War II, almost certainly in a Stalinist camp) and quite a few in-laws in Moscow. I knew that she made many friends in Moscow, and I knew her as a true child of the romantic American revolutionary mood which had flourished before and during World War I. That was about all I really knew. As time went on, I put more pieces together.

She was the daughter of a well-known American clergyman, a widower who managed to interfere with and distort Anna Louise's relations with men, including a violent love affair with Roger Baldwin, then a handsome young man out of Harvard, later dean of American civil liberties. I knew Anna Louise had played a passionate (whatever she did was passionate) role in the turbulent IWW battles of Seattle before and during World War I.

Anna Louise had come to Russia in the 1920s because Lincoln Steffens had said: "I have been over into the future and it works." (That was a good many years before Ella Winter married Steffens.) Steffens told Anna Louise to go to Moscow, and she did. Anna Louise knew Louise Bryant and John Reed. She was of the generation that came out of the Wobblies, Harvard, and Greenwich Village. There was not a revolutionary cause which this statuesque and beautiful (in those years) woman did not grace.

From Moscow Anna Louise had gone to China. After the fall of Red Hankow and Chiang's violence against Communists and Russians, she made her escape in 1927 with Borodin across north China, into Mongolia and finally on to Russia.

I heard the story much, much later from Percy Chen, then a distinguished man in his upper seventies living out his years in Hong Kong. Percy was the oldest son of Eugene Chen, and he drove Borodin out of China and over the Gobi. As he remembered, Anna Louise swooned over Borodin, then a handsome bold revolutionary (once a Chicago schoolteacher). She sang "Nearer My God to Thee," to Borodin, beside a desert campfire until he dissolved her into tears by shouting: "For God's sake, woman, why don't you sing the Internationale!"

Anna Louise came back to Moscow, settled down in the Metropol along with the Chens, with Borodin, with Madame Soong Chingling and the others. Sooner or later all went their ways, but Anna Louise stayed, joining Borodin in founding the *Moscow*

News, writing sloppy books about Red Russia and Red China, coming back to the U.S.A. every year for lecture tours, praising Communism, living on with blinded eyes and (possibly) clenched teeth as her friends vanished in Stalin's purges. Her books are filled with the names of those who would die. She took a trip to the Pamirs in 1930, and almost everyone she mentioned would soon be dead—her friend Dubenko, a leader in the Bolshevik uprising of November 7, 1917 (shot with Marshal Tukhachevsky in 1937), the geneticist Vavilov (arrested in 1940, died in prison, 1943), Bill Shatov the burly and ebullient American IWW who helped build the Turk-Sib railroad. She sat with Bill Shatov in his private railroad car in 1930, listening to him play on the Victrola his latest record from Tin Pan Alley:

> "She's the meanest Queen
> I've ever seen
> Josephine."

Shatov died seven years later before one of Stalin's execution squads.

There was no way Anna Louise could not have known this.

Anna Louise went to Yan'an in 1946 to sit at the feet of Mao, where she transcribed the essence of Mao's philosophy, his characterization of the atom bomb as a "paper tiger," and his definition of "Chinese Marxism." She put it all in a book called originally *The Thought of Mao Zedong.*

It was the only important book Anna Louise ever wrote, and I suspect she knew it. It declared the independence of Mao and the Chinese Communists from Stalin and his Party line. It was quickly published in the United States and China, and taken for publication in Eastern Europe—but not in Moscow.

She arrived in Moscow in October 1948, en route back to China. She hoped to be in Beijing to witness the Communist takeover.

She told her Moscow friends, as I learned, that it was ridiculous that the Russian and Yugoslav Communists were not getting on, that Stalin should make up with Tito. She said she preferred the Chinese Communists to the Russians. Her friends clapped their hands to their ears. They didn't even want to hear this dangerous heresy. She met Borodin a time or two. He tried tactfully to make her realize that she was treading on dangerous ground. She did not listen. Her exit permit to China did not come through. She proclaimed that she was going to see Stalin and tell him a thing or two. Some petty bureaucrats, she thought, had taken important affairs into their hands.

How she could not have noticed the fear in Moscow in late 1948 and early 1949 I cannot imagine. Everyone I knew had his or her head down. The "anticosmopolitan" campaign (against Jews) was at its peak—Jews being publicly denounced, dismissed from jobs, arrested, imprisoned, sent to Siberia, and executed. The "Leningrad affair" was in progress—the top leadership of Russia's second city (Politburo members among them) arrested, secretly tried, and shot. The Jewish anti-Fascist case was underway—twenty-five leading Jews, World War II heroes, writers, scientists arrested, tried, and shot. Preparations for driving Tito out of Yugoslavia had reached a climax. Arrests of foreign Communists were beginning again. What else might have been going on at that time, I cannot recapitulate. I can testify, however, that Moscow was more sinister than I ever saw it—except for the period just before Stalin's death.

It was into this Moscow that Anna Louise projected herself. Small wonder that people literally fled (as some whispered to me) from the sound of her powerful voice; small wonder old friends shunned her; small wonder only a few brave souls (including Borodin) tried quietly to shut her up. To no avail. She persisted against all caution.

Some god smiled down on her. She was arrested. She was held only a few days. Her room at the Lubyanka was as comfortable as a room at the Metropol Hotel. She was not tortured. She underwent no midnight interrogation. She did not have to don prison garb. On February 19, 1949, the Kremlin announced she was being expelled from the Soviet Union as an American spy and an agent of the CIA. She was flown to the Polish border and tottered across.

True, she had to make her own way back. True, the Poles wouldn't help her. True, her world was shattered. She was branded in such a way that not one of her Communist and pro-Communist associates—not even the Chinese—would have anything to do with her. True, the *New York Daily Worker* interrupted serialization of her *Thought of Mao Zedong* in midthought.

But she would find her way back to Los Angeles, find herself befriended by kindly people, and live a not entirely unpleasant existence for the next six years—a pariah, it is true, from those whose association she valued, but physically secure. She would even do a bit of quite profitable speculation.

Not until I returned to the United States in late 1954 and wrote my series in the *Times,* called *"Russia Re-Viewed,"* telling what I then knew about Borodin, the *Moscow News,* and Anna Louise, would she begin to cope with what had happened.

In public Anna Louise had consistently claimed that her expulsion must have been carried out by underlings without Stalin's knowledge—a preposterous theory but one only too familiar to me. Again and again during the Great Purges of the 1930s so carefully orchestrated by Stalin, Old Bolsheviks had gone to their deaths with the phrase "If Stalin only knew!" on their lips. They tried to smuggle letters to tell him that the system had gone out of control. Even in prison camp, again and again, as Aleksandr Solzhenitsyn has recorded, Party members clung to their cri de coeur "if Stalin only knew."

Now with the publication of my article telling of the arrest of Borodin and the *Moscow News* people, simultaneous with her own arrest, Anna Louise directed a pathetic letter to me. It was the first word she had had of "my old friend Borodin and the fact that his arrest took place February 1949." She had, she said, never known "any reason for my arrest—which destroyed my worldwide career." She begged if I had any more information to forward it and asked how certain was my knowledge about Borodin. Regretfully I had to tell her there was no longer a shadow of a doubt. Borodin had been arrested and died in concentration camp, precisely as I had reported.

Did she then grasp that she had played a role in Borodin's death? I do not believe she did, and it is just as well.

It was March 4, 1955, two years almost to the day after the death of Stalin, before *Pravda* finally and, as it seemed to me, reluctantly, announced that the case of Anna Louise Strong had been reviewed, and the charges found groundless.

Another year passed before I had from Anna Louise (in response to one of mine about Nikita Khrushchev's revelations of Stalin's crimes) a long closely reasoned letter, in which she for the first time conceded that she had, indeed, over a period of time noticed telltale signs (which she had faithfully suppressed) of

poor relations between the Russians and the Chinese: the fact
that the Russians did not turn over the arms and matériel they
had seized in Manchuria in 1945 to the Communist Chinese (they
kept it themselves or let the Nationalists have it); the fact that
the Soviet ambassador had followed Chiang Kai-shek from Nanjing to Canton in 1949; that the Chinese consular officers in Siberia in 1949 were still Chiang Kai-shek's men; a Soviet proposal
to Chiang Kai-shek just before Nanjing's fall in 1949 for a coalition Nationalist-Communist government.

She still tried, a bit wearily, to suggest that "what happened
to me" had been "just a blunder of lower officials" but conceded
that, if Stalin was behind it, then it undoubtedly was because she
was boosting Mao all over the map "before Stalin recognized him
and gave a green light." "I really did a job on Mao," she said,
particularly with her *The Thought of Mao Zedong.* It had been
published in America, in India, in China (in 1948 and 1949), and
the Czechs were preparing to publish it in their official ideologi-
cal journal; she had also addressed the important Varga Institute in Moscow in late 1948 on the economic theories of Mao. She
had been, she admitted, "invading the realm of upper Communist theory."

She recalled that then, at a time when her works were appearing all over the world, when she had had requests from East
European countries for everything she had written about China,
in 1948 and early 1949 the Russians were paying little public
heed to the Chinese Communists.

And, she admitted, there had been more personal indications
of trouble—Borodin's fears concerning the attitude of Soviet
officials. All of this was enough—or should have been enough—to
put her on her guard.

There was one more thing, she revealed. Mao himself had
given her a warning in 1946 against going to Moscow again, but,
she said, it was put in so oblique a fashion—just a hint as it
were—that when she came to make her plans to return to China
in 1948, Mao's words did not really leap into her mind.

"I assumed that Mao's warning had not really been a warning, or at least applied only to a brief time," she wrote me. But,
she admitted, she now had to realize that "there must have been
some competition between the two great leaders of world Communism; and that I stuck my head in the way."

She had indeed. Although she never in correspondence with

me was to return to this theme, I think any doubts as to what was going on were finally removed from her mind when, after a fight to get back her passport, she finally returned to China, September 22, 1958. She was bubbling over, and her enthusiasm poured out in long letters in which she, for a time, seemed to think that she might win permission for me to come very shortly to Beijing. She was wrong about that as, alas, she was about so many things.

Anna Louise would stay in China for the rest of her life—an indefatigable propagandist for Mao, as prone to the suspension of common sense as ever. She fawned on Mao Zedong and Zhou Enlai, but once flared up madly at a dirty tablecloth in the Great Hall of the People and compelled waiters to change it in the midst of a state dinner—not quite as imperious as on the occasion in Yan'an when she broke into a meeting of the State Military Council to demand that Zhou Enlai come play bridge in her cave. Zhou gently led her out of the room, telling her he had played bridge with her the night before and that she must not interfere with the business of the State Council. Anna Louise wandered back to her jeep in bemusement, saying over and over like a reprimanded schoolgirl: "Why, Zhou Enlai was really angry with me. He was *really* angry. He told me to go away." She repeated it like a litany.

She spent a fair amount of time playing the stock market, directing her transactions improbably through an offshore account. She was quite successful, as she had been in her operations in Los Angeles real estate. She fought a long war with Soviet authorities, trying to get them to transfer balances in her Moscow bank accounts to Beijing. They insisted she had to come to Moscow to make the transfer. Finally she proudly announced she had thwarted Moscow. She had ordered them to transfer her money to a fund for Vietnam war relief. They had bent at last to her will.

I wrote her long, chatty letters full of American political gossip and my notions of why I should be permitted to come to China. After a time her replies came at greater and greater intervals, but when I reached Beijing at long last in 1972, I found that I was famous in the small court of foreigners that had gathered around Anna Louise. She read the letters aloud as they were received, and there were long discussions of the significance of my observations. If I had known, I would have written more often.

Once I had a letter from Anna Louise containing a special request. Could I obtain a dozen pair of nylon hose for her (I can't remember the size or color) and, so help me, a corset cover, at least, that is what I think it was, an article of apparel so lost in the mists of Victorian feminity that it must have been a companion to the ruffles that Boston ladies once put around the naked "limbs" of their grand pianos. My secretary couldn't find a New York store that carried one.

In China Anna Louise found her heaven. She had long since turned her back on America. She had turned her back on Russia in 1949. Now she had China. She was content, exhilarated, passionate. She threw herself into China, writing, writing, writing.

Then in 1966 China began to change. Anna Louise did not understand it. She plunged into the Cultural Revolution, naïve as a novitiate. She even wore the scarf of the Red Guards and appeared at Tiananmen. She tried in every way to pour what was left of her stock of gilt over the ever-widening cracks in the portrait of Chinese perfection she had painted in her propaganda.

It was not enough. China turned on her in ways too terrible and complex to expound here. Those she trusted went down in the flames of the holocaust, which came close to destroying her along with the whole structure. Anna Louise did not taste prison again, but she did taste betrayal. In the end, bewildered, disillusioned, beset by doubts, fears, and pain, she began to try to return to America. Oh, just for a last trip, she said. But she knew that if she went, she would not come back. Had it not been for the stupid bureaucracy of the American consul-general in Hong Kong, she would have left her last Revolution and come back to the land of her birth.

She was, for practical purposes, a prisoner in her own house, breakfasting each morning on the porch of No. 1 Tai Ji Chang, the lovely house in the courtyard of the old Italian embassy. Rewi Alley, her old New Zealand friend, lived in the apartment just above her—two old friends, who had dedicated their lives to China, trying to understand how it could have happened, what was this madness raging over their chosen land, two old revolutionaries trying to perceive what genie had been let out of the bottle and who had done it, not wanting to confess (or fearful of admitting) that they knew the answer.

Anna Louise was still hoping to go home when she fell ill. Her condition rapidly worsened. One day Zhou Enlai, beset with the worry of the Cultural Revolution, discovered to his horror that she was dying, dying alone without proper treatment. He himself went to the hospital. He lost his temper, roared to the hospital to do everything possible for Anna Louise, roared to his aides to find her nephew, who he knew was somewhere on the East Asian coast (Zhou's own foreign office had denied him a visa to visit his ailing aunt). In vain Zhou tried to hold back the gray shadow until at least one familiar face was beside the bed of Anna Louise. But it was too late. She died March 28, 1969, her great-nephew John Strong not yet arrived from travels in Indonesia. Zhou attended the funeral, his face a mask of weariness, tears falling down his cheeks.

Anna Louise had amassed a comfortable sum from her Los Angeles real estate and her market speculation from Beijing. In her will she left various bequests and the instruction to her executor, the American exile, Frank Coe, that the remainder, a sum of a few hundred dollars, be used "to further the cause of the American revolution." How Coe carried out his instructions, I cannot guess. What I can say is that for all her tantrums, loud shouts, vanity, and childlike naïveté Anna Louise taught me much—about men and women, about life and about the people we call revolutionaries, who try somehow to speed up and change the course of human progress. Anna Louise was the product of a deeply religious, deeply idealistic American faith. Her life was spent in what she perceived to be a great moral struggle to make better the lot of man on earth. If she failed, it was not for lack of passion, and if in many ways she was a foolish woman, at least she tried to leave behind a better world than that into which she was born.

21 | Blindfolded in Room 393

I once boasted that you could blindfold me, put me down anywhere in the Hotel Metropol in Moscow, and I could tell you where I was—which corridor, which floor, which room—by using nothing more than my nose.

In the spring of 1949 when I came back to Russia for *The New York Times,* I didn't have to close my eyes to know that the smell in the Metropol was the smell of fear. The Metropol was peopled by ghosts of Bolsheviks past and present, the victims of Stalin's waves of terror. Especially the ghosts of Stalin's Grand Guignol of China and the Chinese Revolution.

As I sat at the great fumed oak desk in Room 393—the room, now mine, which once had been occupied by Alexander Werth— and thumbed over *Pravda* each morning, a curious sensation ran down my spine. It had been difficult for me to believe that China was the connecting link between Anna Louise Strong, the disappearance of Borodin, and the closing of the *Moscow News,* but the coincidence was too strong to dismiss.

Now as I read *Pravda,* a new realization came over me and this was what sent a tremor down my spine. The Peoples Liberation Army was conquering China. Day by day it was driving Chiang Kai-shek from the field, victory after victory. It had swept down from the northwest, occupied North China, seized Manchuria, marched into Beijing. It was preparing to move south on Nanjing and across the Yangtze into South China. It was the greatest revolutionary triumph since the Bolsheviks seized Petrograd in 1917. *And Pravda was not reporting it.*

Oh, yes, as I went through the papers each day with the help of an interpreter (I was just beginning to learn Russian), there would be the occasional item tucked away on an inside page, the report of a battle here or there, three or four paragraphs. But no reader of *Pravda* could be aware that Mao Zedong, Zhu De, Peng Dehuai, and all the others were winning triumph after triumph. The events which were bannered in headlines in *The New York Times,* in London, in Paris and Tokyo did not engage the interest of *Pravda.* Tiny stories, no commentary, no editorials, nothing to excite the Kremlin or the Russian people.

I am by nature a contrarian. I tend to challenge common assumptions. But I had not until the spring of 1949, studying *Pravda* in that cavernous room, supposed that there might be fundamental differences between Communist China and the Soviet Union. Policy differences, yes. But deep hostility—it had never entered my mind. Of course I did not know the inner history of Mao and Stalin; I did not understand that there had been, since the 1920s, a basic quarrel (sometimes latent, sometimes open) between the two men. I had read Harold Isaacs *The Tragedy of the Chinese Revolution,* but I had paid more attention to his dramatic account of the slaughter of the Communists in Shanghai in 1927 than to his political analysis, and I am afraid I had discounted it as being a Trotskyite distortion.

So regardless of the ghosts of Borodin, of the Chens, of Soong Ching-ling, of Anna Louise, of Rayna and Bill Prohme (all of whom had once lived on the very floor I now inhabited at the Metropol), I found it hard to digest the evidence of what *Pravda* was not printing, but like Sherlock Holmes and the dog that did not bark, I could not ignore it.

I had been brought up with a cliché dinned into my head by my friend Reuben, whose father had been a Bundist radical in Russia. Reuben used to repeat, again and again, in our arguments: "There is a reason for everything." I am sure he got the phrase from his father, who in turn picked it up in the endless discussions of the Russian radicals. I didn't like the phrase, but it haunted me. If *Pravda* was not playing up the Chinese Revolution, there had to be a reason—an important reason, probably a sinister reason.

A month after I arrived in Moscow, I noted in my journal, April 4, 1949:

> From all I can gather the Kremlin still is very unsure of the situation in China. It gets very scanty reference in the press. . . . My opinion is that the Kremlin has its fingers crossed about its Chinese friends and will keep them that way for some time.

A month later I was writing (privately) about the "touchy relations" of Moscow and the Chinese. I tried to convey some hint of this to American readers, but the censors killed my reference to the fact that Moscow was maintaining scrupulously correct relations with Chiang Kai-shek and would do so until he actually left the mainland, the Russian ambassador, unlike the American, following him from Nanjing to the water's edge.

I don't want to overstate my prescience about the antagonisms between China and the Soviets. Yes, I spotted the signs, but because of the Soviet censorship my analysis did not reach the public. My observations were hacked out of my copy. True, a sharp-eyed editor could spot that something was wrong by what I was *not* saying. This is the way Russians had learned to read *Pravda*—not for what was printed, but for what *was not*. But Americans are not skilled in this art. I did circulate copies of the materials killed by the censors to the editors of the *Times* and to my friend, Cyrus L. Sulzberger, chief European correspondent of the *Times*. But I did not make any real mark on their minds.

I do not think this is accidental. All eyes were turned in the opposite direction. The State Department's famous White Paper issued on July 30, 1949 (approved, if not drafted, by Dean Acheson), said:

> The heart of China is in Communist hands. The Communist leaders have foresworn their Chinese heritage and have publicly announced *their subservience to a foreign power, Russia* [my italics]. . . . The Communist regime serves not their [Chinese] interests but those of Soviet Russia. . . .

By March 30, 1950, Senator Joseph McCarthy was saying: "It was not Chinese democracy under Mao that conquered China as Acheson, [Owen] Lattimore, and [Philip] Jesseup contended. *Soviet Russia conquered China* [my italics] and an important ally of this conqueror was the small left-wing element in our Department of State."

Or, as Dean Rusk put it in May 1951:

> We do not recognize the authority in Peiping [sic] for what they pretend to be. The Peiping regime may be a colonial Russian government—a Slavic Manchukuo [sic] on a larger scale. It is not the Government of China. It does not pass the first test. It is not Chinese.

Or as Captain Joseph Alsop, then serving with General Claire Chennault, put it simply and plainly in 1945: "We are childish to assume the Chinese Communists are anything but an appendage of the Soviet Union.''

It is tragic that there was no difference in view among McCarthy, Acheson, Rusk, and Alsop (Alsop later changed his mind). As years passed, there would be a powerful effort to slip the brass ring on McCarthy's porcine pinky, but he was just a flabby Wisconsin pol, the others were classy, educated men who could have known better but, instead, arranged a well-designed stage on which McCarthy could present his rubbishy performance.

The thin grapeshot of my highly censored dispatches didn't pock the seamless surface of post-war American know-nothingism.

Of course, I did not then perceive how deep the divisions were between Russia and China, Moscow and Beijing, Stalin and Mao. But if I, a non-expert in Chinese affairs, possessing scant knowledge of Russia, not one word of the Chinese language, sitting alone, virtually blindfolded in that heavily draped, shuttered, dim-lighted Moscow hotel room could discern enough to suspect that something was rotten between the two big Communist countries is it not reasonable to expect that the President of the United States, his Secretary of State and all the other secretaries, intelligence analysts, members of the Senate, members of the House and assorted wise men would scent a faint clue? Should we not expect that amongst them there would be one who spoke out for reason and common sense; who had the primitive instinct if not expert knowledge to realize that Russia and China were two great nations neither of which would kowtow to the other? In those days, 1949, the CIA was new; we were only spending hundreds of millions not today's tens of billions on intelligence— but what were we getting for our money? (Of course, I know the same question can be raised today). Should we not expect that a man from Missouri like Harry Truman, so savvy in ordinary walks of life, would have said to them: Show Me!

I once met the famous biologist, A.J. Carlson, at the University of Chicago. He was the man who fed patent bleached flour to rats. They died of vitamin deficiency. Our cosmetic milling of wheat had produced a beauteous snowy powder. Unfortunately there wasn't too much nutrition in it.

This commonsensical scientist gave all of his students a test. He commanded them to bring a test tube of urine to class. Then he stood in front with his own test tube: "Watch closely and do exactly as I do." The test, he said, would demonstrate the basic principles of the scientific method. He held his test tube to the light: "It looks like urine, but that is just the first test." Next, he put the tube to his nostrils. Yes, it smelled like urine, but we must not leap to conclusions. Does it taste like urine? He dipped a finger into the tube and put it to his lips. Yes, he said, it is urine. The scholars dutifully followed his example.

"Now," said Carlson, "you have all failed the test. Watch me closely."

He went through it again—held the test tube to the light, smelled it, dipped a finger into the liquid. This time he moved slowly so all could see that the finger he put to his lips was not the one that had been immersed in urine.

"You see?" he explained. "The basis of the scientific method is close observation. You were misled by my words. You must watch closely. That is the scientific method."

No one in Washington—as is so often the case—was watching the test tubes. There can be no doubt that the logic of Acheson, McCarthy, and Rusk did not pass, in Rusk's word, the first test. None had put China to Carlson's test. They may have listened to propagandistic words; they had not paid heed to the deeds.

I have, over years, seen political leaders—American and others—make many mistakes. None, I think, can match the colossal error of the United States on China. It should be clear, forty years after the event, that this was not McCarthy's fault. McCarthy was only a spear carrier. The men whom he counted his enemies (and who saw him as their enemy) were as like as two pumpkins in the blind infantilism of their opinions.

That was not a point of view I could prove in 1949. But it was not long before evidence came in that the relationship between China and Moscow was of a most special nature.

In June 1949, at a time when Mao had taken over Beijing—but had not yet proclaimed the People's Republic—a delegation headed by the important Chinese Communist leader, Gao Gan, came to Moscow, was received by Stalin, and signed an agreement for economic cooperation between the Soviet and the "Manchurian Peoples Democratic authorities."

This struck me as a fish out of water. The "Manchurian Peoples Democratic authorities" did not exist as a government, so far as I knew. Was this a gimmick to establish relations between Communist-occupied Manchuria and the Soviet Union without violating existing diplomatic relations between Moscow and Chiang Kai-shek? Or was it something more mysterious? The censor would not let me speculate. Later, after Stalin's death in 1953 and the arrest and execution of his chief of secret police, Lavrenti P. Beria, the Chinese arrested Gao Gan and some of his associates. They were said to have plotted to detach Manchuria from China and set up an "independent kingdom."

I don't know exactly what went on, but it struck me in 1955 (when I learned of Gao Gan's arrest) that Stalin and Beria had been plotting with Gao Gan against Mao. I think this was the case. The Chinese were very angry in 1955, because instead of standing trial, being sentenced to death, and shot, Gao Gan committed suicide. That, said Beijing, was the act of a traitor.

I think that Stalin and Beria promised Gao Gan his own "independent kingdom" in Manchuria if he went with them. Not exactly the conduct of warm, friendly allies but conduct which went unnoticed by American minds transfixed with the notion of the "Communist monolith." Our specialists were so bemused by McCarthyism they didn't bother to analyze the significance of the Gao Gan affair.

On October 1, 1949, Mao proclaimed the Peoples Republic from Tiananmin Square and finally *Pravda* gave the Chinese a big sendoff. Next day Moscow transferred diplomatic recognition from Chiang to Mao and sent its ambassador scurrying up to Beijing to represent Russia at the court of Communism.

It seemed a curious performance. I didn't even know of the last minute haggling between Chiang and Moscow over the transfer of Xinjiang province to Russia as a protectorate. It still seems strange today. Of course, trying to puzzle things out in Room 393, I could not perceive the long, consistent tendency of Stalin to favor Chiang over Mao. Nor did I know until I learned it in 1984, while interviewing China's leaders about *The Long March,* that just before the PLA moved across the Yangtze in 1949, Stalin sent Anastas Mikoyan to make a last-ditch effort to keep Mao from crossing the river—to leave Chiang in power in south China—warning that otherwise the United States might intervene. Mao refused. He moved south. He crossed the Yangtze. The U.S. did not intervene.

Later Stalin confessed to the Chinese that he had been mistaken. He had thought Chiang Kai-shek was too strong and that the Communists could not conquer him. He had been wrong.

Whether Stalin really was sorry is something else. I don't think he ever trusted Mao. I don't think he ever wanted Mao to win. I don't think he wanted a strong China. I think he backed Chiang because he thought he could manipulate Chiang, and he didn't think he could manipulate Mao. I think Stalin was right about Chiang and Mao, but I was far from thinking that as the dreary Moscow autumn of 1949 moved into winter.

I had heard rumors that Mao was coming to Moscow—natural enough in the circumstances. Lots for him and Stalin to talk about. On December 16, Mao arrived by train with a full entourage, accompanied by Soviet Ambassador N. V. Roshchin. Mao had come, it was said, to pay tribute to Stalin on his seventieth birthday, December 21, and for diplomatic negotiations.

Mao graced Stalin's birthday party at the Bolshoi Theater, where an old chestnut, *The Red Poppy,* had been refurbished for Mao's entertainment—a clodhopper ballet about Russian sailors helping the Chinese make their revolution, a blend of canned chauvinism and poor music, which I don't believe Mao enjoyed. Probably that was why Stalin ordered it performed.

After a few ceremonial exchanges, Mao vanished from the pages of *Pravda.* I knew the protocol of state visits. It never varied. The ceremonial greeting. The trip to the Kremlin. The talk with Stalin. The laying of a wreath at Lenin's tomb. The pro forma negotiations by underlings (the real business, of course, transacted before the guest's arrival). The evening at the Bolshoi. The visit to a factory (usually the Trigornaya Textile plant), the trip to a model collective farm near Moscow. A quick trip to Leningrad. Back to the Kremlin to sign the treaty, a Kremlin banquet, an exchange of toasts, farewell at the airport. Home after five days.

Not so for Mao. He simply vanished. There was a vague suggestion he was sightseeing in the countryside. No communiqués. No reports. *Pravda* was silent. Days passed. Finally I went out to the big Chinese embassy to see what I could find out. Nothing. The Chinese were very polite, but when they found out I was an American, it was "So sorry." I left a personal letter to Mao, a request to visit the People's Republic. I went on sending letters and telegrams for twenty-three years until I got to Beijing in 1972.

Mao's visit lasted two months. One night he came to the Metropol for a formal reception, which the Chinese gave for Stalin in the grand dining room. I didn't even catch a glimpse of Mao. Negotiations went on and on. After Stalin died, Nikita Khrushchev revealed that Mao had gotten so angry because Stalin treated him like a petty petitioner that he would have broken with Russia and gone over to the American side, had it not been for our ostentatious hostility. Knowing what I know now about relations between the men since 1927, I am inclined to accept Khrushchev's story.

A treaty of friendship and mutual defense was announced St. Valentine's day, February 14, 1950, but not until after Mao had been joined on January 21, 1950, by Zhou Enlai and a complement of Chinese that included the mysterious (to me) Gao Gan. It took three weeks more to hammer out a treaty. Never before, or since, had a diplomatic visit to Russia lasted so long. I didn't know what the delay was about, but I didn't think it could reflect anything but disagreement. When the terms were announced, I was sure I was right. The treaty only slightly broadened the provisions of the existing Sino-Soviet treaty of 1945 (signed by Stalin and Chiang Kai-shek). It preserved almost all of the old Russian Imperial privileges in Manchuria—the treaty ports and the Russian-operated railroads, the colonial treaties giving Russia control of minerals and air rights (51 percent owned by the Soviets). The defense clauses were slightly broadened to become operative not only against Japanese aggression but by powers allied with Japan. A niggardly $60 million a year for five years was promised in economic aid, about what the U.S. gave each year to second-rate Latin American countries.

I put my negative comment as strongly as the censors would permit and stated them much more strongly in private letters to my colleagues, but my version was buried under a sensational report by Cyrus L. Sulzberger that "secret clauses" gave Moscow command over all Chinese armed forces and control of strategic facilities in China, and reduced Beijing to a puppet state. There was not one word of truth in Cy's report. Whether or not it was CIA disinformation, I never found out.

My view was that the agreement displayed "extreme chinchy-ness" by Stalin and that Mao, far from proving a Moscow pup-pet or Soviet agent, demonstrated that he was a head of state and his own man.

Once again I found myself in disagreement with the establish-ment. I was far from understanding the basics of the Stalin-Mao relationship, but I stood even further from the Acheson-Rusk-McCarthy assessment that China was Moscow's pawn.

England and France had recognized the People's Republic. We were moving in that direction, I knew, from conversations with Admiral Alan G. Kirk, our ambassador in Moscow. Acheson had polled him and other ambassadors on recognition. Kirk and most of the others favored it. I strongly agreed; delay could only push China into dependence on Stalin. I was sure the China card was ours to play if we would only play it. But Truman decided to delay until he could get a few important bills through Congress. He knew the Republicans, already toying with the war cry "The Democrats Lost China," would raise a row. It was a fatal, disas-trous delay.

I went off to the United States in May 1950 on a brief leave. I was at Pyramid Lake Ranch, about sixty miles from Reno, Nevada (for the usual reason), in late June when news came of the attack on South Korea by North Korea.

The attack was a total surprise to me and I suspect our re-sponse, Truman's decision to defend South Korea, was a surprise to Stalin. He obviously knew (although I had not noticed) Ache-son's declaration at the National Press Club in Washington, D.C., January 12 and again at San Francisco March 15 that the American defense line in the Pacific ran from the Aleutians to Japan to the Ryukyus to the Philippines. He omitted any men-tion of Korea (or Taiwan). He did this first before Stalin signed his pact with China and repeated it after Stalin signed the pact. The inference seemed obvious: Korea is not included in the area of our defense.

I hadn't even heard of the Acheson declarations nor had any-one in Washington whom I knew. It seems to me that no one had been watching the store but Stalin.

I hurried back to Moscow as fast as I could. It was obvious that a world crisis was at hand.

I have studied the Korean episode for many years and I have evolved a theory which I cannot prove but I believe it is correct.

I believe that Stalin started the Korean war to put Mao in a military nutcracker. Russia already held North Korea for practical purposes. It circled North China from its positions in Siberia and the Maritime provinces. North China and Beijing were almost in Stalin's hands. By making the deal with Gao Gan he had Mao almost surrounded.

If Stalin could put the whole Korean peninsula in Soviet control, he could squeeze Mao out like the pip from an apple.

Most Americans assumed—especially after China sent 1 million men into the war—that it was touched off by a Korean-Chinese conspiracy. I disagreed. I thought it was Stalin's doing and that his target was China, not the United States. I think he believed Acheson's twice-stated declaration putting Korea outside our defense perimeter. If Acheson was stating U.S. policy, why shouldn't Stalin take advantage of it and use North Korea as a cat's-paw to strengthen his stranglehold on China?

When, contrary to American declarations and Stalin's expectations, Truman rushed American forces to Korea, Stalin played his Machiavellian hole card—he involved China. He knew, as Americans seemed to have forgotten, that Mao had long favored close relations with the U.S.A. Stalin knew, as we didn't seem to understand, that Mao was his stubborn, implacable antagonist. What better than to inveigle China into war with the United States?

I have found much evidence to support my Korean hypothesis. The strongest has come from the Chinese. Once I got to Beijing and began to talk to high-ranking Chinese, I found that contrary to Washington commentators and my skeptical State Department friends, the Chinese were most comfortable with my thesis. They had, they said, come to the same conclusion themselves. For many reasons, they had not thought it tactful to publish their suspicions.

A Russian friend once said he thought sometimes America acted like a blindfold giant. I don't think this is entirely true, but in the case of China we went even further—we figuratively put out the eyes of our best China specialists just as, according to legend, Ivan the Terrible put out the eyes of the architects who designed St. Basil's in Red Square (so that they might not design a church so beautiful for anyone else). We blinded ourselves and by so doing stumbled into two terrible wars—Korea and Vietnam—neither of which need have been fought. We were

led out of the paranoid world we created only by that most unlikely of Pied Pipers, Richard Nixon, who with the aid of Henry
Kissinger, managed to get to Beijing in 1972 and put us on the
right track at last.

22 | Who Lost China?

When Borodin returned from the failed Chinese Revolution, he was not summoned into Stalin's presence, denounced, and summarily shot. He was not arrested and sent to the dread isolator at Vladimir or the Arctic Solovetsky islands from which no one returned.

He was given a sumptuous two-room suite on the third floor of the Metropol Hotel, which he occupied with his wife and two sons (one of whom was killed in World War II and one of whom joined the secret police). He sat in his suite for two years, writing and rewriting reports, waiting for Stalin to decide his fate.

It was a tricky decision for Stalin. Half the people in Moscow were calling Borodin a Trotskyite and/or a Menshevik. In a later period, Stalin would have had Borodin shot without notice. But he was a little new at the terror game, and Borodin was so much the instrument of Stalin's China policy that he decided against execution. He let Borodin sit and sit. After two years Borodin was denounced—as a fool, not as a counterrevolutionary. That saved his life. He was shunted into small jobs, never again to handle anything Chinese. He was forbidden to speak of China or meet with his old China friends.

But if Borodin's career was ended in 1927, he was most fortunate. His fellow *sovetniks* (as Russia's China hands were called) began to fall by the wayside; some were arrested; even before 1930 a few were shot. It was Stalin's first tentative purge of his China men. Soon he would make Joseph McCarthy look like a pantywaist.

As I ultimately discovered, Stalin purged his China experts three times (and there was a post-Stalin purge in the early 1960s). Why should Stalin do this? Because Russia, thanks to its perfidious experts, had "lost China" three times. Let me repeat for emphasis: Russia had "lost" China three times, and Stalin put the blame on the China hands.

But wait a minute. Something must be wrong. We Americans "lost China." That was what McCarthyism was all about. Didn't

Joseph McCarthy present a list of "Communists" in the State Department? Didn't he blame them and the wimpy Democrats like Truman and Acheson for losing China to Russia? Wasn't that it?

What was going on here—Russia was losing China to whom? To us, of course. And we were losing China to whom? To Russia, of course.

If only I had known what I now know, what I uncovered not in China, not in Russia, but by scratching my fingernails to the bone, digging through old documents, American and Soviet—obscure references in long forgotten or unread Soviet scholarly journals, tracking down the biographies of Soviet men and women who worked in China with Borodin in the 1920's, seeking out the fate of those (many of them survivors of 1927) who were sent back by Stalin in the mid-1930s to help Chiang Kai-shek. (Stalin had a stunning respect for the Generalissimo who had killed so many Chinese Communists—was that one reason?) And then ferreting out the survivors of the 1930s, the ones who lived to be executed or exiled or imprisoned in the 1940s.

When earlier I called Stalin's China policy a Grand Guignol, that was an understatement. It was Lewis Carroll's *Through the Looking Glass,* the mirror image effect. We saw Russia doing what Russia saw us doing. Rashomon? Yes, in a sense but a Rashomon viewed through a prism.

We destroyed our incomparable corps of Old China Hands, men and women, most of them of China background, born there, sons and daughters of missionaries or Standard Oil families, scholars with the Chinese language and decades of firsthand experience, military men who knew the China battlefields, the Chinese generals, and the Chinese fighting men. It was a savage loss. We drove them out of government (in legal battles, many over the years got back their posts): careers and families were wrecked; there were suicides; a handful sought refuge abroad; character and work was vilified. But no American victim of McCarthy suffered as badly as did Anna Louise at the hands of Stalin. No American was imprisoned or sent to a labor camp for the "loss of China"; no American was shot or died under circumstances still unknown.

I do not suggest that Stalin's conduct should be seen as a

standard against which to match our own venal and self-damaging idiocy. But when Stalin purged, it was permanent. No wasting time on legal niceties. No appeals.

Physical reprisals in Russia after the 1927 failure were not great. A handful of Red Army men were cashiered, and a few were shot, probably on charges of being Trotskyites. Among civilians the damage was greater. Borodin was not the only expert to be detached from China. There was a vast shake-up among Far Eastern specialists of the Comintern. This had much to do with Stalin's feud with Trotsky. Trotsky men had run the University of Toilers of the East, where Chinese and Russian specialists were trained. There was a wholesale purge. None of the Comintern's Far Eastern team survived. All were replaced at the direction of a young Ukranian hothead named Pavel Mif, Stalin's new point man for China, taking over Borodin's responsibilities. Out of this shake-up came the naïve "twenty-six and a half Bolsheviks," the young Moscow-trained Chinese (the "half" was for a very small young man) who were sent back to wrest the Party from the hands of Mao. They came close to destroying the whole movement.

As far as I have been able to establish, the Chinese revolutionaries, while grateful, in general, for Russian help, never thought of themselves, as Stalin and McCarthy did, as "belonging to Moscow."

Russia's second "loss of China" was vicious. It accompanied Stalin's violent purges of the late 1930s. Down went a forest of major figures: Marshal Vasily K. Blyukher, Borodin's military counterpart, by then Soviet Far Eastern commander, General A. I. Cherepanov, General Albert Ivanovich Lapin, Blyukher's deputy, Vitovt K. Putna, later Soviet military attaché in London. Colonel Georgy B. Skalov (Sinani), an early victim, was shot in 1935. The list goes on and on and on. In 1938 Stalin purged his whole Far East command, taking the lives of Generals Shtern and Yegorov and scores of officers who had served in China. Many of the officers were two termers. They had been sent out in the early 1920s to help the Communists and were brought home after 1927. Then, with the united front against Japan of 1936–37, Stalin sent back to Chiang Kai-shek the survivors of the first tour and many more.

This second wave suffered severely. Just as Stalin wiped out most of the officers and advisers he sent to the Spanish Loyalists, so he took the lives of the military men who knew (and in many cases loved) China.

Of course, he did not halt with the military. He wiped out the whole cadre of early Bolsheviks connected with China, diplomats and Comintern men: Lev Karakhan, one-time Soviet foreign minister who preceded Borodin to China, Grigory Voitinsky (he preserved his life but not his responsibilities), Sergei Tretyakov whose crime was to write the famous revolutionary play *Roar China,* N. V. Kuibyshev, chief Soviet adviser for all of South China and brother of the Soviet President, V. V. Kuibyshev, and, improbably, Mira Sakhnovskaya, the only woman graduate of the Frunze Military Academy, who bore two children during her China service. Even Pavel Mif, Stalin's fair-haired China expert, went down the drain.

There is no need to reel off name after name. Most can now be found in the memoirs of Madame Vishnaykova-Akimova, whose husband was a military adviser, she a twenty-year-old interpreter; they were married in China. She wrote of her colleagues: "Few of them survived the repressions of 1937–38. The war finished off the others."

Russia's greatest loss was in expertise. McCarthy put a chill on American China studies (academics warned young students against specializing in China; the odds of harassment were too high). Stalin went further. He obliterated not only the China Hands but China itself. I mean he literally stamped out the word "China." The blackout on news of the Chinese Red Army's triumphant progress across China was typical. For years *everything* about China was suppressed. Nothing appeared in the newspapers. Books dried up. Scientific articles disappeared. Scholarly work vanished.

A surviving Soviet Sinologist G. Y. Efimov recalled that political conditions in the 1930s became "so unfavorable" that not one doctor's dissertation in Chinese history was defended until 1953 (the year of Stalin's death). Scholarly studies were simply adjourned. Not one study on Chinese history (ancient or contemporary) was published between 1941 and 1948. Many works completed in the 1930s and early 1940s did not see print until the late 1950s and early 1960s, long after their authors had died in prison or concentration camps. China vanished from Stalin's world. If "China" was uttered aloud or put on paper, the act could be punished by imprisonment or exile.

During Stalin's confrontation with Yugoslavia in 1948, he had exclaimed: "I can snap my finger, and Tito will disappear!" Tito did not vanish. He outlived Stalin by many years. His was the first Communist country to declare its independence from Moscow. Nor could Stalin make China vanish from the globe. But he could make it vanish from the Soviet Union just as he had "vanished" Mao from *Pravda* during his two-month stay in December 1949–February 1950.

I have examined a bibliography of Soviet scholarly works on China, compiled by N. V. Nikoferov. It lists 982 books, articles, and monographs published on what he calls "China problems" in the Soviet era. Eliminating works by Marx, Engels, and Lenin and those published before 1920 I counted these totals:

1920–29	303
1930–39	177
1940–49	73
1950–59	92
1960–69	183

If you break down the decade of the 1930s you find that almost all the articles appeared in the four prepurge years. For 1937, 1938, 1939 only nineteen articles appeared. Materials on contemporary Chinese affairs vanished. Nothing on the Chinese Party or the Chinese Red Army. Not one scholarly article appeared between 1944 and 1949.

Twenty years after Stalin's death, serious Soviet studies in the China field still limped badly. To compile the extraordinary necrology presented by Madame Vishnayakova-Akimova, her memorial to the lost generation of Soviet Sinologists, required the effort of most of the handful of surviving Soviet experts.

Why did we not see what was happening? How could we have been so negligent and, let's be honest, so stupid?

In part we had inflicted comparable wounds on ourselves. When the State Department finally accepted my findings of 1959, the Sino-Soviet split, based on my observations in Outer Mongolia followed by the open polemics between China and the Soviet Union, Khrushchev's withdrawal of experts from China, and the rest, it decided to inventory its resources, to see how many specialists were competent in both Soviet and Chinese affairs. The survey didn't take long. It produced three names. Two were middle-ranking officers whom I knew, both were basically China experts (ex-missionary brats). Both had been posted to Moscow to get them out of the line of fire, to protect them from McCarthy's offensive against China Hands. Both had learned Russian in Moscow. Neither was now serving in the Russia or China fields. The other man was a beginner. He'd had a duty tour in Moscow and now was studying Chinese at the University of Washington.

I thought to myself, when one of my State Department friends told me of this, How can any government with an atom of concern for national security, with even a primitive notion of responsibility, permit such dangerous ignorance? If one gunboat in the Navy went out of commission, the admirals would clank into Congress and demand six replacements. Here we were, sailing blindfold in a world so tiny that the slightest twinge in Eurasia could mean life or death—and we were careening grandly down the path of simpering idiocy—the President didn't know and didn't care, the Congress hadn't a clue, and the public was glued to the tube, anchored to the Superbowl and beer. Well . . . what can I add?

I know that in these pages I sound like a know-it-all, a Cassandra forever finding things out, making shrewd deductions, breaking the secret enigmas, exposing the daze and laze of the Government. I know that there are fine minds in the State Department, in the Pentagon, and in the analytic sections of the CIA, particularly on the Soviet Union (I am not so impressed with their China work).

For years the U.S. consul-general at Hong Kong comprised the best group of China analysts in the world. True, when Charlotte and I paused in Hong Kong in the spring of 1966 on our orbit of China, the Cultural Revolution already underway for four or five months, the specialists still had not figured it out. They knew it was big, but they had no coherent idea what was going on. I condone that. They were working like spit, but half of the jigsaw was missing. I met many Chinese in the years that followed who were just as baffled.

But on the question of relations between China and Russia, between the two great Communist empires, it seems to me that we continually and habitually lag behind our necessity.

One reason is that the Kremlinologist approaches the problem with a Soviet bias. No, he does not take the Soviet view, but he comes close to taking the "Russian" side. The Sinologist comes in with his Chinese bias. They can't get their heads on right.

That's one reason why I have kept hammering away on the Sino-Soviet question. I spent two or three years collecting the information on "Stalin's loss of China" before I finally published my conclusions in 1971. The symmetry of Stalin's and McCarthy's "loss of China" was so delicious, the ignorance so colossal, the implications so profound I still can hardly believe it.

But I am not so naïve as to suppose that my single article in *The New York Times* jolted American public opinion or the think tanks, governmental and academic, which try to monitor such questions.

As for Presidents and secretaries of state—forget it! They are too busy and/or too ignorant even to understand when they don't know something or to evaluate the quality of information their staffs feed them.

Not much has changed since George Kennan's classic study in *Russia Leaves the War,* his analysis of how the United States reacted to the Bolshevik takeover in Russia in 1917 and the Brest-Litovsk treaty by which Lenin and Trotsky took Russia out of World War I. Kennan demonstrated that not one American decision was based on real knowledge of the situation by Woodrow Wilson or his secretary of state, Robert Lansing. Every American act flowed from some seat-of-the-pants intuition unsupported by accurate information; every dispatch the U.S. received from Minister Francis in Petrograd, a genial St. Louis businessman who relied on his intelligent black valet for 95 percent of what he knew of the Russian Revolution (the valet got it from fellow valets and cooks) was baseless, distorted rumor, gossip, or nonsense. Wilson and Lansing paid little heed to the reports and did what they thought was best, acting out of personal ignorance and prejudice.

Kennan's work is based on high precision research. No doubt in my mind that similar research would find that most major decisions today are based on the same flimsy foundations, no matter how many billions we spend for NSA, CIA, DIA, and other secret alphabetical agencies, and—as I hope these pages reveal—this did not start with Ronald Reagan, his "evil empire," and the Contras. It went forward under Eisenhower, Kennedy, Johnson, and Nixon. What a President thinks he knows when he enters the White House has always taken priority over the real world.

I don't believe that kind of government is good enough. It is terrifying in an age when communications are measured in millionths of a second, when satellites bring to us any part of the world live and in color, and electronic gear lets us hear a click when a cat knocks Gorbachev's telephone off the hook, a click when a Soviet sergeant enters his missile silo, a click when the oxygen tank is turned on at the bedside of a dying statesman, a click when a Middle Eastern general phones his mistress.

But the politicians are too lazy or ignorant or prejudiced, and the public doesn't know what it doesn't know. Or what its President doesn't know. No number of exposés seems to drive the lesson home.

As I have said, I figured out that there was bad trouble between Russia and China sitting in my bugged interior courtyard Room 393 at the Metropol. I put together the intricate history of Stalin's effort to wipe the name of China off the Russian map, sitting in my study in Taconic, Connecticut. If I could do this, I think our intelligence community could do it better, do it quicker, comprehend it more deeply and even—this is the hard part—get the message over to the White House.

Why could reality about Russia and China sail past us in the 1940s, 1950s, and 1960s? Part of the answer can be found on our side of the mirror image. Stalin had put out his China eyes and waved China out of existence. We had not gone that far, but if you calculate that we turned our backs on John Carter Vincent, John S. Service, John Paton Davies, Jr., O. Edmund Clubb, John Melby, Colonel David Barrett (a classic case: denied his brigadier's star because of his magnificent reports on Communist China, branded a spy and vilified by the Communists, refused permission to retire to Taiwan by the Nationalists—a three-way loser, but not so big a loser as his own country, deprived of his unique insights), John Emmerson (perhaps the only Foreign Service officer with credentials to China, Russia, Japan), Ray Ludden, Arthur Ringwalt. No need to mention all the names. You cannot fire your first team, obliterate your second team, and forbid the formation of a third string without paying a price.

We paid that price, venting our anger on the men who brought (what some in the U.S. considered to be) the bad news. As the Luddites of nineteenth century England smashed the new steam engines with their hammers and crowbars to halt the advance of the machine age, so we destroyed the men who stood on the tall hills, spied out the land, and told us years in advance that Mao Zedong and his Red China was coming. By destroying our Old China Hands we did not halt for one day the advance of Mao and Communist China. Nor did Stalin halt the creation of the People's Republic by wiping the word "China" out of the Russian language.

One reason why we were so blind to the reality of Russia and China was that, like Stalin, we put out the eyes and ripped out the tongues of the men who could have raised the alarm. Stalin achieved the silence of the graveyard. We stuffed our fingers in our ears and put gags over the mouths of the men who told the truth.

When I returned to New York from my first trip to China in 1972, my telephone rang almost immediately. A Soviet diplomat wanted to lunch with me. He was, I discovered, a survivor, one of Moscow's China hands. He had been posted to Beijing for several years, knew the Chinese language, and had served in China during the Cultural Revolution.

I was not entirely surprised at the call. I knew the Russians were famished for information about China. They had, by the legacy of Stalin's dementia, found themselves in the 1960s with virtually no experts on China, no decent research, no means of knowing what was happening inside the country which had begun to loom more real than Stalin could have imagined.

The Soviets had nothing like the China studies at Harvard, Columbia, Yale, California, and Stanford, which had survived McCarthy's worst and gradually begun a recovery. Nor had Moscow created anything like the Hong Kong consulate-general and its remarkable research and intelligence potential.

What to do? As I had long known, the Russians were barred from Hong Kong. The British, with an eye to the great mainland just behind them, did not permit Soviet citizens entry. In this critical situation Soviet freighters began to "break down" just off Hong Kong Harbor. They were, of course permitted to enter for emergency repairs. When they dropped anchor, a crew member or two—who "by chance" happened to be Soviet specialists on China—slipped off for shore leave and contacted every China watcher they could find. In the few hours they were permitted ashore, they bought Chinese-language newspapers (both Nationalist and Communist), talked to as many experts as they could, then boarded launches back to the freighters and were off.

With the Nixon opening to China, Soviet China specialists turned up on the roster of the U.N. mission in New York and the Washington embassy. They pumped every American correspondent and traveler back from China. They began to invite American scholars to lecture in Moscow. The hunger for information about China was insatiable.

It was heightened, as I learned, by a new minipurge. When Sino-Soviet relations got worse in the 1960s a security drive, once again, was launched against China specialists and scholarly institutes. Once again the institutes were closed. Professors no longer were permitted access to current literature. Periodicals were not even delivered. The whole academic apparatus was put on hold. No physical reprisals this time, no one, as far as I could learn, put under house arrest, but research on China ground to a halt.

Some academics, famished for the bread of their trade, made visits to Prague and Warsaw to use their libraries (not affected by the minipurge).

The security campaign relaxed after a few months. Someone in the Kremlin suddenly realized that, in a time of crisis, more—not less—information was needed about China. Gradually with the slowness characteristic of a creaky bureaucracy, the institutes got going again, word was circulated to the specialists to collect every scrap of data possible. Teams of experts began to seek invitations to meet with their counterparts in the West.

But the minipurge was a significant event. It told me again what I had long understood—in time of crisis, a bureaucracy reacts in panic; it puts blinkers on its eyes when it should be reaching for a telescope. The first instinct is against those who know most about the potential enemy. They are seen not as resources, but as a nest of possible spies.

In 1972, Stalin had been dead for nineteen years, but his spirit lived on in the headquarters of the Party on Tsentralnaya

Ploshchad and up the hill in the Lubyanka, where the secret police still have their headquarters. Their first instinctive move was against the men who might once again "lose China." Only after that could the Kremlin turn to the problem of how to cope with its great rival to the East. It was in the idiom of a great Russian scientist a true Pavlovian response.

23 | War Between Russia and China

I was brought up in the tradition of the scoop. The scoop was dinned into my head by my first city editors, Leslie M. Harkness and Bill Mason, an old Hearst man, on the *Minneapolis Journal*. The scoop was exhalted into a cult by the United Press. First was not only best, it was everything. UP was built on this philosophy: first on the story; first, if even by seconds or minutes, but first.

This was an absolute, and it was the only way the United Press, a shirt-sleeve news agency fighting the mighty Associated Press, could survive. UP didn't have money, didn't have experience, didn't have manpower. What it had was a corps of excitable, underfed, underpaid, lean youngsters who could run faster, think quicker, and write more speedily than anyone. No time for second thoughts. No depth. Just get the story onto the wire a hair's breadth ahead of the stuffy AP, and write it in machinegun bursts of bullet words—a one-sentence lead paragraph and no sentence over ten words. We were trained to be the toughest, fastest competitors. No money but quick warm praise, a band of brothers.

Our obsession with First was just shrewd commercial instinct. If UP's teletype chattered out the story first, the chances were a newspaper's telegraph editor would send it to the composing room, and it would be on its way into type before AP waddled in.

Of course, being first is a cliché of reporting. Its roots go back to the Pony Express and before. The first messenger to bring the news of Napoleon's defeat carried the power of wealth or bankruptcy in his pouch. The first great news agency was founded by Julius von Reuter to transmit commercial information by pigeon post between Aachen and Verviers, Belgium. The House of Rothschild prospered because its network of informers was bigger and swifter than its competitors'.

There was no way I could enjoy missing a First on China. I had, I thought, positioned myself well to beat the field. True, I was not an Old China Hand. I did not have the advantage of long close connections, which so many correspondents had woven before World War II and during the war in the caves of Yan'an and the bomb shelters of Chongqing. I did not have the Chinese language. I was, let's face it, a Johnny-come-lately.

But I had built up assets in the long years when China was closed as an oyster to the West, when China was a forgotten story and no one was paying attention. I had worked like a coolie, studying the country from the outside, developing my contacts and establishing a presence for myself. By 1971 I had spent twelve years working on China from that moment of Nadam, July 11, 1959, when I climbed the staircase of the Government Palace in Ulan Bator and found the Russians lined up on one side, the Chinese on the other. From that time forward, I had carried on my campaign month by month, year in, year out, with as much originality and perseverance as I could muster.

All this reached a crescendo in 1969. That was the year Charlotte and I made our second trip to Mongolia (the fourth for me). That was the year Soviet-Chinese tensions hit a peak, and this, of course, was why we were visiting Ulan Bator again. Why the United States had not established diplomatic relations with Mongolia I did not understand and do not to this day. I had strongly raised the question with the State Department in 1959. It seemed so obviously in our interest, and there were those in the department who agreed that Ulan Bator was a listening post par excellence on the Sino-Soviet scene. The department even assigned two young officers to learn Mongolian, but years went by and nothing happened. Not until 1987 did we agree to exchange diplomats. Every major country had long recognized Mongolia. Not us. This stupidity (there is no other word for it) is exceptional in the catalog of American diplomacy. At first it was explained that we could not do it, because it would anger Chiang Kai-shek. Later, it was claimed we could not do it because we would offend Beijing which, of course, had long had its own diplomatic ties to Mongolia. The real answer may be buried in inertia and possibly the veto of some individual with unfathomable personal resentments. It's a real puzzle.

Our trip to Ulan Bator in 1969 proved a ten-strike. The border fighting had begun between China and Russia in the winter and seemed to be escalating. In Hong Kong on our way to Ulan Bator, we had seen Chinese newsreels of the fighting on the Ussuri and the Amur. The Chinese had attacked Soviet positions on the Ussuri islands in heavy snow and white camouflage uniforms. They destroyed Russian tanks, armored troop carriers, and artillery posts. It looked like large-scale warfare. On the Amur, Chinese in rowboats and launches sallied out against Russian gunboats. The Russians, grins visible in the pictures, turned high pressure water hoses on the Chinese, but the Chinese had the last laugh. They clambered aboard and cut the hoses with axes. The Chinese audience in Hong Kong cheered and leaped to their feet.

The casualties in this were not small. I heard that they ran into hundreds and thousands and that one Soviet division had been badly cut up.

The propaganda between the countries escalated. The Chinese called the Russians the "New Czars." Moscow called Mao "an Asian Hitler." Each contended the other had abandoned Communism and embraced Capitalism. Moscow claimed Mao had never read Marx. Beijing said Moscow's god was Wall Street.

As our plane touched down on the familiar Ulan Bator airfield, I was astonished to see a squadron of Soviet advanced MIG fighters parked at the edge. A Soviet military transport came in as we gathered our luggage. Soviet Army trucks loaded with troops and supplies passed us on the aspen-lined asphalt road into Ulan Bator.

In the days that followed, we traveled widely. Never before had I seen the *purga,* the duststorm of the Gobi, great brown clouds that smeared a dirty scum over the sky, reaching to the horizon. There was dust between our teeth. A gauze nose bandage did not keep it out of Charlotte's lungs. At night we hardly dared open windows. Just a crack let in three or four inches of dust. The whole Gobi was blowing off to north China, the grass steppes ravaged by Russian plows.

But it was not the dust that captured my attention. It was the Soviet army. It was everywhere. Here they were rushing to build a *voenny gorodok,* a military encampment, a permanent camp with wooden houses (the lumber must have been brought from Siberia), there an air strip on the flat steppe. Along the roads technicians were installing complex equipment in cement chambers buried in hillsides facing away from China. I had never seen such equipment, but I knew it must relate to an advanced weapons system. (When I got back to the U.S.A., I telephoned the CIA and said that if they would tell me what the equipment was, I would tell them where I saw it. They refused, so I called a friend at the Defense Department who readily explained: It was high-tech transmission relays, for use, he felt certain, with nuclear missile installations.)

Diplomats in Ulan Bator told me the buildup had been begun during the winter in such a hurry and in such numbers there could be no concealment. Travel south to the Gobi was interdicted. Everywhere the diplomats went, they found the Soviet military, airfields being built, barracks complexes, the streets of Ulan Bator roaring with military trucks and tanks. "They are getting ready for war," one diplomat said. So it seemed to me. This was not a Potemkin show, a show to frighten the Chinese. This was for real. No disagreement among the diplomats about that. When I got back to Moscow, I found plenty of support. The Soviet military were, I learned, advocating a "surgical blow" against China, a calculated nuclear strike to "take out a few Chinese cities" including Beijing. Better strike now, they said, before the Chinese get too strong. It reminded me of what some U.S. generals were saying about Russia at the end of World War II.

War was in the wind. Of this I was certain by the time I got back to New York. It well might break out at any time. The fighting on the Amur and the Ussuri was followed by fighting on the Xinjiang-Kazakhstan border. By this time I was at work writing a short book giving the background of the Russia-China conflict, the ancient national enmity, going back to the earliest contacts of the two powers along the Amur River in the summer of 1650, at a small settlement called Albasin. Neither side had any notion of the identity of the warriors it was fighting: The Chinese had never heard of Russia; the Russians had no idea this was an outpost of the new Manchu dynasty of China.

I traced the hostility between the empires, recalled the unequal treaties imposed on China through the nineteenth century, under which she was compelled to cede to Russia possibly 1.5 million square miles of territory—the emirates of central Asia, the Maritime Provinces, much of Siberia east of Lake Baikal, and Mongolia. I explained the conflict of the two Communist parties and of Stalin and Mao (I didn't know much about the early rows of the 1920s and 1930s). I offered my hypothesis of the double-dealing by which Stalin maneuvered the Chinese into war with the United States in Korea. And I recited the steady rise of hostility in the decade since the 1959 break between Khrushchev and Mao. It was succinct, concise, and complete. I proposed to call the book *The Coming War Between Russia and China.* My editor, Evan Thomas, was so alarmed by what I wrote he feared that war might break out before he could get the book into print. He changed the title to *War Between Russia and China.* The more phlegmatic British brought it out under the original title. Breaking every rule known to the publishing industry, Thomas managed to get the book out by mid-October 1969.

By that time, as is now evident, the peak of the crisis was passing. Ho Chi Minh had died September 3, 1969. The chiefs of the Communist world gathered at Hanoi for the funeral. With border fighting escalating, Moscow had sent a circular telegram to the Communist countries of Eastern Europe and the big parties of France and Italy, warning that the situation might lead to war. The Chinese were feverishly building air raid shelters under their big cities. They knew they had no defense against the nuclear weapons Moscow had targeted on the main Chinese cities. The whole population, schoolchildren and all, was thrown into the task. The lovely old city walls of Beijing were tumbled down and the stones used to hold up the shelters. When I finally got to Beijing in 1972, stacks of stones and steel reinforcing rods lined the streets, shelter building was still going on. We were taken to the busy shopping center, and there, from a trapdoor in the rear of a dress-goods shop, entered the labyrinth of the multilayered shelter system, complete with electricity, power plants, water supply, hospitals, workshops, dormitories, and factories. We saw a shelter at Huhehot in Inner Mongolia big enough for trucks and buses to drive miles under the city to deep mountain caverns, blasted from granite, far outside. (I still doubt that many would have survived a Soviet strike.) The Chinese had zeroed their own nuclear missiles on industrial cities in the Urals and Siberia. Their rockets could not yet reach European Russia.

The moment I heard of Ho's death, I cabled Pham Van Dong for permission to come to Hanoi. I got no reply. Several months later I learned from Marc Ribou, the French photographer who had happened to be in Hanoi at the time, that the Vietnamese had cabled me to come but, alas, the cable must have gone astray.

At Ho's funeral the Communist leaders called on Moscow to make one more effort to avert war with China. Zhou Enlai had deliberately left Hanoi before the Russians could arrive. Now Kosygin cabled Beijing asking permission to fly there and meet with Zhou. The Chinese response was delayed (deliberately?) until Kosygin was airborne on his flight back to Moscow. The message, however, was forwarded, and he received it at a refueling halt at Tashkent. He switched plans and flew 2,500 miles east to Beijing and met Zhou in the lounge of the Beijing airport.

By this time the Russians had massed a million or more troops on the China frontier, including crack armored divisions, missile forces, and their most advanced air elements. They were poised to strike. The Chinese probably had close to 2 million on the frontier. Their equipment was far inferior. Their hope was to make up in manpower what they lacked in metal.

Zhou and Kosygin talked for six hours. They did not leave the airport. They agreed to engage in diplomatic talks to attempt to resolve the border disputes. The talks were to open in late October. It was, in essence, a standstill agreement for one last effort to avert war. When the Russians and Chinese met in late October, they agreed on only one thing—to meet again. They could not even agree upon an agenda. The meetings would continue intermittently for the next twenty years—they were still in progress in 1987. No agenda had yet been agreed upon. For two decades nothing happened.

I took a sardonic satisfaction in these endless, frustrating conversations and the frozen faces which the Chinese brought to the conference table. Leonid F. Ilyichev had been named chief Soviet negotiator. For years he was put through a devastatingly rigid diplomatic experience. It was cruel and inhuman, but I thought he deserved it. He had been editor of *Pravda* before Stalin's death and then was shifted to head the Soviet Press group under Khrushchev. He and I had become enemies. He, it was, who had barred me from Moscow for many years. He had sworn that I would never set foot on Soviet soil. It seemed to me fitting that he be subjected to the Kafkaesque trauma of meeting again and again with Chinese diplomats who never smiled, never spoke an unnecessary word, and never budged from their position during the sixteen years in which he was compelled to meet with them.

* * *

The war between Russia and China did not come to pass, but long before I arrived in Beijing, my book, as I was to discover, had made its way there, had been translated, read by Zhou Enlai and the highest government circles, probably including Mao himself, and had been made compulsory reading for everyone in the Foreign Office. The first hint I had of this came from Scotty Reston, who got to Beijing in July of 1971 simultaneously (although he did not know it) with his friend Henry Kissinger, who had slipped into China secretly via Pakistan in the first move of President Nixon's "opening." Zhou told Scotty that he and others had read my book and found it good.

What Zhou did not tell Scotty—and what I later learned from Qiao Guanhua, China's foreign minister who later fell from grace for casting his lot with Mao's widow, Jiang Qing—was that my book had become the subject of dispute between the Russians and the Chinese.

Objective as *War Between Russia and China* was, in my opinion, the Russians disliked it as much as the Chinese liked it. At a session of the Sino-Soviet border meetings in 1970, Soviet Deputy Foreign Minister Vasily Kuznetsov marched into the conference with a copy of *War Between Russia and China* tucked under his arm. He slammed it on the table and charged that it was a cooked-up work of propaganda, a provocation that the Chinese had put me up to. Delightedly, Qiao Guanhua told me, the Chinese assured the Russians they had nothing to do with the book, had never met me, but thought I had done an excellent and objective job.

After I came back to the United States from China in 1972, I chanced to mention to a Soviet diplomat that I was interested to know that my book had become the subject of a dispute between Moscow and Beijing.

"Who told you that?" the man said angrily.

"Well," I responded, "I heard that in Beijing."

"Oh," said the Russian, "I thought that must be the case. The Chinese have done it again. They have broken their word. We have an agreement that neither side will say a word about what happens in our talks. Now the Chinese have been talking. It's typical of them. You can't trust them."

So it is possible, I suppose, that Zhou Enlai was speaking the plain truth when he said I had lost my chance to be No. 1 into Beijing, because the Chinese thought that my notoriety with the

Russians would put another drop of vinegar into an already high acid mixture.

But I think the situation was more complex. The final dash to Beijing was touched off by the Ping-Pong Championship in Tokyo in April 1971. When the Chinese won the championship, most of the teams asked if they might visit Beijing. Zhou Enlai put the matter to Mao Zedong. Zhou—so he told me—didn't think much of the idea. Mao did. He said: Why not? Then he wanted to know about the Americans. The Americans hadn't asked for a trip. Mao said, never mind, get hold of them. Let them come too. Which they did, and when that news became public, half the reporters in the United States (myself included) cabled Beijing seeking permission to come to China.

Once again Zhou bundled up the requests and went to Mao. Once again Zhou, or so he said, was negative on the idea. But Mao overruled him. Let them come, Mao said. Give permission to some of them.

In reality, it is easy to see now, Mao—and I have no doubt Zhou—were opening the way toward relations with the United States. Mao had hinted at this to Edgar Snow in the fall of 1970. He had said that President Nixon was welcome to come to China for a vacation—a phrase that had not escaped the notice of Mr. Nixon and Henry Kissinger. I am sorry to say that the *Times* did not carry Snow's interview, after a squabble supposedly over the sky-high price demanded by Ed's Paris agent. I say "supposedly" because at one point, Ed offered to let the *Times* print the Mao interview for free. It was a document of world importance, but the text was ultimately run only in *The New Republic*.

So—despite Zhou Enlai's disclaimers—I think that the Chinese were carefully orchestrating signals to the White House that it was time for a change.

When Mao gave Zhou the go-ahead (and this comes from Zhou himself), he decided that the first wave would be Old China Hands, men and women who knew China, who had been there in the 1930s and through the war years, and whom Zhou knew personally. Telegrams went out to a handful of them including Jack Belden, once a *Time-Life* man, long since ill and retired in Paris, and Tillman Durdin and his wife, Peggy, of *The New York Times*. Zhou Enlai had been dining with the Durdins in Chungking the night his own quarters were bombed out by the Japanese. They were old friends even if the Durdins had been quite friendly with

Taiwan. Never mind, said Zhou: Find Till Durdin. I want him and Peggy in the first group to come to Beijing. This was not easy. Durdin was finally located in Sri Lanka. He and Peggy did, indeed, join the first wave, although because of Peggy's illness, their stay in China was cut short. Belden made it, but wound up with three months in a Beijing hospital.

Till got into China April 15 and was followed by a small covey of *Times* people. Audrey Topping, wife of Seymour, foreign editor of the *Times,* arrived in China ten days later with her father, Chester Ronning, born in China of a missionary family, an old friend of Zhou Enlai and former Canadian ambassador. In a couple of weeks Audrey's husband, Seymour, joined the party at Zhou's invitation.

Then it was decided, probably by Zhou, that there should be a second wave—not of old-timers but of new men, men of influence, columnists and/or editors. First, Joseph Alsop was considered. He was an Old China Hand, in a sense, having been in China during World War II on the staff of General Claire Chennault. He was a distinguished columnist, had a wide following, but he had become so violently anti-Communist and pro-Chiang that his name was put aside for that of James Reston, who had equal distinction as a columnist for *The New York Times* and, so far as was known in Beijing, a reasonably objective point of view. That was how Reston came to get the nod, I was told by the Chinese.

So it turned out that I became a tortoise and not a hare on China.

24 | The Long March

In the winter of 1972 Charlotte and I made plans to visit Italy. Charlotte had lived there for a while, and she wanted to introduce me to the Renaissance. Then I got the letter from Moscow on March 20, and everything changed. The North Koreans were inviting me to come to Pyongyang.

My interest in Korea, north or south, I confess, was not intense. We had visited Seoul in 1966, and Charlotte had suffered a stomach upset so severe I feared for her life. It was over in a few days but left an aftershock. Neither of us was in a mood to trade Leonardo for heroic statues of Kim Il-sung, the North Korean dictator.

But there was a catch. To get to North Korea I would have to transit China, and at this late date I had not yet managed to get to Beijing. In fact, the invitation to North Korea was the product of a convoluted strategy I had initiated in 1970 about the time I launched the Op-Ed page of the *Times*. I had become convinced that my sometime hero, sometime nemesis, Abe Rosenthal, had decided to get a correspondent other than me—anyone would do—into China before I got there. Today this may seem a paranoid notion, but at the time I believed it might be true. So, in my usual contrary fashion, I decided to try the back door to Beijing—via Pyongyang.

Of course, North Korea had been on my shopping list for a good many years, but now I began to forward hand-carried messages to Pyongyang, reminding Kim Il-sung of my deep interest in North Korea, especially now that, as it seemed, the glaciated texture of Communist Asia was beginning to thaw a bit. I subjected him to the usual barrage of cables, renewing a campaign I had carried on at intervals since 1961 or even before.

So when one morning I found on my desk an invitation to Korea, postmarked Moscow and signed by the North Korean Journalists Association, Charlotte and I set about rearranging our lives. Whether I could turn the two-bagger (Pyongyang) into a homer (Beijing), I did not know, but I would give it a college try. Charlotte went off to Italy with her daughter, Charlotte, and I stayed behind to negotiate with the Koreans and the Chinese.

May 1, 1972, found me aboard Northwest Airlines Flight 3 to Anchorage and Tokyo, Charlotte in Italy with her Charlotte, and my mind pounding with unanswered questions. Could I get a transit visa through China to North Korea, or would I have to go by way of Moscow? Would the Russians, who had been remarkably hostile to the idea of visas for me in recent years, give me one if the Chinese wouldn't? Would the Chinese let Charlotte and me make a reporting trip in China after Pyongyang? If they wouldn't, could I go back to Vietnam (Nixon had just escalated the war again)? Could I, if all else failed, go back to Mongolia for a new look? (Tsedenbal quickly said no.)

I had mixed feelings, I noted in my diary, as we flew northwest following the still frozen Mackenzie River. I was meeting John Lee, the *Times* correspondent in Tokyo, who would accompany me. There had already been publicity in the Japanese (and some European) papers, and my trip was being taken as having an important diplomatic significance—which, I supposed it had, although exactly what that significance might be I did not know. There had not been an American reporter in North Korea since World War II (except for the war correspondents who accompanied MacArthur in the swift American drive to the Yalu river followed by the even swifter American retreat when Mao sent 1 million Chinese "volunteers" over the border). As far as I could discover there had been no U.S. or western non-Communist correspondents in North Korea since the 1930s. The Japanese had kept the area tightly sealed. So, if nothing went wrong, the trip would be another "first" for me, another hermit kingdom penetrated, a good and important story, but, as I noted, "not a great consolation prize for the loss of being first in China—but a nice one, an interesting one," and I should at least get a glimpse of China even if I didn't win permission for a real look. The permit for Korea was, I knew, a tail to the opening up of China. If Nixon could go to China, well then, I could go to North Korea.

I thought of the many times I had set out on missions like this, how many times I had sat in the plane, taken out my notebook, and tried to pull my thoughts together and figure out what it really meant to me. I had been doing this since 1942 when I flew to England in the marvelous old flying boat with the built-in bunks and lounge and white-jacketed stewards, fine steaks, very dry martinis, vintage wines, and overnight stops at Bermuda, the Azores, and Lisbon. In those days I was an excited youngster off to the great adventure of my generation—the War. Now another kind of war, Vietnam, was still in progress. "It is the bitterest taste of my life," I wrote, "on, on, on, in spite of all we do."

A North Korean delegation met me at Tokyo airport with a great bouquet of red carnations—there would be red carnations all along the route to Pyongyang. I got to the Okura Hotel about midnight. Hardly had I dropped off when David Schneiderman, my assistant at Op-Ed, called from New York. Mr. Kao of the Chinese embassy in Ottawa wanted to talk to me. In ten minutes I had him on the line. I noted: "The jackpot! Chinese transit visas for John Lee and myself and a trip through China for Charlotte and me when I return from Pyongyang. Now the trip begins to have a real purpose."

Next day I telephoned New York and caught Charlotte as she walked into our house at 349 East 84th Street from Italy. She had just put her bags down when the telephone rang—me, calling from Tokyo: "Go up to Ottawa to the Chinese consulate, get your visa, and meet me in Beijing."

I had made the trip to Lo Wu, the Hong Kong boundary town, in 1966, climbing to the security deck of the railroad station and peering gingerly into Shum Chun, seeing the grim-faced PLA men, the barbed wire, and the peaceful peasants tending water buffalo and chickens along the little creek that separated Communist China from Hong Kong's Leased Territories.

Now, heart racing with excitement, I rode the suburban electric train toward China, passengers thinning out until only a handful were left at the border. John and I picked up our bags and typewriters, marched out across the railroad bridge, halted by solemn PLA men, waved on inside the Shum Chun station. Miraculously we walked into China!

Veteran of a hundred crossings into Russia and other Communist countries, I dreaded the grim customs examination. I hauled my bags up on the counter and started to open them. A young Chinese woman smiled at me and said, "The customs examination is completed."

I could not believe my ears. But it was true. So it was all the way to Beijing—and beyond. Good humor, courtesy, charm, informality, problems dissolving with a word and a smile. *This* was Communist China? This was the forbidden land of the red peril? This was the scene of the *luan,* the madness of the Great Proletarian Cultural Revolution?

Something was wrong. Of course I had read all the accounts by my colleagues, but nothing prepared me for this benign atmosphere. John and I had hardly gotten to Beijing when we were received by Ma Yuzhen, the Foreign Office press chief. That evening, with no interpreter, no guide, I called a taxi at the Hsin Chiao Hotel (I hardly knew the name) and drove off under a velvet sky through streets so empty I thought I had come to the end of the world, no policeman at intersections, millions of people sleeping all around but not a sound, hardly a light in the buildings, two solitary bicycles the only sign of life. I knew not a word of Chinese, my driver not a word of English. No one knew where I was, not even myself. A quick turn from dark street into a darker *hutang,* and I could vanish beyond any finding. Just vanish.

The Foreign Office was bright and alert, Mr. Ma on duty, brisk and smiling, newsmen bustling in and out, a Japanese from the Kyoto news agency, an Agence France-Presse man, a North Vietnamese, I was in the traffic stream, no big news, but a good page 1 story, a Chinese protest against Nixon's escalation in Vietnam. I rode back to the hotel, called New York, got the desk in twenty minutes, dictated my story, and lay awake for hours excited as a child on Christmas Eve. I was in China at last. I was in Beijing, the enormous and mysterious city of which I had dreamed all my life. I was covering the news, writing stories, plunging out into the unknown streets to a Foreign Office whose name I could not say in Chinese, whose location I could not have told if my life depended on it, writing and dictating as I had for a lifetime. Of course I could not sleep. I heard a deep rhythmic pounding. I thought it was my heart, but when I went to the window, I heard a switch engine in the distance chuffing away as the switch engines had in the railroad yards just beyond the old house at 107 Royalston Avenue in Minneapolis.

I lay back in my snug bed and relaxed. My worries about Charlotte arriving alone in Beijing dropped away. Mr. Ma had asked about her before I could even raise the topic, had promised to take care of her if I was late in getting back from Pyongyang.

He asked me to telegraph him from Pyongyang what I would like to do in China, and he would make the arrangements.

I was on a high. I was still, I thought, a romantic, but I was something else as well. I had not engaged in this long, long struggle with all its dramatic twists and turns just for the sake of adventure. I believed then (as I believe now) that the world's future lay in Asia, that Asia and specifically China would determine our fate. This, I thought, was the significance of the century—not, as Henry Luce had thought, the American century but the prelude to the Asian century. We were witnesses to a tidal shift in world power, comparable to the shift to Europe when she mastered the technology of the gunpowder which China had invented, when she armed her galleons and frigates and privateers and adventurers with their letters of marque and set them to plundering the East.

Now, I was confident, the Asian renaissance was at hand. World War II had liberated the continent. Every great nation had won its freedom. We Americans had fought the final battles: we defeated Japan only to lay the basis for her extraordinary rise; we had tried but failed to dictate the future of China; we had tried but failed to hold the line in Korea; we had lost in Indochina although the terrible toll was still going on.

This was what underlay my interest in the continent. With all of China, as it seemed, asleep around me, I was so wide awake that I did not drop off until I heard the first sounds of the waking city, coughing and hawking, the shuffle of slippers on the sidewalks, the creak of carts, the muffled greetings, the dim clang of tin pails, and the slowly rising rustle of people riding to work on their bicycles.

I spent two weeks in Korea, angered by the gross anti-American propaganda, hating the *kimchi,* the Korean national dish, a kind of pickled cabbage which seemed to me to smell like an open sewer, and revolted by the manner in which children were taught songs such as "Let's Mutilate the Americans" and the "fact" that the U.S. had been the enemy since the visit of the warship *General Sherman* in 1866. On the night before we were to meet Kim Il-sung, I got into such a row with my escorts that I expected to be hurled over the border at dawn. In the fortnight's stay I had not met a single Korean peasant and not a single worker, until I had protested so loudly that they turned up four men carefully rehearsed to denounce the United States and its capitalist, imperialist leaders. When I told them that President Nixon was then in Moscow engaged in cordial discussions with Brezhnev, they were nonplussed. The event had not been reported in Korea. One afternoon in Kaesong, John Lee and I slipped out of the hotel and got 100 feet down the street before an alarmed escort caught up with us. It was our only unescorted walk. We were warned that we might be attacked by North Koreans, whose hatred for Americans could not be restrained. I hardly endeared myself by suggesting that there was much in common between Koreans and Americans—both of us were violently disliked by the Japanese. A poll had rated Koreans the most disliked foreigners, with Americans a close second.

There were a few light touches. We did meet Kim Il-sung the morning after the big row and had a long dull interview. We were late because our escorts had never been to Kim's palace and took the wrong turn. Kim opened the conversation by saying I had written him ten years before (actually it was eleven) saying I had some questions to ask: What were they? When the official photograph appeared in the paper next day, I was puzzled. It showed me sitting next to Kim—which I hadn't been. I looked more closely and saw that the picture had been spliced to eliminate the interpreter (English very poor) who sat between us. Kim Il-sung's photo dominated every issue of the newspaper. Most of them displayed spaces where participants had been blanked out.

Despite the show of bad feeling, the Koreans hounded me to stay longer. I refused, saying I had a date to meet Charlotte in Beijing. Finally Kim put a personal plane at our disposal. Even so Charlotte had been waiting a day in Beijing alone before I got back.

It was drizzling as the Korean plane touched down on the runway and taxied to a halt. I saw Charlotte standing on the airport steps with red umbrella and raincoat under a great portrait of Mao Zedong. I jumped out and raced to hug her. Rendezvous in Beijing! It took a few moments before I saw two Chinese and two Koreans (with big bouquets of red carnations) waiting to shake hands. One of the Chinese was Yao Wei, the Foreign Office man who was to be by our side for nearly two months and became a close friend. We rode to the Chien Mien Hotel, a marvelous grubby place, filled with PLA men and Overseas Chinese, dirty table linen and cheerful carefree waiters. I can't remember when I have been so happy as when Charlotte and I made our way to our big plain room with its big plain furniture, its big plain bed, its big green thermos jugs of hot water. We couldn't open the windows at night, the fumes from the next-door chemical plant were so gaseous.

I had telegraphed Ma Yuzhen of the Press Department a few days after getting to Korea with suggestions for what I wanted to do in China. "I would like very much," I said, "to visit the route of the Long March and Yenan as well as Chairman Mao's birthplace (Shaoshan)." Of course, I wanted to talk with Zhou Enlai and Madame Soong Chingling and to catch a glimpse, even at a distance, of Chairman Mao, but the Long March of Mao and the Red Army in 1934–35 was No. 1. It had been on my mind for years. Charlotte remembered me "babbling about it" as I came out of the operating room, still under ether, after a minor operation in 1971. And it was still on my mind when we dined with Zhou Enlai. I noticed that he wore leather sandals and walked with an easy gait, which I imagined he developed on the Long March. I felt sure that despite the years he could pick up his pack and start out in the morning and walk all day without a pause. When I said good night to him that evening, I told him I very much wanted to retrace the Long March and talk with the survivors. He looked hard at me under his inky black eyebrows, a quizzical look which I could not fathom, and made no reply.

I mention my request and Zhou's reaction not to demonstrate once again my habitual perseverance (stubbornness, if you will) in working toward reportorial goals, but as a sign of my ignorance of what had been and was going on in China.

I learned a good deal about Mao in China. I think I began to understand his character, his early character, after visiting his birthplace, Shaoshan, and the city of Changsha, where he began his career as a teacher and as a rather eccentric reformer and revolutionary.

I knew about Mao's struggle in the 1950s with the hero of the Long March, his old associate, General Peng Dehuai, and I knew something of the rise of the enigmatic Lin Biao whom Mao had named as his successor. I knew that Lin Biao had vanished from the scene in a mysterious plane crash in Mongolia in September 1971. But I did not understand what connections, if any, existed between Peng Dehuai and Lin Biao. I sensed there must have been a struggle between Lin Biao and Zhou Enlai, but I had no measure of its depth. Even now the circumstances of Lin Biao's death were a matter of rumor, and there would be no official announcement until after I left China in early July, quixotically believing it more important to get back to the U.S.A. and the national political conventions than to stay on and get more insight on China.

I did not know that the Cultural Revolution, in effect, *was still in progress*. It had, I thought, come to an end in 1968 and 1969, sort of petered out. Lin Biao? Well, he seemed to be an aberration. Now he was gone. The term "Gang of Four" had not come into use. Zhou Enlai seemed very much in charge. He had, I believed (and still think), engineered Nixon's visit to China. He was, so far as I understood, riding high in the aftermath of the Nixon rapprochement. It seemed to me that Mao was quietly receding into the traditional role of Elder Statesman and that Zhou in the chairman's name had his hand on the helm. Zhou publicly adopted a reverential attitude toward Mao. "We are all his students," he said solemnly during our dinner at the Great Hall of the People, "but we cannot do as well as he." I accepted this as a sincere expression of Zhou's devotion to his teacher. Now when I know so much more about Mao, the terror and paranoia of his last decade, the very strong signs that he sided with Lin Biao against Zhou (Mao was "jealous of Zhou's reputation in the world," one of the Old Guard told me in 1984), the petty (and not so petty) torment Mao inflicted on Zhou in the months before Zhou's death—well, I wonder. I wonder a great deal, and I wrestled with the enigma of Zhou almost every foot of the way when Charlotte and I finally took the Long March in 1984. I must have asked a thousand questions about Zhou and got no very convincing answer. I tried and tried to interview Zhou's widow, Deng Yingchao. She was one of the handful who did not see me. She had nothing to add to the official record. I wonder about that. No one—well, only one survivor of a martyred Party leader—was willing even to hint that Zhou had failed in any way to meet his high ideals. No one, I came to believe, was going to raise this question. In the debris of the Cultural Revolution and the Gang of Four, Zhou Enlai provided an icon for China to live by.

There is so much to ponder. Take the question of the Long

March and the proposals I made the moment I got to Beijing in 1972 to retrace its path and its politics. What naïveté! No wonder Zhou looked at me with that Mona Lisa smile. I did not know that the Cultural Revolution (if we are to use the conventional phrase—"Mao's Vengence" might be a more accurate one) was far from over. Yes, some victims had been released from prison and hard labor and placed under forced residence, usually in remote places in the countryside.

But what I was asking of Zhou was something of colossal gall—that Mao give me permission to exhume the bodies and reputations of his most illustrious victims, the men (and women and children), tortured or left to die in appalling circumstances. All of this Zhou knew, all of this had been done by his "teacher," part of the continuous struggle, sometimes hidden, sometimes not, which had been in progress for fifteen years and would run another four years until 1976, the year in which both Zhou and Mao would die.

What can I make of this? Was it one more case of ignorant journalist and sophisticated diplomat? Or was it, as I believe, something more complex. I had been through this kind of thing in the Soviet Union, the paranoia of Stalin and the outrages perpetrated by him on his people, those closest to him, his long-term associates.

Was I simply unwary in this new situation? Or did I face again a Rashomon in which the truth was so bent by refracting crystals of distance and time and space that there was no real way to relate Zhou's truth and my truth.

I have not found the answer to this question, but not from failure to talk to men and women who were Mao's victims, the walking wounded, the crippled survivors of the Cultural Revolution. I spoke with many on every trip we made to China and particularly on the Long March in 1984, but there are still gaps in the patchwork.

Perhaps naïveté has its uses. It held me on course—the course to the goal of retracing the route of the Red Army in 1934–35. Within a year or so I understood much of what lay behind Zhou's quizzical smile. I knew enough about the Cultural Revolution to realize I was not likely to achieve my ambition while Mao lived, but I plowed ahead. In 1973 I acquired an ally—John S.

Service, the famous Old China Hand, the diplomat the State Department expelled in McCarthy days but who fought in the courts and got his job back. Jack was born in Chengdu where his father headed the YMCA, had lived in China much of his life, and walked the mountains of Sichuan as a young man, knew and loved the country. In Yan'an days, he met Mao and the other Communist leaders, and his dispatches to the State Department are classics of information and judgment. No one—Chinese or American—can write about China without drawing on Jack's insight.

Jack and I knew each other only casually, but when my book, *To Peking and Beyond,* was published, he liked it. He wrote that he and his wife, Caroline, were thinking of another trip to China (they had been there in 1971) and perhaps we might join forces. He liked to walk. How about going on a walking trip along the Yangtze? I liked to walk too, but I had a better idea.

"One thing which I thought would make a wonderful framework for a trip," I wrote, "would be a reconstruction of the Long March. We could do that, walking, in part, jeeping in part, and covering other areas by train or plane so as not to take two years! I was thinking about the possibility of doing this this coming fall. What do you think?"

I told Jack that Yao Wei, our friend and companion of 1972, had just been to the United States. I had discussed the March with him. He thought a walking trip would be too hard. We didn't, he said, understand how difficult conditions were in the countryside. Yao Wei, I conceded, might be right, but why didn't we try anyway? As years went by, Jack and I lobbied our project with any Chinese official who would listen.

The more I learned, the more I wanted to document the odyssey of Mao and his Communist movement. I had to begin at the beginning, and the beginning was the Long March. That had given birth to the movement, that had shaped its form, had crystallized its spirit, and placed Mao at its head. It was, I was convinced, an epic of our time—the 6,000-mile retreat over terrible mountains, terrifying deserts, devilish rivers, impenetrable swamps across China's outer reaches, the lands which climb up to the mountain core of Asia, the heartland of which MacKinder wrote, the Himalayas, the Pamirs, the Tien Shan, the cruelest barriers nature has erected against the passage of man.

* * *

Again and again Charlotte and I went back to China. We traversed the length of the northern periphery with the Soviet Union—Manchuria, Inner Mongolia (so like yet so different from Outer Mongolia where we had often been), the endless deserts and oases of the Northwest, the old Silk Road, Xinjiang, and up to the Soviet frontier, Tibet and the then almost impassable stone trail from Lhasa under the brow of Everest to Kathmandu (we had to hike around great landslides like those that had barricaded us in Sikkim). There wasn't much of China we hadn't seen—except the beauty spots.

With Mao dead, Zhou dead, Zhu De dead, so many of Mao's heroic Long March commanders dead, I confess I began to wonder if our Long March would ever come about. Charlotte hoped the project was dead. She didn't think we could survive it. We were too old. I had acquired a pacemaker. Jack Service had had a bad heart attack. Neither his wife nor his doctor thought the Long March would be a good idea.

So on August 17, 1983, I got a telephone call from a Chinese correspondent in New York. Was I still interested in going on the Long March? Will a duck swim? If so, I was invited. Could Charlotte come, too? Of course. How about Jack Service. No problem. To say that Charlotte was overjoyed would not be correct. I was coming up to seventy-five, and, as it transpired, she would celebrate her seventieth birthday in Beijing as we prepared, in March 1984, to take off. Jack, a year younger than I, miraculously got the agreement of both wife and doctor and joined us.

The Long March was difficult. I developed a heart irregularity in the back country, but thanks to Charlotte's nursing (the Chinese called her "a model wife"), some fine Chinese doctors, and long distance consultation with my doctor, Peter Schrag in New York, it did not prove serious. We continued the March, and it was, in the end, worth the grinding pressures, the years of nagging, the physical stress of saw-boned mountains, jungle heat and June blizzards on the bend of the Yellow River. "I enjoyed it," Charlotte said. Jack agreed. It was the experience of our lives—and those of our remarkable Chinese companions, General Qin and interpreter and friend, Zhang Yuanyuan. We emerged with the story—not just the exploration of 6,000 miles (we traveled 7,400 miles on land by jeep, land rover, minibus, mule, horseback, and by foot) but the historical record, all that was preserved in the memories of the survivors, high and low, the top men of Deng Xiaoping's government, and the ordinary men and women who made the march at sixteen or seventeen and lived to become the steel core of Mao's movement. We explored the archives, such as there were, correlating our findings with those of the official historians.

It gave me not only a cavalcade of the history of China for the past half century but an extraordinary insight into China today and its problems, a panorama of life in the remote, almost medieval back country, where we were the first Westerners since the missionary era, a territory long off-limits, visited by few Chinese from outside. Not until we blazed the trail had a Chinese (or anyone else) thought to follow in those footsteps of 1934.

Edgar Snow, after hearing tales of the Long March from Mao and Zhou and Zhu De and the others in the caves of Pao'an in 1936, wrote in *Red Star over China:* "Some day someone will write the full story of this exciting epic." He had hoped to write the story himself but never did, and not until *The Long March: The Untold Story* appeared, had the narrative been put together. Only when the book was translated and published in China, first serialized week by week in a publication called *Reference News* (circulation 5 million) and then in hard cover and paperback editions by the Military Publishing House, did Chinese readers have access to more than brief reminiscences, usually of hortatory character (*Chairman Mao on the Long March,* written by his batman). Publication of *The Long March* in Chinese generated a powerful demand among Chinese historians and scholars that they be given equal access to sources and equal freedom to publish factual history.

China specialists and nonspecialists have asked me how I knew I was getting at the facts. Good question, one I have raised myself. Of course I did not get all the story. But I got a great deal more than anyone ever had before—including the Chinese. Again and again by dint of questioning, of skepticism, of what I can only call police reporter tactics, of comparing and contrasting differing versions, I have been able to get close to what really happened. Again and again Chinese specialists who helped to dig out the facts were astonished to find that, after I had rejected the first version and insisted on deeper digging, they did in fact find evidence that made sense.

The Long March raised more questions than I could possibly answer. There remain passages of Chinese history with which I am not satisfied, including those shadowy patches in the biography of the man whom I so admire—Zhou Enlai. There are the contradictions in the philosophy of Mao Zedong. There is the still puzzling story of Lin Biao, of Chiang Kai-shek's kidnapping December 12, 1936, at Sian, of the rivalry between Mao Zedong and Zhang Guotao (did Zhang really plot to kill Mao?), of Zhu De and Mao, of Jiang Qing and the Gang of Four. There are 100 unanswered questions still waiting, and there is China, the giant of Napoleon's epigram, no longer sleeping, shaking off the sloth of centuries, moving ahead under that contradictory and extraordinary little man, Deng Xiaoping, five feet tall and packaged like a bundle of dynamite. Nothing will keep me from going back again and again to China so long as those questions haunt me.

25 | A Verray Parfit Gentil Knight

He moved, I thought, like a panther, puissant, supple, swift, his dark eyes showing flecks of gold, a man of grace, a man whose wit flashed like a tanager's wing, hands sensitive and lips that could be cold as iron. No man I have met in a lifetime has left so deep a mark on me. He was Zhou Enlai, scion of a decayed noble family, Premier of Communist China. For nearly ten years, 1965–75, only his pliant mind and steel will kept his country from the abyss.

The image of Zhou as I saw him first on the evening of July 28, 1954, at Spiridonovka House in Moscow is fixed in my eye as though with an engraver's tool. He was fifty-six years old, dark hair not touched with gray, face smooth, heavy black eyebrows, sparkling eyes. In the half-hour I observed him at a reception given by Vyacheslav M. Molotov, there was not a pause. He was moving, gliding, talking, teasing the Russians, sometimes Peck's Bad Boy, sometimes grave as Buddha. Like so many Americans—Edgar Snow, Teddy White, Anna Louise Strong, John Hersey, General Stilwell—I fell in love with Zhou on first sight.

July 1954 was a moment of triumph in Zhou's life. He was on his way home from Geneva, where he had negotiated the accords that ended (for a time) hostilities in Indochina. By Zhou's side that evening in the old Spiridonov Palace in the Arbat quarter was Pham Van Dong, the Premier of North Vietnam, whom twelve years later I would meet in Hanoi in the midst of the war. On this evening he was quiet, retiring, almost an invisible tail to Zhou's comet.

It was an evening that stayed in my mind, and as I was to discover, it did not vanish from Zhou's. I remembered it with delight, Zhou with sadness not for the prankishness with which he tweaked the Russians but for what happened to Vietnam after the agreement which he persuaded Pham Van Dong to sign against Pham's better judgment. But that came later. On the night at Spiridonovka, he was skittish as a colt, taunting the Russians. The party was given by the stone-faced Molotov, who hadn't laughed since Lenin died in 1924. The whole Politburo was there: Nikita Khrushchev; Georgi Malenkov, soon to depart for distant Kazakhstan to run a power station, confessing, in his letter of resignation, that he lacked the experience to be Premier; Anastas Mikoyan, dark, cynical, looking, as his comrades often said, like an Armenian businessman ("In America," they said, "you'd be a millionaire"; they probably were right). There were the others: Lazar Kaganovich, not yet ousted by Khrushchev, tall, heavy-shouldered, glum; Nikolai Bulganin, drinking a little too much as always; and, improbably, the British, Indian, and Swedish ambassadors, invited because they maintained diplomatic relations with China.

I was not invited to this inner circle, but in my reporter's way I had sidled from room to room, from the big reception hall where I was supposed to stay, through the outer inner reception room, filled with low-ranking Chinese and low-ranking East Europeans, through the middle inner chamber (higher-ranking Chinese, Russians, and East Europeans), and to the holy of holies, the inner inner room, the Politburo room. A plainclothesman barred the door, but I could look over his shoulder and see and hear what was going on. I got an earful.

Zhou Enlai was gliding about the room, clinking glasses with the Russians, but he was saying, "Bottoms up!" not the Chinese *Gum Bei* or the Russian *Do adno.* He was speaking English, which none of his hosts understood. The only ones who knew what he was saying were the Western ambassadors—and myself, leaning in the doorway.

His hosts were not exactly pleased. "Why don't you speak Russian, Zhou?" Mikoyan said testily through an interpreter. "You know our language perfectly well."

Zhou responded saucily, "Look here, Mikoyan, why don't you learn Chinese? I've learned Russian."

"Chinese is a difficult language to learn," Mikoyan grumbled.

"No harder than Russian," Zhou snapped. "Come down to our embassy in the morning. We'll be glad to teach you Chinese."

Kaganovich, never noted for drawing room manners, exploded with a bit of Russian *mat',* a coarse mother oath. Zhou was not ruffled. He went on speaking in English, his remarks translated into Russian by a deft Chinese interpreter. "There's no excuse for you people," he said. Then he drank toasts with the ambassadors, the soul of politeness and protocol.

I was astonished. I didn't know whether Zhou was just indulging in high spirits or whether, as I suspected, he felt tired of Russian chauvinism and that, after China's debut on the international stage of Geneva, it was time that Russia began to treat China as an equal. Zhou believed then that China had scored a success at Geneva. The negotiations had brought the French war in Indochina to an end. There would, he seemed to suggest, be more victories in the future. No longer was China just a junior partner to Great Russian seniors.

There were many undercurrents that evening. One was Zhou's pride that he had met and bested John Foster Dulles. I learned a lot about that after Zhou's death from Wang Bingnan, one of the bright young Foreign Office men who accompanied Zhou to Geneva.

Wang had been entrusted with preparations. It was China's first appearance in the international world. She had been in purdah since October 1, 1949, and Zhou was determined that she would display her maturity and sophistication at Geneva. The Chinese delegation must be properly dressed and properly briefed. Wang was sent to the best Beijing tailor and ordered severe, dignified black tunics and trousers for everyone. When the Chinese went for their first stroll beside the lake in Geneva, the Swiss doffed their hats and bowed. Later the Chinese learned that the good burghers had taken them in their solemn black clothing to be a delegation of Chinese clergymen.

One thing, Wang told me, the world got wrong. John Foster Dulles did not snub Zhou by refusing to shake his hand. Zhou never offered his hand. In fact, Zhou had formally instructed all of the Chinese delegates and, indeed, Chinese diplomats around the world, not to shake hands with Americans unless the Americans extended their hands first. The rule was strictly followed at Geneva. Moreover Wang selected a route from the Chinese delegation office to the council room that avoided the path Dulles would follow. If, by chance, Zhou saw Dulles approaching, he would quickly turn away so no informal encounter would occur.

But, Wang said, the No. 2 in the U.S. delegation, Walter Bedell Smith, did not follow Dulles' stern example. Smith had told reporters that the closest contact the two sides had was that they used the same roller towel in the men's room. But one day, after Dulles had gone back to Washington, Bedell and Zhou met in the delegates lounge and exchanged small talk. There was no handshake because Smith had a cigar in one hand and a coffee cup in the other.

On the last day Bedell sought out Zhou and told him of his pleasure at meeting with him and his high regard for Chinese art and culture. He did not shake hands with Zhou, but he seized Zhou's arm and shook it several times, emphasizing his personal friendly feelings.

Despite the nonsense about handshakes, Zhou was pleased. The French and the Vietnamese had agreed on an end to the fighting and on elections. Informal diplomatic contacts had been made with the United States—quiet talks about exchanges of prisoners and detainees—and a threshold had been crossed which soon would lead to open and formal diplomatic meetings, the fifteen years of talks in Warsaw, conducted on the Chinese side by Wang and on the American side by a succession of ambassadors.

A lot of history rolled by before I would see Zhou Enlai again, much of it history which I perceived only dimly (or not at all) at the time. In those years China went through the Great Leap Forward, the Blooming of 100 Flowers, the Great Proletarian Cultural Revolution, the fall (and death) of legions of the Old Guard, Ping-Pong, Henry Kissinger's secret 1971 trip to Beijing and the visit by President Nixon to China in February 1972, before I got to China and saw Premier Zhou again. He invited Charlotte and myself to dinner in the Great Hall of the People, and as was the imperial custom of the day, we were recalled from Sian to Beijing, traveling by train because the Chinese did not trust their air service to insure our presence in Beijing. We were not told until a few hours before that we were to dine with Zhou, but we guessed from hints and protocol that this was what awaited us—at the end of a day spent in seclusion at our hotel expecting a telephone call summoning us into his presence.

Zhou Enlai had gone through much since I had seen him. There were times during the Cultural Revolution when he seemed, so far as I could discover, the only sane man in China's leadership. He looked older but relaxed and as self-confident as he had been at Spiridonovka House. Charlotte spotted a button missing from his tunic and later I heard stories of his dropping in at the kitchen of the Beijing hotel, just off Tiananmen, for a

quick bowl of noodles before the nightly state dinner or political
session at which he would be too busy to catch a bite to eat.

I did not know then, as later was revealed, that during the
Cultural Revolution, he had once been surrounded at the Great
Hall by 1 million Red Guard demonstrators—the same mob that
had forced so many of his comrades to bow in the "airplane posture" (arms fiercely drawn behind the back and the victim's head
shoved to his knees, deluged with filth, verbal and literal, tortured and sometimes killed). He engaged in fierce debate with his
tormentors for more than twenty-four hours before he finally
talked his way to release. Zhou's wit and tongue saved him from
a howling mob, just as his wit and tongue had saved China from
anarchy in those days, without a hand being raised to support or
rescue him by Chairman Mao and his right-hand-man, Lin Biao.

I did not know on that night in the Great Hall, so elegant
behind silk-embroidered screens depicting the wonders of ancient
provinces, sitting at the great round table with its silent, efficient
waiters, tasting delightful unknown delicacies with ivory chopsticks, that my host had for months and years walked a tightrope
between life and death, between honor and dishonor, somehow
keeping a balance which, I am certain, no one in China could
have managed. He had saved—for a time—the life of a Long
March hero, He Long and his wife, hustled the famous writer,
Ding Ling, to safety in a remote Manchurian military camp,
tried vainly to soften the torture of Liu Shaoqi, the fallen Party
leader, sent a threatened diplomat to the countryside to protect
him from torture by the Red Guard, warned an exposed cabinet
minister to take refuge before the storm broke, and, alas, only
too often found no ingenious way to save old comrades and their
children, try as he would.

I could not have guessed that many close associates, old Party
leaders, grizzled commanders in the battles of the Long March
and the anti-Japanese War had been tortured and killed (or still
languished in prison or camp) nor how many wives and children
had been sacrificed, their blood swelling the terrible toll of those
years.

There was no sign of this in Zhou's suave behavior, his quick
compliments, his politeness to the ladies, in the charm and vitality of a man relaxing in an evening of banter and occasional seriousness, which he said reminded him of what now seemed the
golden days of Yan'an, the days in the caves of northern Shaanxi

in the 1930s and 1940s when he first learned to enjoy Americans and their freewheeling talk.

When I match the Zhou Enlai I met that night, June 16, 1972, with what he had passed through—and indeed with what lay ahead in the last four years of his and Mao's lives—my wonder mounts.

Neither I nor anyone could have been aware that 1972 was Zhou's last good year, the last before the diagnosis of cancer of the bladder numbered his days and cut short the energy which he had ceaselessly poured out for China. Even with my limited knowledge of the complex, hidden mysteries of Chinese politics, I knew that the death of Lin Biao, once Mao's constitutionally designated heir—in a phantasmagoria which (if the official version is true) included a Wild West plot to dynamite Chairman Mao's train and Lin Biao's fatal aircrash in Mongolia (after Zhou himself had penetrated Lin Biao's plot and raised the alarm)—had given Zhou a clout he never before possessed. That evening Zhou looked and acted like a man in command. It was easy to believe that nothing was beyond him, that if he had not formally displaced the ailing (some said doddering) Mao, it was simply because of his exquisite tact.

Zhou Enlai had never wavered in his support of Mao since late 1934—almost 50 years. Before the Long March of the Red Army began in October 1934 Zhou Enlai had been a competitor of Mao's. He had stood with Mao's enemies who had removed Mao from leadership of the Communist Party and its Red Army. But only a few weeks after the March started Zhou began to incline toward Mao and at the decisive meeting in Zunyi in January 1935 when Mao Zedong was again placed in command Zhou stood at his side, never wavering no matter what the crisis, what the pressures, even in the worst days of the Cultural Revolution. Zhou had been at Mao's side for many years. He would not humiliate the old man in his last lingering years. If this is what Zhou decided it was the first time his quicksilver mind had betrayed him.

What did we talk about on this sultry summer evening of 1972 when the men, at Zhou's command, liberated themselves of ties and jackets? What didn't we talk of! There were eight Chinese and nine Americans, some Old China Hands like John and

Wilma Fairbank, some new like Charlotte and myself, and Dick and Helen Dudman. We talked about Chinese students coming to the U.S.A. Zhou worried that they would bump into Taiwan Chinese; he did not foresee the thousands from mainland and Taiwan who would fill our universities, mingling freely. Cigarette smoking (he was almost as much a chimney as Chairman Mao and didn't believe in any connection between cigarettes and cancer). Nixon (whatever Americans might think, Nixon had done the right thing in China and China wouldn't forget). Mao Zedong ("We are all his students"). The Vietnam war (I said it never should have been started and could be ended any time the United States wanted it to; he agreed). The Korean war (he quoted American generals who said it was the wrong war in the wrong place at the wrong time). American politics (he didn't understand our politics). China and Vietnam (China had invaded Vietnam many times over the centuries but, Zhou said, finally gave up because of the fierce resistance).

No subject so preoccupied Zhou as Vietnam. He took upon himself great blame for signing the Geneva accords of 1954 and persuading Hanoi to withdraw its forces from the South; his only excuse was his inexperience. "We were deceived [by Dulles]," he said. As he spoke of the massacre of North Vietnam families left behind in the South, his voice shook. "We made a mistake," he said. "We were greatly taken in at that time." He paused. "We must stop this discussion, or it will become too emotional."

Zhou's mind ranged over the horizon. He philosophized about the role of accident in man's affairs, paying only lip service to Marx's theory of the inevitability of economic-social change. Chance, he thought, was the main thing. It was chance that Mao had suggested that the American Ping-Pong players be invited to China, chance that telephone communications with Tokyo were good, chance that word caught the Americans as they awaited the bus to take them to the airport and a flight back to the United States. It was chance that had triggered Chiang Kai-shek's kidnapping by the young marshal at Sian in December 1936, chance that Chiang was compelled to join the Communists in fighting Japan. If Chiang hadn't gone to Sian to organize a campaign against the Communists, the opportunity would not have come. It was chance that China got into the United Nations in 1971 instead of 1972 as he had expected (he admitted his younger colleagues had predicted it, but he did not realize events were moving so swiftly).

"All events," he said, "have an inevitable cause, but it may be through an accidental turn that the inevitable happens."

I thought that Zhou in a few words had summed up the Chinese view of the dialectic: pragmatic, sensible, nondidactic. Marxian theory was OK but good luck helped a lot. Yes, the Russians were Communists and, yes, the Chinese were Communists, but a continent divided their way of thought.

Zhou pondered the difficulty of forecasting events, the difficulty of foreseeing the future. Neither Chiang Kai-shek nor he could have forecast the Sian kidnapping nor the speed of the United Nations action, and no one could have predicted that poor Prince Sihanouk of Cambodia would be ousted from his country and spend year after year in exile in China.

No one could have predicted the last years of Zhou's life. A year after our dinner, by which time he had been given the diagnosis of his illness (but showed no outward sign), he dined with his old friend, Chester Ronning, onetime Canadian ambassador, born in China of missionary parents, and Iphigene Ochs Sulzberger, the irrepressible daughter of Adolph S. Ochs, founder of the contemporary *New York Times,* paying her first visit to China at the age of 81.

To make small talk, as Iphigene said, the Premier asked about her family. She said she had all kinds of racial and ethnic strains among her descendents. "But no Chinese. How can I get a Chinese?" The Premier said he didn't know. "Can I advertise in the newspapers?" Iphigene inquired.

"No," the Premier smiled. "Our papers don't print ads."

"What if I should put up a Big Character poster?" Iphigene asked.

"Heavens," said Zhou. "Please don't do that. It would cause a riot."

Zhou was the parfit gentil knight and so would glow in Iphigene's memory. No hint of illness, no hint of problems. Within the year, his prestige still unimpaired, he summoned Deng Xiaoping back from exile to share his burdens. But treacherously soon, the fateful knives of Mao's wife, Jiang Qing and her comembers of the Gang of Four, were being sharpened. New winds of persecution had begun to blow. The first whispers of an assault on "Confucius"—Zhou Enlai—had begun in the feverish corridors of Chinese power.

On June 9, 1975, Zhou struggled out of his sickbed and attended a memorial service for He Long, his Long March comrade, one of the great heroes. Despite Zhou's best efforts, He Long had been tortured to death by Mao's men. On this day, so weak his trembling hand could hardly sign the memorial book, Zhou spoke to He's widow, Xue Ming. "I failed," he told her, voice quivering. "I failed to keep him out of harm's way."

Zhou lay dying. The "struggle with Confucius" raged on. Zhou asked that they play for him "one more time" a classic song of the Long March written by a Red Army general, Xiao Hua. No, ordered Jiang Qing, wielding her Dowager Empress' power. Zhou lay dying, but Mao Zedong did not visit his bedside. Zhou died January 9. Mao did not show himself at the mourning ceremonies. Jiang Qing did, wearing a casual body-glove sweater. That evening Jiang Qing arranged to have two of her favorite Western films shown in her residence in the Western Hills.

On Qingming, the April holiday for "sweeping graves" and showing respect for the departed, China erupted. Millions thronged Tiananmen in tribute to Zhou; mountains of flowers were heaped at the heroes' monument; thousands of poems were placed on the walls. After four days, a midnight sweep by police cleared out the flowers, tore down the posters, scrubbed off the slogans, beat, and arrested those standing vigil.

The tribute to Zhou was erased. His right-hand man, Deng Xiaoping, once again was hurled from office. The Gang of Four reigned supreme, but only for a moment in time. Mao died September 9, and China reclaimed Zhou for her own. The Gang was arrested, tried, and imprisoned. Deng returned to Beijing and power. Zhou was hailed as China's true patriot, the man who kept the faith, who served the people and the Revolution.

26 | A Great Lady

Charlotte and I were sitting at the great round table in the dining room of an old Manchu palace beside Back Lake in the tangle of streets and *hutangs* that once formed a perimeter of the Forbidden City. The date, although we did not think of it at the time, was September 5, 1977, almost the first anniversary date of the death of Mao Zedong.

The gardens of the palace had been tended by Henry Pu-yi, the last Manchu emperor and one-time Japanese puppet, who had been returned to China by the Russians who captured him in Manchuria in 1945.

We were guests of Soong Ching-ling, the second of the Soong sisters, widow of Dr. Sun Yat-sen, China's first president. She was now Vice President of the People's Republic of China.

Madame Soong was one of the world's great ladies. Henry Leiberman, who had covered China for *The New York Times,* once told me that every American correspondent there including himself had immediately fallen in love with the sparkling Rosamond. That was the Christian name Charlie Soong and his wife, devout Methodists, had given to their daughter.

I had known Madame Soong for several years, first by correspondence and then, when we finally began to come to China, in person—dining in this room with its "Palace lights," in Madame Soong's pejorative phrase, tasseled teak and painted-glass creations. They reminded me of the fake chinoiserie in the Nanking Café, a chop suey joint in Minneapolis in the days of my youth.

Madame Soong spoke her mind forcefully and had been doing so for many years, just how many I was not absolutely certain. When I wrote a story about her in 1972, I asked the New York desk to put in her age. I had been too timid to ask her myself. I guessed late seventies; the desk made it early eighties. She was not amused, telling me the Chinese Nationalists had been carrying on a campaign of disinformation for years about her age. New York said they got the figure from the reference books. Madame Soong said that was the problem. The KMT had falsified the books. Finally, I sent a "red ticket" letter, which was placed in her folder in the *Times* morgue, to warn future writers to give her age as she specified—seventy-nine at the time, born January 27, 1893.*

The Manchu palace was not to Madame Soong's taste. She disliked the heavy old Chinese decor, her official duties (receiving ambassadors, attending official receptions, entertaining important guests whom she did not know or like), the lack of ease and privacy. Most of all she missed the house on Avenue Molière in the old French concession of Shanghai, where she had lived with Dr. Sun Yat-sen and for years and years after his death in 1925, in the heart of a city which bubbled with life, excitement, and revolution.

On this evening in September 1977, however, she was in fine spirits. Nothing in China had upset her so much as the Cultural Revolution. She had never been close to Mao Zedong; their temperaments could not have been more different, he earthy, peasant manners, permitting more and more power to flow into the hands of his wife, Jiang Qing. Madame Soong, no peasant, educated abroad, liked good manners, good speech. She despised Jiang Qing. Ching-ling was very close to Zhou Enlai and knew how badly Mao and Jiang Qing had treated Zhou in his last years. She hated them for it.

Soong Ching-ling made little effort to conceal her feelings although she had been cautious with her talk during the Cultural Revolution, certain that "the third ear" (microphone) was listening. The last letter I received from her in the winter of 1981 accompanied an English translation of the trial of Jiang Qing. Three months later Ching-ling was dead. Now on this evening, a year after Mao's death and the arrest of Jiang Qing and the Gang of Four, Ching-ling indulged herself by telling what had happened at Mao's funeral, which she, of course, had attended.

Mao's widow, dressed, as Madame Soong thought, most inappropriately in a costume of black with a black scarf theatrically whirled around her neck and over her head arrived with a large wreath which was inscribed, "To the revered Master Teacher"

*Sterling Seagrove in *The Soong Sisters* gives the date as January 27, 1892. This date was used by Xinhua, the official Chinese news agency. But tributes to Soong Ching-ling make it 1893. There are variations of up to ten years in the birth dates given for Mae-ling, Ching-ling's younger sister who married Chiang Kai-shek.

from "your student and comrade." To this she had appended, after her own name, the names of half a dozen Mao family members.

A violent row broke out, as Madame Soong related. Wang Hairong, Mao's niece, daughter of his brother Zemin, objected to Jiang Qing's inscription. The two women traded epithets. Wang Hairong (who had been serving Mao as English interpreter) flew at Jiang Qing, clutching at the flowing scarf. She gave it a tug and, said Madame Soong, with unrepressed glee, off flew Jiang's wig. Mao's widow was bald as an egg.

It was the most Chinese of stories. It was, Madame Soong assured us, precisely true. She had seen it all. It had revealed the nakedness of Jiang Qing in her fateful struggle to succeed Mao and become China's first Communist Empress.

Madame Soong was herself, in a sense, a kind of dowager empress but not a Communist one. She had become the symbol of China's struggle to rise from the feudal darkness of the Manchus. She was the common denominator of China's battle—the wave which brought Dr. Sun Yat-sen to power, then Chiang Kai-shek (Madame Soong's brother-in-law, married to the third of the Soong sisters), and finally the Communists to whose cause Ching-ling had long given her support but not her membership.

All of contemporary China was epitomized in the life of this petite woman, radiant and beautiful as long as she lived: fire-lit black eyes, rosy cheeks, flashing white teeth, a wit that cut through pretensions like a sword, perfectly poised, totally knowing, aware of her position in China and the world. She was no longer the slender girl of her romance with Dr. Sun but she still remained romantic in her maturity and age.

When she heard that Red Guards had broken into her house in Shanghai while she was away, she asked what they had wanted. They wanted, she was told, to cut off her long jet hair, perfectly pulled back from her broad Hakka forehead (her father Charlie Soong had been born on Hainan island from which he made his way to Boston in the 1880s).

"I'll cut their hair!" she exploded, and no one who heard her doubted that she would. Premier Zhou deployed a company of PLA soldiers around her Beijing Palace. No Red Guards attempted to break in across the high walls and barbed wire.

It was in the house on Avenue Molière that Madame Soong had waited, foreign friends sleeping on the floors as a kind of makeshift bodyguard, in 1949, fearful that as the last of Chiang Kai-shek's troops hustled out of Shanghai, they would stop off and put a bullet in her head.

Madame Soong retreated to the big garden of the compound. An American manned the telephone. At the first sign of Nationalist troops, he was to call the foreign correspondents. They would rush to the house. Their presence, it was hoped, would deter an attempt on Ching-ling's life.

The telephone rang. The American answered it. "They're here!" a voice rang out. But it was Madame Soong, and she was not reporting on Nationalist troops but on the arrival of the Chinese Red Army units of Marshal Chen Yi.

The full history of the house on Avenue Molière will never be written. It was to this house that she and Dr. Sun came after their marriage in 1915, and it was to this house Ching-ling returned again and again after the travail of Dr. Sun's Revolution, the upheavals in Canton, the setbacks in so many places, and finally after his death in 1925. From this house she fled when Chiang Kai-shek turned on the Communists in the Shanghai massacre of 1927. And to this house she returned after exile in Moscow, to sit for nearly thirty years in the center of a web of conspiracies, giving shelter to Communists and radicals on the run. She became a kind of last ditch fall-back for the Communist Party after its apparatus was wiped out by Chiang Kai-shek's police (except for the rural revolutionaries under Mao).

For years the house was watched day and night by three or four sets of agents—the secret police of the Nationalists, agents of the Japanese, of the British, and of Madame Soong's own brother, T. V. Soong. In the hall of mirrors which was Chinese politics, T. V., a dedicated Nationalist, was guarding the life of his sister, a dedicated Communist supporter, against attack by his commander, Chiang Kai-shek, who was his brother-in-law and Soong Ching-ling's as well.

Only when I began to study the politics of medieval Florence did I find complexities of families and clans as divided as those of China.

In the days when there was no Shanghai Communist apparatus, Party agents sent out from Moscow by ill-informed commissars ducked into the house on Avenue Molière for a night's sanctuary. Ching-ling helped agents get into the Communist bases and out of China. When all Communist wireless communications were disrupted by Chiang's police, a substitute transmitter-receiver was installed either in the attic of the Avenue Molière house or an adjacent one. Survivors argue about the precise location.

The Avenue Molière house was the starting point of Edgar Snow's famous expedition to the Communist bases in Shaanxi province which produced *Red Star over China* and brought to the world (and China) the first word of Mao's movement. Madame Soong played a key role in setting in motion the complicated arrangements by which Snow made his dangerous mission. She did the same for Dr. George Hatem (now a Chinese citizen with the Chinese name Ma Haide, known around the world for his spectacular campaign to rid China of leprosy). In those days he was an American of Lebanese origins, trained in Buffalo, North Carolina, and Switzerland. In these endeavors Rewi Alley, Madame Soong's long-time friend, a New Zealand sheepherder who cast his lot with Chinese reform and revolution after seeing the horrors of Shanghai's slums, played a leading role.

Charlie Soong, Methodist-educated in the United States, a man of extraordinary charm, had made a fortune in turn-of-the-century China, printing and selling Bibles, then going into big business. He had been a major supporter of Dr. Sun Yat-sen but was hardly pleased at the marriage of his twenty-two-year-old daughter and his sixty-year-old friend. Sun divorced his wife of long standing prior to marrying Soong Ching-ling. The marriage created bad feeling in the Soong family, but looking back over fifty years Ching-ling could find nothing but loving words for her father. She never tired of talking to me about him. Her older sister, Ai-ling, had worked for Dr. Sun as a secretary but left to marry H. H. Kung, a lineal descendent of Confucius, later enormously wealthy and a major financial figure in Chiang Kai-shek's government. Ching-ling took her older sister's job as Dr. Sun's secretary. They fell in love despite the age difference.

I did not know, when Madame Soong told me of her marriage, what a row it had stirred up in Methodist Chinese and missionary circles—so much so that it was still a political hot potato.

When I wrote in *To Peking and Beyond* that Dr. Sun had divorced his first wife to marry Ching-ling, I found out.

I had offended Ching-ling by reporting her age incorrectly. Now I got into worse trouble by writing that Dr. Sun had obtained a divorce specifically to marry her. She wrote me a tart letter about "the reactionaries and missionaries" who tried to "smear and slander" Dr. Sun and herself. When I corrected the reference in later editions, she relented.

But I discovered how touchy this issue was. She had kept in a strongbox in Shanghai the records of her marriage to Dr. Sun and of his divorce from his first wife. When she had to flee Shanghai and then Hong Kong ahead of the Japanese, she was unable to take her papers. After the war some of them turned up and were acquired by the Beijing Museum, which put them in its archives. Still sensitive about the ruckus over her marriage, she sent a friend with a copy of the documents to Hong Kong to show them to foreign correspondents. This time she was afraid the Nationalists would launch propaganda against her. The documents proved, she said, that Dr. Sun divorced his wife before she went to Tokyo and became his secretary.

I never had a conversation with Madame Soong without the topic of her sister, Mae-ling, the Generalissimo's wife, coming up. Over the years the sisters (and the third sister, Ai-ling, wife of H. H. Kung) had kept in touch at second or third hand. I suspect that there were occasions when they exchanged direct messages, but no one would admit this. There were jealousies. For years Mae-ling had top billing as wife of China's ruler, Chiang Kai-shek. But with the triumph of the Communists, Soong Ching-ling became No. 1.

Family plays an enormous role in China, much more than in contemporary America or Europe. The row over Jiang Qing's wreath was familial as well as political, and there was a family skirmish when Soong Ching-ling died in 1981. The government tried to assemble the whole Soong tribe, including Mae-ling, but she refused to come unless she could bring Chiang Kai-shek's ashes and place the urn in a memorial at Nanjing. Beijing turned her down. There was squabbling among the relatives, none very close since Ching-ling had no natural children. She had adopted two wards, Yolanda and Jeanette Sui, daughters of a bodyguard-secretary. She had raised them in her family as her own children. The blood relatives and the government gave the

Sui girls second-class treatment. Finally after some argument about Madame Soong's will, the government sent the relatives on their way with a good deal of bad feeling and gossip.

How the Chinese love gossip! Some relatives lifted eyebrows at Ching-ling's "deathbed conversion" to Communism. In her eighty-nine years, she had not joined the Party. In her last moments she was admitted to the Party and named China's honorary president. Some said Ching-ling had lost consciousness before the "conversion." They asked why, if she had wanted to join the Party, she had waited until the last hours of her life? It was not a question likely to receive an early or satisfactory answer.

Soong Ching-ling's bequest to her country was her undeviating spirit in support of change, modernization, the transformation of a backward, illiterate country into one taking some first steps toward sophistication, education, advanced science, and an end to ignorance, superstition, and anarchy.

She saw no redeeming features in the besotted mire, which was the China into which she had been born. She admired beyond measure her father, a poor, poor boy who had risen in life through wit and work, who had supported reform and revolution and who believed in the American way. If, perhaps, she was not so strong a Christian as was he, she was as strong as he in believing that American education—*learning things,* learning the easy American approach to life, breaking with traditional customs of domination of daughters by mothers-in-law, of the marriage broker, of the harem rectitude of traditional Chinese life—was the first step toward a better China.

She had no tolerance for superstition. Nor had she a tolerance for bad manners. There were, she once told me, no decent servants in China anymore. Young people thought service was beneath them, that proletarians had no need for manners. There were no good cooks. The best Chinese restaurant was in Paris. Young people lacked what she regarded as the Christian or Chinese work ethic. She saw no difference between the two. She liked warmth and openness and informality. Over and over she talked of the joy of her days at Wesleyan in Macon, Georgia, her earlier times at a preparatory school in Summit, New Jersey.

I never saw Ching-ling more happy than at dinner on July 22, 1980. From my journal:

"She looked *marvellous*. No other word for it. Beautiful, easy, and radiant. We have never seen her so relaxed. In part it was because of the young people. She adores the Sui girls. In part because of us: 'I wish you would come over every year.'

"Warm, easy talk about cornbread and hominy grits and turnip greens, which she loved, and Southern fried chicken and sledding and sleigh riding in New Jersey in the winter."

She talked a lot about Premier Zhou Enlai that evening and pointed to a photograph on the wall of the Premier with Yolanda and Jeanette, aged six and three. "It is such a shame," she said of Zhou. "He should have had children. He loved them so."

Yolanda, a beautiful girl, svelte and supple, was getting married in a few days. She worked in a film studio and her husband-to-be was an actor. She and her younger sister, Jeanette, studying in America but back home for the wedding, and an American friend, Beth Wells, made Soong Ching-ling's eyes sparkle. She looked twenty-two again and about to elope with Dr. Sun. The wedding was going to be a Southern dream, a mixture of Chinese and American styles—rock 'n' roll music from tapes brought back from New York by Jeanette, a wedding cake designed by Jeanette with a little bride and bridegroom atop, a satin wedding gown just as Soong Ching-ling remembered wedding gowns from her Macon days, lots of young people, including another young American, Arthur Golden, grandson of Iphigene Sulzberger who happened to be in Beijing. I would have given a lot to stay over and attend, but we had to be off to Tibet.

All of this touched the old-fashioned, naïve but gloriously American chords in Ching-ling. Her father had always told her that no one resembled the Chinese more than Americans of the South, whom he had met in the last century. I think Ching-ling sometimes liked her Americans at Macon, Georgia, even better than her Chinese.

Ching-ling had never lost her American accent. She read every scrap of American print she could get her hands on. Even during the Cultural Revolution, I sent her via Hong Kong *The New York Times,* and, later, *The New York Review of Books.* When Moscow finally began to publish memoirs of Russians who had come to China to help Dr. Sun Yat-sen—the widow of Mikhail Borodin and others—I got copies, translated some into English, and sent them on to her. In most cases it was the first she had heard of the fate of her Russian friends.

(After Madame Soong's death, the palace was turned into a museum, but upstairs her quarters remained as when she was alive. One day in 1984 we were permitted to visit her living rooms, strewn with books, well-thumbed and read, among them some of Charlotte's and my own. There were piles of American magazines. Her dressing table was still cluttered with perfumes, a bottle of Revlon's Charlie among them, American music sheets lay on the piano. It might have been the apartment of a well-to-do, rather old-fashioned lady on Commonwealth Avenue in Boston.)

A few days after our dinner Yolanda was married in that same big palace dining room, decked with flowers and looking as much like a Wesleyan College wedding scene as Ching-ling and her wards could make it.

We talked on that night of July 22, 1980, of her coming to the United States. She wanted very much to do this. She had put on a good deal of weight, was fat as a butter ball, and had bad arthritis in her knees. It was hard to get up and down and hard to walk. Still I encouraged her. I thought she could manage, and I knew it would be the greatest moment in her life since eloping with Dr. Sun Yat-sen. For years, Wesleyan had been trying to persuade her to come. Now, at long last, in the excitement of Yolanda's wedding, she began to think that it might really happen.

Alas, by midwinter it was too late. She had not been told immediately of the diagnosis, but it was cancer. She never did get to her Wesleyan reunion, but no college girl carried in her heart a warmer image of peach trees in bloom and young voices singing college hymns. She had long had a print of *Gone with the Wind*. I don't know how many times she had watched it on the small projector in the entrance hall of the Palace. Quite a lot. Some time that winter she had it threaded onto the projector, the lights darkened and for the last time she saw Scarlett O'Hara and Rhett Butler and the glory of Tara. She was a very great lady, as fine a blend of China and America as we will ever see.

27 | The Little Man Nobody Mentioned

I confess that, when I went to China for the first time, the name "Deng Xiaoping" rang no bells. Yes, I had heard of him. I knew that he had been a target of the Cultural Revolution. President Liu Shaoqi was called the No.1 Capitalist Roader and Deng was called the No.2. The pair were supposed to have conspired to turn China away from Communism and back to Capitalism.

That was about it. In the tens of thousands of words I jotted down you will look in vain for the name of Deng Xiaoping. I never asked a question about him, and if he was mentioned, it was only as a hyphenated add-on to President Liu Shaoqi. Deng is not even listed in the index of my *To Peking—and Beyond*. It had never occurred to me in March 1953 that Nikita Khrushchev would succeed Stalin; it didn't occur to me in May 1972 that Deng would succeed Mao.

I try to keep this in mind when I am tempted to make prophesies. Grand politics is beyond tidy formulations. The odds defy even the science, if that's what it is, of advanced polling technology. No one in 1987 knew who would be elected U.S. President in 1988.

No one in China in 1972 was eager to talk about what would happen after Mao Zedong, but I concluded that he would probably be succeeded by Zhou Enlai, then in vigorous health, no hint of the cancer yet. Mao looked slack and sloppy, overweight and tottery, sprawling in his armchair in baggy clothes, his mouth slightly agape. I thought Zhou had pretty much taken over the day-to-day running of China and that before long Mao would shuffle off the stage. It would be a long shuffle. Mao would hold the spotlight for four more years, and Zhou would precede him to the land of the immortals by eight months.

My idea was that Zhou would have a free hand and time to tidy up the mess left by the Cultural Revolution, then the era of the Long March, of the men who had come to power with Mao, would end. The successor generation, I came to believe, would emerge from the dynamic Shanghai leadership, which had carried out the Cultural Revolution.

This notion was reinforced by a meeting in Shanghai with a man called Zhu Yongjia, dark-haired, handsome, quick grin, sharp wit, a no-nonsense way of talking. He wore a well-tailored gray Mao tunic, and I guessed his age at thirty-two or thirty-three. He held one of those cumbersome titles which seemed to disguise more than it told. He was a member of the Standing Committee of the Shanghai Revolutionary Committee. That meant he was one of the top men running Shanghai, just below those soon to become known as the Gang of Four.

Zhu Yongjia looked me in the eye as he spoke, and I could see that his frankness was rooted in both authority and knowledge. We dined in a cream-and-gold suite in the Park Hotel (now the Peace), a first-class English residential hotel before 1949 and still, if a little declassé, a four-star establishment. We dined well, the linen white, the silver gleaming, the waiters quiet and efficient, one splendid dish after another, a menu in exquisite calligraphy on rustling sheets of gold-and-red paper. The pièce de résistance was a vegetable plate decorated with twin pheasants carved from winter melons, a trompe-l'œil of the kind Shanghai hotels had been famous for long before the Revolution.

After this glorious meal, seated in an adjacent room with a bowl of fruit, fine cigars, and brandy, Zhu turned to me and said quietly:

"I can tell you something about the Cultural Revolution in Shanghai. I only participated in it here. I wasn't in other parts of China. But it is true that it all began here."

It had been, as he recounted it, the splashiest Revolution since the Paris Commune of 1870.

Again and again I had asked to be given a briefing on the Cultural Revolution. Now, in a swift and flowing narrative Zhu told the story. It was a lucid, logical account of extraordinary complexity, but he danced through the twists and turns without hesitation. He met my skeptical questions in stride, never the slightest hesitation, like a runner taking the high hurdles. It was, I thought, the kind of briefing a young Andrei Vishinsky might have given me on Stalin's purges, every point neatly tucked in place, no loose ends.

The conversation went on until 1 A.M., an outlandish hour in a city that went to bed by 9 P.M. He and I were prepared to go on to dawn, but Yao Wei was exhausted. So was Charlotte. I was enthralled. Zhu seemed as fresh as when he started.

The story Zhu Yongjia told was a classic exercise in paranoia. If you accepted his basic premise—that Liu Shaoqi had been a hidden traitor from the earliest days of the Revolution, say, since 1927—the rest mortised like a Chinese puzzle box. But the premise was as bizarre as the premises of Stalin's delusional apparatus. It was cut from the same psychotic cloth. Zhu's tale reeked of Othello, the sickly suspicion with which I had become so familiar in Moscow, as dark and dangerous a drama as any of those confected by Stalin and his murderous executioners, Yagoda, Yezhev, and Beria. All this Zhu Yongjia presented to me with businesslike assurance, a total commitment to his tale that took my breath away.

As I traveled back to our hotel past the haunted pillars of Britain's once imperial establishments along the Bund, I felt I had caught a glimpse of China past and China future. Perhaps I was wrong, perhaps Zhu only affected to believe the story he had so deftly spun, but I doubted that. He plainly was a major player in what I thought (and feared) would be China's next act—the coming to power of a band of thermidorian revolutionaries, armed with intelligence, driven by paranoia, superior, I suspected, in every way to Stalin and his cronies but infected with the same lunatic views and possessed of far more vigor than any other group I had found in China. That long talk at the Park Hotel, I thought, had lifted a curtain and given me a glimpse of what to expect.

I recall no mention in Zhu Yongjia's narrative of Deng Xiaoping nor do I find his name in my notes.

The ambitions of Zhu and his Shanghai associates were not to come to pass. There were many reasons for this, but the most important had to do with the little man who was not there, Deng Xiaoping. In the days after the death of Mao Zedong, September 9, 1976, it was a very close thing, very close indeed, as to who would win out. But the chips fell against Shanghai and Jiang Qing, and as I ultimately was to discover, Zhu Yongjia would play out the last scene in the fall of the Gang of Four.

Things moved with great speed after Mao died. Everyone knew that supreme power was up for seizure. It was the moment Jiang Qing, Mao's widow, had been awaiting. Her forces were ready. But so were those of the Old Guard, the handful of survivors of the Long March who still held key positions, military men and an equivocal politician named Hua Gaofeng.

By lightning strokes, cloaked with deceits straight from that classic of China *The Romance of the Three Kingdoms* (so long a favorite of Mao's), the Old Guard arrested Jiang Qing and her three Shanghai collaborators on the evening of October 7, 1976, in Beijing—a secret sweep not revealed to anyone outside the core of the Old Guard. In Shanghai the second tier of leaders— suspicious but unaware—stood by awaiting a call to action. One by one they were summoned to Beijing on plausible pretexts and placed under control of the Old Guard.

Finally, Zhu Yongjia, my cool, confident Gang of Four man of the Park Hotel, was left in charge by the conspirators, to handle whatever might come: a rising against the Old Guard in Beijing, an order to mobilize against attack—who could know what might happen in these frightening times? It was his duty to call out the workers' militia (some estimated the Shanghai defense force at 1 million), to prepare for combat, to rally the masses behind Jiang Qing and the Gang (not a whisper of their arrest had seeped out), and to hold the Shanghai bastion of Revolution, come what might.

Single-handedly, no directives from his chiefs (now held incommunicado), unable to reach any reliable ally in Beijing by telephone or coded message, Zhu Yongjia pulled together the remaining cadres of conspirators, suppressed all news coming from Beijing (propaganda had been his special responsibility), invoked a blanket censorship, halted the Shanghai edition of the *People's Daily* (the national Communist Party organ), jammed all incoming radio transmission, distributed arms, placed defense detachments at newspapers, radio stations, communications centers, battened down the hatches.

For five days Zhu Yongjia held the fort in the face of waves of rumors that the cause was lost, hoping against hope, drafting proclamations declaring that Shanghai had taken up the flag of the Revolution against usurpers.

This was his final act. On October 13, one week after the arrest of Jiang Qing and her collaborators in Beijing, Shanghai capitulated.

Much of the detail about Zhu Yongjia's last stand was reconstructed by Roger Garside of the British embassy in Beijing. I am not certain of Zhu Yongjia's fate. Probably he is still in prison.

So ended the ambitions of the bold but fatally paranoid group that hoped to ride into power with Mao's death. And so much for my ability to fathom the complexity of China's politics. I had sensed correctly that Zhu Yongjia and his associates were high rollers.

But not one item of my scenario came true. Nor did theirs. Instead we had what came close to a Chinese version of *Aida*.

Who did become Mao's successor? Not the ambitious men of Shanghai, not Jiang Qing with her hope to become China's new empress, not the slow-moving, uncharismatic provincial politician Hua Goofeng, whom the doddering Mao had improbably installed as surrogate in his last days ("With you in charge I am at ease").

The one who leaped to the top was Deng Xiaoping, the man whom nobody had mentioned in 1972.

I make no apology for the blank page in my 1972 portrait album. In that time not a word, not a line about Deng had appeared in the Chinese press for years—not since he was thrown out of office and daubed with wagons of verbal nightsoil in 1966. Deng had vanished, just as the No. 1 Capitalist Roader, Liu Shaoqi, had vanished. Not a word of the fate of either had circulated outside Zhongnanhai, the government compound within the Forbidden City. The two men had slipped from the face of the earth. Liu Shaoqi was dead, dead since 1969 at the hands of Mao's torturers. No one knew that. Deng Xiaoping was alive. No one knew that.

My ignorance was total in those early days. I didn't even know what questions to ask. In fact it was not until 1984, when I took the Long March and met the colleagues and friends of Liu Shaoqi, Deng Xiaoping, and Mao Zedong, that I was able to put the picture together. When I did that, I found the rise of Deng beat the traditional Chinese classics for pure melodrama.

In the quiet late spring days of 1972, when I first came to Beijing (as Deng's daughter, Deng Rong—"Maomao" was her family nickname—was to reveal in 1985), Deng's spirits had begun to rise. After his arrest and disgrace in 1966, he and his wife, Zhou Lin, had been kept under twenty-four hour guard in

Beijing, subjected to interrogation and physical harassment. Then, without warning, they and Deng's elderly stepmother were bundled onto a plane under armed escort and flown to Nanchang, capital of Jiangxi province. Here they were harangued by the governor-general, then taken to an abandoned infantry school in Xinjian county closed down in the Cultural Revolution in 1966.

They were confined in a brick house, which once had been the residence of the school's director. In this remote spot, forbidden to speak to anyone except their guards, cut off from communication with any authority, virtually without money, they had to struggle for existence. In a nearby tractor plant, Deng got a job as a machinist, a trade he had learned as a work-study student in France after World War I. His wife worked as a common laborer, washing and cleaning coils of wire. They dug a vegetable plot and raised chickens, selling the eggs in hopes of putting by money to bring their children to them. Deng broke up ten-kilo hunks of coal to feed the stove.

The five Deng children had been scattered to the winds. The oldest son, the brilliant Deng Pufeng, physics senior at Beijing University, had been hurled from a fourth story window by the Red Guards. His spine was damaged, paralyzing him from the waist down. Denied medical treatment, he was confined to a dirty hostel north of Beijing. He lay flat on his back weaving baskets of thin wire, which he sold to buy food.

In 1971 Pufeng was permitted to join his parents. Medical aid was still refused, but Deng bathed his son and massaged his back and legs. That year, too, the youngest daughter, Maomao, was permitted to join them. The Deng family will always remember November 5, 1971. Guards escorted Deng and his wife to a Party meeting. They had no idea what might be happening—perhaps another struggle session. The children waited in concern. About noon their parents returned, saying not a word, their manner grave. Maomao caught a signal from her mother and followed her to the kitchen. The guards were still in the house, but her mother seized Maomao's hand and traced on her palm four characters that meant: "Lin Biao is dead." Then she put a finger to her lips. When the guards went outside, Deng let his emotions come to the surface. "Justice could not have allowed Lin Biao not to die," he said. "Even heaven won't tolerate him."

Things began to move. The Lin Biao officials who had held Deng and his family in custody were replaced. The new officials paid a formal call and apologized for the harsh regime. They removed the armed guards. In April 1972 permission was given to bring Pufeng to Beijing for treatment. Maomao accompanied her crippled brother.*

In Beijing there were more signs that the clouds were lifting. Wang Zhen, one of Deng's comrades of the Long March, sent word that he wanted to see Maomao. Himself a victim of the Cultural Revolution and still "set aside"—that is, forbidden to work—Wang Zhen told Maomao that times were changing. He was writing to Mao asking that Deng be reinstated. (Later, with the death of Mao, Wang Zhen entered the Politburo.) Maomao told her father, when she went back to Jiangxi, that not since the start of the Cultural Revolution had anyone treated her so warmly.

All of this was going on while I was having my long talk in the Park Hotel with Zhu Yongjia.

For the Dengs life went on in the red brick barracks near Nanchang, cultivating their garden, Deng reading at night from books he had been permitted to bring with him, sometimes Marx, sometimes not, listening to the evening news on the radio, following events with great care.

In December 1972 they had a vacation—a sightseeing trip to the mountain top of Jinggang Shan, 200 miles southwest of Xinjian county, the redoubt where Zhu De and Mao Zedong assembled their ragged bands in what would become the first formation of the Communist Red Army. Deng had served in the Red Army through the Long March, the war against Japan, and the final victory over Chiang Kai-shek and was one of those who stood with Mao on October 1, 1949, in Tiananmen.

After the visit to Jinggang Shan, Deng and his family went back to the Xinjian barracks, back to their quiet routine. In late afternoon as the declining sun cast long shadows on the courtyard, Maomao watched from her window as her father emerged for his constitutional, forty turns around the square. Deng, head slightly bent, hands clutched behind his back, walking briskly in the path his feet had worn in the red soil, day after day, deep in thought.

*Deng Pufeng was brought by his father to America for diagnosis. U.S. physicians said nothing could be done. He did undergo physical therapy in Toronto. Since 1979 Pufeng has headed an association for aid to the disabled, the first China has ever had.

"Watching his sure but fast-moving steps," Maomao recalled, "I thought to myself that his faith, his ideas and determination might have become clearer and firmer, readying him for the battles ahead."

Deng was pondering, there can be no doubt, the future of China—what must be done to set the country back on the track, what steps he would take should he once again rise to leadership.

One evening in April, 1973, a banquet was given at the Great Hall of the People for Prince Sihanouk. Nothing special about the banquet. Sihanouk was periodically so honored, partly to boost his morale, partly as a gambit in the complicated political games around Vietnam and Cambodia. Nothing unusual about the dinner except for one guest—Deng Xiaoping. The Little Man (Deng is slightly under five feet tall) once again had bounced back. No explanation, no reversal of the verdict which had declared him a vile traitor, a scab, a pernicious weed. Deng simply walked in and sat down at the table as if he had just returned from a long vacation in the country—as, indeed, he had, but of a special kind.

No one, except perhaps Zhou, knew China and its problems as did Deng. There was not much of China he had not seen since his birth in Paifang village a few miles from Guang'an, a district town in Sichuan about sixty miles north of Chongqing.

No one had been up and down the political roller coaster so often. Deng was small physically, but when I finally met him in 1977, he had the bounce of an India rubber ball. I could imagine him on the court in his favorite sport, basketball, and I wasn't sure he could not hold his own against the six and seven footers. Years later a Russian told me of an encounter between Deng and Mikhail Suslov, the tall, gaunt six-foot ideologue of the Soviet Union. The two men, Deng so short and Suslov so long, had engaged in violent debate over Soviet and Chinese versions of Marxism in the late 1950s. Suslov was Moscow's premiere dialectician, but Deng had boned up on Marx. Nikita Khrushchev later grumbled to Mao: "Your little guy floored our big guy." Mao smiled. "Never underestimate our little guy. Our little guy led the Second Field Army in a battle with Chiang Kai-shek in which Chiang lost 1 million troops." Deng was political commissar. One-eyed Liu Bocheng was the general. Together they won the Hwai-Hai battle that sealed the defeat of Chiang Kai-shek.

To underestimate the little guy was a common mistake. Deng was small, but his energy never ran down. When he entered a room, he charged the air with electricity. When I saw him in 1977, he bounced across the floor, and I felt vibrations on the back of my neck. We shook hands, and the current flowed up to my shoulder.

When Deng was knocked out politically, he came back on his feet—always. Most people talked about Deng having been knocked down three times. They didn't know what he had survived in his early years. In 1926, having made his way back to China from France via Moscow (he studied for a while at the Sun Yat-sen University, where Jiang Jingguo, Chiang Kai-shek's son, was a classmate—"not a bad fellow," Deng recalled sixty years later), Deng was sent into a very tricky area on the Vietnamese border. Twice he was dragged into inner Party intrigues, but both times he shook off the charges and moved on up the ladder.

On the eve of the Long March, Deng was arrested on trumped-up charges (actually because he supported Mao whom his accusers did not dare attack openly). He was beaten, held in a bare-walled room, and given only a cup of rice and a cup of water a day. He refused to confess any crime (he would do the same when he was accused in the Cultural Revolution thirty years later). So he was beaten again. One day, as he was being led back to his cell, he encountered a Communist woman who was an old friend. "I'm starving to death," he told her. She bought two chickens, cooked them, and made his guards give them to him.

Deng's persecutors stripped him of rank and sent him to duty in a dangerous no-man's-land. They hoped he would be killed. Deng's principal accuser persuaded Deng's wife to get a divorce and marry him.

Of all Deng's downs this was the most dangerous. But he survived. He was brought back as a common soldier when his enemies became fearful he might defect to Chiang Kai-shek. Deng started the Long March like all the other soldiers, carrying his own pack, a twenty-pound food bag, forty pounds of bullets, and his rifle. There were rumors he was made to serve as one of the 5,000 porters who toiled under 200-pound burdens. That doesn't seem to be true. His load was heavy enough, but he had developed strong muscles working in the Renault factory in Paris and as a locomotive fireman in France.

The Long March gave Deng the brisk pace Maomao noticed as her father walked around and around the barracks courtyard. He learned a lot in those years.

The first thing I heard about Deng in 1974 was that he was a man in a hurry. "Sometimes he moves too fast," my Chinese friend said. Deng had just become Zhou Enlai's chief deputy. "That's what I am afraid of now. He may get into trouble."

He did. But Deng could no more take a snail's pace than he could transform his hot Sichuan temperament. Mao cursed at him, said that Deng was deaf and that he deliberately sat in the back of the room so he could not hear Mao's instructions. But Mao also said that Deng was like "a needle wrapped in cotton." He was a sharp man but gentle, "a rare and talented man." Deng had ideas, and he was capable of finding responsible solutions to difficult problems. He was a good fighter. He was a good fighter against the Russians. Not many like him, Mao said.

Deng did move fast. Possibly it had something to do with his stature—very small, very quick. He thought his growth had been stunted by his student years in France when he worked as a laborer and often had nothing but a croissant and a glass of milk a day. He developed a fondness for croissants, and when he finally made it to the United States in 1974 for a United Nations session, he went home via Paris, bought 100 croissants, and took them back as a gift to Zhou Enlai and others who had been his comrades in France.

I learned a lot about Deng as time went on. He had started the Long March under an evil cloud, but he bounced back. When Mao took command in January 1935, Deng was pulled out of the ranks and resumed his own long march to the top. By the end of the epic in October, 1935, he was a trusted young lieutenant of Mao's. He went on to play a leading role in the battle against the Japanese in 1944–45 as Liu Bocheng's political commissar in the famous 129th Division. At the close of World War II the 129th Division was expanded into the Second Field Army for the struggle against Chiang Kai-shek. When Mao proclaimed the People's Republic in 1949, he named Deng proconsul for the vast regions of China's South. Up and up and up Deng rose only to fall to the depths in 1966. Again he went up in 1974, taking charge from Zhou's failing hands, then with Zhou's death in 1976, he fell to the pits where he would have perished but for Mao's timely death a few months later.

Why, Charlotte asked a Chinese official, do you respect Deng so much. He has been up and down so many times. "Ah," he said, "that's why we trust him."

In 1976 it was a question of life or death; he fell like Lucifer. Whether he would survive, no one could be certain. He had one advantage. He had never lost his friends in the Red Army. After Deng returned to power, he demurred at becoming chairman of the State Defense Committee. "It should go to one of you military," he said modestly. But the military men smiled. "You are one of us," they rejoined. With his life in danger from Jiang Qing, Deng was given protection by Xu Shiyu, commandant of Guangdong and South China, one of the toughest Red Army commanders, called Old Ironsides by his troops. In Guangdong Deng had the support of the Party Secretary Wei Guiqing. All this would have availed Deng nothing had Jiang Qing won. It gave him temporary protection, and in Beijing he had the quiet backing of Ye Jianying, second only to the ailing Zhu De in the armed forces. Other stalwarts secretly sided with Deng, including Li Xiannian who was to become President.

The three great men in China died in 1976—Zhou in January, Marshal Zhu De in July, and Mao Zedong in September. Deng resembled none. He set himself four-square against Mao's leadership style. No cult of personality. You could travel from one end of China to another and never see his picture or statue. The old Deng home in Xiaxiang village housed three families, no museum, no little Red Book of Quotations from Chairman Deng, no calligraphy on the walls, no poems by Deng. He didn't give interviews, and he refused to have his biography written. He was not effacing. He just didn't want to be overblown like Mao. He had a flair for easy relations. He liked to play bridge, had liked to since his days in Yan'an where bridge and poker were introduced by Americans like Edgar Snow and Anna Louise Strong. But Deng was no ordinary bridge player. He was world class. He played to win. And he played two or three times a week with some of his old friends like Wang Li. No money stakes, but the loser had to crawl under the table. Deng seldom lost, and when he did, his friends told him he didn't have to get under the table. No, he would insist. "It is a rule of the game," and would crawl under—not so difficult for a man of his stature.

"I concentrate on the cards," Deng has said. "That way my mind gets a good rest." Deng likes to swim, too, and has told his friends "The fact that I can swim especially in the vast sea [the Yellow Sea, at Beidaihe] proves that I am healthy; the fact that I play bridge means that I still have a clear brain." He fell in love with soccer (European football) when he was in France and once pawned his jacket to buy a ticket for an important match. In later years he watched championship games on TV. He took a daily cold water bath until he was seventy-five. Mao also liked to swim. Cold baths and calisthenics were closely linked with revolutionary activity in China. One of Mao's early works was on physical exercise. Deng comes from sturdy Hakka stock, the Hakkas being a special ethnic group of Hans who migrated from north to south many centuries ago. They are usually small, dark in color with ruddy cheeks. They are numerous in the area around Hong Kong and Canton, the women wearing fringed lampshade hats. Deng came from a middle peasant family. His father led a local defense detachment.

This was the background of the Little Man Whom Nobody Mentioned in 1972, the Little Man who could never be kept down. It took him about two years to reach the top after Mao's death, and he was already racing ahead with the pragmatic, daring program which he had turned over and over in his mind as he paced those forty rounds of the courtyard on his barracks home. It was a fast track program, and it broke through conventions, both Communist and Chinese. It was, in a sense, more Chinese than Communist, and that was, in the tradition of the Chinese Communists, Marxist but *Chinese* Marxist—Marxism of a special kind, building a Communism tailored to Chinese needs (which is one reason why Stalin and his successors disliked and distrusted China).

Deng said: "It does not matter whether the cat is black or white so long as it catches the mice." What he meant was that, to drive China to technological rationalization by the year 2000, he was ready to take techniques, methods, devices, ideas where he found them. If that meant abandoning Mao's blue-ant communes for private farming and private profits—OK, he did just that. When I followed Mao's Long March into the deepest and most remote places in China, I saw the results: booming market towns, private houses going up like Levittown, television antenna thick as willow branches, red-slippered girls trotting off to the paddies to transplant rice, more money than the countryside had seen in the last 5,000 years. The slogans: "Make the Peasant Rich— Make China Strong," "To Get Rich Is Glorious."

Deng opened the doors to foreign investment, private industry, joint ventures, "special economic zones" (free trade areas where Chinese and foreign entrepreneurs operated in a style more like Hong Kong than anything seen since 1949 in mainland China).

New stock exchanges in Shanghai, Tianjin, and Shenyang, private trade, private business, private restaurants, private beauty shops, private shipping companies, private production contracts for factory workers.

It happened so fast it took China's breath away and possibly even Deng's: stock market reports in the official English language newspaper, a bridge column, beauty hints, classy international style hotels, a golf course beside the Ming tombs. Well, it took my breath away, too. It brought with it a husky dose of graft, corruption, prostitution, black marketeering, smuggling, foreign porn, and VCRs.

Deng's new China dazzled my eyes when I first saw it. I discovered I missed blue ants, hundreds, thousands of peasants bending over in the rice fields, no way to tell man from woman, the plaintive strains of Jiang Qing's primitive eight operas, *The White Haired Girl, The Taking of Tiger Mountain by Strategy, The Red Regiment of Women.*

I found it hard to imagine a man better suited than Deng to guide China into the passing lane, to overcome the devastation of the Cultural Revolution and motivate 1.1 billion Chinese to the tasks of what he called The New Long March.

I was not confident that Deng would succeed in all his goals, but I did not think there was anyone in China so competent. When in 1986 and 1987 there arose a moving and shaking in China, when Hu Yaobang, Deng's handpicked chief lieutenant, was compelled to resign as Party secretary, when a miniwave of repression was ordered against the more free and talented writers, when young people were reined in (a bit) and some brakes applied to the economic joy ride, I did not see Deng Xiaoping as threatened. More likely, I thought, Deng and his old Army cronies had decided to pull up before China took off into the clouds.

I was prepared to believe that the new mode had been touched off by pragmatism. Deng headed a coalition government even if his voice was the most powerful. I did not have to believe that a group of Party Old Boys (and women), led down to Shenzhen to see Hong Kong honkytonk flourishing under the aegis of Communist puritanism, had risen up against Deng. Rather, it seemed to me that they had done the job (if they had done it) *for* Deng and not *against* him.

China, so I thought, would stay on Deng's course, the one he worked out during those long walks in the Jiangxi courtyard, the one which had already won him three *Time* magazine cover stories (one excerpted from my *The Long March*) and the title of 1985's Outstanding Achiever, awarded by *Success* magazine, the trade journal of young U.S. executives, which voted him the Success Story of the Year and ran a profile written by me under the title "China's CEO."

Success he surely was. CEO he was. I put my money on his getting China up and away toward a new kind of economy, which might be Socialist in description but one seasoned with enough free enterprise to place China firmly among the rising Pacific rim powers, Japan, Korea, Taiwan, Hong Kong, Singapore, which would make the twenty-first century their own.

28 | **Rosenthal Redux**

We are sitting in the dark, empty lounge of the Century Club. It is 9:30 A.M. on April 27, 1976, and we go upstairs to see if they have any coffee. No luck. No one but porters cleaning up the dining room from the night before. We sit down not too comfortably on a brown leather sofa and begin to talk about the *Times.* But we approach the subject gradually, as if we are a little shy about coming to the point, which is, of course, A. M. Rosenthal himself.

We skirt around like dogs sniffing uncertain terrain. We talk about the splashy story in the papers this morning about Dorothy Schiff and her relations with FDR and about Congressman Hays of Ohio, who has made the headlines with one of those periodic Congressional tabloid yarns about a young woman. We ponder a couple of sex scandals which we think are going to be hitting the papers soon, and I advance the notion that politicians are very animal people. They like bodies. They like to touch, to put their arms around human beings, male and female. Yes, says Abe, and mentions John Lindsay's new novel in which the hero-politician must have a woman every six hours.

From there our talk wanders leisurely over John Ehrlichman's first novel, which neither of us has read but think we should, and about Bob Semple's observation that Ehrlichman was the most humane of Nixon's White House gang. Semple had covered the Nixon White House for the *Times.* Not an easy job, and Bob had been shocked to learn what had been going on. He had never had any idea.

Finally we get down to Abe and his stewardship of *The New York Times.* I was writing a book about the *Times,* called *Without Fear or Favor.* We began talking about the *Times's* publication of the Pentagon Papers in 1971, the biggest story of Abe's career. The conversation flowed smoothly, each of us interested in what the other had to say. Abe spelled out the tension, the trauma, the dangers, the fears he felt over the publication, his warm relationship with Neil Sheehan, the impacted but extraordinary correspondent who had brought the papers into the *Times,* the frustration of his, Abe's, relationship with David Halberstam, whom

287

he had felt was his protégé and who, he also felt, had turned against him. Before we noticed, it was coming up to 11 A.M., and we had to go.

Abe said he had enjoyed the talk enormously. So had I. We agreed we would meet again soon. We did. Again and again and again. In my lifetime as a reporter I never interviewed anyone at such length, such depth, such frankness, as I interviewed Abe Rosenthal. We talked and talked and talked, in 1976, 1977, 1978, and for weeks on end in 1979. I think I must know Abe Rosenthal better than almost anyone, except of course, Ann, his wife of thirty-six years (until 1987) or Artie Gelb, his old friend and faithful right arm who for twenty years spent almost every waking moment with him.

I wish I could explain our relationship better. It was important to us over the years—very easy for a long, long time, then a bit prickly after Abe came back from Tokyo to become city editor in 1963, but not always and never entirely. We usually worked with harmony, respect, and often something much warmer. Our starting point was a dedication to *The New York Times* and to covering the news as Adolph S. Ochs proclaimed "without fear or favor." To Abe, as Jack Chancellor once said, "*The New York Times* is a kind of religion." As years went on, Abe and I began to define the *Times* and the news in somewhat differing terms.

I was always much more the gung-ho reporter, a drop-dead scoop artist with deep roots in the Chicago style of *The Front Page*. Abe was philosophical and conceptual, not a street reporter. I loved to chase ambulances, fire trucks, or squad cars with wailing sirens. I got a kick out of the Chicago morgue with its formaldehyde and cement floor, white rubber sheets concealing the staring eyes of Gangster No. 26 on *The Chicago Tribune*'s hit parade. Abe's first job on the *Times* had been writing the news bulletins for the electric sign that circled Times Tower. I don't believe he ever climbed through a window to filch a photo of the deceased from a bedroom dresser. I loved that stuff. I wanted to be a great war correspondent—but was not. I saw a lot of fronts but not a lot of action. I reported the war: London, the Eighth Air Force, North Africa, all the Russian fronts the Moscow censors let me cover—Leningrad, Stalingrad, Kharkov. I only saw a little bombing in North Vietnam and never got to the South. War was my kind of story. I cut my teeth on Richard

Harding Davis and one-eyed Floyd Gibbons of World War I. Stephen Crane's *The Red Badge of Courage* was my bible. My World War II heroes were Webb Miller and Ed Beattie, Jr., of the UP, Ed Murrow and Bill Shirer, Walter Cronkite and Bill Stoneman. In Vietnam it was Halberstam, Sheehan, Charley Mohr, and of course the all-time best, Homer Bigart. I don't think those reporters would make Abe's Best Ten. I don't believe he had a Best Ten. He was younger, didn't join the *Times* until 1944, missed the war, and his early years were a tribulation, playing second-fiddle to Tom Hamilton at the United Nations.

Abe was a writer's writer, not so much a spot news man, but a joy with a typewriter, schmaltzy to be sure, but turning out a stream of 14-carat words as fast as the keys clicked. We could enjoy each other's talents, but at close quarters the hair sometimes rose on the backs of our necks.

At first glance Abe and I seemed to come from very different backgrounds. I was a WASP from the Midwest, of old New England and Welsh origins. He was a child of Jewish parents, who emigrated to Canada from Bobruysk in the Pale of Settlement. He remembered friends coming to the house and saying, "Oh, that's Abram Shipiatsky's grandson." Abe's father had changed his name to Rosenthal. ("Shipiatsky" was an old Russian name, probably deriving from *ship,* meaning "hush, hush" or from *shipok,* a tavern.) Abe was born in Sault Ste. Marie and didn't become an American citizen until 1951. For a while his father, a big expansive man, a great storyteller and gambler, was a fur trader, going out into the bush with a dog team. Then they moved to the Bronx, and he found work as a painter.

I grew up with Abe. I don't mean that literally, but I grew up in the Jewish ghetto in Minneapolis, and my best friend was a boy whose father was a house painter who made his way to Canada from a shtetl in the Pale of Settlement, a man of revolutionary sympathies like Abe's, a nonreligious Jew like Abe's, a man who hailed the Revolution of 1917, as Abe's had, because it liberated the Jews and brought an end to the czars' pogroms. I knew exactly the kind of talk that raged around the Rosenthal table of an evening—Abe, his parents, his sisters (all older than Abe), his cousins, his aunts, his uncles. Abe's father had helped seven brothers get out of Russia.

Abe grew up poor, ambitious, bright, argumentative, aggressive, loving books, carting them home from the public library by the armload, haunting secondhand bookstores, working at odd jobs, the family always on the ragged edge.

I was a goy, but there was not much about Abe's childhood that mine didn't match. His was not a family of religious Jews. His father was an atheist. So was mine. There were more fits than not in our backgrounds. I don't know whether Abe ever understood this, but he must have grasped something of it during our endless talks. Abe did not go to synagogue; he was circumcised but had no bar mitzvah. He married Ann Marie Burke, a lively Roman Catholic girl. Ann's class at Textile High School at 18th Street and Eighth Avenue forecast she would be the "first woman editor of *The New York Times*," and so, in a sense, she ultimately was. She beat Abe onto *The New York Times* by two years. She was hired as the *Times*'s first copygirl in 1942 and worked with Abe in the *Times* United Nations bureau.

Abe and Ann's marriage was conducted by Ann's favorite young priest. Ann told him her husband-to-be was an atheist, but the priest took little account. They were married at St. Catherine of Siena, at First Avenue and 67th in New York* with only Ann's father and mother and sister present. There was the usual agreement about bringing up the children as Catholics. They didn't. The children were raised ecumenically. Ann instructed them in the Jewish faith and sometimes took them to a Catholic church.

By the time Abe retired as editor of the *Times* in 1986, shortly before his sixty-fifth birthday, I don't know what he considered his religion to be. He was a passionate Jew, however that might be defined, consistently asked himself of an issue "is it good for the Jews?," supported Israel, and had long ago turned his back on the radicalism of his father and the flaming Communism of his favorite sister, Ruth. He had quarreled with Ruth violently just before she died in 1940, after giving birth to a son. To the end of his days, I think Abe will carry that guilt. Ruth was married to an Abraham Lincoln Brigade commander named George Watt. Abe in 1979 told me of his hatred of Communism but called the Spanish Civil War *his* cause, the cause "for all of us" of that age. He admired George Watt. "God, how I admired

*From the Second Avenue tower to which Abe moved when he and Ann broke up he could look right down to St. Catherine's.

that man," he said. As executive editor of the *Times,* he published an article almost every year about the Lincoln Brigade.

No one could accuse Abe of being a devout Hebrew. He and his second wife, Shirley Lord Anderson, were married in a civil ceremony, and a Jesuit priest and a rabbi offered blessings. Atheist, agnostic, nonconformist—describe Abe as you will—he found his Jewishness a handicap on the *Times,* a newspaper refounded by a Jew, Adolph S. Ochs, owned by a large and prominent Jewish family, numbering many Jews on its staff, but never until Abe's elevation, a Jewish managing editor. Abe had to overcome the patterned non-Jewishness protectively decreed by Mr. Ochs and faithfully followed by his successors as publisher, Arthur Hays Sulzberger and Orvil Dryfoos.

This pattern—never, so far as I know, spelled out in words— could be observed in the workings of the *Times.* For many years with the notable exception of the Episcopal convert, Mr. Arthur Krock, the Washington chief, the great names of the *Times* were almost ostentatiously non-Jewish. True, there was a Jewish city editor, David Joseph, and a Jewish (but largely invisible to the the public) Sunday editor, Lester Markel, but few were the Jewish signatures over the stories. Abe knew that the *Times* of the 1940s would never publish a story signed "Abraham Rosenthal" on page 1. His middle name, Michael, might have made "Rosenthal" acceptable, and earlier, his sister urged him to use it. It would have gone well later with his Irish rose, Annie. Yes, Michael Rosenthal might have passed muster. Or A. Michael Rosenthal. But in the event the city desk simply took the easy way. They signed his name A. M. Rosenthal, and that is it to this day.

Abe believed, I think with justification, that for years he was denied a European assignment because of the opposition of the chief European correspondent, Cyrus L. Sulzberger, who was supposed to have said: "One Jew in Paris is enough." (Cy denied the remark. He said his opposition to Abe was based on a row Abe had had with a Paris hotel. Cy thought Abe naïve and lacking in language skills.)

This internal *Times* discrimination was struck down by Arthur Ochs Sulzberger, who succeeded his brother-in-law on Dryfoos' sudden death in 1963. Punch thought the *Times* should stop sticking its head in the sand. Abe felt the same. Fueled by Abe's tendency to hire and promote reporters and editors whom he saw (for a while) as "Young Abe," the pendulum shifted until page 1 of the *Times* became a thicket of Jewish names. When Abe retired in 1986, the changing of the guard brought in Max Frankel as executive editor, with Arthur Gelb as his managing editor, and Jack Rosenthal (no relation to Abe) in as editor of the editorial page with Leslie Gelb (no relation to Arthur) as his deputy. The names would have made Adolph Ochs's eyes bulge.

But, you might ask, what are the principles on which Abe Rosenthal conducted the *Times?* How did he define the news and the responsibilities of the great newspaper he was editing? Not much of a clue—or was there?—in his first successes. They were pop stories: an exposé of "cooping" by police officers, that is, sleeping in their squad cars at night when supposed to be on alert; the thirty-nine witnesses, the neighbors who did not respond to a woman's screams for help when she was being murdered; articles that brought the New York homosexuals out of the closet onto Third Avenue; a yarn about a doctor, nicknamed Doctor Feelgood, who catered to the fast track crowd.

Serious sociopolitical studies for which the *Times* had become famous took second place. Politics got the Roman candle treatment. There was a blazing infatuation of Abe and Arthur Gelb with John Lindsay, which whimpered out as fast as it flared up, leaving lasting scars on both sides. Mary, John's wife, once told Scotty Reston that Abe'n Artie "cost my husband the Presidency of the United States." She may well have been right. Scotty himself told me he thought the coverage "unfair." Daniel Patrick Moynihan became the golden boy after Punch rammed an endorsement of him onto the editorial page over the violent objection of Editor John Oakes. Then it was Mayor Ed Koch's turn. Zabar's and gentrified delis got as much space in Rosenthal's *Times* as Amundsen and the South Pole in Mr. Ochs's.

A volcanic feud erupted between the *Times* and *The Village Voice,* a publication never before even noticed at 229 West 43rd Street, over the novelist Jerzy Kosinski, when *The Voice* published a story that Kosinski, a native of Poland, had help in putting his novels into proper English. The *Times* weighed in with a ponderous essay purporting to demonstrate that Kosinski, a close friend of Abe's, had been the victim of Polish Communist hit men.

* * *

What was going on here? For the first time since Mr. Ochs bought the dying *New York Times* in 1896, the paper and its editor became the focus of cheap publicity, gossip columns, speculative articles in weekly magazines. Mr. Ochs had had to contend with rumors that he was a pawn of J. P. Morgan or the British.

The contemporary glitz focused on Rosenthal. Some reporters claimed he had put the fourteenth executive floor off-limits so they could not go over his head.

Abe was only too well aware of this clatter. He conceded that his predecessors as editors had adopted a reined-in, stiff-upper-lip style. "I'm too smart not to know that at least part of this must come out of myself," he told me. "It can't always be someone else who is at fault." He knew he fought and bled and shouted and cried and agonized in public. "If the bull didn't bleed," he said, "they wouldn't torment him. I know I bleed easily."

So there was no end to the stories, stories that seemed to me bereft of aim or pattern: how he had sent famous reporters to rusticate in Ottawa (two Beijing correspondents in succession, Christopher Wren and John Burns); how Ray Bonner was pulled out of Nicaragua and put on the New York financial desk "for seasoning"; how Jim Sterba went from pillar to post—Houston, Hongkong, and Beijing—before joining *The Wall Street Journal.* Abe ordered M. S. Handler to stop reporting Malcolm X, about whom he had written some remarkable stories. Malcolm X disappeared from the *Times* and ultimately was assassinated. Handler sadly wasted into retirement. Roger Wilkins took a run at writing an urban column but was out of the paper more often than in. Alden Whitman, virtuoso of death (he had invented the superobituary under Clifton Daniel's tutelage), was pulled off and the beat scattered to a dozen winds. Once Abe walked out of 229 West 43rd Street in a dudgeon just before edition time because he was so angry at Theodore Bernstein, champion of the bullpen and the man who first nominated Abe for the city editorship. Not so long afterward, Bernstein retired, not very pleased with his protégé. The signature of Ben Franklin, a Washington reporter, was banned from the paper, restored, banned again, then restored after Abe's retirement. The scathing social criticism written by Charlotte Curtis under the guise of reportage about the rich and nouveau riche had bothered Russell Edwards, the society editor for whom Charlotte nominally worked. He asked Clifton Daniel how to handle her. Daniel had an easy answer: "Let her cover the stories, write them up, and print them." But when Curtis began to write a column, Abe limited it to once a week and buried it deep in the paper. Daniel's style was not Abe's.

On one occasion Abe became convinced that he had uncovered a homosexual-Communist conspiracy on his staff and roared at a terrified young staffer in the center of the city room that he would root it out and destroy its participants.

Nothing exceeded in ups and downs the career of Seymour Hersh, the country's No. 1 investigative reporter. Abe bought Hersh's classic of Vietnam, the My Lai story, and made him a staff reporter. In Watergate days Hersh gave the *Times* a competitive edge, but in the end Sy wandered away, and I think Abe felt a sense of relief.

Sometimes the *Times*'s Kremlinologists tried to find a pattern underlying all this. I am convinced there was none. It stemmed from the contradictory personality of a remarkable man. Abe took to describing himself as a "bleeding heart conservative," and gossip writers labeled him a neoconservative. "I'm a liberal on civil rights," Abe told me, "and a conservative on taxes." He was beyond labels. The *Times* boasted two brilliant critics, Ada Louise Huxtable on architecture and Hilton Kramer on art, both certifiable neoconservatives. Both left the paper, Ada Louise after winning a MacArthur grant. She was out of the paper for five years until Abe retired. Kramer resigned and founded *The New Criterion*. The *Times* probably would have lost Gene Roberts, who became editor of the *Philadelphia Inquirer,* and Bill Kovach, editor of the *Atlanta Constitution,* Abe or no Abe. The same might be said of some of Abe's early stars—Halberstam, Fred Powledge, Richard Reese, Gay Talese, J. Anthony Lukas who plunged into writing best-sellers and hot magazine pieces. Lukas lingered as a contributor to the *Times* magazine. Halberstam delighted in reediting the *Times* at dinner parties, but was not permitted to write for the paper for ten years—until Abe's retirement. Talese maintained a personal friendship with Abe but wrote seldom. He took a hand in persuading Abe to buy his suits at Brooks instead of off-the-rack at Harry Rothmans. "You are the managing editor of *The New York Times,*" Talese said. "You must dress like the editor of the greatest newspaper in the world." I asked Abe once whether the Brooks suits were custom-made. "Geezus," Abe said, "I never had a made suit in my life." That was 1979. Times would change. Before he retired, Abe was patronizing Paul Stuart, and his suits were made to measure.

Abe hotly denied he maintained a black list. "I have no hit list" he told me. But many writers complained that their books no longer were reviewed in the *Times* or were assigned to critics certain to blast them. Some publishers privately said they were afraid to complain for fear of reprisals. *The National Book Critics Journal* devoted nearly ten pages of its February 1986 issue to an exhaustive study largely devoted to complaints about the *Times* book review and its critics. Sometimes there was juggling of theater reviews. *Dancin'* got a roast and was given another chance by being assigned to a dance critic who also bombed it. The dance critics' review was not published. When a food critic gave the Café des Artistes a less than four-star review, he quickly discovered it had been Abe's favorite for years. I shared Abe's passion for Beverly Sills but wondered how hanging her poster outside Abe's office affected the music critics.

When Sydney Schanberg came back a hero from Cambodia, Abe recognized in him a true reincarnation of "Young Abe." He took Sydney to the mountaintop, spelled out his future, set him on the track by making him city editor. It was a stormy passage. Once Sydney regained his status by hiring a Scots piper to pipe through the block-long city room to Abe's office (Abe had observed that he had never been piped by a piper). But came a day when Schanberg was sent up to the tenth floor to write a column on city affairs. Schanberg did not hang there, twisting slowly, slowly in the wind. He became the talk of the town, the symbol of Civic Virtue, exposing the evildoer, naming the slumlords, pillorying the privateers who with Mayor Koch's benign inattention were taking Manhattan.

In all *Times* history, columnists had enjoyed total editorial freedom. No one edited their opinions or told them what to say. They had lifetime—well, say, to age seventy-five—tenure. That had been the *Times* principle since the days of Mr. Arthur Krock, the first columnist. There was no doubt that Schanberg stirred up a lot of dust. New York's real-estate interests are not blushing violets. There were plenty of complaints about Schanberg's tough columns, threats of lawsuits, pressure. Publisher Sulzberger was hardly pleased. Still a shudder ran through the *Times* staff when on one autumn weekend in 1986 Schanberg's column was abruptly terminated. The man who took the heat was Sulzberger, although he was conveniently absent in Alaska. His associate, Sydney Gruson, conveyed the word to Schanberg. There was a great fuss and much negotiation, but in the end Schanberg left the *Times.* He blamed Abe's influence as the decisive factor—a contention not totally susceptible of proof. The Schanberg case was the newspaper scandal of the year but Schanberg lived on as the symbol of Civic Virtue, blazing away— on *New York Newsday,* the newest *Times* competitor.

One afternoon in 1979 I stood beside Abe outside his office as he looked out on the city room and heard him say: "Why do people hate me so?" He was speaking from his heart. He was looking out over the room he loved more than his life, *his* room, *his* territory, *his* people, and asking the question to which only he possessed the answer. People did hate him, even some who had been bullied into sycophancy—the ones who, once he was gone, hurried to say they had not been close to Abe, they had been for Frankel all along.

In the winter of 1987 I chatted with Abe, as I have so often, in his new office on the tenth floor, a lovely office bright with his Japanese prints, a bower of flowers on his desk and blooming under the big window to the west. He sat comfortably behind his desk, jacket off, cheerful new red suspenders, his hair sculptured in a koala cut, face round and rosy, not a trace of that skinny needle he once had been (127 pounds when he joined the *Times*) and listened as he told me what he missed. "I miss that room," he said, "the life, the room, the city room. The people. The whole world was there. Schoenberg—that was music. And Rich—that was the theater." He went on ticking them off, but there weren't too many names. It had been a cri de coeur when he uttered those words: "Why do people hate me so?" And now it was a cri de coeur because they were still at their desks on the third floor, and he was not at his.

How had Rosenthal carried out his mandate to run *The New York Times?* "I kept the paper straight," he liked to say. "I kept the paper straight." But what did he mean by that? That he kept it out of the hands of reds, radicals, revolutionaries who plotted to take it over? Or those young people at Columbia, for instance?

Never in history had a managing editor of the *Times* boasted

that he had kept the paper "straight." That went without saying.
Mr. Van Anda had not said that, nor Mr. Birchall, Mr. James,
Mr. Catledge, nor Mr. Daniel.

Did Abe mean he kept the paper straight from forces that
would have corrupted it? Wheeler-dealers? The Mafia? Bias?
Prejudice? No other managing editor had felt he had to make
such a declaration. I think Abe believed in conspiracy theory. I
think he believed the yarn he told me about the plot of the Columbia radicals. He had spelled it out. The friend whose name he
could never recall had told him that the media was the most
tempting target for the student left. The *Times* was the most
tempting part of the media, and Abe personified the *Times*. Then,
as he told me, it had happened, just as his friend predicted—it
had happened *just like that*. He meant that Columbia burst out
with anti-Rosenthal banners after his Grayson Kirk story.

He went back to this theme again and again. He returned to it
at the time of Chicago, 1968. It was not the police riot that disturbed him so much it was the young demonstrators. He saw
them as the villains. Nor did this response vanish. His greatest
triumph was the publication of the Pentagon Papers in 1971, but
his first concern had been that the papers might have been fab-
ricated, as he said, by 1,000 young antiwar people sitting in a
basement typing all night. Or the KGB. Again in 1979 he compelled his editors to tear apart a commemorative piece on Wood-
stock, because it credited the young people with a coherent social
philosophy. He didn't see them that way. They were more of a
mob. He always denied he was uncomfortable with minorities—
blacks, women, you name it. He contended he had done more for
them on the *Times* than anyone else, a contention they did not
accept. As for the young, I think he was always somewhat uncomfortable with them. Once he told me that he had never questioned that the *Times* was the Best. But the young people of the
late sixties were different. They wanted direct action. They did
not possess the *Times* mystique.

Abe Rosenthal wanted it *all*. He told me once that his ambition was not just to be managing editor, executive editor, boss of
the news. He wanted everything. He wanted to be *publisher*. Of
course that never was to be, never could be. But once ambition
began pounding in his veins, it was ambition unlimited. At first
he had not even been sure he wanted to be an editor. At first he

thought city editor was a step-down from the glorious role of foreign correspondent. He didn't lose that quickly. He had, to his surprise, loved being an editor, but he still wanted it *all*. He wanted to write as well as edit. Once he told me: "You went off to Hanoi, and became the most famous correspondent in the world. I saw you come into the room. You were fulfilling my dream. I said: 'Harrison, what have you done? Who did what to whom?'" The question was never to be answered.

I don't know how good a portrait I have drawn of Rosenthal. I know him too well to be sure. Of one thing I am certain: Neither his friends nor his enemies really understood him. Nor did he himself. Once he began to talk to me about a dream he had had, a dream about women. He said that he liked women, liked them very much. He had grown up with women, his five sisters, now all dead, and himself. "I get along with women," he said. "I feel at home with them." But, he went on, just the other day he had suddenly realized that in a dream all the characters are yourself. All of them, men and women. There is nobody else in the dream but you in different forms.

He was right, of course. But I could not fathom what had sent this thought into his restless mind.

When Abe said to me, "Why do people hate me so?" it was a genuine question, not a bit of posturing. He could even understand that people did hate him, but he could not accept the hatred because, I think—in a paradox which his friends, most of his associates, and surely his enemies did not understand—his inner psyche was founded on love. What no one, perhaps not even Abe, could fathom was the swiftness with which love, that most capricious of emotions, could change at a flicker of an eye, a word, a gesture, from milky almost maudlin affection to Othellian paranoia, suspicion, fear, hate. Only Shakespeare could limn such a man.

Rosenthal knew no limits. He took the curves with his foot on the accelerator. He had accomplished a small miracle with the *Times*. Never had it been so readable. No one had so outrageously stolen ideas, and he made no bones about it. "We swallowed *New York* magazine," he said. "I'll steal any idea from anybody if it's not nailed down." No one had so completely broken with his own standards (Abe had loved the good gray *Times* on which he went to work in 1944; it was perfect—he had hated the idea of change). No one had changed it more—blasted open the columns, brought in graphics, given space to art and pictures, surrounded them with masses of dazzling white. When Abe came in as city editor, he hated to use space for any thing but words. Writing—that was what the *Times* was about. Space was not to be wasted on art.

He was a quick learner. When I introduced graphics on the Op-Ed page in 1970, broke all rules about makeup, he had nothing but ridicule. But within a year graphics, drawings, artwork blossomed throughout the paper. He designed and redesigned section after section until the paper had an open and inviting aspect. He fought like a terrier against the plans of Business Manager Walter Mattson for a four-section paper, but when Punch Sulzberger ordered it for economic reasons—the paper was just bumping year by year at the red-ink level—Abe and his faithful Artie whistled up a prairie fire. Mattson wanted to run grocery ads, which the *Times* had never carried, he wanted to tap new revenue sources. Abe threw himself into the task and invented a newspaper with enormous appeal to upwardly mobile readers, suburbanites, and the new Manhattan cliff dwellers with extraordinary budgets for restaurants, designer clothing, million-dollar apartments, top dollar interior decorators, what Thorstein Veblen called conspicuous consumption.

I told Abe on the day he became editor that he was the first editor in *Times* history whose main problem would be money. That remark stuck. He and Mattson, under Punch's driving incentive, made the greatest *Times* turnaround since the day Mr. Ochs bought the paper. They turned the *Times* into a money machine, treading new ground, *inventing* new ground every step they took. It was and is an economic miracle.

Abe's genius became the code word for the phantasmagoria I have recited. I agree that Abe is a genius and that without his transformation the *Times* might not have survived. But I do not believe that it could only have been achieved by institutionalized chaos.

I had an extraordinarily close relationship with Abe during his formative years in charge of the *Times*. Each morning I wrote him a brief critique about the paper—blunt, unsparing, no punches pulled, praise for the good, contempt for the shoddy. He wanted that. I insisted on it. The memos drove him out of his mind—as they would have me—like having a portion of chopped barbed wire with your orange juice each morning, but he came back each day for another dose. Once or twice, voice heavy, eyes glowing, he asked me if I couldn't find anything good to say (sometimes I couldn't). But scanning the memos today, I find many cheers—every one deserved—to balance the daily noggin of acid and castor oil.

Once, he scribbled:

> As for you, sir, the annual Managing Editor Ass-Kicking award for 1969, than which there is no higher. Salisbury, if you ever go up to that tenth floor office [I was getting ready to move from the third floor to the tenth in preparation for launching the Op-Ed page] you will have to take me with you!

That took balls—and grace.

Soon I did go up to the tenth floor, but I kept sending my critiques to AMR for several years. The Op-Ed page was a one-man band. At the start I had a single assistant, David Schneiderman, an apprentice whom I picked off the foreign desk, where he was a temporary news clerk in the summer of 1970, just out of Johns Hopkins, bright as buttons, thoughtful, quiet, responding to challenge like a Chesapeake retriever. Today he is publisher of *The Village Voice.* He would tackle anything and had to. In late January 1972, inspired by endless talks with the young people on the *Times,* he sent a three-page single-space memo to Rosenthal:

> To be young and working at the *Times,* it seems to me, is to be on the very lowest rung of the newspaper and I wonder if this is necessary. . . . Getting onto the staff no longer possesses the magic among young people that it once had. . . . What the *Times* considers news is, for me and many of my peers, boring and often irrelevant to our lives.

David said the answers to what he and his friends were interested in—the Pertola Institute, Mick Jagger, the Lyman Family, Ken Kesey and the ex-Merry Pranksters—could be found in *Rolling Stone, The Whole Earth Catalogue* (which Digby Diehl of *The Los Angeles Times* and I steered that year to a National Book Award, causing much establishment gnashing of teeth), and other alternative publications. He wrote:

> Young people with the proper training are energetic and resourceful enough to do investigative reporting and muckraking.

. . . this generation is highly idealistic and anxious to do this sort of writing if given a chance.

Then, David spoke of experience on the Op-Ed page, his delight in such odd chores as translating from French a piece by Prince Sihanouk on deadline.

There are scores of young journalists out there who would jump at the opportunity and make a magnificent contribution to this paper. But they must be given the chance soon as the number is dwindling every day. Is there something to be done?

I saw this memo (to me it seemed quite thoughtful) only after David had received Abe's instant same-day reply:

Oh, no, Mr. Schneiderman, I will engage in no discussion, ever, with anybody who opens with hostility, insult, arrogance and assault. I would demean myself by writing further.

When David showed me this correspondence, I dropped Abe a note: "Don't tag David as 'arrogant'; have a word with him and see yourself in the 1972 version."

To which Abe responded:

It was not his comment on the *Times* that disturbed me—I have heard and made far worse myself and can recognize where his biases and perceptivities are at play. What did deeply disturb me was the insight I believe it gives into him. . . . This is not a matter of age or youthfulness. . . .

I feel there is an enormous amount of hostility in the world, and that, indeed, this hostility is the major sickness of our time . . . I must confess that his note literally made me ill to the point where I skipped the front page conference. Again, it was not the comments on the *Times* that sickened me, but what I consider the warp in Mr. Schneiderman. . . .

"I refuse to take part in verbal aggression. . . . This is by no means a matter of turning the other cheek—quite the contrary. It simply grows out of a belief that if people who did not believe in assault refused to engage in discussion wherever possible with those who opened with assault, then the assaulters might eventually change their ways.

What was there to say? I often thought of Abe's words when someone told me the latest horror story from the city room. I knew that Abe was absolutely honest in his anger. That was how he saw the world around him, and it was no good to say that it was a mirror and not a window into which he gazed. I tried to shut my eyes to this image. I could not drive from my heart the young Abe whom I had known in the beginning days at the United Nations, facing up to his big competitors, alone, vulnerable, small, thin, with brown eyes whose plea for help you could not deny. Lord Acton, I think, was right. There is nothing more difficult to guard against than the alchemy of power, the more absolute the more intoxicating.

29 | Where's the Rest of Me?

The evening of April 25, 1984, Charlotte and I had reached a place called Xishui on our 6,000-mile journey retracing the route of Mao Zedong's Long March of 1934–35.

We were deep in Guizhou, a province where, tradition says, there are no three li* without a hill, no three days without rain, and no man has three silver dollars in his pocket. It was back of beyond. In prerevolutionary days everyone smoked opium, and babies became addicted at the breasts of their half-naked mothers. We halted overnight at Xishui on our way to Mao Tai, a village where the Red Army on its long march first discovered a local booze called mao-tai, made from sorghum mash, said to be 190 proof. It became the national drink, imbibed (usually) in minute quantities at official banquets. I wanted to check a dubious rumor that Mao's teenage soldiers were so naïve they soaked their blistered feet in mao-tai instead of pouring it down their parched throats. They may have, I found, used some mao-tai on their feet but more went down their gullets.

Charlotte's meticulous diary records the events on the evening of April 25. She saw her first rat in China, and she saw Ronald Reagan on Chinese TV. She was not making a political comment. The rat, a grayish creature, flashed across her feet when she visited the improvised toilet that had been set up for her use. (Charlotte knows rats; she has lived on a farm and in New York City and has coped with rats in both places.)

Ronald Reagan was making his first trip to China, and in remote Xishui, roughly 1,000 miles west of Beijing, we had hardly expected to catch a glimpse of him. I was interested in the President's visit. Nixon had left an indelible mark on his 1972 trip, and I wondered how Reagan would play in Beijing. He was more anti-Communist than Nixon and on entering the White House had made no secret of his preference for Taiwan. Some Reagan friends were last-ditch Taiwan supporters. I knew that many Chinese were excited about the President's visit, but I was

*The li is a Chinese unit of measurement, about half a kilometer long. Three li is the rough equivalent of a mile.

amazed when our hosts told us that he was going to be on TV and that somehow in this remote corner they had obtained a set so we could see him.

Sure enough, after dinner they led us into a kind of barren lounge, and there on a table in front of a lumpy davenport and several chairs was a small TV. Quite soon, Mr. Reagan appeared on a grainy screen, a bit ill at ease, but Mrs. Reagan seemed to be having a fine time. I thought that was very important.

Charlotte and I and our Chinese friends listened to the end. Our companion, Jack Service, former Foreign Service officer, Old China Hand, McCarthyite victim and Californian, fell asleep. The Chinese seemed amiably impressed with the President, but not until we got to Xi'an seven weeks later did I talk to a Chinese who had actually seen him in person. The President, like most tourists, had made a side trip to Xi'an to see the famous terra-cotta warriors.

Reagan had left a strong impact on Xi'an and, as I later found, in Beijing as well. The Chinese had been amazed at the remarkable security arrangements and split-second timing. They had never seen anything like it. They could hardly believe that the President's bullet-proof limousine had been flown across the Pacific to Beijing and then to northwest China for the short ride from a military airport to the archaeological museum.

And the President himself. "Oh, that wonderful cowboy smile," one young man exclaimed. That was it, the cowboy smile, even in post-Mao China, it was the symbol of America, etched deep by thousands of Western movies. Here was Mister Cowboy himself, Mister America, if you will. How could they not like him? They went for him for the same reason so many Americans did—for that smile, for his big American image, his friendliness, the wave of his hand, and all the imperial trappings.

I was not as surprised as some might have been. I felt that, except perhaps in England and Western Europe, Reagan's cowboy image was a national heritage. It reminded people of the cowboys and Indians they had grown up with, the Lone Ranger, all the wonderful child's mythology. When Reagan or his handlers or Nancy Reagan nixed a proposal that he go to Moscow for the Brezhnev funeral, I could hear the Kremlin sigh with relief. His cowboy smile on Moscow TV would have been worth a thousand Star War pitches. No Russian man or woman could have been convinced after seeing his "wave from the saddle" that he had ill intentions toward what he had foolishly dubbed "the evil empire." If Nixon had wowed the Russians, Reagan would have knocked them dead.

Reagan scored a hit in China, but not with everyone. In Beijing in June we dined with Hu Yaobang, general secretary of the Communist Party, in his residence in Zhongnanhai, in the Forbidden City. Hu told me he had met three American Presidents—Nixon, Carter, and Reagan. He rated Nixon No. 1, Carter No. 2, Reagan No. 3. Nixon had made the "opening" to China, Carter had established diplomatic relations. Reagan still had not lost all the aura of his Taiwan sympathies. The upper Chinese were still a bit suspicious.

I had never been close to Reagan. My opinions were all secondhand. I saw him as one of those special products of California, which in politics as in plants are distinguished by showy colors, uncertain flavor, and dubious nutritional values. The politicians had not come out of the plant-breeding experiments of Luther Burbank, but they somehow seemed related to boysen berries, pomatoes, and avocados.

The first California politician I heard of as a child was Hiram Johnson, a Bull Moose Republican, always out of step with everyone; he eventually helped Henry Lodge to scupper Woodrow Wilson's League of Nations. There were California politicians and businessmen involved in the Teapot Dome scandal of Handsome Harding. Herbert Hoover, disguised in starched collars, was half do-gooder, half entrepreneurial pirate, a lot more California OJ in his veins than Iowa corn.

The depression brought the California quirkies to the top. It gave us Upton Sinclair, socialist muckraker, author of *The Jungle* and *The Brass Check,* as candidate for governor. Dr. Townsend scared the daylights out of solid citizens by proposing $200 monthly pensions for the elderly. All this, I thought, was natural in the land of Aimee Semple McPherson, a new frontier of low-budget imagination, populated by a mixture of the elderly and the young in search of nirvana and a free ride.

When a new generation of California politicians began to sprout after World War II, they seemed to me to wear the colors of their predecessors. Richard Nixon fitted in nicely, although on the other side. He defeated Helen Gahagan Douglas, too sensible a lady to make it in day-glow politics. Nixon had no easy time, but thanks to his dog Checkers stayed on Ike's ticket and entered the realm of destiny. He was followed by the song-and-dance man, George Murphy, who managed to serve in the Senate without leaving any detectable trace of having been there. Then came Jerry Brown, a true product of Luther Burbank, a cross of 1960s rebel, Hollywood, the Jesuits, and Zen. And no one wore the California colors with more flash than Tom Hayden and Jane Fonda.

It was within this framework that I placed Ronald Reagan, first as governor, then coming on like Gangbusters—real Gangbusters—against the unfortunate Jimmy Carter, who may have had the last laugh, having bequeathed Iran to his vanquisher.

To find the real man within the cocoon of political legend is never easy. The politician himself loses his ability to tell what is flesh and what is plastic. The task is even more difficult if the man is both politician and actor. There is, of course, a close connection between acting and politics. One element of the art of politics is to create an image that is attractive to the general public and wins their backing for the politician and his policies. Harold Macmillan put it neatly in answer to an American reporter's question as to what he thought of electing an actor President. Macmillan smiled behind his bushy moustache and said: "Why, my dear boy, we are all actors on the world's stage, aren't we?"

He was right, and television has brought more and more stars of the electronic world into public office. The blending of stage and politics is not without hazard, of course. Introspection and self-examination are not highly developed on the stage. There are apt to be more Jesse Helmses than James Madisons in the future.

Before Mr. Reagan launched his Hollywood career, he spent some years as a sports announcer on WHO radio station in Des Moines, Iowa. He broadcast football and baseball games play by play with the aid of telegraphic bulletins. The report was offered with all the excitement of the real eyewitness play by play, although the listeners were told it came off the wire. There was no deceit in this, but the announcer's trick was to make it sound so exciting the listeners forgot it was all secondhand.

Early in his career Walter Cronkite performed the same chore in Kansas City. One evening after a White House interview, Walter told the President about the awful moment when his telegraph line broke down. He expected it to come back in a minute or two and went ahead, making up trivial detail, five-yard penalties, incomplete passes, failed line plays, time-outs. It was the Notre Dame–University of Southern California game, and to Walter's horror the wire stayed down—five minutes, ten minutes, fifteen—finally coming back after a twenty-minute interruption. He discovered that Notre Dame had scored a touchdown in the interim. In Walter's imaginary game, USC had the ball deep in Notre Dame territory. It took him another three nervous minutes to get Notre Dame's touchdown racked up. It was, Walter said, the worst time he had ever had on the air.

A few weeks later, Walter was going over some outtakes of a minor speech by Reagan and heard him telling about "my worst moment as a sports broadcaster." It was, Mr. Reagan said, during a Notre-Dame–USC game . . ." Reagan told it very well, Walter conceded.

Actors and politicians take their materials where they find them. Cronkite suffers from loss of hearing in one ear. He told Mr. Reagan he dated the trouble to a moment in World War II when a GI on the battlefield discharged a shot only a foot from his ear. Not too long after that, Walter heard the President talking of his hearing difficulty, which was caused, he thought, by a rifle shot close to his ear. The President, to be sure, saw no combat during World War II. He was first assigned to a cavalry unit and then to an Air Corps detachment, where he made morale films for the troops.

A storyteller's tales are not necessarily true, although he may earnestly assure his listeners that they are. He consciously heightens suspense, colors the drama, and often casts his story in the first person. It was *his* adventure, *his* escape, he it was who slew the dragon. We do not mind the deception. We suspend belief in order to increase our own enjoyment. This is tradition, and this is how the bard held his place at court, amusing the king and his courtiers.

No one minds if Reagan puts on the mantle of Cronkite to tell a good joke. But where to draw the line? A friend of mine had a magazine assignment to interview Mr. Reagan. He was well received. Mr. Reagan enjoys telling tales. The conversation strayed onto race relations. Well, said Mr. Reagan, this America of ours is a wonderful place. Do you remember how on the day after Pearl Harbor, FDR integrated the U.S. Armed Forces—just like that?

But, demurred my friend, I think there is something a bit off here. I believe that President Truman integrated the military, and there was quite a row over it.

Mr. Reagan was patient with the writer. Oh, no, he said. You must remember that Negro cook on the battleship at Pearl Harbor? The Japs were attacking, the crews had been killed or wounded. He picked up a machine gun and shot down a Japanese Zero. The very next day FDR integrated the armed forces.

My friend did not press his point. He knew exactly what Mr. Reagan was talking about. The President had it dead right. But he was talking about a movie, not real life.

Or there is the story about the Israeli Prime Minister who was seeing Mr. Reagan for the first time. He came out of the White House aglow. He told the reporters that the President had described how he took part in the liberation of the Buchenwald concentration camp. "I'd never known that," said the Prime Minister. Back at the embassy his colleagues explained to the Prime Minister that the incident had not happened that way. Mr. Reagan had not been in Europe during the war. The liberation occurred in a movie, not at Buchenwald.

I was in Moscow just after the Summit at Geneva in 1985. One of Mr. Gorbachev's close aides invited me to his office. He was walking on air over the Gorbachev-Reagan meeting. They had been very worried. It was Gorbachev's debut. How would he stand up to Reagan? They briefed him to the ears with everything they could think of about Reagan. Then the two men met, one on one, an interpreter, no aides. Gorbachev was on his own. So was Reagan. They began with small talk, then Gorbachev switched to the subject of movies. He told the President he had seen some of his films (as he had in the briefing sessions). Mr. Reagan beamed. Hollywood was home ground. Yes, Gorbachev mused, I have seen some of your movies. "There was one," he said, "which I liked best. I think it was called something like 'The Best of Me'."

That was the ballgame. Gorbachev was talking about *King's Row*, the best picture of Reagan's career, an adult, dramatic totally professional performance. Reagan had not been nominated for an Oscar, but he might well have been. On late night TV reruns the picture is sometimes called *The Rest of Me*. In it Reagan undergoes a double amputation, both legs off above the knees, wakes up from the anesthetic and exclaims: "Where's the rest of me?" It was the best line Reagan ever uttered, and he knew it. In 1964 when politics began to preoccupy his mind, he called the biography which a free-lance writer named Richard Hubler had turned out for him: *Where's the Rest of Me?*

The Rest of Me, I think, was a watershed in the life of Ronald Reagan, as much of a watershed as the poliomyelitis attack which FDR suffered. True, it was not a real amputation. It was make-believe, but it was an experience that changed everything, philosophy, role, expectations.

Gorbachev and his advisers were shrewd, well-informed, but I do not think they were *that* shrewd or *that* well-informed. I do not believe they understood that *King's Row* opened a direct route to the Reagan psyche. It put Gorbachev and Reagan on a plane of intimacy and understanding. Fears melted. Each man now felt he knew who he was talking to. It was not just Reagan who had seen the image of the Evil Emperor dissolve. It was Gorbachev who saw the Capitalist Enemy vanish. They went on to talk of critical matters like Star Wars. Reagan spelled out his views and his vision of a world from which nuclear peril forever vanished.

As he listened, or so my Moscow friend told me, Gorbachev made a profound discovery. Reagan really believed in his dream. He was not dissembling. He saw Star Wars as a peace project, not a device to bring the Soviet Union to its knees. "Listening to Reagan talk, Gorbachev understood that this was no trick," my friend told me. Reagan might be mistaken. He might be ignorant. He might be badly served by his advisers, but he was not trying to wipe out Moscow. He wanted to saddle up and ride into the golden west of Peace, stirrup to stirrup with his Russian *friend.*

I do not know whether this is the whole story. I don't know whether Mr. Reagan was as naïve and sincere as Gorbachev was represented as thinking. But I do know that the two men hit it off. For a while until the wrecking crews on both sides—the professional arms experts, diplomats, ideologues, and military—got to work, it looked like a real breakthrough.

I think that the intimacy of the talk about *The Rest of Me* was genuine and that it underlay the curious events of Reykjavik when Gorbachev and Reagan, again one on one, negotiated a virtual nuclear-free world to the amazement, alarm, and horror of their advisers, who rushed into the breach and torpedoed the friendly, human, and mind-boggling achievement.

Yet, it was not entirely smashed, and as time went on, quiet words, hints, and a little hardball applied to the antagonistic negotiators freed one element after another for a new and grandiose deal. Edged by memory of an event that never happened—an almost catastrophic but theatrical amputation—the world moved inch by inch toward sanity.

I did not meet Mr. Reagan until 1985 when (to my surprise) I was twice invited to the White House. It had been years since I had been a guest there, and I found a lot of changes. In New Deal days and until the Kennedys, there was a kind of Jacksonian scruffiness about the place, especially backstage, in the offices and press quarters: cramped cubicles, reporters dashing for phones, impromptu news conferences, people sauntering in and out of the offices of the President's staff, little or no security, a pleasant, sleepy White House policeman at the door. People left tennis rackets and packages from Woodward & Lothrop's department store on the big Philippines mahogany table in the entrance hall. Copypaper was balled up and tossed toward the cuspidors beside the old leather chairs, where visitors waited and waited for their appointments, which were always late.

All that was gone now—most of it before the Reagans, but the President and his wife put a seal on it. The press quarters reminded me of CBS at 524 West 57th or the *Today* studios at 30 Rock, combed down, hot lights, security guards, no wandering.

I found the social quarters of the White House spiffed up and very well run. Efficient, pleasant, well-groomed young men and women of the armed forces escorted guests through the metal detectors and up to the reception rooms. Quiet, careful waiters and an air of relaxed elegance I'd not seen even in the Kennedy era, smooth as a Cunard liner in the great days. The White House had become, if you will, an excellent stage: superb dinners, fine after-dinner entertainment, lots of show biz guests, Liz Taylor, Beverly Sills, Robert Mitchum, you name your favorite.

My first visit was a luncheon honoring the Eagle Scouts. I had been one a great many years ago. The President had a handsome black Eagle Scout at his right, an elderly Jewish scoutmaster from the lower East Side on his left, and at the table a button-eyed black Cub Scout and a brace of towheaded Nordics. A balanced selection.

I couldn't place one guest at my table, a French lady, author of a book about nuclear war. I couldn't figure out how she related to the Scouts. Why was she there? Pat Buchanan filled me in. She was going to have a quick photo opportunity when the President left the room, a little promo for her book. I thought of that later on when stories appeared about people wangling Reagan handshakes through low-ranking White House officials.

Still, I liked the the way the Reagan White House ran, except for the press part. The grubby old days were better.

I got a closer look at Mr. Reagan and his White House July 23, 1985, when Charlotte and I were invited for the state visit of President Li Xiannian of China. The President had been operated on for cancer of the colon ten days earlier, and this would be his first public appearance.

His gesture would long be remembered by the Chinese, who venerate age. Mr. Reagan turned it into a tour de force. He had never seemed more fit. (Although I spotted a fold-up wheelchair just inside the entrance to the East Portico, where the elderly Chief Executives met, whether for Reagan or Li who could say?)

We spectators had been handed tiny red flags with golden stars to wave when President Li appeared. Red flags in the Reagan White House? What next? I wondered. Then I remembered that Mr. Reagan had shown his friend Warren Beattie's picture *Reds* (about John Reed and the Bolshevik Revolution) in the White House. When someone asked him how he could show such a Communist paean, he responded: "But I thought it was *anti-Communist!*"

Wave our red flags we did when the Presidents emerged, Mr. Reagan bouncing up the four steps to the rostrum, Mr. Li assisted by an attendant. There was a twenty-one-gun salute and the respective national anthems. When "The Star Spangled Banner" rang out, the Americans briskly placed their arms over their hearts, all but Charlotte and me. We hadn't been brought up to do that. We stood at stiff attention. A hundred times I had seen President Reagan thrust his arm proudly across his breast. Not today. For the first and only time, he betrayed a reality beneath the hearty exterior. He must have had his mind on his operation. Like Charlotte and me he stood with hands firmly at his sides. Only Donald Regan's quick eye caught the President's lapse. He too stood at stiff attention. Going down the steps, Mr. Reagan gave President Li a hand. Another fine mythologic photo opportunity. No White House correspondent bothered to report Mr. Reagan's single lapse. Perhaps they did not even notice it.

It was, all in all, a good performance, and in the evening he gave another. He and President Li made a private pact to skip the entertainment. His decision should have been shared by Charles Z. Wick, USIA director, who snoozed through Grace Bumbry's songs from *Porgy and Bess* despite Mrs. Wick's repeated jabs of the elbow.

The evening had the identifiable Reagan signature. At my table I sat beside Mrs. Michael Deaver, worrying about the fall-out from the Bitburg scandal. Her husband had vetted the President's ill-fated visit to the Nazi cemetery, and there had been some talk about Deaver's purchasing several BMWs at export prices for Washington friends. I told her not to worry. Little did I know what lay ahead, the indictment for perjury.

Earle Jorgensen, an elderly, frail but frisky California businessman, was standing alone at Table 8 when I approached. He introduced himself as one of the five men "who got Ronnie to run for governor."

"At that dinner," he told me, "I told Ronnie, 'You will be in the White House one day.' I didn't believe it, and he didn't believe it. None of us did. But here he is, and here I am."

He explained that he had grown up poor, hadn't money to pay the rent when he went into business. He had two suits. He pawned one to pay the first month's rent on his office. "And now," he said proudly, "I have forty-two suits in my closet. That's America for you."

I agreed that, indeed, it was America. As other guests joined us, I heard him repeating the story. Finally, he came back to me, introduced himself, and told me the story again. I thought it was a pretty good story. I knew that Mr. Reagan's kitchen cabinet was made up of self-made men, some more self-made than others. Mr. Jorgensen was a good example of the Horatio Alger legend, and he had every right to be in this house, which was—as John Hersey pointed out to me that evening when we were wondering a bit sheepishly how we happened to be there—the People's House, not just the President's House.

* * *

It seemed to me that the Reagan saga was a blend of legends, not just the cowboy legend but the rags-to-riches legend, the clean-scrubbed Boy Scout legend, the Ah, shucks, high school football hero legend. All of it. I grew up reading *The American Boy.* Mr. Reagan could have been the hero of every one of the Clarence Buddington Kelland serials, his legend every bit as rich an American invention as those banana splits the corner drug-store used to serve, marshmallow and cherry topping, a sprinkle of nuts, and maybe a dash of chocolate sauce. There was a lot of boy in Reagan. In Sacramento after dinner with legislators in the Governor's mansion he used to invite them down to the base-ment to enjoy his electric train. It was a super-duper.

How could anyone—the President, his wife, or his California friends—know what was real and what was dream, where reality and where unreality met? There was no way of sending it to the laboratory for scientific analysis.

As I tried to grasp the secret of it all, I found myself again and again sucking air like a pump in a dry well. I turned at last to Mr. Reagan's one effort, with the help of his ghost writer, to discover himself and put it down on paper. Early in the pages of *Where's the Rest of Me?* Mr. Reagan or Mr. Hubler had written:

> So much of our profession is taken up with pretending, with in-terpretation of never-never roles that an actor must spend *at least* [my italics] half his waking hours in fantasy, in rehearsal or in shooting.

This, he added, gave to the imaginary world an exaggerated importance. It became harder and harder to distinguish between real life and imaginary life on the stage. In fact, he said, it was the very trauma of his experience in *King's Row* that caused him to decide to leave the film world for politics.

Now, as the political leader of the greatest nation in the world, as the leader of what he liked to call "the free world," could he distinguish the boundary between fact and fiction?

Sadly, I concluded, he probably could not. He could rise from a cancer operation, his life in danger, and play a glittering role of a President overcoming the harsh reality of the physical world. He could, when the political world was collapsing about him, telephone Colonel Oliver North and congratulate him as a "real hero," adding the greatest of accolades: "It would make a great movie." But was there, indeed, a line between what should have been in his mind, the real world of the White House, and the "never-never" world in which he had spent most of his adult years?

Did Mr. Reagan know that the answer to his cry "Where's the Rest of Me?" was a terrible truth: It did not exist.

30 | The World of Op-Ed

On a spring morning in 1970 I sat at my typewriter and looked out over the upland field that borders our old orchard, and my eyes were filled with the splash of golden daffodils, the eight hundred that Charlotte and I had planted, one by one, backs bent, in the late fall, fading a little now but bowing gently in a western breeze. Beyond the field birches blazed white against the dark pines. In my study the sun slanted over the wide planks of the floor and spackled the walls.

It was a bit of heaven, but as I hammered the keys of my typewriter I saw not flowers but fountains of earth and flame thrown to the sky by the 2,000-pound bombs that gouged the red soil of Cambodia in this hallowed season of the Plowing of the Sacred Furrow. It was the time when Prince Sihanouk and his forebears had moved across the emerald paddies behind a shimmering pair of gray bullocks, hands on the wooden plow, moving through the watery earth in the ancient fertility rite. Beyond the paddy the buffalo would nuzzle bowls of maize and soya and rice and water and wine set out for them. If they ate the grain and gulped the water, all would be well, a fine crop, plenty for the people to eat, peace in the world. But woe if they drank only the wine! Disaster would strike as it had in the drought of 1959.

Now in this year of 1970 the buffalo neither ate nor drank. The sacred furrow was not plowed. Sihanouk was gone, overturned by a plot, and we Americans and our technology of war, our B-52s, were turning the gentle land into inferno.

Charlotte and I knew Cambodia and loved it, the raffish capital of Phnom Penh, its unkempt boulevards, fleets of Mercedes bought with money from American aid, gay, eccentric Sihanouk with his homemade movies and his beautiful ladies, Angkor Wat (only the Russian word *dremuchii* catches its drowsy, dreamy gloom), the jungle silently tearing apart the ancient stones year by year. We had waded through the "sanctuaries" along the Vietnam border, which now trembled as our B-52s, weapon of the gods, ravaged paddies, forest, vines, people, buffalo, carp, thatched huts and palaces, all going up in thunder.

315

The thunder of Cambodia that spring echoed over America, rifle fire on our campuses, Kent, Ohio, and Orangeburg, South Carolina, teargas, men in helmets, clubs in hand. I could not wipe from my mind the picture of that girl kneeling beside the body of her Kent State friend, weeping, arms outstretched, face etched forever with grief and the question: Why? Why?

That spring I was preparing to launch the Op-Ed page of the *New York Times.* It finally appeared September 26, 1970, three months after I had abandoned the unquiet realm of the third floor and gone up to the tenth to create a new world. It had been a long time coming, debated for years but thwarted by bureaucracy. Three powerful editors—John Oakes of the editorial page, Lester Markel of the *Sunday Times,* and Turner Catledge (and later Abe Rosenthal) of the *Daily* had fought for jurisdiction. In 1970 Punch Sulzberger decided to start the page and put it in my hands. I packed my things and moved off the fine old warehouse third floor, now raddled with hutches and cubicles, and up to that gothic relic of Mr. Ochs' enchantment with the *Times* of London, the editorial boardroom. In Mr. Ochs' day the editors (beards and frock coats) each morning sat and decided upon the policies of the day. I inherited the mullioned windows, oak cabinets, and, for a while, the great oaken table where the fate of nations had been pondered. I don't think Mr. Ochs or his editors would have liked the work to which I put my hand.

I created Op-Ed at a moment when the country had entered an uncharted, unproclaimed, and largely unrecognized revolution. Each day conflict engulfed another institution—the Pentagon, the CIA, the White House, the State Department, Congress, the Supreme Court, the legal system, the Catholic Church, most other faiths, universities, the educational system, social and racial relationships, banks, corporate America, the great foundations, Rockefeller and Ford, the moral system—marriage, the family, sex, life-style—the arts, the way we dressed (jeans) and the way we cut or didn't cut our hair. Nothing shattered nerves as did hair. Establishment America was under siege. From the watch post of Op-Ed, we brought the latest bulletins to the readers of the *Times.*

That was not exactly what I or anyone intended when the long debate (it lasted seven years) over the Op-Ed page was going on. My idea (and that of Punch Sulzberger) was that it would pre-

sent an alternate opinion to those expressed by *Times* editorials
and columnists. It was to be opposite in the true sense. If the
Times was liberal, the Op-Ed articles would be reactionary or
conservative or radical or eccentric. The page would offer a window on the world, particularly that scene which for one reason or
another (usually the parochialism and timidity of editors) the
Times was not presenting in its news pages and editorial comment.

I am sorry to say that, with the passage of time, Op-Ed has
lost most of its Op quality. It has become a wallow of predictabil-
ity. Not so the page of the early days. Op the page was from its
start, and the revolutionary nature of the epoch put it on the
crust, the breaking edge of the issues that spewed like volcanic
lava from the depths of America. The page was a hit, quickly
becoming (next to page 1) the most read section of the *Times*.
Within a year every paper of consequence in the country had
adopted Op-Ed. Even TV and radio and the news weeklies were
trying to create imitations. *The Washington Post* was so eager to
get into the game (on hearing the *Times* was launching Op-Ed)
that it threw out a haberdasher's ad which had run for forty
years across from its editorial page and started its own Op-Ed a
few days before the *Times*.

By spring of 1970 the view from 43rd Street was tinted with
alarming colors. President Nixon's Cambodian "incursion" hit
America and the university campuses with an explosive power
not unlike that unleashed by the B-52s in the jungles. Kent and
Orangeburg rocked the country. Sitting in Taconic, I wondered
how we were going to get out of this—and if we would. I could
not admit that thought to myself, but in spite of everything it
crowded into the edges of my mind.

I had not felt such agony since February 1933 when, every
bank in the country closed, I rode the train from Chicago to Detroit bringing a satchel of nickels, dimes, and quarters so the UP
bureau could go on covering the news. As I rode into Detroit, I
saw a city abandoned, not a factory wheel turning, not an assembly line moving, tens of thousands of men huddled around pots
of slumgullion in the Hoovervilles along the banks of the dirty
Detroit River. I thought the factories were closed for keeps. I
didn't think the chimneys would smoke again. I didn't believe the
men would work again. America was busted, its spring broken

like a mechanical toy. The system could not be fixed. That is what I thought.

Cambodian spring was, in a way, more terrifying. Detroit had been passive. Now smoke and fire and rifle volleys echoed over the land, soldiers shooting young people. I thought of St. Petersburg in 1905. How could our nation be made whole? This was a thought I could not accept. In my hasty book, *The Many Americas Shall Be One,* I tried to argue that somehow a way would be found. We would strike a path to unity and wholeness through the thickets of division and anger and confrontation. By the time I had finished the book, I had almost convinced myself.

I convinced myself by turning back to the past. I think of history as our only guide to the future (which is why the disappearance of history from the curriculum of our schools, even from many universities, fills me with foreboding). I turned back to Dickens' *A Tale of Two Cities,* the first great novel which I read, and to Dickens' opening words, so familiar to all: "It was the best of times, it was the worst of times. . . ."

Then, as few do, I read on:

It was the age of wisdom, it was the age of foolishness, it was the epoch of belief, it was the epoch of incredulity, it was the season of Light, it was the season of Darkness, it was the spring of hope, it was the winter of despair—we had everything before us, we had nothing before us, we were all going direct to Heaven, we were all going direct the other way. In short, the period was so far like the present period that some of its noisiest authorities insisted on it being received for Good or for Evil, in the Superlative degree of Comparison.

I am not so sure today that Dickens is telling us as much as he seems to be telling us—except that at any moment, no matter how dark the murk, light can be found and that in the deepest despond we can find grit with which to build anew. It is testimony to the extent I had been shaken that I sought encouragement in this commonplace commonsense.

The world as seen from Op-Ed was far from commonplace. It was the world of C. D. Darlington and Patrick Buchanan, of B. F. Skinner and Milovan Djilas, of Anaïs Nin and Charles Reich *(The Greening of America),* of LBJ and Hannah Arendt, of Walt

Rostow (who shared all-time tops in frequency of appearance on
Op-Ed with Mary Mebane, the black North Carolina writer), of
Bernadette Devlin and Yukeo Mishima, of Robert Bly and
Yevgeny Yevtushenko, of Buckminster Fuller and Aleksandr
Solzhenitsyn, of Loren Eiseley and William C. Westmoreland, of
Andrei Sakharov and Bernadine Dohrn, of Roger Wilkins and
Spiro T. Agnew, of Fred Hampton (the slain Black Panther),
and Halldor Laxness (Nobel writer of Iceland).

The world of Op-Ed expanded at the rate of almost 100 names
a month, and a great many were not names anyone would recognize, had ever before heard, or ever would hear again: a Mississippi doctor's letter to his freshman son at Tulane, promising
that if the boy was shot in a demonstration, he would grieve, but
he would buy a dinner for the National Guardsman who pulled
that trigger; from an Ohio father whose daughter, Sandy, was
shot and killed at Kent State; from a man fighting to save a Connecticut mountain from despoliation by a power company; from
a drug addict, writing of a fourteen-year-old girl addict and
prostitute; from a professor fed up with the slobism of his students, male and female; from prisoners in jails and camps from
Siberia to Central America; from a man aroused at the destruction of the Newark he grew up in and a woman lamenting the
loss of the prairies of her Midwestern childhood.

There was not much that did not get said on Op-Ed. I had
feared we might run out of materials and piled up an inventory
of 150 articles. I was stupid. We got 100 to 200 submissions a
week. Everyone in the country wanted to speak out, and we let
their voices be heard.

Op-Ed educated me—and I hope many Americans—as to
where we had arrived by the seventies and where we might be
going. No one who read Op-Ed failed to understand the moral
dilemmas of our society—a dilemma of which Richard Nixon
emerged as a classic symbol, embodying, as he did, the contradictions of his age. In this sense the publication of the Pentagon
Papers in June 1971 prepared the state in a Sophoclean way for
Watergate, a year later.

The Pentagon Papers were LBJ, Watergate was Nixon, but
both were rooted in the desiccation of American political morality, the growing gap between our belief in American virtue and

the spirituality of the democratic process and the reality of a society turned sordid. Long since we had moved away from that soaring vision of John Winthrop, drawn from Matthew:

> Wee shall be as a Citty upon a Hill, the eies of all people are upon us; soe that if wee shall deal falsely with our god in this worke wee have undertaken and soe cause him to withdrawe his present help from us, wee shall be made a story and a by-word through the world.

We had dealt "falsely" in Winthrop's words, and we had become a "by-word." If Pentagon and Watergate were personal shocks, there was little in me to indict only two men, Johnson and Nixon, and their associates.

I might find blame in Rusk and Rostow and Westmoreland; I might shudder at the thought of men like Mitchell and Haldeman and Ehrlichman in the White House circle. But what of us—of myself and my fellow citizens? We had elected Johnson and Nixon. It was our choice. Yes, they were flawed men. So was Reagan, waiting in the wings, but were they more flawed than the society for which they spoke? We Americans had collectively chosen them out of the 200 million men and women of our nation. Each was elected by a landslide. It was, I thought, too cheap, too slick to put the blame upon these men alone. We had made them Presidents. We had voted them our proxy and our power. We knew their flaws. They had not sprung unknown on the scene. They had been around for years. We could not pretend that we had been deceived. I didn't think we had much to cry about— except our own sorry selves. Mr. Nixon had not suddenly become a sly political trickster when he walked into the White House. Nor had LBJ. We knew their character. On balance, matching Nixon's wisdom in foreign policy (except for Vietnam) against his abuse of the secret agencies (CIA and FBI) and the creation (like Reagan) of his own private security apparatus, I think he performed better than we had a right to expect.

We cannot cast off our responsibility by saying, Well, I didn't vote for him. We live in a democratic world, and if democracy provides us with ignorant, incompetent, and venal leaders, we have no one to blame but ourselves.

Not long after Watergate, I rode one evening through the bluegrass country of Kentucky with a college student. He came from Pelham, New York, son of parents in the publishing world, product of what he called a wonderfully comfortable and even exciting home.

"My God," he told me, "you don't know how lucky I've been with parents like mine and a younger sister and younger brother."

We drove through the October dusk, and he talked and talked and talked as though he would never stop. It all came out.

"I like it a lot here in Kentucky," he said. "I might even relocate here. I've learned a lot. Not so much in classes [he was a sophomore at Centre College] as out. Do you know there are people here in school who watch daytime television? Honestly. Daytime TV. TV—that's what saps our imagination. It turns our minds into jelly."

He turned to me, lumbering the big college station wagon into the fast lane.

"You were lucky," he went on. "You grew up on radio. That extended your imagination."

"True," I told him. "Radio was like the old-fashioned story-teller. It gave you the words. You provided the pictures."

He had been, he told me, a Nixon supporter, a believer. He worked in the campaign of 1972. He hadn't thought a word of Watergate was true. Then something happened. He and some others were called in by the Nixon staff. There was going to be a breakfast meeting. They wanted the young people to help, to come in as waiters. Of course, everyone volunteered. Then they were told to wear suits and jackets and ties. He thought that was peculiar. But when they turned up, he saw that the neatly dressed young Nixon people were being used to demonstrate that young people were still supporting the President—nice young people, the right kind of white button-down shirts and rep ties and J. Press suits. It gave him a strange feeling, he said. Then came the tapes and all the rest.

"You don't know how that made me feel," he told me. "I felt as if I had been betrayed. It was terrible. I can't get over it. Sometimes I read Lincoln, the Gettysburg address, and I get all choked up. And I have a tape of President Kennedy—the inaugural address. I can't play it without crying."

Sometimes, he said, he felt so bad he even thought of joining the Socialist Party or the Communists.

"Don't do that," I said.

"No," he said, "I won't. But you don't know how terrible it is. I'm only nineteen, and what is there to believe in? I don't think much of Ford or Reagan or any of the Democrats. I haven't any faith. Not in anything."

He told me that the people of the 1930s like myself were the lucky ones. Things were bad then, but we had faith. We weren't disillusioned. We believed that things would come out all right in the end.

"That's right," I told him quietly. "That's right."

But was it right? Today I am not really sure. I had never expected to see the Ford assembly lines working again or smoke from the River Rouge plants. Did I have faith that everything would come out right in 1931 when I scampered down the staircase to lower Michigan as the mounted police were riding into the demonstrators outside the *Chicago Tribune* tower? Did I have faith when I walked past the silent rows of jobless men sitting on the curb of Halsted Street in Chicago? When I found my father had pawned his gold watch and cufflinks and was borrowing money from the loan sharks to make the mortgage payments?

Did I have faith? I just don't know. But I am glad I told the young man I had. I felt that telling him might give him faith, too, something to help him through this fool's turn into which our country had careened.

I did not know whether I had had faith in 1933. If I did, it was the faith of youth and ignorance and natural optimism. And now, talking to that young man in Kentucky, I found I had faith in him. I recognized him and his seriousness of seeking. This, I thought, was what America was about. Americans had their doubts, their disillusions. We fought our way through bogs of despair and broken idols toward a new level of consciousness.

But what to make of another young man, a bit older, who drove me from Newport Beach, California, to Pasadena one morning not long after. He was not driving a college station wagon. He was driving a black car, a stretch with bar and built-in TV. He wore a chauffeur's cap and the manners of the black car driver—obsequious, catering to the millionaires who infest Newport Beach.

He did the routine: offered to adjust the TV, could he mix me a drink? He put a copy of the *Los Angeles Times* on the seat beside me. I didn't want TV, I didn't drink, I had read the *LA*

Times. We started to talk. He came from Indiana and worked at driving black cars and did odd jobs. His wife worked in a hospital. They lived "on the beach." Well, it turned out, they lived two miles from the beach, but they spent their lives on the beach. It was a wonderful free way of life. They lay on the beach, played on the beach, ate on the beach, had sex on the beach, sometimes went into the water. No way he would go back to small town Indiana.

But he was not happy. He and his wife wanted to travel, wanted to go to Europe, wanted to see the castles. They wanted that very much. But how? They could not earn the money for a year in Europe, and that was what they wanted.

So, he said, why shouldn't the government give everyone a year off to do what they want—go to Europe, go to Hawaii, loaf, travel, play. Just for one year. Give them the money; then they would come back and work for the rest of their lives. He and his wife would be happy to do that. Nothing else they wanted, nothing else they would ever want. Just a year in Europe to see the castles.

No, he said, he wasn't much interested in politics. He didn't read the papers. Watched the tube a bit—*Dallas, Dynasty,* things like that. But what he liked was the beach. That was life. He and his wife had a good many friends. They all felt like that. There ought to be some way the government could work it out.

No one looking back on these last years can give us high marks. That cliché of Pentagon, Watergate, and the Reagan days—"the system worked"—is true only by the kindest extension of belief. The system has been abused by people, ordinary, middle, and high, who put their personal interests ahead of those of the country. There was and has been an abandonment and/or distortion of patriotism—twisted away from concern for all to the interests of the few or the individual.

I see this not as an indictment of the system but of society—of bigness and greed, selfishness from vulgar top to wasted underclass.

I see myself as constant critic of American life and of American institutions. And as their strongest supporter. I have examined the other systems at first hand and conclude with Winston Churchill that there is no poorer system of government than democracy—excepting all the rest.

So long as there exist in America young men who can be devastated by the perfidy of a President and can weep at the words of John Fitzgerald Kennedy's inaugural, I cannot in my heart take too seriously the beach people who would give their lives to slavery, if you will, if government would only give them a free year to see the castles of Europe.

31 | "Death for Noble Deeds Makes Dying Sweet"

On the Fourteenth of July, Bastille Day, 1975, I tossed a notebook and a briefcase into a rental Chevy at the East 76th Street Hertz, took the FDR drive to the Bruckner, and headed up the New England Thruway. It was muggy, humidity high, a Jones Beach day, sky hazy, the usual clutter of vacationers and rec vehicles on I-95.

I had embarked on a journey of discovery—Good-bye, Moscow, Good-bye, Beijing, Good-bye, Hanoi and the uglies of the world, I was taking the high road back in time and space to explore my own country. I had a copy of De Tocqueville in my briefcase, and I was seeking detail and images for a portrait of America, where it had been and where it had come in the 200 years since Lexington and, I hoped, some clues to where we were headed.

My first stop would be Chepachet, Rhode Island, eighteen miles west of Providence through a corridor of franchisers, auto lots, furniture barns, and big ticket appliance spreads. I had never been to Chepachet. No one had heard of Chepachet, but that was where the Salisburys spent the first 150 years of their life in America. I was going to follow the Westward Ho! of their trek across the continent and then retrace my own peregrinations from the Hoovervilles of depression days to the battlegrounds of civil rights and Vietnam, Birmingham, Berkeley, and the rest. I would use this as a chart to the two centuries of the American experience. Not exactly the way De Tocqueville and Trollope had done it, but the best scenario I could invent to expose the hardscrabble of American history.

Travels Around America set off a flash fire, not over my reporting but the circumstances. Xerox Corporation, which had given much funding for public television, proposed an experiment—to try the same technique for print. They gave *Esquire* magazine a hands-off public service grant to be used for creative writing, they being permitted to run a commercial notice, just as they did on PBS. I liked the idea. Almost all the magazines I had grown up with had been killed by TV. There was hardly a periodical left that published creative fiction or serious nonfiction. This brainstorm might, I thought, turn the tide.

Alas, E. B. White, a man whom I revered, thought otherwise. He wrote to his hometown paper, the Ellsworth, Maine *American* (every paper in the country picked up the article), that Xerox had hatched a dastardly plot. Next, the Big Corporations would be sitting in the editor's chair, dictating to ink-stained wretches what to write.

I thought E.B. was dead wrong. I thought a good many editor's chairs were already occupied by the devil he invoked. I thought E. B. was living back in the days of Ida Tarbell, Lincoln Steffens, and TR's "malefactors of great wealth." But I had too much love for White to say that, except for *The New Yorker,* the serious general magazine was almost extinct, the survivors a ferociously endangered species headed for the scrapheap where already rusted *The Saturday Evening Post, Colliers, Life, Scribners, Century,* and the *Harpers* of William Lyon Phelps. But there was something wonderful about E. B. White, the little man from North Brooklyn, Maine, slaying great big Xerox. E.B.'s letter killed the experiment, but he wrote to tell me he had enjoyed *Travels:*

> When I last investigated America, I was in a Model T Ford, with the prairie grass up around the hubs of the wheels. The scene has changed, all right, and not all of it for the better. But we still have the explorers, like yourself, and the people looking for the answers and not finding them.

Sadly, magazines went on dying and even *The New Yorker* took on a sickly cast and ultimately landed in the pocket of the Newhouses, Biggest of the Bigs.

The great hero in the America which I portrayed was my "Uncle Hiram." It was on his account that I had headed for Chepachet. Actually he was my father's great-uncle, born in 1779, three years into the Revolution. He died in 1860, one year short of the Civil War, a span of extraordinary years in American history. The more I discovered about Hiram—and eventually I discovered a great deal—the more he came to symbolize for me that early breed which had laid the foundations of the country.

Not that he was exceptional in any way in his time and place—and that, I believed, was his significance.

I arrived in Chepachet with a copy of Hiram's journal in my briefcase. The parts which I possessed began October 19, 1815, describing a journey from Chepachet to Buffalo, New York and back—a peddler's trip. He wrote his account (I later found), in a neat hand, with black, slightly rusty ink in a small calf volume which he had purchased in Providence October 6 "15 days after the tornado of Sept. 23rd" as he noted. He kept that journal until May 9, 1819. A second segment began January 1, 1825, and ended December 20, 1844. Two or three segments were missing. So were the original rag-paper journals.

Hiram kept a day-by-day record of his life. He was thirty-six years old in 1815, and he would write regularly, journal and letters, until he died at eighty-one. His last letter was posted only three months before his death. His style was sparse, exact, thrifty, details of his work, sums earned, sums owed, salty comments, horizon narrow, not a mention of Europe, seldom of Washington or national affairs, the record of a yeoman's life and times, debts, weather, deaths, births, crop failures, bank failures, suicides, and occasionally crimes.

Hiram was all the things my generation was not. He went into the woods, hewed timber, fashioned chestnut and oak into lumber, trimmed beams with his ax, raised houses, forged his nails, gathered old iron and smelted it into bolts and hinges, surveyed the land, built gristmills and schoolhouses, constructed coffins (a steady source of cash), fashioned chests of drawers and bedsteads, plowed the land, cut the hay, sowed wheat, barley, and oats, planted beans (his winter fare was beans and molasses), chipped a plow, carved a gunstock, fixed clocks, built wagons for himself and his neighbors, collected taxes, wrote deeds—not much he could not do. I listed seventy-eight skills in a casual run-through of his journals. He sheared his sheep, made cheese from the milk of his cows. Hiram was that "upstart American" of whom Daniel Boorstin wrote—Mr. America of his day. He fought in the War of 1812 as his father had fought at White Plains with George Washington, as his grandfather had fought in the French and Indian war, and his great-grandfather and uncle (I believe) had fought and died in King Phillip's War in 1675.

Like his family, Hiram was plainspoken, never rich, never poor, working every day, Sundays included, no holidays, no vacations (once he took a three-day trip to Boston), celebrating only Independence Day, the Revolutionary War still close, drinking a little too much rum on New Year's Eve. No Christmas. No Easter, an ecumenical man who heard every preacher who came to Chepachet, once or twice a Catholic and once a Jew preaching a Sunday service.

He possessed a small, serviceable library, a speller bought for half a shilling (he was a good speller except for writing "choir" for "chore"), an almanac, a couple of arithmetics, a trigonometry, a psalter, a book on elocution, and a couple of readers. He was a literate, well-spoken man.

The life of his wife, Diane, was hard, and like so many she went mad and died early. Death was close to women in those times, especially in childbirth. In Hiram's day the babies died, one after another. In the cemeteries you find graves of three or four wives, and a tatter of infant children with their tiny stones. When I learned of the peril which the Chinese women faced on the Long March, the danger of pregnancy, of death and the death of the babies, I thought of Hiram, his wife, Diane, and the other wives of those grubbing days.

Since childhood I had heard stories of Hiram, but not until I came to Chepachet did I get the feel of the man and his times. Behind a veneer of motels and gas stations along Route 44, Chepachet lived almost unchanged, the old names, the old houses, the great-grandsons and daughters of those Hiram mentioned in his journals. His Masonic lodge, Friendship No. 7, survived. So did a table of his handicraft in the parlor of a neighbor, a writing desk in another, the lectern he made for Friendship No. 7 still used in the town hall.

I found Hiram in Chepachet. And I found two of his original journals, lost for fifty years. I possessed only typescripts copied by my Aunt Sue. With the aid of a family connection, Hazel Hopkins, one volume of the journal was tracked to Alaska and to Massachusetts. That took a couple of years. Then, miraculously, a second volume turned up five years later in Florida, along with a dozen books of Hiram's library, more of his records and correspondence. I've not given up on the missing segments.

* * *

There was no way in which I could have written or understood the 6,000-mile Long March of Mao Zedong's Red Army without crossing the 100 rivers and 1,000 mountains of the Chang Zheng. There was no way in which I could understand the origins of the American legend without walking in the footsteps of the men and women who created it. I followed every step of the ice-clad roads from Chepachet west across Connecticut and Massachusetts, over the Hudson and along the Mohawk trail west to Canandaigua and north to Buffalo, traversed by Hiram in his peddler's ventures. I examined the site where Hiram's father and brother Amasa farmed at "No. 9," just outside Canandaigua (the house they built still standing). I walked the streets of Buffalo where Hiram's brothers, Smith Hamilton and Hezekiah Alexander (their second names commemorate Alexander Hamilton), founded the first newspaper in Buffalo in 1809, escaping west to Black Rock with their press when the British attacked in 1812. I journeyed along the Erie Canal and the Great Lakes to Milwaukee, where my great-grandfather Amasa removed in 1843. I inspected the house in Oregon, Wisconsin, where he lived and the little red brick house in Mazomanie, Wisconsin, where my father was born. I went to Minneapolis where I was born, the old Victorian home bulldozed with the whole Victorian neighborhood, curved streets, elms, and all.

There was continuity in this progression. I am not so certain of the continuity of my own life: my childhood in the Jewish ghetto Royalston Avenue became; the straight-arrow Scandinavians of high school days; my North High School classmate, Farrell Dobbs, catapulted out of the teamsters' strike of 1934 to Trotskyite leader (he had never heard of Trotsky before, had barely heard of a strike or a union), who went on improbably to run four times for the Presidency as candidate of the FBI-ridden Socialist Workers Party; my university political mentor, Harold Stassen, as bright a man as ever came out of Minnesota, who ran even more times for the Presidency than Dobbs but failed, sadly and finally farcically.

I tried hard to define what I called the Minnesota spirit. I conceived this as an amalgam of Hiram's work ethic—honesty and pragmatism—blended with the Scandinavian socialism of the 1880s and the flinty doctrines of the Mainites, Vermonters, and Massachusetts men who came to Minnesota a bit earlier and grabbed the iron ore, savaged the timber, and milled the wheat.

I believe in it as an entity, the agrarian ecleticism which has given us honest, rather lumbering politicians: Humphrey, Mondale, Eugene McCarthy, Stassen, McGovern, and earlier Floyd Olson. None quite made it. Many reasons for that. One, I think, is that they were naturally honest men, lacking that oil of hypocrisy which has come to be, I fear, an essential ingredient in an era of television politics.

The heroes who made up my iconostasis were not, in any case, mainstreamers, those who made it to the top. There had not been in my family a professional man, a man with a college degree, until my grandfather got his M.D. at Michigan after the Civil War. Until then it had been a yeoman's family, farming the land since we arrived from England in the mid-seventeenth century and probably for generations before. The first deviation came with my Buffalo great-uncles, Smith and Hezekiah, and their newspaper. Their papers regularly folded every two or three years only to appear the next day under a new name with (usually) a new partner.

But this was the fabric of America until the mid-nineteenth century. No corporations. Business was individual. My pantheon of America contained two or three wonderfully talented blacks—the writer Mary Mebane for one—women who had fought heroically against the stream, a handful of radicals, students and some who were not students, voices of the 1960s, Charles Reich, the now forgotten author of *The Greening of America,* the unclassifiable Tom Hayden, his wife Jane Fonda, an improbable but miraculous blacksmith named Werner Thiers of Mazomanie, Wisconsin, finally and overwhelmingly Lawrence and Sue Brooks.

Lawrence and Sue Brooks, when Charlotte and I met them, were in their upper eighties. Each died at over 100. If Hiram was Mr. America of the 1800s so the Brooks were the flame which lived on into the late twentieth century, pure Quaker honesty, pure New England ideals, clear blue eyes that spanned the years from the Civil War to the dying embers of Vietnam.

The first time we met them at Pleasant Bay on the Cape, at their wind-weathered shingle house, not changed (except perhaps for electric light) from the day the family had moved in in 1888, Charlotte dissolved in tears. Here was her childhood miraculously preserved in outward dress and in inner moral. Lawrence and Sue Brooks never bowed their heads except to God. They were born with absolute pitch for good or evil, quiet, firm, warm, always knowing on which side to gather, always knowing by instinct bred by Puritan, Pilgrim, and Quaker blood what was false and what was pure.

But hearty, laughing people, mountaineers who took us into the Adirondacks to Putnam camp, where they had first met in 1905 and where Charlotte, as a child, had gone with her Boston parents, a rough unpainted cluster of buildings, two pools in an icy mountain stream, separated by a hung blanket, one for men, one for women, and Mount Marcy to climb. Lawrence and Sue led us up the twisting trails, surefooted as goats, each with a cane, never faltering, never breathing hard as we puffed and slipped behind. And on the Cape, hurrying down the steep path to the beach before seven in the morning for a quick dip before the water got warm, and sailing summer-long back and forth across Pleasant Bay in their skipping *Quawk,* a catboat cousin of the one Charlotte had sailed on Buzzards Bay in her teens.

We worshipped the Brooks and their covey of children, grandchildren, great-grandchildren, their oatmeal porridge, race ribbons bedecking the living room, the judge sitting at the Yamaka piano which he got for his eightieth birthday, hammering out the songs of the 1880s as the family joined in chorus. It brings tears to my eyes to write about them.

Sue was a Hallowell of Philadelphia. Her grandfather was a merchant and an abolitionist. Most of his customers were Southerners. He put a sign on the wall: "I do not sell my principles with my goods." His customers boycotted him, but he held high his head. His son, Sue's father, was wounded together with Justice Oliver Wendell Holmes at Antietam. The parents of Lawrence and Sue were born in Hiram's lifetime. These two sets of lives span the years of the Republic.

I cannot say that Lawrence or Sue had much use for our more recent national leaders. Both had been brought up as staunch Republicans (as had I). Judge Brooks had known Teddy Roosevelt. The judge thought he was the McGovern of his day. Try as the Party might—and he thought men like Nixon, Goldwater, and Reagan had tried very hard—the GOP was not going to go back to McKinley. He did not expect to live to see it (he didn't), but he felt confident that a sense of equity and justice would return to public life, that fortunes like those of Getty and Hunt would wither away (as has Hunt's), that in another fifty years the rich would not be so rich, the poor would not be so poor, that education would begin to bring us up from the doldrums. He did not minimize our lack of public morality, and he was shocked by the racism of his beloved Boston (then at the height of the school-busing crisis). He liked to go to the Boston Common and look at the Saint-Gaudens statue when he was feeling particularly low about the "Southies." It gave him reassurance.

One day I followed Judge Brooks' example. I walked onto the Common on a cool autumn day. Behind me was the gold dome of the State House where, I knew, Hiram had climbed on the one vacation of his life and looked out over the harbor on November 19, 1817, his eye taking in Charlestown, Castle Island, Dorchester Heights, the Glass House, and the clipper *Independence*.

I stood before Saint-Gaudens' bas-relief of Robert Gould Shaw and his mounted black infantry. Some sidewalk artist had carefully embossed a heart in blue crayon on Shaw's horse and each trooper's canteen carried a white crayon star, circled in blue. Not defacement, homely enhancement.

Three young people were sitting on a bench beside the statue, eating their lunch. They moved aside so that I could copy the inscription: "Death for Noble Deeds Makes Dying Sweet."

I thought then, as I think now, that the heritage of our first 200 years is not going to be eroded by the sleaze of speculators, corruption of men in high office, the hypocrisy of television, or the aimlessly evil deeds of random actors on the national stage. Our fundaments are secure and will serve as a refreshing spring for renewal of the simple, unadorned truths of the men and women who have been building the country, stone by stone, life by life, these past centuries.

I agree with De Tocqueville:

Future events whatever they may be, will not deprive the Americans of their climate or their inland seas, their great rivers or their exhuberent soil. Nor will bad laws, revolutions and anarchy be able to obliterate the love of prosperity and spirit of enterprise which seems to be the distinctive characteristic of these men or extinguish altogether the knowledge that guides them on their way.

32 | The Winged Eye

On a sunny morning before Christmas, 1985, I was entering the hall of Botticelli in the Uffizi in Florence, my eyes adazzle and my head spinning. I had never seen Florence, the Uffizi, or Botticelli, and I thought I could stand in that doorway forever, transfusing into my consciousness the glory of Venus and the poetry of Primavera.

For twenty years Charlotte and I had dreamed of Florence, and now we were here, in its heart, the blood of the Renaissance surging through my veins, my whole philosophy of life galley-west. I knew as I looked into that room, inspired by Michelangelo and designed by Vasari for Cosimo, that I would never be the same; I had crashed like a jerrybuilt condo. I felt, it seemed to me, as Moses must have in the presence of the Revelation. Nothing I had seen, nothing I had experienced possessed any weight on these scales of gold.

As I stood intoxicated, my eyes brimming with joy, my mind in turmoil, I bumped—literally—into Christopher Lydon, he too in a trauma. I had last seen him when we were making a television record, June 8, 1978, of the commencement in Harvard Square, listening to Aleksandr Solzhenitsyn intone his indictment of the West, pronouncing anathema on that mixture of Good and Evil which he proclaimed "made space for the absolute triumph of absolute evil in the world."

It was the voice of doom arising from the bowels of Russia, resounding like the iron bells of Moscow's 700 churches, proclaiming the Apocalypse.

The decline of the West, Solzhenitsyn thundered, began in the Renaissance with the birth of a humanist view of the world, the abandonment of the absolutes of the Middle Ages. We had taken the wrong turn. We had raised the false banner of a philosophy which, he believed, had caused the West to abandon in totality "the moral heritage of the Christian centuries."

I had not entirely understood what Solzhenitsyn was driving at, standing in the gusty spit of rain in Harvard Square, aware (because I had tried to reassure his wife) that he feared he might be pelted with stones and hurled down by the ranks of radical youth, professor-atheists, and debauched citizenry which he imagined to constitute the audience for the hallowed Harvard ceremonial. It was a moment. I felt as though I was witnessing Savonarola preaching perdition as he was led to the flames in Signoria Square (not five minutes from the Uffizi where I now stood).

I sensed the relief (and puzzlement) with which Solzhenitsyn concluded his address. He was received with the polite applause due a celebrity, the courtesy (a few boos very faint from the extreme rear) awarded a great man, and congratulations (many had not really understood his words, the loudspeakers, as usual, defective). The temple had not fallen and its elders, if later to express some irritation, had not been shaken.

Oh, to have Aleksandr Isayevich beside us now in the Uffizi! I exclaimed to Christopher. Oh, that he might breathe into his lungs the joy of man's most soaring creations, savor the Renaissance at its ultimate eloquence. How would he respond? I did not believe mortal soul could come into this presence without being born anew. But that most stubborn of men? The iron will of Aleksandr Isayevich had not been bent by Stalin, and his spirit, snug and secure in the granite hills, snow, and birches of Vermont, had not been lured by the sirens of American materialism. To Aleksandr Isayevich, the spot where Christopher and I stood truly marked the Great Divide of Western civilization, that place at which the Church of Rome turned west. The Church turned to humanity (away from revealed truth, as Solzhenitsyn believed), embraced the explosion of human talent, the broadening of human minds, which under Cosimo and the others created in Florence and Italy and Europe that civilization (so deeply fertilized by Athens and Rome) that gave our modern world its exhalted spirit. For the Renaissance was as profound an event (I believed) as the birth of Christianity itself.

Solzhenitsyn was not mistaken in his remarks at Harvard. Here at the Uffizi, we did stand beside the crevasse that sundered the world, Rome looking to the future, the church of Constantine looking inward to the past, to that literal doctrine which the missionaries Cyril and Methodius preached to the Slavs, founding the Orthodox faith of Russia. A faith untouched by the Great Rebirth of human vigor and thought, by what, as I now realized, had been a Revolution as profound as if the earth had been struck by a comet. In that moment I realized how absurdly pedantic and teutonic had been Karl Marx. What a coven of pretentious bigots he had summoned forth, the believers and the antibelievers. How Cosimo would have laughed at the spectacle, Botticelli turning his head in embarrassment at such mawkish naïveté.

The Renaissance hit me like fireworks at the Minnesota State Fair ("The Last Days of Pompeii," "The Battle of Waterloo"). It is a measure of the poverty of my education and, I'm afraid, the narrowness of my preoccupation with the contemporary that Renaissance had been for me a word without content, the Medicis only a synonym of wealth, Lorenzo a metaphor of cloth-of-gold magnificence, Cosimo only the faintest of echoes.

I did not know that the wisdom, the classics, the literature, the philosophy, the culture of Greece and Rome had been strangled by the Dark Ages as if it had never been. I did not know that Cosimo and his friends, Niccolo Niccoli and Poggio Bracciolini, had ransacked Europe to discover, preserve, and revive the art and knowledge of the classical world—as if Dante, Villon, Chaucer, Boccaccio, Shakespeare, Michelangelo, and Botticelli had vanished without a trace for hundreds of years and suddenly been found by an expedition financed by J. P. Morgan.

Only now at the Uffizi, under the impact of Solzhenitsyn's words at Harvard, did I comprehend that the Renaissance *was* a Revolution, *the* Revolution. It recaptured the human body and human spirit for art and man and God. It broke the one-dimensional parameters of a Church sunk in blackness. It blasted open minds like pockets of ore. It created a tide on which, 500 years later, our society still rode at flood. The humanism against which Solzhenitsyn inveighed had become the way of mankind from the day Cosimo began to reclaim those worm-eaten parchments from the stone cellars of the mordant monasteries of Switzerland and Greece.

Only in Florence did I realize that the Revolutions of my day—1917 in Russia, 1949 in China, and all the sputterings before and after—were only summer squalls on sand-saucer lakes compared to the oceanic force of the Renaissance. Only, perhaps, the American Revolution, its founders familiar with Greek, Hebrew, and Latin, conscious of history and philosophy, caught a whiff of what had been born in Florence in the fourteenth and fifteenth centuries.

Florence illuminated like lightning the essence of the modern debate. Solzhenitsyn's argument echoed that of the Albizzi family, the enemies of Cosimo, who hated and feared the wildfire spread of the new philosophy, contending that the Greek and Latin classics threatened the pillars of Christian faith. But the Church followed Cosimo, not the Albizzi, and in its patronage and scholarship supported the new against the old—but not Byzantium, not the Eastern Church to which Russia adhered.

Russia knew neither Renaissance nor Reformation. It plodded on in the tracks of the Middle Ages, arguing whether the sign of the cross should be made with two fingers or three, spawning schismatics who believed in self-flagellation, self-castration, immolation by fire (the congregations assembled in their wooden churches and burned themselves up), and in redemption through sin, as Rasputin preached to the Romanovs.

I cannot but wonder whether Lenin's Marxism, its intense insistence on purity of dictum, discipline, the "divine word" of Party, did not have its real roots in that Eastern Orthodox world which had never known challenge, change, or Florentine charisma. No one, of course, can resolve these questions of Church and Communism. Instinct and prejudice cut too deep. But Florence taught me how shoddy are our discussions of the political issues of our day, how poorly we reason, how shabby our education, how weak our standards, how little I—who have spent a lifetime on the pseudo-ideological frontiers of the world—know of genuine thought, of history, and of the rich, exquisitely convoluted society which we humans have created. I have not, I fear, possessed even the vocabulary to describe it.

Charlotte and I spent not quite two months in Florence. How could I have taken so long to let her lead me there? How could I have visited Tirana, 100 miles across the Adriatic, in 1957 and not see Florence till thirty years later? What sense did it make?

How could I have spent my life arguing about Democracy, Fascism, and Communism and never studied the originals of these doctrines in Athens, Rome, or Florence? What manner of world have we Americans created with our opulent universities, brimming museums, extraordinary electronic skills yet nurture a people as ignorant as myself, not even knowing what books to take from the shelf and, too often, possessing neither shelves nor books to place upon them? We have become, I fear, too much like the Romans in their turbulent barbaric days.

I have poked my nose into almost every corner of my country: to bloody Harlan County, Kentucky, with its dying coal fields and dying miners; to the abandoned iron range of Minnesota where the richest high school of America once stood, funded by royalties of ore mines now extinct; through the West Side slums of Chicago, desolate when I first saw them and more desolate fifty years later. Those magnificent arch-windowed, red-brick New England factories, closed for forty or fifty or sixty years, shatter me; so do the thin-lipped slate-faced men and women sitting on their porches, rocking, rocking, rocking, in the cricks and hollers of West Virginia, waiting for work that will never come.

I have watched our parades for popes and pennant winners, our Presidential polls and electronic politics, the mindless spectacles with which we celebrate the bicentennial of our Independence and our Constitution. But what about our minds? My mind, in particular. How can we expect to create a new or better world if we possess only cartoons of what is going on—an image of the American flag, buoyant in the breeze, patriotic bombast, talk of morning in America, commercials of cowboys riding into the Golden West, peddling light beer, low-tar cigarettes, and ever-lower taxes?

This is what Florence has come down to? This is why Hiram spent his life plowing the land, building houses, and selling notions on icy trails until he died at eighty-one in 1860?

I sit at this Remington portable which I have used for forty-five years. I have spent hundreds of dollars to keep it going. I hate to think how many words I have pounded out, how many ribbons I have worn to rags, how many quires of paper I've used. It has been faithful to me, has responded when I battered at it in deep Siberian forests, on a plane I thought for sure was going down over New Guinea, in an air raid shelter in Hanoi, in a pigsty on Roswell Garst's farm in Coon Rapids, Iowa.

It has been faithful to my use. Have I been faithful to it? I am not so sure. It seems to me that a lot of mile-wide, inch-deep conclusions have sailed off these keys. How often have I got down to bedrock? Not as often as I would like to remember, except when I reported what I saw or heard, the Hanoi bombing, the *Andrea Doria* disaster, the bloated German bodies gently rising and falling in the Black Sea off Sevastopol, the Shook-up gangs in Red Hook. I can tell you what Stalin said and looked like, the way he held his shoulders, but it took me five years to realize that no one in the Politburo was taller than he (he was very short) and that this was no accident. I knew Nikita Khrushchev better than I have known most American Presidents. I never did a portrait of him in words that caught his schoolboy's gaucherie, his sly peasant curiosity, and the haunting look in his eyes. I thought Ike was a naturally nice guy who turned into kind of a fake because of his ambitions. (Never put that down on paper until now.) I think Richard Nixon is the most complicated, smartest, and stupidest President of our times. (Never wrote it before.) I thought Carter (before he was nominated) was the most attractive candidate since Wendell Willkie. I didn't write it and am glad I didn't. I was wrong.

I've been writing and talking and arguing about Russia for nearly fifty years. I know what I'm talking about. I've never found the right words to convince people that it is Russia's burden of history, not Communism, which makes her so difficult. No one likes to hear that there is more Mongol than Marx in Communism. We clutch our clichés to our bosoms, and I have never found a grenade to blow them free.

I look out over the orchard and wonder if we'll have any apples in the fall. Often we don't, I haven't a clue as to why. Neither, it would seem, do the cheerful young men who come to prune the trees. I would not think of writing an article on apple culture. But I will analyze the Afghan situation at the drop of a hat. I once spent ten days in Afghanistan; I love the Afghans; I shouldn't open my mouth about their plight. Of course that doesn't keep Presidents, Prime Ministers, and Pundits from uttering long, weighty, didactic absurdities. They don't have to know a thing to pontificate. Sometimes they get us into wars.

I do know a lot about Russia, China, and the United States. I am sitting right at the apex of that triangle. I have spent three decades studying the United States, China, and Russia. I have been over the ground. It is my territory. I have seen it from every side and over a long time. I know the history. I have known a great many of the players, the men who have made policy, who have committed troops, who have disposed their forces. I have known many of the diplomats who have negotiated on the problem or segments of it. I have even, at times, been part of the problem in polemics between the Russians and the Chinese.

The US-USSR-China triangle weighs more heavily on the world's future than Grenada, the Falklands, the Persian Gulf, the India-China frontier, the trumperies of North and South Korea, the edgy debate over Libya or the question of bugs at the American embassy in Moscow. I speak about it frequently, but no one in Government *thinks* about. The press doesn't devote five minutes a year to it; the public never asks about it.

The rottenness in our government, the growing deceit, blundering, and hypocrisy since World War II has made me a First Amendment absolutist—that is, I oppose any government restrictions on the press except for what is called the "troopship exception." No one, I hold, has a right to publish the date of a troopship sailing in wartime or war crisis. I agree with wartime censorship but only on military operations. I would forbid publication of the fact that we have broken a hostile state's code but insist on publication of bumbles of our own expensive intelligence apparatus, even if sometimes this seems harmful to immediate interests, in the long run it would serve us well. I would prohibit the government from concealing its blunders and embarrassing mistakes. I believe with Jerome Wiesner, former head of MIT, that democracy and secrecy are incompatible, that people will not in the long run permit the kind of government cover-ups which have become so common. Without William Howard Russell of the London *Times,* the command-made horrors of the Crimean war (including the Charge of the Light Brigade) would never have come to light. Newspapers revealed the rotten beef and dud bullets of the Union Army. Without Upton Sinclair the meat industry would have buried its victims unheeded. The press exposed Teapot Dome. It alerted the nation to the incompetence behind Pearl Harbor, and tardily it began to tell the truth about Vietnam and is still getting hell for it. The press brought us the Pentagon Papers and Watergate and trembled at its audacity. It exposed the Bay of Pigs but tread softly about Grenada and Nicaragua. To its shame it has never told the full story of the United States in Iran (where the money went). It hasn't bothered to winnow the thousands of documents exhumed by Tehran from the secret files of the U.S. embassy.

The New York Times electrified the nation in 1871 when it exposed the financial crimes of Tammany and the Tweed ring. It dozed through the Koch years, even sending its outraged and brutally honest columnist, Sydney Schanberg, to the showers. The press drowsed along with the government and its opulent contractors until *Challenger* blew up. Nearly twenty years ago Emma Rothschild in *The New Yorker* forecast the demise of Detroit. It took David Halberstam's book to detail the sordid story not of Japanese skill but of American sloth. The press slept.

I could go on and on. The world of electronic journalism, once sparkling with men like Edward R. Murrow and Walter Cronkite, slipped into the gray wasteland, with bottom-line barons taking it over, men whose testicles seemed to have been replaced by puffballs. No one in the Fourth Estate ventured to don the mantle of the certifiably eccentric Colonel Robert R. McCormick of *The Chicago Tribune.* McCormick wittingly or unwittingly gave away, in anger at Roosevelt, the secret of our breaking Japan's Purple code. FDR decided not to send the Colonel to jail, for fear of tipping the Japanese to what they had missed. J. Edgar Hoover has been in his grave for a decade. Mysterious events—fires and strange deaths—have, it is said, burned the archives and eliminated witnesses. The press yawns. Candidate after candidate rolls out of the electronic image processors. Nobody hires Sy Hersh to see what skeletons lurk behind their gussified hairdos. I mean real scandals, not Gary Hart trifles.

And no one complains of all this. Not the public, not Congress, not the White House—heavens, no, not the White House. Not opposition parties. Not the princes of the press—with a few honorable exceptions: *The New York Times, The Washington Post, The Boston Globe, The Los Angeles Times.* The others are too busy with their accountants and tax lawyers. We sleep. Oh, a few eccentrics raise a paranoid cry of Conspiracy. But nothing breaks the somnolence. We are, it seems, as Lincoln Steffens found Philadelphia, corrupt and content.

If anyone had a clue to national interest and national security, he would be spending, let's say, billions analyzing and studying this country itself, the United States. The menace of our own malfunctioning, it would seem to me, is the only serious menace to our own well-being and survival. We spend tens of billions on ultratechnology, pennies on those who are supposed to manage it. Schools close, universities turn into drug-ridden, commercial sports farms, and only a dwindle of men and women capable of manning new-age miracles escape the rush to Wall Street's megabucks.

We can do anything. We possess the know-how, the manpower, the thought power, the laboratories, the concepts. We do nothing. We rarely even bring to trial the men in government and out whose concentration on self-promotion and extravagant profit margins trash our prestige abroad and our integrity at home.

There is no story—literally none—which the great electronic news media and the billion-dollar press aggregates cannot extract, be it from the Kremlin or the Pentagon, and bring to the public of America. Instead, they tinker with sitcoms and four-color ad pages. Priorities? Forget it.

On Christmas Eve, 1985, Charlotte and I walked through the streets of Florence, awash with people, young, old, rich, poor, gay, and serious, through the throngs and into the great Duomo, that wonder of the world, where Florence has gathered on this holy eve since the fourteenth century. Tonight the vastness is filled, and the music lifts up to heaven. We stand breathless as the priests and princes of the church utter the incantations, the prayers, the music swelling, the tapers alight, the incense filling the air.

Finally, we make our way back through the people, very close, walking slowly, the sense of the moment filling our hearts, out into the square, deep with young people, happy, abandoned, holding hands and arms around waists, teasing and joking, no ribaldry, a festive night. We walk down Via Santa Maria, in the center of the street, no traffic, only sauntering people. We walk up onto the Ponte Vecchio, as lovers have for a thousand years, pausing in center bridge to look up the Arno to Ponte Santa Trinita and beyond, one bridge after the other, each a work of art, each as it has been for centuries (but rebuilt and rebuilt, especially after the German destruction) and then around the corner to our *pensione* just down the street from Pitti Palace, looking out over the slanted gray roofs, just as did Cellini and Leonardo and Brunelleschi and Donatello and, I suppose,

Cosimo. It is a long, long way from Minnesota. Or even Boston. I know that Florence possesses us and will to the end of our days. We are very close.

I read a good deal that winter about Florence. I could not get enough. I was transfixed by the city and its men, none more than the architect Leon Alberti and his concept of man, unlike any I had ever heard. He saw man as a ship, designed for long, arduous voyages, sailing to the edge of the earth, and back, driving himself each year of his life, because there was so much to do and so little time in which to do it. He was painting a self-image I am certain. For his own device he took a winged eye because only an eye with the wings of a bird could see as much, see as far, and see as fast as man could travel. He borrowed, he said, a concept from ancient Greece, the idea that "man is born not to mourn in idleness but to work at magnificent and grandiose tasks."

That, I resolved, was a theorem for me. So much in the world to see, so much to report, so much to write, so pressing time and strength. I must hurry if I am to return quickly to Firenze and walk again the ancient stones of the pavement and let my imagination float freely over the beauty and wisdom of man's finest hour.

Index

ABOUT THE AUTHOR

Harrison E. Salisbury is a product of Minnesota, where he was born, grew up, went to school, and had his start in journalism. His earliest ambition was to go to China and work there as a newspaper man, but instead his career took him in the opposite direction.

He worked for United Press International in Chicago, Washington D.C., and New York City. In World War II he became a foreign correspondent in London, the Middle East, and Moscow. He joined *The New York Times* in 1949 and won a Pulitzer Prize for international reporting after returning to the United States from a six-year stint in Moscow. He then spent several years in investigative, social, and political reporting in the United States as well as broad coverage of the Communist Bloc.

From 1959 onward his attention turned more to China and Southeast Asia, stimulated by his discovery in Outer Mongolia of the first signs of the great rift between Soviet Russia and Communist China. Beginning in 1972 he has made frequent trips to China and has traveled extensively along the Sino-Soviet border, the extreme Northwest China, Tibet, along the rocky road from Lhasa to Katmandu, and in 1984 covered 7,400 miles along the routes of the Long March.

In 1987 he returned to China for extensive travel and interviews on a new work about China to be called *The New Long March*.